The Diary Novel

The *Juſt Vengeance* of *Heaven*
Exemplify'd.

IN A

JOURNAL

Lately Found by

Captain *MAWSON*,

(COMMANDER *of the Ship* COMPTON)

ON THE

Iſland of Aſcenſion.

As he was Homeward-bound from
India.

In which is a full and exact Relation of the Au-
THOR's being ſet on Shore there (by Order of
the Commodore and Captains of the *Dutch*
Fleet) for a moſt Enormous Crime he had been
guilty of, and the extreme and unparallel'd
Hardſhips, Sufferings, and Miſery he endur'd,
from the Time of his being left there, to that
of his Death.

All Wrote with his own Hand, and found lying
near the SKELETON.

L O N D O N:
Printed and ſold by the Bookſellers and at the
Pamphlet-Shops of *London* and *Weſtminſter.*
(Price Six-pence)

The diary novel

LORNA MARTENS

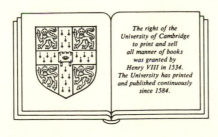

The right of the
University of Cambridge
to print and sell
all manner of books
was granted by
Henry VIII in 1534.
The University has printed
and published continuously
since 1584.

CAMBRIDGE UNIVERSITY PRESS

Cambridge
London   New York   New Rochelle
Melbourne   Sydney

Published by the Press Syndicate of the University of Cambridge
The Pitt Building, Trumpington Street, Cambridge CB2 1RP
32 East 57th Street, New York, NY 10022, USA
10 Stamford Road, Oakleigh, Melbourne 3166, Australia

First published 1985

Printed in the United States of America

Library of Congress Cataloging in Publication Data

Martens, Lorna, 1946–
The diary novel.

Bibliography: p.
Includes index.
1. Fiction, Autobiographic–History and criticism.
2. Diaries–History and criticism. I. Title.
PN3448.A8M3 1985   809.3   84–23216
ISBN 0 521 26656 4

To my students at Yale, for their encouragement

Contents

Preface

When one thinks of the diary novel, it is mainly famous twentieth-century examples that come to mind: works like Rainer Maria Rilke's *Notebooks of Malte Laurids Brigge,* André Gide's *Pastoral Symphony,* or Jean-Paul Sartre's *Nausea.* But is the diary novel a twentieth-century genre? It is true that the diary novel has become particularly popular in the twentieth century. In fact, however, the diary novel has a long history, one that originates in the eighteenth century. One of the main purposes of this book is to trace that history. The diary novel is an important subgenre of the first-person novel. Any typology or theory of first-person narration would benefit from some insight into one of its prominent forms, and interpretations of specific works would profit from information about the horizon of expectation against which a work was written. Although several articles and dissertations have been written on the diary novel as a genre, however, no history even of a limited period of time, such as we have for the epistolary novel or the picaresque novel, exists. Not even as much as a bibliography is available. The only exceptions are Peter Brang's short survey of diary fiction in Russian and Valerie Raoul's bibliography in her book on the French fictional journal.[1]

To compensate for this lack of information and to provide theoreticians of narrative and critics of the novel with a basis from which to work, I give interpretative summaries of the main stages of the history of diary fiction from the eighteenth to the mid-twentieth century in roughly chronological sequence, concentrating on the development in England, France, and Germany. The considerable Russian and Scandinavian traditions are beyond the scope of this study; they are mentioned only in passing. Titles of French and German diary novels are cited in the original languages. Other foreign-language titles are given in English if a published translation exists. Quotations from foreign-language sources are given in English translation in the text. The translations are mine except where otherwise indicated. For reference, and for those interested in pursuing the study of the genre, chronological bibliographies are given near the end of the book.

By showing a concrete pattern of change, the study provides new insights into factors that influence genre development. I discuss theoretical issues in Part I. The reader may well wish to read Chapter 2 (on genre theory) and Chapter 5 (on the interpretation of first-person narrative) of Part I last, after having finished the rest of the book, because these sections do not specifically concern the diary novel but address more general theoretical questions. Genre is conceived not in strictly typological or "logical" terms but as a historical manifestation. I agree with the premises of structuralist genre theory: Genre should be viewed as a set of historically constituted norms that serve as a frame of reference against which individual works are written and understood. Structuralist studies tend to emphasize the synchronic aspect of genre at the expense of history, however. I believe that any characterization of a genre should take into consideration its diachronic dimension. Some of the questions I ask are: How does a genre originate? How does it change? To what extent are our reflections on literary typology, on the abstract "logic" of literary forms, confirmed by the actual history of these types? The enterprise of tracing the history of a genre reopens theoretical questions that have hitherto been treated mainly in the abstract. Some speculative questions that should not be ignored or quickly settled merely for the sake of completing the study at hand include the following: How does one define the constitutive features of a genre? Where does this initial definition lead? Depending on the formulation of the object of inquiry, the investigation can go in very different directions. The question of generic definition, of generic closure, thus becomes a question of the specific nature of generic openness, or in other words, of a genre's relation to other literary and nonliterary systems.

Other literary systems constitute a horizon that, at a given point in time, permits or limits the realization of a given form's potential. In the historical chapters I attempt to show not only how writers used the diary form in fiction but to what extent the diary novel was influenced by its model, the actual diary, and by the historical horizon for fiction. The presentations of material are linked by certain themes: the relation of narrative to narrated time in periodic narration, and the use of the present tense; the fiction of writing; and the implications of secrecy. One central issue of wider scope is the question of authority in first-person discourse. In first-person narratives we hear only a single voice. How are we to evaluate what the narrator says? I address this traditional question by discussing various techniques for establishing consonance (where the author validates the narrator) and dissonance (where the author undermines the narrator).

Some of the chapters are devoted to interpretations of well-known or particularly significant works. Chapter 14, on unreliable narration, for example, focuses on an interpretation of Gide's *La Symphonie pastorale,* in which the narrator, assuming the role of reader and interpreter, draws his entire milieu into the specious world of his discourse. Chapter 15, on reliable narration, focuses on Rilke's *Die Aufzeichnungen des Malte Laurids Brigge,* a mosaic of Malte's perceptions, visions, and memories in which Malte, in Rilke's metaphor for creative power, holds up a mirror to the invisible. In Part IV, on the contemporary diary novel, I select three works for close analysis: Max Frisch's *Stiller,* Michel Butor's *L'Emploi du temps,* and Doris Lessing's *Golden Notebook.* These works are particularly successful realizations of a traditional form. The authors disengage the structural attributes from their traditional functions, and so exploit the diary's potential for discontinuity and open-endedness. The resulting construction is designed not just to carry and reinforce the plot but to express a message obliquely, through form.

I wish to thank several people for reading the manuscript and making useful suggestions and criticisms: George Schoolfield, Peter Demetz, Jeffrey Sammons, Dorrit Cohn, W. Wolfgang Holdheim, Valerie Raoul, and H. Porter Abbott. Special thanks go to Howard Stern for his painstaking critique of several chapters. I am grateful to Klaus Martens, Ulli Johst, and Angela Odenwald, who helped in the early stages of the project with the dusty job of searching stacks in the university library at Göttingen, as well as to Sarah Westphal, Gary Wihl, Tony Niesz, and Saïd Chébili, who helped at a later stage with proofreading, and to Olga Bush and Nancy Pollak for their help with the Russian bibliography and transliterations. Finally, I would like to thank those people who gave their time, energy, and moral support in the final stages of the project: Geoffrey Hartman and Chuck Grench for their invaluable practical advice, and Sam Fleischacker and, above all, Betsy Kolbert for helping me edit the manuscript when I was under great time pressure.

PART I

Problems of Definition, Method, and Interpretation

I

Is the Diary Novel Definable as a Genre?

Today we think of the diary as a periodically kept, secret, or at least private notebook in which the diarist writes down anything ranging from intimate details or introspective self-assessments to descriptions of the events of his day, random observations or aperçus, outbursts of anger, aphorisms, drafts for poems, or even quotations. If we think of a diary novel, we probably imagine something like Jean-Paul Sartre's *La Nausée*—an individual's record of his self-searching and self-finding, written by a reflective, perhaps even alienated, character; for a more self-certain person, a person of action, would live his life confidently and record his experiences later, if at all, in a memoir. The diaristic *in medias res* implies a state of turmoil or excitement, an inability to predict the future, an urge to master and purge overwhelming experiences or intense emotions. Obviously, however, we cannot expect diary novels written in earlier historical periods to conform to expectations aroused by recent diary novels. Especially in the earliest diary fiction, or what one might more cautiously call the earliest recognizable ancestors of our modern diary novels, the word "diary," the periodic first-person form, and the autobiographical or confessional content we have come to associate with the diary novel did not all neatly converge.

How does one approach the question of deciding what a diary novel is, for the purpose, for example, of tracing its history? In other words, what exactly is the phenomenon whose history we want to trace? Or is the question best put the other way around: Does historical investigation yield a definition?

These questions bring us to the problem of genre. Despite the disagreements that exist between the various schools of genre theory, it is generally argeed that a genre is a set with a high degree of homogeneity. We speak of a genre when we perceive a group whose members resemble each other to a significant degree. Certain twentieth-century works—for example, Rainer Maria Rilke's *Die Aufzeichnungen des Malte Laurids Brigge* (1910), Sartre's *La Nausée* (1938), André Gide's *La Symphonie pastorale* (1919), Georges Bernanos's *Journal d'un curé de campagne* (1936), Hjalmar Söderberg's *Doctor Glas* (1905), Simone de Beauvoir's *La Femme rompue* (1967) – are usually cited by critics as diary novels, and they could be seen to constitute such a homogeneous set. Among the characteristics they have in common, the predominant characteristic is the diary form – or, to give a more technical description, a first-person narrative that the narrator writes at periodic intervals and essentially for himself.

This provisional descriptive definition appears promising, especially from a typological point of view. If we look aside temporarily from the word "diary" and also from any connotations it might bear in terms of content, and define the diary novel exclusively in terms of formal characteristics, we have isolated a type of the novel that is similar to other recognized types, yet is distinctly different from any of them. Let us define the diary novel more precisely in terms of form: It is a fictional prose narrative written from day to day by a single first-person narrator who does not address himself to a fictive addressee or recipient.

This definition is based on the accepted distinction between first- and third-person narration. Within first-person narration, certain types of works purport to be *written* by the narrator. There are three main types of such works: memoir novels, epistolary novels, and diary novels. It is possible to describe the differences between these types in terms of a "narrative triangle" based on the communicative triangle of sender, receiver, and message. The poles represent the fictive narrator, the fictive reader, and the narrator's subject matter, or what one might call the narrated world:

The diary novel is distinguished from the memoir novel by the narrator's relation to his subject matter. The memoirist or autobiographer is at pains to give an account of past events. The present moment, the time of writing, is itself of little or no interest. The memoirist rolls out the past like a rug, and the cohesiveness the chronological march of events projects, the unfolding of a "life," provides the novel with its ordering principle. The diary novel, in contrast, emphasizes the time of writing rather than the time that is written about. The progressive sequence of dates on which the diarist writes gives the narrative its temporal continuity. This present-tense progression tends to dominate the subject matter, so that the diarist usually writes about events of the immediate past – events that occur between one entry and the next – or records his momentary ideas, reflections, or emotions.

In its temporal structure the diary novel thus resembles the epistolary novel. As in the diary novel, the time of writing in the epistolary novel, represented by the sequence of letters, establishes the dominant temporal order; and what a correspondent writes in his letter is generally limited to what has happened to him since he wrote the last letter, or to his sentiments, ideas, thoughts, and recollections that reflect his present temper. But unlike the epistolary novel, the diary novel does not presuppose a fictive reader. Letters are by definition addressed to a recipient; diaries are normally private.

Is it possible to draw any conclusions from this typological definition, and from these distinctions? We can say, before actually looking at examples of diary novels, that the diary form offers a certain abstract or logical potential different from that of other narrative types. Potentially, the diary novel presents the possibility of something approaching the collapse of the communicative triangle as it is found in fiction. For the diarist does not have to bridge a gap between his writing self and his "subject" – his younger, temporally distant, different self – as does the autobiographer; nor are his utterances circumscribed by the presence of an addressee whose character and relationship to the narrator are apt to influence the content and color the tone of his communications, as are those of the letter writer. In the extreme case, instead of a narrator who creates a narrated world and addresses himself to a fictive reader, we have a narrator who takes himself as subject and is his own reader. When we consider that the narrator can take his *present* self as subject, the result is something like a folding over of the subject of discourse on himself. We can imagine a modification of the schema presented above:

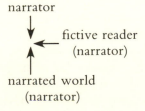

The interior monologue and stream-of-consciousness technique come even closer to collapsing the distance between the narrator and the narrated world than the diary, for by doing away with the time it takes a thought to slide from the mind into the pen, they eliminate all temporal distance. But, unlike the diary novel, they place the reader under the strain of suspending his disbelief. The reader is implicitly asked to accept the convention that the thoughts got on paper somehow and not to inquire about the scribe. In contrast, the diary form is mimetic of what could be a real situation. No other form of narration can achieve comparable closeness between the narrator and the narrated world without being identifiably fictive.

With our provisional definition of the diary novel, then, we seem to have a tool, a working hypothesis, with which we can go looking for further examples. Even if we look aside from the diachronic dimension of the genre, however, and remain within the synchronic cut of twentieth-century diary novels, where the likelihood is greater that we will find repeated instances of a relatively stable organization of elements, it must be stressed that our provisional definition does not give us a criterion for deciding whether any given work is a diary novel or not. If we consider the entire time span during which diary novels were written, there is an even greater possibility that we will encounter examples that are not clearly either inside or outside the genre as we have defined it. By assessing the empirical evidence in a fairly impressionistic way, we have arrived at a definition of what might be regarded as the *ideal* characteristics of the genre. But we have not drawn borderlines around the set. The diary novel, like any genre, has blurred edges; and by defining the form more "precisely," by enumerating attributes we call constitutive of the type, we have at the same time complicated the issue; we have multiplied the borderlines, or facets, that can be blurred.

One finds, for example, countless shadings between diary novels and other types of first-person narration. In the context of a large work like the novel, sequential time structures and retrospective narration can easily be combined. An author may wish to establish complex parallelisms or present a special kind of psychological development by emphasizing both past and present time. Thomas Mann's *Doktor Faustus* (1947) could not be considered a diary, although the narrator-biographer Zeitblom frequently interrupts his account of his friend Leverkühn's life to speak of current political events and to complain of his hand that trembles as he writes. Gerhart Hauptmann's *Phantom* (1922) with its day-to-day writing about a single, consecutive past event, interspersed with present comments, is a borderline case. John Updike's *Month of Sundays* (1975), a day-to-day record kept by an institutionalized clergyman mainly about the past, and François Mauriac's *Le Noeud de vipères* (1932), in which a confessional memoir-letter changes gradually into a secret record of the events of the increasingly recent past, are more diarylike. Finally, Wilhelm Raabe's *Die Chronik der Sperlingsgasse* (1857), whose first-person narrator presents his extensive but chronologically disorganized recollections as well as day-to-day events in a present-tense framework, is a work a bibliographer of diary novels would be likely to include.

Likewise, the fictive reader may be more or less absent. In particular, the borderline between the diary novel and the epistolary novel is fluid. An epistolary novel like Guilleragues's *Lettres Portugaises* (1669), in which a single correspondent directs letters to a recipient of ill-defined character who does not respond, approaches the diary form. If the recipient in an epistolary novel is a confidant, an alter ego whose personality does not affect the tone or content of the letter writer's utterances, the fictive reader all but disappears. Werther's letters to Wilhelm in Goethe's *Die Leiden des jungen Werthers* (1774) and Hyperion's letters to Bellarmin in Friedrich Hölderlin's *Hyperion* (1797–9) are examples of this type of communication. On the other hand, a diarist may intend the "secret" diary for another person, perhaps posthumously, as does Sophie in Johann Martin Miller's *Siegwart, eine Klostergeschichte* (1776), who bequeaths the record of her unrequited passion to the man she loves. A diarist may even hope to publish the diary, as Célestine in Octave Mirbeau's *Le Journal d'une femme de chambre* (1900), who is writing an exposé of her employers, hopes to do. The "secret diaries" of husband and wife in Jun'ichirō Tanizaki's *The Key* (1956) are, in a peculiar sense, letters: Each spouse knows that the other surreptitiously reads his or her diary, and consequently each one uses his or her journal as a roundabout means of communication.

Similarly, the diary convention that the first-person narrator is actually writing on a page of paper may be more or less strictly adhered to. We may have trouble imagining how a narrator finds the opportunity and implements for writing when, for example, he is shipwrecked at sea. Eighteenth-century letter-journal heroines often stretch plausibility by writing in moments of crisis or in other unlikely circumstances. The fiction of the written document was an eighteenth-century convention; the only existing technique for thought transcription was to have the narrator impart his thoughts by speaking or writing them. In later periods the convention of the written document was to prove more and more of a hindrance. In the late nineteenth century, before the autonomous interior monologue had found wide acceptance, works whose style was all but indistinguishable from stream of consciousness appeared in the traditional guise of diaries. In the twentieth century, the need to ground the narrative in a mimetic fiction, or even to establish a unified point of view, vanishes. In Sartre's *La Nausée*, Roquentin keeps a diary, but many entries are unconvincing as pieces of diary writing. In

L'Etranger (1942), Albert Camus leaves it unclear whether the narrator, Meursault, is writing or not; and he perplexingly changes his perspective from one contemporaneous with narrated events to a retrospective one.

Finally, even the question of voice, of first-person narration itself, is not unambiguous. A first-person narrator can write chiefly about himself, but he can also write mainly about events or other people. In Emily Brontë's *Wuthering Heights* (1847), for example, Lockwood's diary, the frame narrative, is scarcely more than a vehicle for recording the gossipy Mrs. Dean's oral serial story about the lurid goings-on at Wuthering Heights and Thrushcross Grange through three generations. Lockwood's personality colors the story, but Lockwood himself is not of essential interest. A "first-person narrator" can shade imperceptibly into the "intrusive narrator" of a third-person story. In general, the dividing line between first- and third-person narration is not so clear as is usually supposed; these terms deserve a more precise and critical differentiation than they are normally accorded. Within the field of diary fiction one also finds juxtapositions of first- and third-person narrative; for instance, Uwe Johnson's *Jahrestage* (1970–3) is a work divided into daily entries but only in part written in the first person.

2

The Impasses of Genre Criticism

The concept of genre, then, is not an especially useful tool for converting empirical data into neat, abstractly describable divisions. In trying to set limits, one constantly arrives at the impasse described by Armand in André Gide's *Les Faux-Monnayeurs* when he tries to find "the dividing line, below which nothing exists."[1] This is the evident flaw of any genre theory that tries to satisfy typological requirements and at the same time retain its descriptive applicability. Even though a typological definition may be derived from empirical evidence, it cannot effectively be reapplied descriptively. An even more serious objection to a typological use of the concept of genre is that we have no reason to suppose that real genres, as they emerge historically, yield a contrastive system of types. Whatever mechanisms produce historical genres, conformity to an abstract scheme of contrasting types – or, for that matter, to any other abstract scheme – can hardly be supposed to be one of them. One could go so far as to say that insisting on the subsumption of actual genres in an ulterior order is a denial of their historicity, a suppression of the acts of repetition and modification that produced the resemblances between the texts. Even though the formulation of that order may originally have been the outcome of description, it cuts short inquiry into why resemblances between literary texts exist by subordinating such continuities to philosophical or taxonomic considerations.

Theories that view genres absolutely, prescriptively, or ideally are of course inimical to a historical explanation of genres. This is notably true of theories that stand in the tradition of the deductive and speculative poetics of the German Romantics, which reached its anti-empirical extreme with Friedrich von Schelling and is known for postulating a "holy trinity" of genres.[2] But even contemporary structuralist genre criticism tends to overemphasize the systematic aspect of genre at the expense of history.

9

Let us take Tzvetan Todorov's theoretical argument in his genre study *The Fantastic: A Structural Approach to Literary Genre*. Todorov maintains that genre criticism must reconcile theory and description; according to him, such criticism "must constantly satisfy requirements of two orders: practical and theoretical, empirical and abstract." Yet his contention that "everything suggests that historical genres are a sub-group of complex theoretical genres" shows that he favors theory.[3] For Todorov, theoretical genres are defined according to a contrastive model, in terms of the presence or absence of features. He formulates the relation between real and theoretical genres in such a way as to give priority to the originally derivative order of theoretical genres. Todorov continues:

> The genres we deduce from the theory must be verified by reference to the texts: if our deductions fail to correspond to any work, we are on a false trail. On the other hand, the genres which we encounter in literary history must be subject to the explanation of a coherent theory. . . . The definition of genres will therefore be a continual oscillation between the description of phenomena and abstract theory.

I would argue that it is misleading to contend that the principal task of genre criticism consists in reconciling description with a systematic and deductive theory. The empirical task of describing texts and the abstract project of constructing a system, coming as they do from entirely different points of departure and serving different interests, are fundamentally irreconcilable. Wishing to reconcile them reflects a scholarly desire to bridge the gap between the two dominant critical traditions of genre theory, between the inductive, descriptive Aristotelian tradition and the deductive, speculative Romantic tradition, rather than an attempt to deal with texts themselves. In fact, if we are interested in actual genres, it seems to me that "theoretical genres" can be left to one side entirely. Todorov himself makes a similar point in a later essay, where he asserts, in contradistinction to his theory in *The Fantastic,* that it is a mistake to confuse genres (which are found inductively, through "the observation of a period of literary history") with types (which are postulated deductively, starting with "a theory of literary discourse"), and to describe genres as if they were types.[4]

Converting an empirically won definition into a typologically satisfactory definition is, I would argue, not difficult. Any perceived literary type can be defined in contrastive, typological terms if we choose to define it that way. Such definitions are useful as heuristic devices. As we have seen, they can be used to illustrate the abstract potential of one form versus another. Yet as far as descriptive or historical study is concerned, they yield hypostatized categories that the concrete constantly threatens to elude; the more perfectly they suit the requirements of a system, the more rigid and unsusceptible they become to modification by actual texts. They do not lead back to works in their specificity and also do nothing to illuminate the relations between works belonging to the same genre. They are not, therefore, a satisfactory first step with which to approach historical genre criticism. But where does this disqualification of typological definitions leave us? Can it not be extended to all definitions? Even the most purely descriptive definition is, obviously, at the mercy of new evidence. Does the difficulty in drawing up boundaries put into question the idea of genre itself – or, in other words, is the idea of genre the wrong question? Yes and no. Provisionally, we can say that definition is not the end of genre criticism. Making definition the end would be to superimpose a critical concept, a critical convenience, onto actual relations between texts. Rather, definition is at most a beginning, a working hypothesis. But this essentially *critical* problem of definition does not put into question the stubborn repetition of forms and themes in literary history, a fact we cannot overlook even though the process does not seem to submit to any easily discernible order.

At this point one might do well to consider how resemblances between texts actually come into existence. We can assume that, aside from whatever factors, like social conditions or market changes, create favorable circumstances for the emergence and popularity of certain art forms, imitation is an irreducible component in the explanation. If genres exist, it is because people imitate one another. The only other possible explanation would involve assumptions about human nature and its natural expression; such an account, which would explain the existence of genres in terms of an ever repeated spontaneous genesis, seems manifestly improbable. It also suggests that literary genres are analogous to biological species, an equation that contemporary critics of genre are – understandably – explicitly anxious to avoid.[5] One might complain that citing imitation as an explanation is to remove the problems surrounding genre to an even shakier ground. One can, however, swiftly limit the types of imitation involved in the creation of genres to two. The first, more limited case would involve the imitation of specific models. An artist may study an "original" in order to create a similar work. Such acts of direct imitation alone do not suffice to explain the existence of genres, however. The second, more general case involves imitation in the broader sense of encoding. The artist locates his activity with reference to already existing types; he brings his creation into conformity with a certain type, where this type is in turn determined by the existence of other objects of the same type.

The notion that imitation in this second sense is responsible for the formation of genres plainly underlies, at least implicitly, the widespread conception that genres can be viewed as codes. In 1916 Viktor Šklovskij asserted that texts are written against a background of other texts.[6] Other Formalist critics went on to discuss genre in terms of conventions, codification, and norms. There is an unclarified theoretical issue in this discussion: When Jurij Tynjanov and Boris Tomaševskij speak of genres, they mean groups of texts,[7] yet they also see genre as a "system," or a constellation of formal devices that exists in the abstract.[8] Genres thus have both an empirical and a conceptual mode of being. It was the systematic aspect of genre that interested the Formalists most, however. Although Tomaševskij attacked the notion of "theoretical" genres and advocated descriptive and pragmatic study in its stead,[9] the Formalists did not focus on such study. Their primary aim was to formulate a theory of literary evolution that would account for the mechanisms responsible for literary stasis and change, and they situated their discussion of genre within this broader context. They were interested principally in how genres as "systems" changed and evolved, rather than how genres as groups of similar texts emerged.

Structuralist critics and semioticians have widely adopted the Formalists' views on genre. "A genre is a model," Claudio Guillén writes, "a traditional model or conventional pattern."[10] Again there is a shift in emphasis, however. Structuralist critics are interested less in the theoretical question of generic evolution, and still less in the actual formation of genres, than in the role generic conventions play in constituting meaning. The analogy between Tynjanov's designation of genres as "systems" and Ferdinand de Saussure's conception of "langue" as a sign system is apparent. The relation of the individual text to the generic code can be seen as homologous to the relation of "langue" to "parole," where "langue" constitutes a set of norms against which specific utterances are comprehended. Thus Jonathan Culler writes: "Once genres are treated as sets of norms or conventions which make possible the production of meaning, much as linguistic norms do, then the notion of genre is restored to a central place in literary theory. Generic conventions account for the meaning that is produced when a work violates or evades these conventions, and generic codes are postulated in order to explain the way we treat details in different sorts of works."[11] With this particular focus on constituting a context for meaning, then, genres can be equated unproblematically with codes.[12]

The conception of genres as codes has certain evident advantages. It provides a plausible explanation for the existence of literary types, and it takes history into account by suggesting that genre is a motivating force in the production and reception of literary texts. Generic conventions constitute the contexts against which works are written and read. They are communicative aids, guidelines that ensure that works will be understood and that readers will not wander in an uncharted jungle of uninterpretable signs. From the maker's point of view, they are sustained by the desire to make "one of something," to create a specific, recognizable entity – for example, to write a *novel* – rather than create a nebulous, indefinable something. From the reader's point of view, generic codes appeal to a desire for orientation, the desire to know what one confronts.[13] Yet generic conventions do not necessarily exert a prescriptive force. Communicative contracts exist to be broken: The author can transgress the guidelines and even choose purposely to disorient the reader, and nothing compels the reader, in turn, docilely to respond as generic signals suggest.

This conception of genres as codes brings with it certain implications for the relation of individual texts to codes. One implication concerns the ontology of the text vis-à-vis generic codes. A work is never completely subsumed by, but always includes elements that exceed the requirements of, its genre. Whether one conceives of these elements as uncoded, individual, and unique, or instead, as Roland Barthes states polemically in *S/Z*, "articulated upon the infinity of texts, of languages, of systems,"[14] they obstruct a transparent reading of texts as "messages" against their codes. Jurij Lotman has discussed the differences between natural languages and what he calls the "secondary modeling system" of literature at length and persuasively in *Die Struktur des künstlerischen Textes*, drawing attention to multiple coding and "untranslatable surplus information" in literary works and to parallels between art and play.[15] But at the same time the relation of texts to genres is absolute: A work can never fully elude a relation to a code or codes.[16] Thus one finds generic conventions just as readily in periods that privilege originality or novelty as in those in which adherence to prescribed rules is a criterion of value. Even in the age of the avant-garde, the very institutionalization of the avant-garde might be understood as a genre convention.

Another implication of the identification of genres with codes has to do with the composition of the codes themselves. It will be useful to return to the analogy between generic codes and Saussure's "langue." "Langue," it will be recalled, is an essentially mental construct, a system of signs that exists in the collective consciousness of speakers of the language. It is of a different order from "parole," or individual speech acts. Yet "langue" and "parole" exist in a relation of interdependence: The system of language makes speech acts intelligible, while it itself is constituted by such speech acts and also modified by them.[17] Generic codes have the same ontological status as "langue." They are perceptual norms rather than actual works, yet they owe their genesis to works and can be modified by further works. Wittgenstein's observations on the nature of language can be applied to the nature of genres. Wittgenstein writes: "Our language can be seen as an ancient city: a maze of little streets and squares, of old and new houses, and of houses with additions from various periods; and this surrounded by a multitude of new boroughs with straight regular streets and uniform houses."[18] The city, in other words, owes its existence to houses, and the addition of new and different houses changes our conception of the city. This is as much as to say that codes change; they are not eternal norms but are subject to modification, and this modification has to do with the production of actual texts.

The conception of genres as codes obviously provides a useful tool for the interpretation of literary texts. For the reader, works of art acquire meaning through reference to preexisting norms, including generic norms; generic conventions constitute a horizon against which individual works are understood. These conclusions are so widely accepted and uncontroversial that not only structuralists but also critics who have profound disagreements on other scores concur on them. Thus one finds the idea of generic norms in the background of a theory of interpretation like E. D. Hirsch's *Validity in Interpretation,* and the question of interpretation in the foreground of Jacques Derrida's recent contribution to genre theory, "La Loi du genre."

From any critical point of view other than textual interpretation, however, a conception of genres as codes brings problems with it. Most particularly, problems arise when the critic wants to study the codes themselves, that is, place in the foreground what has hitherto been designated as background. The trouble is that codes cannot be equated with groups of texts. Codes are, as we have said, norms. Texts of course play a crucial role in constituting these norms, but other factors enter the picture as well. The particular standpoint of the observer, the historical period he lives in, and individual factors like his age and his degree of acquaintance with or susceptibility to the code, will all affect his perception of the norm. For literary codes can scarcely be seen to be mental constructs as universally, fundamentally, and ineluctably present as the rules of our mother tongue. If Lotman and others distinguish between the literary work and the speech act, a distinction between the system of language and the literary code is equally necessary. Beyond that, the perception of codes has to do with what might be described as a certain distance. At a certain distance we see simple, clear shapes; if we step closer, the degree of distortion that was present in the view from afar becomes apparent. Thus (to return to Wittgenstein's metaphor) the "city" as such is visible only at a distance; at close proximity one sees only houses. It is not only a question of dissolution into detail, however, of the proverbial difference between the woods and the trees. Individual works can be code-constitutive to varying degrees. A single work can create the perception of a code, while another work may have no effect on it whatsoever. Representations of texts may form the perception of codes just as well as texts themselves. Strictly speaking, one need never have read a detective novel to have a fairly clear idea of what such a novel is. Thus there is a fundamental and irreconcilable disparity between genres conceived as codes and genres conceived as groups of texts. The set of "code-constituting" texts is by no means necessarily, and probably will not be, identical with the set of similar texts.

Let us look at what happens when the critic tries to make descriptive use of a code perception, or, in other words, to validate his perception of the code by referring to texts, in the name of descriptive criticism. The critic starts with an impressionistic initial concept of the genre, or sense of a code. He attempts to make this concept more precise by decomposing what he perceives as the code into the individual texts he believes participate in it and scrutinizing them. The business of converting a code into texts is, of course, a subjective and ontologically questionable procedure. Even if the critic feels confident in pointing to specific texts he believes constituted the code, a degree of distortion that figured in the original perception of the code is lost when he takes a closer look at the texts. Decomposing the code into specific texts brings with it a loss of the illusion of simplicity and uniformity created by distance. The texts prove less uniform than they initially appeared, while at the same time in their concrete specificity they greatly exceed the generic concept.

The critic hopes that looking at the texts more closely will have a corrective effect. His task, he believes, consists in discerning what all the texts really have in common and then modifying the original impressionistic genre idea so that it conforms to the actual examples. The upshot will be a slightly off-focus, but empirically validated, version of the original code – or, in other words, a "descriptive" definition of the genre.

The critic thus arrives at a description of a set of texts – the chosen ones – that says: "These texts have such and such in common." This brings us to the second problem: Issuing as it does from a generic idea, the descriptive definition is not genuinely descriptive. Rather, it has superimposed the idea of a genre – the critic's idea of a genre – on a set of texts. One might compare the results of the critic's procedure with the outcome of a more empirical process, that of looking at all the books in a library that has maintained a practice of regularly acquiring books.[19] If one looked at the literary landscape as a whole rather than concentrating on certain chosen texts, one would find not so much genres as what Wittgenstein calls "family resemblances." The critic, then, has artificially tied a string—the genre concept—around a certain group of works. If he looked at a large enough selection of works "outside" the genre, he would find that the works inside the genre have features in common not only with one another but also with works that are outside.

The critic's first problem, which arose when he tried to identify a code with texts, is one that he cannot circumvent if he wishes to work with codes: There is a disparity between codes and texts, and one cannot be converted into the other without a loss. His second problem, which consisted in creating a dubious set, was simply a result of fallacious reasoning. The critic was misled by the quest for an invariant. By analogy to textual interpretation, where the code functions as an invariant against which the individual text or variant can be measured, the generic code seemed to represent such an invariant. The conversion of the code into texts seemed to promise a group of texts whose similarity was guaranteed. The similarity, the code-invariant, could then be re-written as a definition. But one cannot convert a code perception into a ready-made genre, or assume that a group of texts possessing a certain similarity is the concrete equivalent of a code. Instead of using codes to explain textual resemblances, the critic used his own code perception to superimpose relatedness onto texts. He misused codes as a principle of closure, as a circuitous and seemingly more sophisticated means for arriving at the definition he failed to arrive at otherwise.

Apparently, then, the real problem the genre critic faces is not the irreconcilability of "description," conceived as a purely empirical method that lacks organizing principles, with "theory," conceived as a method oriented toward systematic ends. Rather, the problem lies within descriptive criticism itself: It consists in an irreconcilability between genre, understood as an idea or norm, and any description of texts. In the specific case, this means a discrepancy between a generic conception or code idea and a set of similar texts.

What does the genre critic study—codes, or groups of texts that have features in common? Plainly, he must study texts. The idea of studying codes per se seems to contradict the very notion of study—of progressing from the general impression to more precise and differentiated information, or from the particular perception to the general conclusion. There is one sense in which codes can be studied, namely, in the sense of describing the code principle or mechanism. Thus, Todorov can show that the "fantastic" operates according to a principle by which the reader is forced to hesitate between a naturalistic and a supernatural reading of events, and I can show that the "diary fiction," conceived in ideal terms, has certain implications, such as the collapse of the narrative triangle and the folding over of the subject of discourse on himself. Describing the code principle in this sense has exactly the same virtues and shortcomings as the typological definition, however. It is heuristically useful, inasmuch as it provides us with a basis for speculation about the potential of a certain type. Its shortcoming is that it has little to do with actual texts. Again the disparity between the relation of literary codes and literary works, and that of the system of language and speech acts, becomes apparent; if we isolate a linguistic rule, this rule tells us a great deal about a certain group of speech acts, whereas isolating a literary code principle tells us relatively little about texts. With a demonstration of the code principle, we have not described texts, nor have we shown anything about the varieties or extent of the principle's occurrence.

> You can never get more out of your classification
> than you put into it.
>   E. H. Gombrich, *Norm and Form*[20]

There are cases where glaring discrepancies between a code perception and a genre do not exist—namely, where a group of texts gave rise to the code perception to begin with. The texts in the group manifest a high degree of homogeneity, and the code perception encompasses the text, so that a given text in its entirety is a more or less perfect realization of the code. A formula is repeated with very little variation from one work to another, so that a cluster of very similar works comes into being. Some critics find it expedient to speak of genres only in such cases. They propose a stricter concept of genre, one that insists on a stable, that is, repeated, organization of elements as a criterion. A single point of similarity, such as a formal element, would be insufficient as a basis for a genre; it must be "completed" by other similarities, for example in tone, theme, devices, implication, and so forth. Thus, Wellek and Warren write: "Genre should be conceived, we think, as a grouping of literary works based, theoretically, upon both outer form (specific meter or structure) and also upon inner form (attitude, tone, purpose—more crudely, subject and audience),"[21] and they give as examples for genres the historical novel (which is tied to Romanticism, nationalism, and historicism) and the Gothic novel (which has a limited subject matter, a stock of devices, and the single aesthetic intent of thrill). Such genres could be seen as a special subset of the more general phenomenon of textual resemblances. The texts are similar and also related; they mutually constitute the code perception for one another. In this strict sense of a stable, repeated organization of elements, genre is obviously an essentially synchronic phenomenon. Other codes, new fashions, have not had a chance to interfere with the production of the formula. Any genre, if traced over a long enough time span, will dissolve, or, stated differently, the longer the time span over which the constellation of elements is traced, the less this constellation appears stable or consistent.

In other genres – of which the diary novel is one – the picture is more confusing: The texts appear to have something in common, but it is difficult to specify precisely what, how much or how little, and the examples are spread out over a long period of time. A classic example of such a muddy genre is the novel itself; it has often been said that novels written from the sixteenth century to the present have little in common except the name. Other classical genres like the ode, or types that have received enough attention recently to be accepted into the canon of genres, like the grotesque, are similarly elusive. Or we can propose our own categories, based on our own perceptions of similarities, rather than adopt traditional ones; we can speak of open-ended dramas, or political novels, or metapoetic poetry. Studies that compare several works as examples of a "category" proliferate.

How do we study these genres? We are back at the classic problem, often cited by theoreticians of genre, which we phrased earlier in terms of definition versus history. We can now formulate it in terms of similarity versus bibliography. When we actually set about the task of doing our research, which of the two comes first? We need a point of resemblance in order to be able to find a group of texts, and we need the group of texts in order to study the resemblance. Neither comes ready-made. We have certain examples, and an idea based on these examples – a code perception. We would now like to enlarge our bibliography. Our aim is not to press texts into false conformity with a definition. Nevertheless, just in order to be able to find further texts, we need something similar to a definition, though less ambitious: a point of departure, a point of resemblance that enables us to find similar texts.

First, can we dispense with codes? There is at least one sense in which we cannot. Codes not only explain the relatedness between texts; they are also a *critical* inevitability, inasmuch as they enter into the very process of finding similar works. Even if the critic uses the most empirical method for finding textual similarities, a method that renounces any a priori organizing principle, his perception of similarities will at some point modulate into a code idea, namely at the point where he scrutinizes a new text in order to compare it to an already existing group.

But can we nevertheless – bearing in mind that the act of comparison implies a certain simplification – single out a feature or features that our initial group has in common, or convert our initial "larger" code perception once and for all into such features, and then go looking for further examples? As a practical method and an expedient, yes. We can certainly arrive at a bibliography that way, always keeping in mind that we are not trying to arrive at a closed group, one that suggests an "inside" and an "outside."

Among the possible objections to this method, one in particular stands out. How can we guarantee objectivity? How can we conclusively refute the charge that we may have fabricated a genre, arbitrarily imposed relatedness onto a set of texts, all the while ignoring more salient, more genuine, and more interesting textual relations? How do we convince the reader that the feature or features we have singled out, the point of similarity, reflects an actual relatedness between texts and is not merely of our own concocting? In other words, how do we convince the reader that we are not comparing a cat, ink, and the frying pan because all are black?

Thus the project of studying genres, as distinct from arriving at recognitions about the nature of genres, brings problems with it, and these problems assert themselves at the simple level of finding an object of study, defining it, and justifying it once found. To be sure, we know that textual similarities exist. Yet how do we isolate and study these resemblances? If we start by assuming that something as delicate and elusive as encoding is responsible for textual similarities, any attempt on our part to convert the psychological into the concrete seems to violate the spirit of the theory itself. Moreover, any given concretization brings with it the accusation of subjectivity. Paul Hernadi in *Beyond Genre* makes the point that genre study foregrounds some particular aspect of works, and classifies the "genres of genre criticism" into four broad types, those that emphasize form, or content, or mood, or response. One of the potentially most persuasive arguments against genre criticism is that such categories are of questionable validity. For unlike works, such characteristics are not necessarily agreed-on units; they are concepts of arguable status, apparently arbitrated by the beholder. They seem to be constantly open to dispute as fading into one another, and, taken singly, seem susceptible to being redivided. If there has been a school of criticism (typified by Croce) persistently opposed to genre study, it is because such study "dissolves" the single work, drives a wedge into it, and attempts to posit new and less obviously tenable units in its stead.

Yet it is possible to counter such objections inasmuch as they are ideological, rather than strictly methodological. No approach to literature can claim rigorous objectivity; every other approach, including intrinsic criticism, is open to the same accusations that are leveled at genre study: that its method selects one way of looking at things to the exclusion of others, that the mapping it chooses preordains conclusions of a certain type, and that the method is self-validating in the sense that it brings with it a mapping or set of examples that prove it. Every approach to literature makes a connection that is "loose," that rests on faith.

What is really at issue is traditional mappings – ones that have hardened, that have become conventional and accepted, and that no longer alarm us because we are used to them – versus new ones. One can very well argue, in defense of new mappings, that restricting oneself to accepted categories for talking about literature, to "normal discourse," amounts to limiting oneself to expectable results.[22] Productive and interesting new ways of assessing evidence, one could argue, should be sought out, not avoided. Is there not, at the bottom of the urge to classify, an urge to compare, because sparks come out of the comparison – even the comparison of the cat, ink, and the frying pan? Do comparative studies, studies that establish "categories," really testify first and foremost to a rage for order – or are they not, rather, motivated by a delight in recognizing similarities and comparing differences?

Genre study, then, should not be rejected because it fails to live up to an unattainable objectivity. I have criticized one traditional type of genre study, rather, for operating in the name of objectivity but in the actual service of critical convenience, for imposing a preconceived notion of genre onto texts even though this notion manifestly does not conform to what we know about how genres come into being. The problem we confront now is essentially a different one. It concerns practical methods, and consists of a need to resolve a discrepancy, or at least find a compromise, between the assumptions we hold about genre on the one hand and the actual methods we have for studying the material on the other. For, as we know, there is no "pure description." Description always involves, if not an ideological decision, at least a methodological decision that will influence the outcome of the study. Even if we are conscious of the assumptions underlying our project – even if we avoid an unquestioned, self-validating mode – we are nevertheless obliged, when we begin practical genre criticism, to choose one method or another, each of which will prejudice our results.

> C'est une mauvaise méthode que de partir des mots
> pour définir les choses.
>> Saussure, *Cours de linguistique générale*[23]

One should not confuse methodological criticism with ideological criticism, to the extent of arguing that because a project is difficult or seemingly undoable, the enterprise itself lacks value. There is also no reason not to attempt a project with the means that exist. One should merely bear in mind that the conclusions one reaches have to be evaluated relative to the means as well as to the aim of the study. We know that textual resemblances exist; we also know that we will have problems dealing with them even if we have only modest descriptive ambitions, and that these problems arise precisely at the level of deciding on the object of inquiry and finding a group of texts on which to base the study. How do we proceed?

Our assumption is that with genre, we are within the broader field of textual resemblances generally. Textual resemblances are not completely fortuitous but are, rather, traceable to encoding. With this insight, we are automatically committed to historical genre criticism. We seem to have the choice between two possible procedures for finding a bibliography and for studying a genre – for the two endeavors are, as has become clear, intimately linked. Each of them would imply limited, but different, results.

First, we could try to make use of the conclusion that textual resemblances result from encoding and attempt to perform this process, so to speak, in reverse. Taking into account all the reservations having to do with reconstructing a past code perception and identifying it with texts, we could, nevertheless, try to identify the codes behind the works we have singled out, and then "dissolve" these codes into further works. (We would thus say: Diary novel A derives from a code that is traceable to work B; work B derives from a code that is traceable to work C, and so forth.) The result would be an approximation of a naturally constituted chain of texts. Using this method, we would avoid an a priori notion of the object of study; instead of starting with a definition, we would investigate presumptive historical relations. Definition, bibliography, and history would, seemingly, be accomplished all in one.

Such a process of studying the dynamic relation between texts may, however, lead away not only from our initial code perception but also from any unified view of the genre. The actual continuities between examples will probably not correspond to what we would imagine as a progressive regress within a single code. The originally isolated configuration of devices that we perceived to constitute the code may well not remain in configuration as we progress from work to work. Each trait is apt to lead in a different direction; one may find oneself in a garden of forking paths where initially unsuspected codes present themselves as routes to follow. The critic can hope to arrive at a related chain of texts, but not a homogeneous group of texts. For – as is true of many novels written as diaries – it is not necessarily the case that the historically prior works of a given set will compose the code for a given work. Potentially, even probably, threading our way through the historical constitution of resemblances between texts will give us a different list of works from that obtained by tracing texts that manifest a certain trait or set of traits.

The second procedure would be to depart from the critic's present code perception and trace its history, using the method for finding a bibliography described in the previous section. (Thus we would set the code "diary novel" equal to a set of features manifested by the group of similar works we start with, and look for further works with the same features.) Let us consider the advantages and disadvantages of following this method. We may begin with a focal point, a concept of the whole, but as we proceed we will lose this orientation more and more. Any clear picture we might have of what the salient features of a genre are dissolves if we look at the genre over a long enough time period. An element will disappear. Others will be assimilated into the configuration. What we originally perceived as "dominant," to speak with the Russian Formalists, will lose its dominant position. In time, our genre may seem to resemble more closely what we think of as another genre than what we perceived as the genre "itself." This phenomenon has to do with the nature of codes and encoding. Encoding implies that types are established but also that type boundaries are crossable; the types can be modified, and also melt into other types. Particularly at the origins of a genre, we can expect to find such crossings and modifications. A genre might typically originate when two codes are merged, when an old fashion is radically modified and that radical modification is copied. Eventually the new fashion is perceived to be a thing distinct from the old; people realize they are writing in a tradition; the genre jells and becomes self-conscious; it is given a name.

When we say that a genre "changes," we mean something like the change of the meaning of a word vis-à-vis its signifier. At any given moment, the word has a certain signification, but the meaning changes while the signifier remains constant. Yet in genre history it is not a question of a simple binary relation whereby the thing changes vis-à-vis a constant signifier. Rather, when we speak of a genre changing, we mean that there is a change vis-à-vis *some* constant. The constant will not necessarily remain the same element; one element will represent the constant at one time, another at another. If we follow the "thread" of our twentieth-century diary novel back to its origins in the eighteenth century, to give a concrete example, at a certain point this thread splits. On the one hand, we have a group of novels that are written in the first person and possess a day-to-day time structure but are not called "journals." On the other hand, we have fiction that is called "journal" and is written in the first person, but lacks the day-to-day time structure.

Which direction should we follow? How should we assess this evidence? Shall we say that the epistolary novel modified the diary novel, or that the diary novel is an offspring of the epistolary novel? We can say either one, depending on our perspective, or both.

When the constant element changes, this of course implies a radical modification in the genre, while the very idea of genre implies that the consistency between texts is greater than the inconsistency. Presumably, if we are to speak of a "genre" at all, we will find a fiber that will form a more consistent part of the thread than the others. It will seem, often enough, that the most constant element actually is the name that has been given to the genre. Thus if we say that the novel changes, what we mean is that the word "novel" remains the same, while this word is used to designate a multitude of different phenomena.

We will not necessarily want to identify the object of our study with such a generic name, however. The moment at which a new genre acquired a name was a privileged moment, the moment at which people recognized its existence as a type and became conscious of it as a code. From that point on, people had the word and its signification in mind when they wrote. The shape of created things (unlike real things) is prejudiced by the existence of the word; these creations are often enough brought into conformity with the word's meaning; people try to adapt what they create to what they imagine when they think of the word. The existence of a generic name both produces and testifies to a certain consistency in the things designated by the name. Yet it is just as clear that there are great variations in the thing designated by the word. The critic should not let the generic name, or other people's consciousness of what is similar, dictate his perception of what is similar. New forms can attach themselves to an old signifier and modify the genre thus named. As Boris Tomaševskij states, "Because works habitually attach themselves to already defined genres, a genre's name remains the same while a radical change comes about in the construction of the works belonging to it."[24] What we perceive as the thing may also persist under another name. For example, we can say that when novels in letters began to be called "journals," a new name was added to an old form. When fiction called "journals" began to be written from day to day, a new form attached itself to an old name. To trace the history of a genre that is perceived as all the works designated by a particular word would be, in effect, to trace the history of the word, and not of a particular thing.

3

The Diary Novel
Reconsidered

How then shall we proceed with the diary novel? Our discussion led us to the point where we had a choice. We can follow the consecutive realization of a trait or constellation of traits, or we can try to reconstruct the process by which textual resemblances are created. These alternative methods for finding a bibliography imply different approaches to studying the history of a genre, as well as different texts. The first method implies that we are studying the history of something in particular, perhaps our present code perception; the second method implies that we are studying the historical relations between texts. With the first method our interest lies in similar texts, and by implication in the differences within this similarity. With the second method our interest lies in related texts.

It is clearly of interest to pursue both methods. My primary intention in this study is to trace the history of something in particular, namely, the twentieth-century diary novel. It is also of great interest, however, to see how this genre intersects at various points with other codes. The question of generic openness is particularly appropriate in the case of the diary novel. The diary novel proves extremely diffuse, and also discontinuous; there was a period in which it nearly died out. This diffuseness and discontinuity should be considered, first of all, in the light of a special aspect of the diary novel's genericity. The diary novel is a *mimetic form*,[25] that is, a form that the system of fiction has borrowed from the system of letters in general. As such it is by no means unique: Other first-person novel genres, such as the memoir novel and the epistolary novel, are similarly mimetic.

The importance of the real diary in the history of the diary novel can hardly be overestimated.[26] The first diary fiction that resembles what we think of today as a diary appeared in European literature in the eighteenth century, but diaries themselves (as distinct from records of state, annals, merchants' journals, housewives' notes, monks' chronicles, and compilations of scientific notations) began to be written in the fourteenth century in Italy, and by the sixteenth century they were common all over Europe.[27] We assume that genres are constituted through acts of imitation. This mimetic hypothesis leaves us with the question of origin: Where does the first example come from? The origin of the diary novel is not lost in darkness; we can pinpoint a first example; and this first example involved imitation of the prior nonfictional form. The earliest diary fiction imitated real diaries, and for a long and formative period in its history, the diary novel continued to be subject to the influence of the real diary. Even after the diary novel became a self-conscious genre and authors showed an awareness that they were writing in a certain fictional tradition, this influence manifested itself. The nonfiction model was always present; even if many authors of diary novels had no intention whatsoever of faithfully imitating the nonfiction counterpart, it was, and is, hardly possible to write a narrative in the first person with a day-to-day time structure and no fictive reader and remain unconscious of the congruence of this form with the form of the diary. Consequently, diary novels have always had something to do with what the authors thought real diaries were – whether they were outright imitations of the real object, whether they merely absorbed certain connotations of the idea of the diary, or whether they used real diaries as negative models for parody or the like.

The diary has conventionally implied not only a certain form but also a certain content, a particular context or specific accompanying circumstances, and an implicit purpose or legitimation. In the mimetic process this changing function was often absorbed by the diary novel. Many novels, in particular trivial ones, adopt the diary as a prepackaged conception, so that mimetic considerations determine both the form and the content of the fictional work.

If diary fiction manifests a peculiar tenacity compared to other fictional genres, it is because the real diary provided a continuously present and ever new point of departure. Because the fictive diary imitated the real diary – in itself a changing and diffuse genre – and always in some measure reflected its real base, the fictional genre took on many different forms. But the diary novel was not only strongly influenced by the changing fashions of the real journal; it was, particularly at its origins, indebted to the influence of another novel form, the epistolary novel. Needless to say, throughout its history the diary novel has also borne the mark of various other current literary preoccupations and novelistic fashions. If the continued presence of the real diary accounts for the tenacity of the fictional genre, its compatibility or incompatibility with such dominant fashions as the psychological novel and literary realism account for its increase or loss in popularity at different times. Originally conceived as a subset of the novel, then, the diary novel crosses over in the alternation of codes and examples both into nonfiction and into other novel types.

While I shall take these extra-generic influences into account, the focus in the following chapters will be on the genre I call the diary novel. The preceding discussion showed that if we want to trace the history of something in particular, we cannot really begin without a concept, an idea of the genre, a point of orientation and a fixed point against which to measure what we find. If we take the relatively homogeneous group of twentieth-century diary novels as our starting point, we have various paths we could follow. Our group of twentieth-century diary novels has in common a certain form, a content that is confessional in its tendency, and the fact that these novels are called "diaries" or "journals." I have chosen to take the diary form as a point of orientation – or, more specifically, the constellation of formal traits I described as a first-person narrative, written from day to day, and without a fictive reader. There are two reasons for choosing this focus.

The first reason is that the constellation of formal elements – which coincides with what we think of today as a "diary," although it does not exhaust the idea – is the feature that makes diary novels most interesting as works of art. Given that the diary novel is mimetic, it is in their use of form that diary novels usually achieve the greatest degree of independence from real diaries. Diary novels very often borrow the conception of the diary – the diary type, the diarist's motivation for writing, and so forth – at face value from real models. The conception of the diary is the most mimetic aspect of the diary novel, so that the reader who would study the diary type or the theme of the diary in a diary novel is usually referred back to genuine journals of the same period. The idea of the borrowed conception is of interest primarily in eighteenth-century diary fiction, because at that time mimetic considerations promoted the use of the form. Diary novels adopt the formal structure of real diaries as well, but they generally do not copy real diaries' *use* of form. The authors of real diaries use the day-to-day structure in accordance with the premise that they are writing a "diary," and thereafter without thought to the artistic potential of the form; they simply accumulate a record of one day after the next. The authors of diary novels, on the contrary, choose the form consciously, and usually with some particular artistic end in view: to convey the impression of immediacy, to show the development of a character, to present variations on a theme, to establish a context for dramatic irony, and so forth. There are, of course, diary novels that play with the current or a traditional conception of the diary and exploit it artistically, but in most cases it is their use of the diary form rather than their use of the idea of the diary that makes diary novels most interesting as fictional works. The most ingenious modern innovations, certainly, have involved playing with the form or the implications of the form.[28]

My second reason for choosing the diary's formal structure as a point of orientation is that this structure has been associated with the idea of the diary for a long period in its history (where content, in contrast, has been quite variable), and yet it *is not* precisely the "idea of the diary." I have chosen not to take the word "diary" and its synonyms as my point of departure for the study of the diary novel – although the appellation "diary novel" would seem to suggest that the object of investigation should be all fictional works labeled diaries, journals, or the like – for I have found that such a delimitation of the subject matter leads only to confusion. It is true that the word is very influential. Its signification at a given time often, in fact usually, has a determining influence on the form, style, and content of what the author of a diary novel writes. But is has a history that is at base separate from that of any of the central elements of the group I call "diary novels," including the formal structure I have already described. The formal structure has been designated by many signifiers, quite apart from "diary" and etymologically related words: "chronicle," "notes," "papers," even "letters" (to look at English alone). The word "diary" has denoted formal structures unlike the one under consideration, for example, retrospective first-person narratives and impersonal predictive texts (almanacs). Furthermore, the word "diary" has signified in its successive usages not only different forms but also not even always primarily a form; sometimes it has signified chiefly a particular kind of content. In short, the thing designated by the word has changed considerably in the course of the word's history. The set of fictional works called "diaries" is potentially a collection of heterogeneous examples linked *only* by the word. Consequently, it is essential to differentiate between the structure – or the element to be studied – and the word, even though it will often seem artificial to apply the distinction, since interpenetration rather than separation is the rule in the history of the genre, and since to a very large degree the set of novels united by the designation "diary" intersects with the set defined by the formal characteristics I have outlined.

A brief survey of the history of the word and its synonyms will help make apparent to what extent usage coincides with, or diverges from, the structural description I have just given. It will also make it possible for us to see how the changing usage of the word affected the history of the diary novel.

All of the words for "diary" in French, English, and German derive from the Latin expressions for "daily," the two adjectives *diurnus* and *diarius*. *Journal,* the dominant expression in French, was historically the first word used to describe diarylike records. The word *journal* has been documented since the fourteenth century. Until the eighteenth century the word occurred most commonly in the compound *papier journal,* and *papier journal* became the standard expression for any relation of day-to-day events. *Papier journal* is typically defined as "memoire de ce qui se fait, de ce qui se passe chaque jour" (*Dictionaire universel,* 1690). No distinction was made between private diaries and public modes, like newspapers and periodicals, of recounting the events of every day, and the emphasis is on the chronological comprehensiveness of the content, not on the formal characteristics of the product. The same is true of the less frequently recorded noun *journal:* Richelet's *Dictionaire françois* (1680) defines *journal* as "recit de ce qui se passe chaque jour." In English four words have been used to describe a daily record: "journal," "journal-book," "diary," and "daybook." All of them came to mean a daily record in the late sixteenth and early seventeenth centuries. The expression "journal-book" is a translation of the French *papier journal* and fell into disuse rather rapidly. "Daybook" persisted as a synonym for "diary" into the late nineteenth century, but its usage became increasingly restricted to bookkeeping. As in French, the English definitions of "diary" and "journal" began by stressing a record of daily events. Samuel Johnson's *Dictionary of the English Language* (1755), for example, defines "diary" as "an account of the transactions, accidents, and observations of every day," and the definition in Webster's American dictionary of 1828 is similar. The German *Tagebuch* originated in 1613, when Kepler created the word to translate the Latin *diurna* (cf. *Trübners Deutsches Wörterbuch,* Berlin, 1956). In 1711, Rädlein's *Europäischer Sprach-schatz* defined *Tagebuch* as a book "darinnen verzeichnet wird, was täglich geschieht." According to this definition the diary is merely a record of what happens every day: There is no indication yet that the content is personal, or even that it concerns the diarist. Adelung's definition (1807–8) does not differ from Rädlein's, but the contemporary lexicographer Joachim Heinrich Campe establishes an emphatic connection between the individual diarist and what he writes in his diary: A diary can contain either "was täglich vorfällt" or "was man bemerkt, beobachtet, thut."

All of the above definitions stress that *each day's* events are recorded. One receives the impression of a rather circumstantial, compendious record in which the events of each day, regardless of how undistinguished, are given their due. The "diurnal" quality of the journal obtained in the nature of the events recorded, rather than in the act of recording them. Thus the journal is a work that gives an account of daily events, rather than one that gives a daily account of events. For example, Daniel Defoe's *Journal of the Plague Year* (1722) is a record of how the plague of 1665 spread in London from day to day. The narrator claims, fictitiously, of course, that the account is based on "memorandums" he wrote down every day during the Plague Year, but the document prepared for the public eye, the finished novel, is in fact in the retrospective form of an eyewitness report. It records daily events, but it is not a day-to-day record.

Beginning around the middle of the eighteenth century, the recorded meaning of "journal" underwent a major and significant shift. The change is first documented in France; for example, *Le Grand Vocabulaire françois* (1767–74) defines *journal* as "relation jour par jour, de ce qui se passe ou s'est passé en quelque pays, en quelque endroit, en quelque négociation, en quelque affaire." There is still no explicit distinction between newspapers and diaries, but the emphasis on daily relation does exclude retrospective types of writing like memoirs or histories. In the definitions of the words for "diary" given in English and German dictionaries, the idea of regular writing replaces the idea of a circumstantial account of each day's events in the nineteenth century.

At different times in different countries, a second major shift in the meaning of the words for "diary" occurred. This time it concerned the content of the diary. Like Campe, lexicographers began to recognize the tradition of the personal diary. Thus the *New English Dictionary* (1897) defines "diary" as "a daily record of events or transactions; a journal; specifically, a daily record of matters affecting the writer personally, or which come under his personal observation." The 1944 edition of the *Sprachbrockhaus* lists "Buch für tägliche Aufzeichnungen über wichtige Erlebnisse." In France the specifically personal content of the *journal* was acknowledged later than elsewhere, probably because the expression *journal intime* came into use to describe private diaries and the simple word *journal* remained relatively free of personal connotations unless linked to the adjective. "Journal" became the preferred expression for a private diary only recently. The change reflects the expansion and diversification of the journal's functions in the twentieth century. "Journal" no longer primarily conveys the impression of a strictly intimate record; it can be anything from a book of jottings or reflections to a published literary work. The *Dictionnaire du français vivant* (1972) defines *journal* as having a personal content in the widest sense: "le compte rendu quotidien ou quasi quotidien de mes occupations, des événements auxquels j'ai été mêlé, des réflexions que j'ai faites, etc." and notes, "on dit aussi, journal intime."

Contemporary definitions like that of the *Dictionnaire du français vivant* show that the diary is no longer thought of as a strictly quotidian

record. The emphasis on regular writing has been dropped. The definition of *Tagebuch* in the 1970 *Duden* mirrors this present-day change in
the concept of the diary: "Buch, in dem man persönliche Erlebnisse und
Gedanken aufzeichnet." Here there is no mention of daily writing at all;
the temporality implicit in the etymology of the word no longer plays
any part in its meaning, for the diarist does not necessarily describe the
events of each day, nor does he describe daily.

4

The Diary Form: Techniques

Up till now I have left one distinction unquestioned in my discussion of the genre that is the subject of this book, the distinction between the real and the fictional document. I have based my argument on the tacit assumption that the distinction between the fictional diary and the real diary is a valid one. In fact, it could be seen to be the most controversial of all the distinctions in which the subject is involved. The concept "fiction" opens up an abyss. Recent critics have justifiably questioned a distinction between "report" and "fiction," especially one based on a criterion of correspondence to actual lived reality. It has been argued, taking autobiographical narrative as a starting point, that the existence of a writing subject in any given kind of narration tends to undermine all genre distinctions; all writing is autobiographical, while fiction is inevitable.[29] Such theories complement avant-garde literary trends of the 1960s and, particularly, 1970s. It has become increasingly fashionable to write works that are neither factual nor fictional, or both, or in some way obscure the distinction between the categories.

The range of works that have appeared under the name of "diary" seems to offer a particularly fortunate case for disputing the existence of a clear distinction between fictional and factual narrative, particularly if the distinction is based on the truth to life of the subject matter. First, and most obviously, there are the many "literary" diaries published in the twentieth century, which have become a kind of genre in themselves. Journals like Max Frisch's *Tagebuch 1946–1949* (1950), a melange of *journal intime,* essayistic pieces, and fiction, were followed by works that defied any kind of categorization, such as Günter Grass's *Aus dem Tagebuch einer Schnecke* (1972), which is partly the diary Grass kept while campaigning for Willy Brandt, partly a novel about an invented character. Even earlier, however, in an age when the distinction between fiction and autobiography was accorded more weight, diaries were published that presented themselves as real but that are open to charges of fictionalization, like Bettina von Arnim's *Goethes Briefwechsel mit einem Kinde* (1835) with its diary, which the author reworked for publication more than twenty years after the original composition. Then there are autobiographical novels, and works like Pierre Loti's semifictional accounts of his adventures in exotic places, collections of glittering sketches cast loosely in diary form. Other works, despite superficial trappings of fiction, in one way or another resist classification as novels. Pustkuchen's rival *Wilhelm Meister,* his *Wilhelm Meisters Tagebuch* (1822), for example, is a collection of aphorisms or thoughts whose title indicates that it was written by a fictitious character, but which lacks any kind of fable. Kierkegaard, who writes a mixture of philosophy, autobiography, and fiction, includes novelistic diaries in two of his longer works, *Either/Or* (1843), which contains the "Diary of a Seducer," and *Stages on Life's Way* (1845), which contains " 'Guilty?'/'Not Guilty?' "

Despite these borderline cases, however, I would suggest that there is an essential difference between first-person novels and nonfictional first-person narrative. It is significant because it provides the possibility for very different kinds of creation. At this point it will be useful to recall Käte Hamburger's discussion of first-person fiction as she presents it in *The Logic of Literature.* Hamburger denies that there is any *formal* distinction between first-person fictional and first-person nonfictional narrative. Basing her argument on a differentiation between first- and third-person narrative – a distinction that is, in fact, not as clear as she would have it – she finds that only third-person novels bear formal signs of fiction. These signs are the use of the epic preterite, verbs of inner action applied to the third person, and narrated and straight monologues. First-person fictional narratives, according to Hamburger, lack these signals. Instead, they are "feigned reality statements." As such, they are formally identical to nonfictional first-person texts. She writes, "It is an innate characteristic of every first-person narrative that it presents itself as nonfiction, i.e., as a historical document."[30] According to Hamburger, we can distinguish first-person fiction from real documents only on the basis of the unreality of the former's content.[31]

It is certainly true that fictional first-person narratives can be written in such a way that they are indistinguishable from real first-person narratives. It is easy enough to write a fake diary – an example would be *The Journal of a Spy,* allegedly written by Raoul Hesdin and published in 1794, but actually written by Charles Fletcher in 1895. I would submit, however, that there is a primary distinction that separates first-person fiction from nonfiction, and that in the novel this essential difference frequently gives rise to formal or technical differences. The distinction becomes particularly clear in the case of the diary and the diary novel.

The diary itself involves the diarist and what he writes; he may or may not show his diary to a reader. The diary novel involves a diarist who is a fictional character, a set of events he writes about, and a fictive reader (who is often lacking). Outside this first narrative triangle, however, there is a second one. The fictional diary purports to be written by a fictional character, but *in fact* it is written by a real author, for real readers. The communicated object in this second narrative triangle is the entire first narrative triangle of fictive narrator, narrated world, and fictive reader. A diagram illustrates the difference:

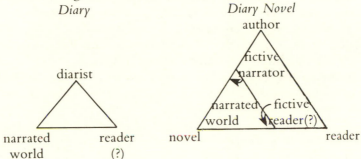

The difference between the diary and the diary novel, then, is based on the existence of a simple communicative situation in the former and a framed communicative situation in the latter. In the diary novel the author is distinct from the narrator, while in the diary he is not. This particular difference has far-reaching consequences.

Let us consider the real diarist's relationship to his form. Writing from day to day, he records his current feelings or thoughts, or events from the immediate past. If he wishes, he can record remote memories. But he cannot foresee what will happen or what he will think on any future date, and if he keeps his diary as a genuine record, he cannot predict what he will write in the future. The diary is thus a form that eludes the author's full control.[32]

The diarist has various ways of reimposing his control on the diary. He can – although the idea is farfetched – decide what he will write in advance. He may structure his perception of the present, and his account of it, according to insights conceived in the past. His past writing may influence his present writing, so that a kind of plot is superimposed on the diary. Michel Butor has parodied such an attempt in his diary novel *L'Emploi du temps*. The possibility – indeed, the inevitability – that fictional structures shape a kind of writing whose overt purpose is to furnish a record of real life has been widely discussed and affirmed in the case of autobiography. Restated in its crudest form, the argument is that whereas real life rarely arranges itself into plots, the autobiographer tends, retrospectively, to superimpose on his past a coherent line of development similar to a plot. He makes his life tellable, and worthy of being told, by turning it into a story. A similar argument has been made for certain diaries and correspondences; it is said that such works as Kafka's diaries and letters or the correspondence between Stefan Zweig and Joseph Roth[33] appear to have been written – or if not written, at least received – as if they were fictional diaries or epistolary novels.

It seems to me, however, that the creeping influence of fictional structures – that is to say, plots – is much less automatic and more problematical in exchanges of letters and diaries than in autobiography. Letters and diaries are defined by a periodic and forward-marching time of writing. It is a psychological truism that it is easy to superimpose a fiction on the past in accordance with some present interest, but the hold of the past over the present, or of the present over the future, is less certain, and its mechanisms are less clearly predictable. It may be true that key experiences may lead to a neurotic repetition of certain kinds of situations, but it is also true that our past preoccupations, for example, the most urgent desires of childhood and adolescence, fade. If psychological determinism exists, it is not the same as artistic determination.

In the diary novel, the fictive diarist has no more control over his material and his form than the real diarist. The author, in contrast, has absolute control. For example, the author can create a plot. He can also use whatever other literary techniques he wants – leitmotifs, allegory, irony. What the presence of the second narrative triangle means for the diary novel, in contrast to the real diary, is essentially the presence of a second voice in the narrative, which we can broadly designate as the voice of the author. This voice will appear in different guises in different novels and can be refracted into several voices: the voice of the plot, of irony, of symbol, and so forth. Even the form can speak. As we will see in the discussions of Max Frisch's *Stiller,* Michel Butor's *L'Emploi du temps,* and Doris Lessing's *Golden Notebook,* the diary's structure itself can be exploited to illustrate and reinforce the novel's thesis, or to undermine the diarist's own intent. Form is not necessarily just a container for other voices; it can become "expressive," and the less mimetic considerations play a role in the history of the diary novel, the more writers tend to use it that way.

The reader of real diaries may, of course, become aware of the sound of other "voices" between the lines. The practice of psychoanalysis is founded on the idea that repressed material is in conflict with the subject's conscious discourse but is recoverable precisely through discourse. An author may also take an ironic position toward himself, and so forth. But there is no way that other voices can prevail as fully, insistently, and coherently in the real diary as in the fictional diary. In this sense first-person fiction is comparable to third-person fiction: There is an author and there are characters, and they are distinct.

How do we read, how do we understand first-person narrative? The fictional allies in which the reader is accustomed to place his trust – the authoritative fictive narrator or the interplay of different points of view – are not there. Ostensibly we hear only a single, subjective voice, that of the narrator. The narrator may change his mind, but it is nevertheless *his* mind; he may doubt or question himself, but it is still he who is doubting; he may narrate events whose full significance he does not understand till later, but it is always he who reports, understands, or revises. The reflective interplay of his consciousness may be shown in hundredfold complication, but it is a closed structure that is subject only to internal refraction and cannot be questioned from without either by "the facts," or by other characters, or by an omniscient narrator.

Nevertheless, as I have suggested, even though we are asked to believe that we hear only the voice of the first-person narrator, other voices may become audible, voices that are undeniably not the character's own. The ascription of the narrative to a single voice, that of the narrator, may be a naturalization of what is in fact a more complicated state of affairs.[34] If we read carefully and suspiciously, we may be able to denaturalize the narrator's discourse and find points in the text that support, belie, or simply enrich a reading based on our voluntary acceptance of the fiction that the narrator alone is speaking. As I have shown, fictional first-person narrative paradigmatically involves two narrative triangles. If we can find points where the second narrative triangle intrudes into the first, we can accept these points of intrusion as indications of how to read the text. Especially if we can identify these other voices as the author's voice, if we find traces of the author's hand, we have entrances into the text.

The presence of a second narrative triangle or framed communicative situation makes possible varying degrees of tension between what the narrator says and the text's own voice. In order to discuss such tension, it will be useful to distinguish between the "story" (the complete account, including information supplied by voices other than the narrator's) and the "discourse" (the story as told by the personal voice of the narrator). This distinction is, of course, a variation on such well-known pairs of oppositions as Šklovskij's "fabula" (the story itself), and "sujet" (the story as told), and Benveniste's "histoire" (a form that excludes the "I-you" relation) and "discours" (a form that uses all personal verb forms, third ["he"] as well as first and second ["I-you"]). The tensions in first-person narrative are generated by allocating the narrative to different voices or, to state the simplest case, to the voices of the narrator and the author.

If an author wishes to avoid such tension, he has a simple means at his disposition. He can make a formal separation between the "story" and the "discourse" by juxtaposing first- and third-person narratives. Many authors who use the journal device adopt this technique, inserting portions of a character's journal into a narrative otherwise written in the third person. In the historical sections that follow, I shall not devote space to discussing this technique, but it is widespread enough to deserve mention here. It was a favorite device in the eighteenth and early nineteenth centuries and persisted on into the twentieth century, even though it often strikes one as somewhat out-of-date after *style indirect libre* was developed. The purpose is almost always the same: The author wishes to have an omniscient narrator recount the story, and thereby keep a firm grip on the facts of the plot, yet at the same time make the reader privy to a character's feelings by quoting his thoughts extensively. For, as one late-eighteenth-century writer puts it, journal passages "being written at the time, and to the moment, . . . give a more lively representation of these feelings of the heart than can be conveyed by cold narration."[35] Walter Scott, interrupting an exchange of letters in *Redgauntlet* to begin a third-person narrative, seizes the opportunity to survey the narrative tradition from the perspective of 1824, summarize the advantages and limitations of first-person narration, and justify his own procedure:

> The advantage of laying before the reader, in the words of the actors themselves, the adventures which we must otherwise have narrated in our own, has given great popularity to the publication of epistolary correspondence, as practised by various great authors, and by ourselves in the preceding chapters. Nevertheless, a genuine correspondence of this kind . . . can seldom be found to contain all in which it is necessary to instruct the reader for the full comprehension of the story. Also it must often happen that various prolixities and redundancies occur in the course of an interchange of letters, which must hang as a dead weight on the progress of the narrative. To avoid this dilemma, some biographers have used the letters of the personages concerned, or liberal extracts from them, to describe particular incidents, or express the sentiments which they entertained; while they connect them occasionally with such portions of narrative, as may serve to carry on the thread of the story.[36]

Scott here suggests that the use of first-person narrative *alone* could prove awkward. It is not suited, he thinks, to recounting plot. He is quite right. As we shall see, the first person sometimes proves a genuine hindrance in early journal novels, where great emphasis is placed on the plot, and where the narrator is not in a position to report certain important facts accurately. It is revealing that in the nineteenth century, the age of literary realism and broadly based plots, the fictional journal fell out of fashion with first-person forms generally, even though the same period witnessed the flowering of the *journal intime*.

In later fiction, where the form is put to more appropriate use than to serve as a vehicle for convoluted plots, techniques for the insertion of the "real story" into the story as told by the narrator, for "telling all" within the framework of first-person narrative itself, became interesting. The sheer ambiguity that can be generated by a situation in which the reader has no authoritative voice to trust gained in fascination, so that the journal form was put to use precisely to sustain this ambiguity, to keep the reader guessing at the plot and the character simultaneously.

The simplest relation between the first and second narrative triangles is that of *consonance* and *dissonance,* to use terminology introduced by Dorrit Cohn.[37] In other words, the author may endorse the narrator and his discourse, or he may choose to undermine him. While these polarities do not exhaust the possibilities for the interaction of secondary voices with the narrator's primary voice, they nevertheless deserve special attention in a discussion of the diary novel, for in the history of the genre there is a strong tendency for works to converge on one pole or the other, for authors either to validate their diarists or to take the opposite attitude of dissent.

Certain aspects of the diary form, I think, invite these opposing authorial attitudes. The form makes the diary especially suited to a sympathetic presentation of the narrator: The lack of a fictive reader suggests uninhibited self-expression, while the periodic time scheme makes possible an immediate and vivid presentation of the narrator's sentiments. But the same periodic time scheme prevents the diarist from predicting the future and thus also makes it exceptionally easy for an author to present a deluded or "unreliable" narrator – one whose insights are undermined by a dissenting second voice, such as the voice of the implied author, or the reader's common sense, or of dramatic irony in the plot.

H. Porter Abbott, who has devoted an article on the diary and the diarylike epistolary novel to the question of authorial endorsement and nonendorsement, places great emphasis on the outcome of novels and the criterion of change in the main character. Abbott shows that a fictive diarist who comes to an honest self-recognition and changes is often authorially validated, while a diarist who does not change is self-deceiving and thus frequently does not have the author's support.[38] As we shall see, authors have many other ways as well for expressing their approval or disapproval of their diarists within the work. All of these methods involve ways of inserting the story into the discourse, of letting the second narrative triangle shine through or surface.

Moreover, the diary's predominant connotation, "sincerity," encourages authors to take a position toward that embattled notion by either implicitly espousing it or explicitly debunking it. It should be stressed that this connotation originated in value criteria rather than in actual historical examples; readers of the first major intimate journal to be published, Henri-Frédéric Amiel's, already noted the ambiguities implicit in "sincere" self-analysis. Nevertheless, the connotation clung to the diary; it accompanied it through the nineteenth-century *journal intime* vogue, by which the diary became a major confessional genre. The assumption is that because the diarist writes secretly he writes sincerely, and that the self in the diary is the "true" self and stands in contrast to the outward facade presented to the public. Even in the twentieth century, writers of fiction often adopted the connotation of "sincerity" in one piece with the diary form. The miniature diary of a girl in Alfred Döblin's *Berlin Alexanderplatz* in two entries, one of which I print in its entirety, offers a good example of this use:

> For a week I've been feeling bad again. I don't know what will become of me if this goes on. I think if I didn't have anyone in the world, I would open the gas valve on myself without a second thought, but this way, I can't do it to my mother. But I really do wish that I'd get a serious illness and die from it. I've written everything down just the way it looks inside me.[39]

Other writers, in contrast, have chosen to emphasize the self-consciousness and thus insincerity implicit in writing about the self, and, more recently, the deformation inherent in the process of writing itself.

5

Saying "I"

Let us imagine that we have a first-person fictional narrative in which the narrator's discourse is not naturalized, but simply natural. We are not asked to suspend our disbelief; the second narrative triangle is not in evidence; we cannot find any points of intrusion; the author is silent; only the character speaks, and his discourse is indistinguishable from discourse we might encounter in a nonfictional situation. Nothing but the jacket of the book tells us that the novel is a novel. This hypothetical situation, which is unusual but certainly not impossible, raises certain questions. Does first-person discourse itself predispose us to read in a certain way? Are there different kinds of first-person discourse, and do they incline us to respond in different ways, to draw different kinds of conclusions? Can the author prejudice our reading without indicating his presence through signals in the text but merely by letting his character speak? To phrase the question in its most general terms, what does it mean to say "I"?

While I cannot consider the different modes of first-person discourse and their use in first-person narrative here either in depth or in breadth, it will nevertheless be useful to examine forms of discourse that have had a tendency to predominate in the diary novel. In particular, I shall consider one type, which I call the "expressive," that occurs frequently in diary fiction but has not yet received attention in the theory of first-person narrative.

In real life, we have few ways to find out what goes on inside another person's head. A person can tell us about his own thoughts, but precisely a person's representation of his own subjectivity is apt to meet with our skepticism. Quite apart from any doubts we might have about the speaker's sincerity, and the distorting effects the presence of a listener might have on his discourse, we of the post-Freudian era are likely to believe that the subject cannot know himself in any profound sense. Critics tend to be skeptical about the truth content of autobiographical writing, and to doubt the authority of the autobiographer. This skepticism comes primarily from two different sets of presuppositions. The one involves preconceptions about the organization of the psyche; the other, a belief in the primacy of language over the self. The self, we believe, is permanently conflicted: Material is repressed for the very protection of the organism. The gaze into the self stops short at the barrier of the censorship and does not penetrate the unconscious. The psyche is so constituted that the self *must* see an incomplete, idealized version of itself. The authority of the autobiographer is discredited, implicitly, by contrast to a hypothetical omniscient point of view.[40]

Recent theoreticians of autobiography argue that the very project of writing, the act of signification itself, alienates the writing self from his subject.[41] Roland Barthes goes so far as to say that there is no referent in the field of the subject; according to Barthes, the self, so called, can at most be written, but not represented: "Do I not know that, *in the field of the subject, there is no referent?* The fact (whether biographical or textual) is abolished in the signifier, because it immediately *coincides* with it."[42] Following Jacques Lacan's rewriting of Freud's metapsychology, critics tend to focus on the deceptive first-person pronoun. Fredric Jameson tells us that Lacan makes the pronoun "I," rather than the Oedipus complex, responsible for creating the unconscious; it causes a split in the subject that drives the "real subject" underground.[43] Philippe Lejeune argues that the first-person pronoun imposes a fictive unity on the self by suggesting an identity between the speaking subject and the subject of the enunciation, whereas, in fact, "the first person . . . always conceals a hidden third person."[44] According to Lejeune, the identity of the two "I's" can be taken literally only in the case of performatives.[45] In other words, language forces the subject to objectify himself as though he were a third person. At the same time, through the pronoun "I," language masks the dubious enterprise of self-objectification the subject is engaged in, suggesting to the listener that he is finding out something about the subject of the statement.

Autobiographical writing is thus discredited wholesale, either on the grounds that it involves a prior cognitive act of self-objectification and thereby of self-distortion, or because it is presumed to rely on a referential model of language, where the "self" is elided into preexisting rhetorical structures. Either way, the autobiographical representation runs counter to what we suppose we know of the ontology of the self. Autobiography today seems fated to comment on the problems of autobiography. Sophisticated autobiographers, like Barthes, dwell on the impossibility of saying anything about the self. In *Roland Barthes,* in a skeptical attempt to avoid the "image repertoire," he orders fragments alphabetically, that is, arbitrarily, and switches back and forth between the first- and third-person pronouns.

In writing that takes advantage of the conventional distinction between fiction and nonfiction and labels itself overtly as fiction, no comparable barriers stand in the way of the representation of subjectivity. As Dorrit Cohn demonstrates in *Transparent Minds,* the representation of subjectivity is the very province of fiction, specifically of third-person narrative. The novelist can avail himself of conventions that allow him to tell us, authoritatively, what goes on inside his characters' heads. "Auctorial narration" (also called "neutral omniscience" or "nonreportive style") commands the reader's belief as a matter of convention. Literary critics and linguists agree that this style involves "no narrator" – in other words, the statements are not taken as representing the judgment of any subject of consciousness. The style prescribes to the reader an attitude of willing suspension of disbelief. The reader accepts what is said and does not question it, of course within the framework of recognizing that the entire work is fictional.[46]

But what, then, is the status of first-person narration? Given the existence of the "transparent mind" convention in third-person fiction, what function is left for first-person narrative to perform, if not to draw attention to the problems of self-representation? In autobiography, where the author, as a rule, believes in his own privileged spectatorship, we encounter consonant structures: The implied reader is meant to believe the narrator. In first-person fiction, in contrast, dissonant structures are common. In view of the many resources an author has to undermine the narrator, the ideal function of first-person narrative seems to be to put into bold relief the problems of autobiographical writing. To assert, however, that first-person narrative is merely the binary opposite of third-person narrative, unreliable where the latter is reliable, is perhaps to apply too much logic to fiction.[47] The "unreliable narrator" in first-person fiction is certainly a commonplace of criticism. But first-person narrative also has dimensions that circumvent the question of credibility and that offer the reader a response other than the choice between belief and disbelief.

Does all discourse about the self force self-objectification on the subject? Are the only language patterns available to the subject those derivative of propositions about outside things? In order to approach a dimension of first-person narrative that transcends self-objectification and referentiality, one might begin by studying first-person statements. This simpler case may then serve as a model for investigating longer and more complex forms of narrative. It will prove expedient to focus on first-person statements in the present tense, where the speaking self is not automatically separated from his subject by temporal distance and where questions of falsification by memory, therefore, do not arise. In *How to Do Things with Words* J. L. Austin deals specifically with first-person statements and distinguishes between "constatives" and "performatives." Performatives (e.g., "I do [take this woman to be my lawful wedded wife]") give us a category of statements that are not referential. Performatives do not describe, report, or constate; instead, the uttering of the sentence is, or is part of, the doing of an action.[48]

Austin does not devote space to discussing constatives, but we can draw some conclusions of our own. Examples of constative utterances might be:

"I'm in the bathtub."

"I'm standing here, dripping wet, with no clothes on."

"I live with my two elderly maiden aunts." In such statements the "I" is indeed the self as seen by the other; the other is implicitly present as a kind of voyeur. The subject distances himself from himself, steps outside himself, and observes himself from the outside as another person would. One might say, "I'm in the bathtub," to someone standing outside the bathroom door, demanding to know what's going on in there. The speaker describes a state of affairs that is hidden to the interlocutor but that, if circumstances permitted, the interlocutor would be able to see for himself. Such a statement is verifiable: If the bathroom door opened, the addressee could ascertain whether or not the speaker is telling the truth about being in the bathtub. The addressee could then say, merely substituting pronouns (and adverbial shifters), "He (or she) is in the bathtub." Such statements do seem to be modeled on third-person statements; the first-person statements could be transposed into the third person without difficulty. Here, the subject really does appear to adopt the discourse of the other for speaking about himself.

By analogy, one can distinguish a subset of constatives, which I shall call constative statements of interiority. This category of constatives will have particular bearing on a discussion of autobiographical narrative. Examples would be:

"I'm a coward at heart."

"I'm usually quite happy, even when alone."

"I often think one thing and do another." Here again, two "I's" are involved. Reflecting on itself, the self doubles itself: The speaking self looks into itself, as into a mirror, and portrays what it sees there, the subject of the utterance, in words.

This type of statement engages an epistemological model in which metaphors of vision play a prominent role. Constative statements of interiority rely on notions of privileged spectatorship and verifiability; the speaker presumes that if the listener could see into his hidden self as clearly as he himself can, he would not fail to agree with his statement. Conversely, appeals to privileged spectatorship and verifiability signal to us that we are in a context where we are meant to read statements of this type as constatives. Rousseau's metaphors of vision in *The Confessions* are an example of such appeal: At the beginning of *The Confessions* Rousseau settles (for himself) the question of authority and thus short-circuits a potentially infinite series of defenses by equating the power of his vision with that of the highest authority, God – "I have bared my secret soul as thou thyself hast seen it, Eternal Being!" he writes. He later invokes "transparence" as a metaphor for his mode of self-presentation ("I should like in some way to make my soul transparent to the reader's eye").[49] The question of self-knowledge is thus transformed into a question of sincerity; we are meant to ask merely whether the first-person narrator is honest in revealing himself to us, not whether he is in possession of the truth.

The field of first-person, present-tense utterances is not exhausted with performatives and constatives, however. It is perfectly possible for what linguists call "expressives" or "emotives" – utterances that express a "feeling or desire"[50] or, most generally, the speaker's "attitude"[51] – to occur in the first person, present tense.[52] Examples might be:

"I'm miserable."

"I'm so happy."

"I'm scared!"

Such utterances could be understood as spontaneous expressions of sensations or emotions. Anton Marty, who coined the term "emotive," argues that emotives are not merely "statements about the inner experiences of the speaker."[53] Roman Jakobson likewise makes a sharp distinction between the "expressive" function of language and the "referential," "denotative," "cognitive" function.[54]

Wittgenstein's theses on the language of sensations in the *Preliminary Studies* and in the *Philosophical Investigations* could usefully be applied to the new category of first-person statements I propose to call "expressives."[55] In the *Philosophical Investigations*, Wittgenstein proposes that it is wrong to assume that the language of sensations is cognitive and referential. He chooses the example of pain. One doesn't *know* one is in pain – expressions of knowing and doubting are out of place in this language game; rather, one *is* in pain.[56] One does not *observe* oneself in pain – Wittgenstein questions the notion of self-observation generally, noting that a certain "giddiness" accompanies the notion of consciousness observing the brain processes – and then *describe* the pain.[57] If we assume that first-person sentences involving psychological predicates are descriptions, we are succumbing to the "descriptive fallacy."[58] Pain, Wittgenstein notes, has its "natural expression," which is readable by others. It has outward signs in living beings, which include the wriggling of a fly, a groan, or "human behaviour" generally.[59] In short, "the human body is the best picture of the human soul."[60] First-person statements, then, rather than describe pain or pain behavior, could be seen to substitute for these natural, primitive expressions of pain: "A child has hurt himself and he cries; and then adults talk to him and teach him exclamations and later, sentences. They teach the child new pain-behaviour. . . . The verbal expression of pain replaces crying and does not describe it."[61] Wittgenstein suggests that a substitutive, involuntary relation, rather than an arbitrary and conventional one, exists between the hidden "referent" and the sign. Language is the last link in this substitutive chain. Wittgenstein does not investigate the arbitrariness of the final connection between pain behavior and words. One could propose, as a tentative solution, thinking of the utterance "I am in pain" as a kind of trope, borrowed from the domain of referential constructions, which substitutes for the natural body sign, the grimace.

The isolation of expressives as a category of first-person statements gives us a new insight into the question of the authority of the discourse of the subject. Expressives present a type of "I" statement that seems to avoid reference entirely. An expressive utterance represents a psychic state without describing it; the problem of self-knowledge is circumvented; self-objectification does not take place. There is no division between the speaking subject and the subject of the utterance, and there is no temporal or reflective distance between feeling and statement. Expressive statements seem not to imply a hearer, any more than a groan would. They are thereby, presumably, not subject to distortion or modification by a listener's presence. Simple and limited in the range of what they express though they are, expressives thus seem to give us a "true discourse of the subject."

It remains to discuss the applicability of expressives to writing, narrative, and fiction. Can we move from the original context, where we ascribed expressiveness to an utterance because we saw a person in pain, ecstasy, and so on, to new contexts where there is only language? Can we make a transition from sentences to longer linguistic units, to passages or entire narratives? Can we say that if the sight of another person's passion inspires our own, then the expression of the passions in a narrative context will provoke a sympathetic reading? Or do we lose everything when we attempt these transpositions? Presumably, the transpositions will be complex, but nevertheless possible. For if we grant that the passions have their true expression, and if we are willing to concede the original substitution of language for more primitive forms of expression, we can allow for more elaborate substitutions as well. Given favorable conditions, there is no reason why expressives cannot be transposed into new contexts, and why a rhetoric of the expressive cannot be developed.

The farther we move from the original situation that occasioned the hypothesis of expressives, however, the less we can argue in absolute terms. Rather, we must argue in terms of history and convention. For such transpositions will ultimately depend on the receptivity of a given historical climate toward expressive presuppositions, toward the notion of a true discourse of the subject founded in the passions, and on its willingness to extend these presuppositions into new and possibly resistant contexts. In the present day, we may want to restrict the idea of speaking from the heart to its least ambiguous manifestations. It may seem to us that autobiographical narrative is a far cry from the shrieking savage, and that the idea of the expressive loses all its value in remote contexts, more elaborate narrative frames, and more sophisticated forms of expression. We may want to align writing with analysis and reflection, and thus oppose it to spontaneity and emotion. Yet there is no reason to impose our own prejudices onto other historical climates. The second half of the eighteenth century, in particular, abounds with men of letters who thought, like Hugo Blair, that "the heart, when uttering its native language, never fails, by powerful sympathy, to affect the heart."[62]

How do we identify an expressive? The original connection between language and the passions was established by context. That is, if we originally attribute expressiveness to an utterance, it is because we actually see a person in a state of pain, joy, fear, etc. Wittgenstein shows that an utterance like "I am afraid" can be understood as a "cry of fear" or a "reflection," depending on the context.[63] Context, then, and not grammatical form, is decisive in identifying an expressive. Indeed, in most cases no formal distinction separates expressives from constatives.

But, presumably, the less the context is clearly given, and the more complex and less self-evidently universal a person's emotional response to a given situation, the more the expression itself will be unambiguously – in the sense of conventionally – expressive of the passions. Within the conventionality of expressive behavior, there is a tendency to substitute "extreme" or "extravagant" for "natural" as the opposite of "conventional." While a response that is conventional in the sense of formulaic or trite is apt to lose its expressive force, we tend to believe in the semiotic value of extreme behavior: the *crime passionel* expresses uncontrollable jealousy, suicide suggests despair, and so forth. We can hypothesize that the same is true of expressive rhetoric and imagine a convention of unconventionality: While formulaic language, even the formulas for genuine feeling, signal the absence of feeling, nonformulaic, extravagant expressions indicate its presence. Longinus asserted that "it is the nature of the passions, in their vehement rush . . . to demand hazardous turns as altogether indispensable"; Meyer Abrams shows that eighteenth-century poetics persisted in seeing a connection between the passions and figurative language.[64]

How can expressives possibly be *written?* Our intuition tells us that the language of the passions is *spoken* (shrieked, gestured); writing would seem inevitably to eliminate expressive spontaneity. Specular statements of interiority, in contrast, strike us as essentially written. Writing would seem to force the subject to create an order, monumentalize the self, establish a conviction about itself, "sign" what it says. But some types of writing may, by convention, borrow the expressive mode directly from speech, for example the love letter and the suicide note, and some forms of mimetic first-person fiction allow it as well.

Finally, to what extent can one generalize from the level of the sentence to that of a passage or a narrative as a whole? What connection can be made between expressives and the interpretation of narrative? To put our discussion into its proper perspective, it will be useful to recapitulate for a moment. Critics have suggested that we can draw certain conclusions about autobiographical narrative based on the hidden implications of first-person discourse. Language, it is suggested, inflicts third-person patterns on the first person, in such a way that the discourse of the subject makes a truth claim for the unverifiable (the subject's inner world), based on the analogy of the verifiability of third-person statements. Whether or not the writer explicitly embraces the notion of privileged spectatorship, he unavoidably subscribes to constative presuppositions merely by using the first person. The reader who has seen through the deceptive nature of first-person discourse will necessarily adopt an attitude of suspicion toward first-person narrative. The writer seems to be saying something about himself, but in fact his discourse tells us nothing about the true nature of the subject.

It goes beyond the scope of these remarks to question the presumption that self-knowledge is impossible and that the known self is a linguistic self. These assumptions are speculative and as such seem highly plausible. Rather, I wish to question a line of reasoning that moves from the use of the first person to the interpretation of narrative. There are two doubtful moments in the argument.

First, as we have seen, the existence of a category of expressives calls into question any absolute connection between the use of the first person and hidden implications (the claim of verifiability for the unverifiable). Expressives show us that it is possible to speak in the first person, to reveal the subject, without automatically making a constative truth claim. If we are disposed to find certain implications in certain kinds of discourse, this has more to do with the conventional significance we attach to them than with the form of the discourse.

The existence of expressives has to do with a willingness to believe in the expression of the passions, in certain locutions as expressive of them, and in the incorrigibility of these locutions. If we are suspicious of constatives, likewise, it is because we are inclined to assign language a certain position within a framework of belief about human beings. Present-day critics oppose the long-held assumption that self-knowledge is possible and can be expressed in language with the intuition that self-knowledge is impossible and that thought does not exist prior to and separate from language. The argument through form (first-person statements) is in fact a detour, a way of drawing conclusions about the implications of language from preconceptions about human beings.

Second, any connection that can be made between the implications of a certain kind of discourse and the interpretation of narrative is necessarily fragile. It would be an error to assume that conclusions about the narrative as a whole can be drawn from an analysis of smaller units. To suggest that a narrative is an additive construct that amounts to the sum of its sentences would be to underestimate its complexity and seriously short-circuit the process of interpretation. We surely react to a narrative from moment to moment, from sentence to sentence, as we read, but we are also disposed to revise our reactions cumulatively from whatever point in the narrative we have reached, and to form different opinions while rereading. Something as simple as a sudden swerve in the story might cause us to change our opinions. Even if much of the discourse in a narrative should appear expressive by convention or context, expressivity does not guarantee that we will emerge from our reading sympathetic to the narrator. Nor does the use of constatives necessarily provoke suspiciousness. There is, presumably, a relation between expressives and consonance: If the expressive was developed as a rhetorical mode, it was surely to enhance rather than undermine a serious and sympathetic presentation of the speaker's feelings. But the relation is not a determinate one. A narrative consisting of disjointed expressives, for instance, might strike us before very long as the ravings of a lunatic. In a work of fiction an author may avail himself of expressive presuppositions to establish consonance in the narrative. He can prepare and strengthen a positive final judgment on a character by moving us to sympathize with him as we read from page to page. But expressives may also occur within dissonant structures, and an author may even use expressives to create such structures.

Fiction plainly presents a climate that is much more favorable than nonfiction for the extended, persistent, and developed use of the expressive. The reason is that in the novel, the narrator's "I" stands not for the author himself but, rather, for a fictional character the author creates. In longer nonfictional narratives, for example, a diary or correspondence, an extensive use of the expressive is not very likely; moreover, we would not expect a writer to publish whatever expressive texts he might have written, or quote his own expressive utterances, without distancing himself from them. For an author to write expressive texts in his own name for publication would be yet more suspect; such a *production* of expressives would be a contradiction in terms. In fiction, none of these barriers to the use of the expressive exist. If an author believes in the expression of the passions through language, he can easily put such language into the mouth of a fictional character in order to give the impression that the character is speaking from the heart. Moreover, longer expressive texts in fiction are quite imaginable. It is the prerogative of fiction to heighten and condense. Fictional plots need not correspond to everyday situations, and discourse in fiction need not be perfectly mimetic of everyday discourse. Inasmuch as fiction borrows expressive locutions from nonfictional writing or from speech, it can borrow them intensively, for example, by increasing the frequency of their occurrence. Fiction can also develop its own expressive conventions. In such cases we are already dealing with intrusions of the second narrative triangle into the first. The expressive imposes a "convention of nature" that bears directly on our reading of the first narrative triangle, however; it suggests that we should understand the first narrative triangle implicit in the narrative as follows:

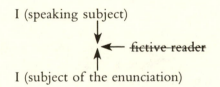

I (speaking subject)

← fictive reader

I (subject of the enunciation)

The expressive "convention of nature" creates an authoritative identity between passion and language, between feeling and expression. It asks us to believe that we are in a privileged context where thought and writing merge.

As we have seen, we cannot in general identify expressives in a formal sense. Rather, context or convention signal expressivity. Expressiveness certainly implies a subject of discourse and reveals the subject's present state (his state while speaking), but the first-person pronoun need not occur, nor must the verb be in the present tense. Even if the narrator is formally referring to the past, expressiveness can be signaled by an emphasis on the narrator's present joy, anguish, and so forth – which may or may not imply a reliving of the sentiments he felt at the time. There is also no reason to restrict the expressive to a particular grammatical unit, such as the sentence. Thus we can speak of an expressive *mode* in narrative. Epistolary and diary fiction obviously represent the ideal fictional locus for the expressive mode. Where the autobiographical subject can reveal himself, at spaced intervals, in his present moment, entire narratives can be so dominated by the expressive mode that the whole work falls under its sway. A good example of a narrative dominated by the expressive mode is *Die Leiden des jungen Werthers*. The following passage is taken from one of Werther's letters to Wilhelm:

> Ich suchte Lottens Augen; ach, sie gingen von einem zum andern: Aber auf mich! mich! mich! der ganz allein auf sie resigniert dastand, fielen sie nicht! – Mein Herz sagte ihr tausend Adieu! Und sie sah mich nicht! Die Kutsche fuhr vorbei, und eine Träne stand mir im Auge. Ich sah ihr nach und sah Lottens Kopfputz sich zum Schlage herauslehnen, und sie wandte sich um zu sehen, ach! nach mir? – Lieber! In dieser Ungewißheit schwebe ich; das ist mein Trost: vielleicht hat sie sich nach mir umgesehen! Vielleicht! – Gute Nacht! O, was ich ein Kind bin!

> [I tried to catch Lotte's glance. Alas, it wandered from one young man to the other, but it did not fall on me! Me! Me! Who stood there absorbed in her alone! My heart bade her a thousand farewells, and she did not notice me! The carriage drove off, and tears stood in my eyes. I looked after her, and saw Lotte's headdress lean out of the carriage window as she turned to look back – ah, at me? Dear friend, I am torn by this uncertainty. My only consolation is: She may have turned to look back at me! Perhaps! Good night! Oh, what a child I am!][65]

The entire passage, in which Werther relieves his emotions at seeing Lotte, combining report with his reactions to the events, is expressive, rather than the individual sentences. *Werther* as a whole could be seen as an extended outcry, meant to move us to sympathy rather than inspire our "belief." We are surely meant to follow the editor's hint when he tells us, "You cannot deny . . . his fate your tears."

Of course, if an expressive statement can also be read constatively – Wittgenstein's "I am afraid" is an example – it can be transposed into the third person as well. The very ambiguity of isolated sentences can be seen as one of the advantages of first-person narrative. The opening sentence of Max Frisch's *Stiller,* "I am not Stiller," is an excellent example of such ambiguity. The novel sustains two stories simultaneously: that of the mistaken identity of Stiller alias "White" and that of Stiller's identity crisis. The first sentence, referential if the narrator is White and emotive if he is Stiller, admits both interpretations.

What rhetorical conventions do authors develop for the expressive?
Rhetorical conventions can be modified by fashion and altered by context. An example of statements that strike us as unambiguously expressive, however, are sentences that use metaphors of the body to express psychic states. Such sentences tend to occur in consonant first-person narratives like *Werther*. Examples are:

"I am poured out like water, and all my bones are out of joint; my heart is like wax; it is melted in the midst of my bowels" (Psalm 22:14).

"Ich halte mein Herzchen wie ein krankes Kind" (*Werther*). ["I hold my little heart like a sick child."]

"Ich wehre mich, obwohl ich weiß, daß mir das Herz schon heraushängt und daß ich doch nicht mehr leben kann" (*Rilke, Die Aufzeichnungen des Malte Laurids Brigge*). ["I defend myself, although I know my heart is already hanging out and that I cannot live any longer."]

"Ich bin gefallen und kann mich nicht mehr aufheben, weil ich zerbrochen bin" (*Malte*). ["I have fallen and cannot pick myself up again, because I am broken."][66]

Such metaphors strike us as plausible only in the first person. In the third person they would be infelicitous and might even be understood denotatively. When uttered by the subject, they engage the notion, familiar from Wittgenstein, that feelings are translated outward into the body and can also be read "backward" by the spectator.[67] Of course metaphors of the body – verbalizations of bodily contortions – are far from being actual bodily contortions; the point is to evoke, through what one might call the conventionalized eccentricity of figurative language, some state of soul or psychic malaise beyond conventional descriptive language, as extraordinary as the bodily distortion indicated in the metaphor. We can understand these bodily metaphors as catachreses – substitutions in the absence of a proper term.

Both the expressive and constative modes are particularly frequent in diary fiction. I do not mean to suggest, however, that expressives and constatives are the only possible narrative modes, just as consonance and dissonance are not the only two possible authorial stances. To discuss first-person narrative in terms of reliability and unreliability, or sympathy and suspicion, is to limit the range of authorial attitudes and reader responses. Calling attention to expressives is meant to counteract a reading that, a priori, doubts; it is meant to suggest that there is in fact no simple shortcut from the use of the first person to textual interpretation. If one argues in extra-textual or ideological terms, it makes more sense to speak of history and convention than to superim-

pose ideas about the ontology of language or a concept like "the impossibility of self-knowledge" onto the work. Alternatively, one can assess
the narrative, and the reader's implied response to it, in terms of signals
built into the text. This method seems particularly appropriate in fiction, in a world that contains no objects of reference but, rather, is
wholly written. For in the case of fictional first-person narrative we
have no actual person to contrast the validity of the self-expression to.
Instead of extra-textual evidence, we have textual evidence, signals in
the narrative that reveal the interaction of the second narrative triangle
with the first and suggest that some readings are more plausible than
others.

Just as there is no direct route from the use of first-person discourse
to a certain kind of interpretation, the analysis of the "logical" implications of the formal characteristics of narrative gives us a range of possibilities rather than a single answer. Let us consider, for example, the
lack of a fictive reader in the diary novel. Why does a person enter into
such a peculiar noncommunicative situation? The answer may be a
disappointingly simple one: The protagonist may wish to communicate
but is unable to because of extraordinary circumstances such as imprisonment or shipwreck. He may desire to deliver a record of these marvelous or, more likely, excruciating events to posterity, or he may long
to smuggle out a description of his whereabouts to a friend or rescue
team. In such cases the diarist essentially writes a *record,* in the sense of
the journal that was prevalent in the seventeenth and eighteenth centuries, of the story he lived through himself. On the other hand, the
diarist may be writing for himself because what he has to say is private,
because the type of information he wants to record is indiscreet, or
because what he has to say is of interest to him and to no one else. He
may be writing to remember, to hold fast events and ideas for the
future or for the leisure of his old age, or to immortalize himself,
consciously or unconsciously intending his journal for posterity. He
may be writing to forget: Writing may serve as a form of catharsis. He
may wish to dominate his experiences by putting them into words. He
may wish to gather his thoughts, compact them into sentences, in order
to reach a decision. He may wish to observe himself over a period of
time and analyze himself, in order to reform his behavior. He may have
several or all of these motivations at once.

Which of these possibilities are used, and in what way any of the
diary novel's formal characteristics are realized in a given novel, will
depend to a considerable extent on historical factors, on current fashions, contemporary values, and the influence of extra-generic models,
as well as on established patterns in the genre itself. The diary novel,
heir to the real diary, manifests a continual tension between imitation

and invention. The influence of other fictional techniques furthers or obstructs the realization of certain aspects of the form's potential at different times. The tensions between the two narrative triangles is handled differently, depending, to a large extent, on historically determined values like sincerity, spontaneity, and reflection. Now that we have considered some of the logical possibilities for the diary form and for first-person discourse, it remains to see how this range of possibilities intersects with diachronic patterns of the form's realization. There is no shortcut from narrative means to narrative ends in works that use the same set of formal techniques, or the same "genre," no deductive method that allows us to draw conclusions from the form about the form's function. Our task in the following chapters, therefore, will be to take the longer, historical route: to see what diary novels were actually written, and when, and what patterns they follow.

PART II

The Diary Novel in the Eighteenth and Early Nineteenth Centuries

6

Diaries and Diary Fiction

Although entire novels in the diary form as we know it today did not appear until the 1790s, and although the type was minor and examples were sporadic until the nineteenth century, diary fiction can be traced back to the early eighteenth century. If a single cause for the origins of the diary novel can be named, if a common source for the scattered and heterogeneous examples of early diary fiction exists, it is the model of the real diary. The emergence and popularity of different kinds of real diaries are directly responsible for the first examples of diary fiction. Fictive journals, whether they were parts of novels, entire novels, or stories, imitated or at least borrowed their appearance from the various kinds of real diaries that were being written and increasingly found their way into print.

In eighteenth-century Europe, diary keeping of all kinds flowered.[1] Travel diaries, which had been written in increasing numbers since the end of the fifteenth century, became especially fashionable with the popularity of travel in the eighteenth. Protestant diaries formed another major type. In England diary keeping had become a standard spiritual exercise in Puritan circles in the mid- and late 1660s, and in the next century the practice was adopted by Quakers, Methodists, and Baptists. In Germany the Herrnhuter Brüdergemeine (the most influential of the Pietist foundations, established in 1727) encouraged sectarians to keep daily records of their spiritual condition. The keepers of personal, non-religious diaries in the seventeenth and eighteenth centuries tended to record events rather than feelings; like Pepys in his *Diary* (1660–9) and Boswell in his *London Journal* (1762–3), they wrote about themselves but were not excessively introspective. The Protestant journals, in contrast, furthered habits of self-analysis. For the Pietists in particular, diary keeping meant vigilant self-observation, designed to protect the Christian from falling into sin. Toward the end of the eighteenth century, introverted secular journals took the place of religious ones.[2]

These intimate diaries became a major confessional type throughout continental Europe, particularly in nineteenth-century France. They absorbed the function of self-analysis and also became a vehicle for self-expression; the secret diary as "best friend" gradually replaced the confidant of intimate correspondence.

Diary fiction imitated these different types of diaries, and intimate journals in particular provided fiction with an interesting model. The confessional mode was widely copied. If the diary novel gained a foothold, however, the reason has to do with the popularity of another novel genre, the epistolary novel, particularly in the second half of the eighteenth century. Early diary fiction derived directly from real diaries, but it found a favorable climate for its reception in the already existing epistolary novel fashion. Series of letters present the same periodic temporal structure as series of dated diary entries. Long before diary keeping itself came to imply daily writing, epistolary fiction introduced periodic narration. Throughout most of the eighteenth century, the diary was not rigorously distinguished from the memoir, a situation religious diaries with their teleological, conversion-based orientation did little to change. The epistolary novel, with its "writing to the moment" or emphasis on the present, introduced a kind of first-person narrative that did not depend on the notion of the conversion or the retrospective temporality that distinguished both autobiography and picaresque fiction. The epistolary novel was the structural ancestor of the diary novel. It initiated a line of development in narrative technique that the diary novel continued, and its conventions exerted a persistent influence on diary novels. The obvious difference between letters and diaries as we think of them today is that letters are destined for a recipient, whereas diaries are private. Yet one need think only of the "dear diary" convention to realize to what extent intimate diary keeping was influenced by letter writing.

There are striking parallels between the way the diary form was adopted by fiction and the way the epistolary novel developed. Historians of the epistolary novel have shown that the use of the letter in fiction began with the inclusion of letters in novels and progressed to the composition of entire novels in letters.[3] In a similar pattern, diary excerpts in novels preceded whole diary novels. Plainly, the climate that fostered the rise of the epistolary novel also promoted the adoption of the diary form in fiction. The epistolary novel drew on the model of actual intimate correspondence, just as the diary novel copied real diaries.

The question that poses itself most centrally is why some of the most popular forms of the eighteenth-century novel, the memoir novel as well as the epistolary and diary novels, copied nonfictional forms. The

eighteenth century brought with it a passion for producing fictive
"documents"; "true histories," "authentic relations," and narratives introduced by fictitious editors abound. But to what end was the convention adopted? The question deserves a study in itself; I shall attempt to
touch on only certain of its aspects here.

Did the novel copy nonfictional forms in order to seek legitimation
for a new genre, not included in canonical poetics and largely frowned
on by critics?[4] It has been argued that the picaresque, progenitor of
first-person narrative forms, adopted the authority of a nonfictional
code precisely in order to legitimate itself as a new genre. Roberto
González Echevarría, in his article "The Life and Adventures of Cipión:
Cervantes and the Picaresque," shows that the picaresque novel
adopted the formula of the *relación,* a legal deposition sent back to Spain
by explorers and adventurers in the New World[5] in which the narrator
"identified himself by telling his life and then told the relevant incidents
in which he had been involved" (p. 20). The picaro, who is often in
trouble with the law, likewise confesses to a temporal authority, like a
judge. According to González Echevarría, "by assuming the form of a
'relación,' the picaresque is implicitly claiming that by doing so it is
truer to life, that it is a document showing a real life enmeshed in the
society of the times" (p. 21). The picaresque's strategy was a defensive
one, González Echevarría concludes: "The picaresque lacked an official
model: therefore it mimicked real, official documents to render effective
its 'performance' of the functions of society's texts" (p. 25). He suggests that "the novel mimicks whatever kind of text a given society
invests with power at a certain point in history" (p. 26).

Mimesis can surely always be seen as a defensive gesture, an attempt
to borrow authority from another source. It is surely reasonable to
suppose, as González Echevarría does, that a new form in particular
will attempt to justify itself in terms of current social values, to the
extent of imitating whatever forms currently incorporate those values.
One could argue, by analogy with the picaresque, that if seventeenth-
and eighteenth-century fiction retains romance themes and structures[6]
but copies the forms of the memoir, the letter, and finally the diary, it
is because these "eyewitness reports," whether of quotidian life, exotic
places, or one's own adventures or the state of one's soul, themselves
embodied the values of society in the age of empiricism. The case for
borrowing in eighteenth-century mimetic fiction could be made even
more strongly: The novel imitated forms that were themselves popular
with the reading public not only because they were factual, but because
they possessed imaginative qualities.

By contrast with the picaresque, however, the epistolary, diary, and
memoir novels present an additional complication. These types not

only imitate real models, they also advertise themselves loudly as true histories and adopt all the trappings, such as the editor's introduction, of the real thing. In other words, their authors not only imitated real documents but also, apparently, tried to disguise the fact that they were doing so; they presented their imitations not as "novels" but as "histories." One kind of writing appears virtually to be hiding in another kind of writing. The analogy of animal camouflage and mimicry suggests itself: Certain species imitate the shape and coloring of other species in order to deceive their predator or prey.

But could one pursue this biological analogy to the point of arguing that such fiction was actually striving to present itself as real? Was the novel engaged in a struggle against competing real published novelties, which it could only hope to survive by subversively blurring the distinction between fiction and fact? Did it react to contemporary value criteria, which favored the empirically verifiable, and to a corresponding interest in drawing a clear boundary between fact and make-believe, by fictitiously displacing its origins to the other side of the boundary? If so, why was the convention often used in such a perfunctory fashion, and why was the imitation itself frequently so transparent? Why was the fiction of the authentic document coupled with stories that were wildly improbable?

Imitation, coupled with the seeming claim of the fictional work to be the genuine article, has led critics to suppose that the novel was actually trying to present itself as real. Vivienne Mylne in *The Eighteenth-Century French Novel: Techniques of Illusion* argues that first-person mimetic fiction, and novels that labeled themselves "true histories," really were trying to masquerade as real memoirs, collections of letters, and the like. She contends that novelists who used the convention of the authentic document were actually trying to convince readers that they were dealing with factual accounts. She asserts that "the forms themselves [memoirs and letters] are an outward sign of the novelist's desire to impose his work as literally true" (p. 32) and concludes, "The novelists were apparently trying to evoke literal rather than imaginative belief" (p. 43). This strategy of eighteenth-century novelists, she argues, corresponded to a contemporary climate of reception that did not distinguish between "literal belief" on the one hand and "imaginative belief" on the other. She writes:

> We now make a distinction between "believing in" a work of literature and "believing in," say, the events of an historical narrative. These two aspects of the activity may be called, for the sake of convenience, "imaginative belief" and "literal belief" respectively. In the seventeenth and eighteenth centuries most critics made no such distinction. Belief for them was a single activity, one that admitted of no differences of kind or of degree. [p. 8]

Mylne sees the authentic-document convention as an early and relatively "crude" strategy for convincing the reader; later in the eighteenth
century, she says, the novel acquired greater sophistication and displayed "more concern for everyday standards of probability and possibility" (p. 11).

According to this explanation, the novel's strategy was radically defensive. Mylne's argument breaks down at several points: The appearance of *Don Quixote* in 1605 testifies that the inability to distinguish
between objects of "literal" and "imaginative" belief was considered
naïve by the beginning of the seventeenth century, while the very mass
production of memoir and epistolary fiction shows that novelists themselves, if not their readers as well, were aware that they were reading
fiction. This mass production also indicates that writers were motivated
to write such novels because they thought they could make a profit.

Some authors, particularly those who used the mimetic convention
before it was widely accepted, may in fact have been trying to deceive
their readers, believing that a work would sell better if it were thought
true. I would like to propose, however, that once the mimetic fiction
became conventional, the phenomenon can be explained in terms of the
novel's emerging art claim. Stated more precisely, at whatever point
the seventeenth- and eighteenth-century novel began to make an art
claim, the use of labels like "true history" and the fact that novels took
the shape of memoirs and letters testify that novelists were trying to
support that claim, rather than to undermine it by presenting their
work as literally true.

In the eighteenth century, art was circumscribed by rules and norms.
The most important of these norms concerned mimesis. Throughout
most of the century, Aristotle's central tenet on the nature of poetry
continued to hold sway; it was taken for granted that art was, and
should be, imitation.[7] Although the mode of imitation and the objects
considered worthy of being imitated were subject to debate and frequent reinterpretation, verisimilitude was universally held to be a criterion for art. The criterion of mimesis is, of course, a defensive strategy;
as Hans Blumenberg writes, "The tradition of our poetics since classical
antiquity can be understood under the general heading of an argument
with the ancient assertion that poets lie."[8] By the same strategy, however, poetry established its own privileged status. The criterion of
mimesis is double-edged: In maintaining a criterion of representation,
imaginative literature does not aim to decategorize itself, but to create a
theory of *poetic* truth that has the effect of legitimating it as art.[9]

Any normative definition represents a way of defending a category as
such, for it provides a criterion for including or excluding prospective
members in a given set. A normative definition of art as imitation thus

presupposes, at the very least, a clear distinction between a category of originals and a category of imitations. It also places value on imitative skills. Here is the source of the muddy waters into which a discussion of the novel falls: These two conclusions, that normative mimesis presupposes a differentiation between copies and originals, and that it accords value to imitation, might be seen in their extreme case to conflict. That is, one could argue that the more perfect the imitation, the more "artistic" it is, the more indistinguishable it becomes from what it imitates, or non-art. Obviously, such an objection could be leveled only at artistic creations that use the same medium as the original. Such art forms therefore tend to draw firm boundaries around themselves, to label themselves as such, for what very closely resembles what it is not must somehow designate itself as being of a different order if it indeed wishes to insist on its difference. A boundary can be a simple physical one, like the edge of a stage in a theater. Today, we are no longer in the age of normative mimesis; the avant-garde trend is to blur the distinction between factual and fictional literature, and to question the distinction between art and non-art. Certain works of modern art insist on presenting themselves as objects for use or simply as objects. Nevertheless, a conservative tendency to uphold the traditional distinctions persists: One sees these works being preserved from self-decategorization – for example, by being placed within museum walls.

The argument that novelists were trying to evoke literal belief by borrowing first-person forms from nonfiction and calling their products "true" is probably inspired by the fact that the novel, in imitating the real document, does not change its medium: Both the document and the novel are written works. But let us consider the eighteenth-century novel within the context of eighteenth-century art generally. A parallel phenomenon to the fictive document in the visual arts could be seen to be *trompe l'oeil*. The *trompe l'oeil* artist paints a picture that momentarily, and from a certain angle, deceives the viewer into thinking that he is looking at the real thing. But an artist who painted *trompe l'oeil* curtains was trying neither to create real curtains nor to perpetrate a permanent or even lasting deception; rather, the viewer was meant to take pleasure in an illusion that lasted for a moment, and then to admire the artist's skill. The cleverness and the artistic status of the representation are testified to by the change of medium: Paint is used, not cloth. Although in literature there is no change of medium, nevertheless, if we do not imagine that something like the spirit of *trompe l'oeil* underlay the "true history" convention, there would be no interest in the imitation. The artist would effectively efface his own achievement by creating something that, without claim to fictionality, also renounced its claim to art.

Just as an element of deception and an aesthetic pleasure in bewilder-

ing the viewer momentarily are part of the very art of *trompe l'oeil,* one
might conjecture that novelists similarly wished to tease readers when
they entitled their works "true histories." The reader who picked up a
novel and glanced at the title page might momentarily be deceived. But
presumably he (or she) would not long remain oblivious to the presence
of a plot, or to the preposterousness of the events purporting to be real.
In the multivoice epistolary novel, the idea of an editor finding or
collecting a voluminous and coherent correspondence was in itself
implausible.[10] The lack of verisimilitude in mimetic first-person fiction
need not be interpreted as crudeness or evidence of incompetence; unlikely stories can be delightful, particularly if we are encouraged to
pretend that they are true, and both the implausibility of the story and
the playful deception can be understood as signals that tell the reader
that he is in the world of imaginative writing.

It would be difficult to defend the point of view that the eighteenth-
century novel eluded the artistic theory of its day or flowered apart from
current poetic norms. Early theories of the novel support the hypothesis
that novels were early trying to inscribe themselves in an artistic tradition, rather than to advance the much more dubious claim that they were
real. In the earliest theoretical pronouncements on the new genre, critics
both defended and attacked the novel in Aristotelian terms as an art
form. Pierre-Daniel Huet in "Lettre-traité sur l'origine des romans"
(1666) explicitly defended the *roman héroique* in terms of Aristotle's *Poetics*
by drawing an analogy between the novel and the epic.[11] In the years
following Happel's German translation of Huet (1682), German critics
followed suit, invoking Aristotle in the novel's defense. The criterion for
the novel became verisimilitude.[12] In the following decades, critics like
Sorel and Du Plaisir used the same criterion to attack the "old" heroic or
pastoral novel, which they found improbable.[13]

Whereas the novel was assimilated to prevailing poetics, the *imitatio
naturae* doctrine itself was modified in the course of the eighteenth
century to accommodate developments in the contemporary novel and
the values that those developments reflected. The seventeenth-century
demand that literature show the probable changed to a demand that it
portray the real. The modification of the "rules" and of literary practice
in the novel thus went hand in hand. Meyer Abrams shows that in
English neoclassical criticism, where critics stood in the philosophical
tradition of empiricism, "imitation" was interpreted to mean that art
was to be true to the world of sense experience.[14] Herbert Dieckmann,
contrasting the seventeenth-century French *doctrine classique* with eighteenth-century French interpretations of *imitatio naturae,* shows that the
sense of both *imitatio* and *natura* changed: Whereas the *doctrine classique*
prescribed the representation of beautiful, universal, typical nature, in

the eighteenth century theoreticians encouraged poets to represent the individual and concrete details of daily life.[15] According to Werner Krauss and Hans-Robert Jauß, the poetics of the novel in France place the same construction on the *imitatio naturae* doctrine as contemporary poetics generally. The demand that the novel be *vraisemblable* changes to a demand that it be *vrai*.[16] Although early critics still attempted to classify the novel in Aristotelian terms as poetry (concerned with the universal and probable) rather than history (concerned with the particular and true), critics of the novel in the second and third decades of the eighteenth century began to call for the representation of quotidian reality, of adventures that happen every day.

The early novel inscribed itself into the norms of contemporary poetics in a direct and unorthodox way, by imitating an "original" in the same medium as itself. The fiction of the document offered a quick appeal to authority: It settled the question of truth to sense experience by presenting a first-person narrator who tells the tale of events he witnessed himself. Later, different ideas of verisimilitude came into being, and simple formal mimeticism was replaced by new conventions for signaling belief, like the effaced narrator. The perplexing imitation of first-person nonfictional forms (with no change of medium) could thus be seen as a half-serious in-joke, by which the novel was trying not to pass itself off as real but, rather, to indicate that it was as good as real, or even better – that the novelist could create situations and characters that were truer to life than life itself.

It is essential to distinguish between the novel's *actual* mimesis of nonfictional forms and its *conventional* mimesis of them. Plainly, the first-person mimetic forms – fictional autobiography, the epistolary novel, and the diary novel – came into being because authors actually imitated existing nonfictional forms. Actual mimesis could be seen as a defense mechanism on the part of a new genre, and what the novel chose to imitate reveals what forms were considered interesting, imaginatively pleasing, and valid. Once the fictional genres were established, however, mimesis became conventional. Formal mimesis was a gesture that in the widest sense corresponded to current poetic norms and gave the novel a claim to artistic status. It is our modern, post-Romantic sensibility that makes us see copying purely as a defensive gesture, undertaken from a position of weakness. In the eighteenth century, as we have seen from the example of *trompe l'oeil,* clever imitation is not at all incompatible with an art claim. Philip Stewart, quoting Charles Pinot Duclos on the appeal of the marvelous and the true, confirms that "deceit becomes a positive literary quality."[17] Copying could thus be seen to legitimate the eighteenth-century novel on two fronts: The novel imitated popular forms, and by the same token it advanced an art claim that was in approximate conformity with accepted norms.

Eventually, novels established their identity as novels by presenting themselves in the guise of genuine documents: A paradoxical situation arose in which the ubiquitous descriptive words "true," "authentic," "secret history" became tags that signaled fictionality rather than its opposite. By midcentury at the latest the convention of authentication was well on its way to becoming an ironic game.[18] In Christoph Martin Wieland's *Agathon* (1766–7), for example, the elaborate references to phony documents – pinned, quite superfluously, to a third-person narrative! – are obviously for the reader's amusement: not only for the reader who is able to catch the Cervantean echo but for the reader accustomed to protestations of authenticity. The narrator, who claims to be writing a true history, invokes a chain of sources: He speaks of a manuscript whose author claims to be using a kind of diary written by Agathon and copied by a friend – but not until after the "editor" in his introduction has announced that he can hardly expect to convince the reader that the story was really taken from an old Greek manuscript.

As far as the diary novel is concerned, the fictive-document convention is already parodied in a late-eighteenth-century example, Moritz August von Thümmel's *Reise in die mittäglichen Provinzen von Frankreich* (1791–1805), where all kinds of mishaps befall the manuscript. E. T. A. Hoffmann plays with the idea of the physical page in "Kreisleriana" (1814–15), where Kreisler scribbles his "extremely scattered thoughts"[19] – in part his personal notes about the events of the day, and in part his views on music – on the backs of sheets of music paper; he carries the joke farther in *Lebens-Ansichten des Katers Murr* (1820–22), where the cat mixes Kreisler's biography up with his own autobiography. Among nineteenth-century authors, Kierkegaard perfects the parodistic game. In *Either/Or* (1843) he parodies the convention of the genuine manuscript that an "editor" finds and publishes by inventing an elaborate story about the genesis of his text. A fictive editor, Victor Eremita, claims that he came into the possession of the papers of the aestheticist "A" and the ethicist "B" by buying an old secretary, which he struck in a heated moment with a hatchet; a secret drawer sprang open, revealing a mass of papers. Kierkegaard carries the joke farther by putting an editor in an editor: "A" claims to be only the editor of the last of his papers, the "Diary of a Seducer." The first editor, Victor Eremita, doubts the second editor's disclaimer of authorship but hesitates to protest too strongly, because the entire question of fictive editorship also puts him in an awkward position: "This is an old trick of the novelist, and I should not object to it, if it did not make my own position so complicated, as one author seems to be enclosed in another, like the parts in a Chinese puzzle box."[20]

7

English Origins

Not surprisingly, the first fictive diaries were written in England. In the eighteenth century all types of the novel developed more quickly in England than elsewhere, and England was also the country where traditions of diary keeping were the most firmly entrenched by the beginning of the century. Private diaries and travel diaries were widely kept in the seventeenth century. Publications tended to be the exception, however. Before 1719, when the first fictive journal insert appeared in Daniel Defoe's *Robinson Crusoe,* only a handful of travel journals, several sea journals dealing with buccaneering and exploration, and some scattered, one-of-a-kind instances, such as the highwayman's diary of 1685 attributed to Thomas Dangerfield, one of the rogues who denounced the Popish Plot, had actually been published.

Of these published journals, the one type that enjoyed popular appeal was the sea journal. Early published sea journals were, in fact, the first genuinely "literary" diaries. In the late seventeenth and early eighteenth centuries they formed a new variety of the established genre of travel books, which at the time were produced in quantity for the market in response to an increasing popular taste for the sensations that voyagers, recently returned from military, scientific, commercial, or piratical expeditions, brought back from exotic parts of the globe. The idea of the sea journal even found its way into a seventeenth-century work of fiction: The hero of Richard Head's unwieldy picaresque novel *The English Rogue* (1665), Meriton Latroon, keeps a sea journal. But like the genuine mariner's journal published before it, John Dunton's *A True Journall of the Sally Fleet* (1637), Latroon's diary is a purely retrospective narrative and is called a journal simply because it records the events of each imaginary day at sea with minute exactitude and bristles with technically worded information about latitudes, longitudes, the degrees and directions of the compass, and the management of the ship.

Until the second decade of the eighteenth century, the published sea journals were all written from a retrospective point of view. Basil Ringrose's sea diary, published in Alexandre Exquemelin's *Bucaniers of America* (1685), and Raveneau de Lussan's *Journal of a Voyage made into the South Sea,* in Exquemelin's *History of the Bucaniers* (1698); William Dampier's *New Voyage Round the World* (1697–1709); and William Funnel's *Voyage Round the World . . . together with the Author's Voyage from Amapalla, on the West Coast of Mexico, to East India* (1707) all conscientiously include accounts of each day at sea, and although the narratives are carefully divided under dated headings, glossed with dates in the margin, or at the very least contain specific references to the date, they are all nevertheless written from an armchair perspective. The sailors probably reworked their journals for publication after they returned to England. Two later sea journals, however, Captain Edward Cooke's *Voyage to the South Sea, and Round the World* in two volumes (1712), and Captain Woodes Rogers's *Cruising Voyage Round the World* (1712), both accounts of the same voyage, consist of present-tense entries that were evidently written from day to day. These works thus introduce a new journal type. They are also far more splendidly "literary" than any of the sea journals published before. By Cooke's and Rogers's time, the publication of an edited version of a maritime journal was an accepted way for a navigator to earn fame and money after returning home from his voyage. Each man introduces his journal much as a novelist of the same period might introduce a "true history": as a product for consumption that will not fail to amuse the reader, yet is careful to conform to the high standard of veracity a discriminating reading public exacts. Cooke protests that his journal is a strictly factual record containing no fabulation whatsoever; Rogers asserts that his version is the official journal of the ship and that it is immune from error because it was "kept in a publick Book of all our Transactions, which lay open to every one's View; and where any thing was reasonably objected against, it was corrected."[21] The authors insisted on the impeccable veracity of their journals; but they also shrank from diminishing sales by including exhaustive records of facts that might be considered tedious. Cooke makes a point of saying in his introduction that he omitted tiresome details about wind, weather, latitude, and longitude so that he could include some more interesting material. Both his and Rogers's journals are embellished with histories of the traveled areas, summaries of other explorers' accounts, descriptions of topography, fauna, and flora, maps, sketches, and plates of exotic animals, birds, and fish. The pièces de résistance are eyewitness accounts of Alexander Selkirk, a member of Dampier's expedition of 1703 who had been put ashore on the island of Juan Fernandez at his own request after quarreling with his captain and who survived alone for four years.

Protestant diary keeping was well established at the beginning of the eighteenth century with the tradition of the seventeenth-century Puritan diaries. William Haller in *The Rise of Puritanism* asserts that "the diary became the Puritan substitute for the confessional."[22] The journal was supposed to be the regularly kept, wholly truthful account of the Puritan's spiritual life, the record of his conversion, his strayings, and the daily mercies Providence vouchsafed to him. Keeping a diary was considered an act of worship and a token of thankfulness to God comparable to prayer. In contrast to the later nineteenth-century intimate diarists, the Puritan did not regard his journal as the place for the spontaneous outpouring even of religious feelings: Keeping the diary was supposed to be a form of self-discipline rather than a means of emotional release. The diary was to be a record of daily conduct, evaluated in terms of spiritual debits and credits. Its kinship to the merchant's account book was recognized, and it was established practice to refer to diary keeping in monetary metaphors. A diary was, as one nonconformist autobiographer observed, "the best preventative Exercise to keep the Soul from running deep into the Debt of Divine Justice."[23] The style of Puritan diaries, like that of Puritan autobiographies and funeral sermons, was not expected to be spontaneous or original but rather formulaic.

Although Puritan diaries were not written for publication, they frequently furnished material for autobiograpies, biographies, and funeral sermons.[24] Sometimes they were quoted in print: The biography *An Account of the Life and Death of Mr. Philip Henry, Minister of the Gospel* (1699) contains long quotations from Henry's diary, for instance, and in the autobiography *Some remarkable passages in the Holy Life and Death of Gervase Disney, Esq.* (1692) the author includes numerous quotations from his journal, although he reworked them to conform to his retrospective autobiographical style. An excerpt from a diary passage from this latter work gives an impression of the approved mode of formulation for such accounts of the state of the Puritan soul:

> 9th. I there bless God for the mercies of that Day, and beg pardon for my sins, and that the Lord will cause me to live better the next Day.
>
> 10th. My Sins stare me in the Face, being many and great; there I find my self begging that I might eye the Blood of Christ, and might, through Grace, be interested in it, being the only Sovereign Remedy for a poor Sinner; yet I am preserved from ensnaring Bonds; and enjoy (through Mercy) comfortable Liberty, and sit under my own Vine with delight.
>
> 11th. This I find a comfortable Sabbath, when Mr. Coats did most sweetly call, invite and encourage Sinners to come to Christ: O! that I

may not stand out; the Lord bless the Sermon of my poor Soul, and pardon my Sins.

12th. No actual Sin that I know of. [pp. 136–7]

The Puritan journals were a seminal type in the history of the diary, and they were also a distinct type, with different aims and a different style from the other major types that succeeded them, Pietist and intimate journals. The Puritan formula of establishing an order in the sense of keeping book has remained a standard motivation for diary keeping throughout the history of the genre. Even diary-novel authors of the twentieth century frequently choose this pretext for having a fictive diarist start his diary. Eveline in Gide's *L'Ecole des femmes* (1929), for instance, writes, "I shall write in order to help myself put a little order in my thought; in order to try to see into myself clearly."[25] Roquentin in Sartre's *La Nausée* (1938) likewise reflects, "The best would be to write the events day by day. To keep a journal to see clearly."[26]

Satires

The first day-to-day fictive diary that appeared in print is a two-page satire by Joseph Addison, the "Journal of a Sober Citizen," which *The Spectator* published on March 4, 1712. An exhaustive, hour-by-hour account of the dressing, eating, sleeping, smoking, newspaper reading, and coffeehouse visiting that fills the "sober citizen's" week, the journal is meant to expose the lamentable emptiness, idleness, and triviality of the existences of many contemporary members of society. Though Addison's aim was thoroughly secular, his conception of diary keeping as an aid to self-discipline and self-improvement recalls the function of the Protestant diaries of the time. Addison makes the point that keeping a week's diary might be a salutary form of self-examination for his readers; it "would give them a true State of themselves, and incline them to consider seriously what they are about."[27] The little satire inspired a number of imitations in the eighteenth century: "Clarinda's Journal" (*Spectator,* 1712); "An Hue and Cry after Dr. S - - - t." (1714) and "Dr. S——t's Real Diary" (1715), two pamphlets ostensibly written by Swift but in fact meant to ridicule Swift for turning Tory; the "Journal of a Senior Fellow, or Genuine Idler" (1758), and a similar journal of a scholar whose author refers to "the Spectator's inimitable productions of this kind"[28] (1759), both of which Dr. Johnson published in *The Idler;* and a journal ostensibly written by a fashionable gadabout and snob, which appeared in an anonymous novel, *The Adventures of an Author* (1767).

Addison's miniature journal set the tone for a type of fictive diary that continued to be written throughout the history of the genre, particularly in England and America. These satiric journals often involve a naïve diarist whose simplistic opinions reveal the emptiness of the social conventions of a certain social class. Thackeray's *Jeames's Diary* (1845–6), for example, is the diary of an only minimally literate footman who makes a fortune speculating in railroads. Thackeray pokes fun at the money-hungry aristocracy, which is willing to forget Jeames's lowly origins and court him for his riches. George and Weedon Grossmith's *Diary of a Nobody* (1892) satirizes the trivial existence of a Victorian clerk in order to condemn the dishonesty of the society around him, which forces well-meaning, gullible, inhibited people like the diarist to make fools of themselves. Mark Twain puts the convention of the naïve diarist to a similar use, to reveal the mutual incomprehension of the sexes, in two humorous pieces, "Extracts from Adam's Diary" (1893) and "Eve's Diary" (1905).

Defoe's *Robinson Crusoe* and the influence of sea journals and Puritan diaries

The first European novel to contain a diary that in any way corresponds to the modern definition of the word is Daniel Defoe's *The Life and Strange Surprizing Adventures of Robinson Crusoe, of York, Mariner,* which appeared in 1719 and is sometimes called the first English novel. Crusoe's journal is an insert of about sixty pages that begins after Crusoe is shipwrecked on the island. The journal can be traced to one of the two chief "real" models of the day, if not to both: sea journals and Puritan diaries. It is generally considered that two sea journals, Edward Cooke's *Voyage to the South Sea, and Round the World* and Captain Woodes Rogers's *Cruising Voyage Round the World,* both published in 1712, were two of Defoe's main sources for the Alexander Selkirk story, which served as the principal inspiration for Crusoe's solitary existence on the island. Defoe probably knew of and had read other travel journals as well.[29] Defoe's exposure to Puritan diaries is less documentable, especially since none were in print until after *Robinson Crusoe* had been published. However, G. A. Starr in *Defoe and Spiritual Autobiography* argues that Defoe, a dissenter, was surely acquainted with the tradition of Puritan autobiography. The autobiographies, conceived as works of piety and destined for the edification of fellow sectarians, often circulated in manuscript form, so that one cannot assume that Defoe was influenced exclusively by printed works. The autobiographies frequently emphasize the keeping of a journal as one of the steps in the direction of spiritual betterment.[30]

The two literary types that presumably influenced Crusoe's journal mirror the two styles that predominate in Defoe's novel as a whole. *Robinson Crusoe* gives the impression of being pulled with equal force in two different directions: toward a realistic story of travel and adventure on the one hand, and toward allegorical religious autobiography on the other.[31] The work is written in the form of an autobiographical memoir, and its plot is liberally interwoven with the sort of pious reflections and references to the workings of Providence characteristic of the widespread genre of Puritan autobiography. Particularly Defoe's use of the conventionally metaphoric voyage and shipwreck themes suggests an allegorical interpretation of Crusoe as a Puritan Prodigal Son, the personification of the errant soul that ultimately finds its way to God.[32] On the other hand, Defoe certainly also drew inspiration from the travel literature of his day. The love of fact so apparent in the novel links it stylistically to the genre of travel description. In fact, the novel's so-called realism, the sheer bulk of purely descriptive detail for its own sake, seemingly unclouded by aesthetic or metaphorical motives, is so overwhelming that it often seems impossible to believe that Defoe aspired to endow it with any allegorical connotations whatsoever.[33]

From the point of view of narrative technique, Crusoe's journal is an odd document, full of structural inconsistencies. Unlike modern journals, it is not a day-to-day record. It is rather a journal in the contemporary eighteenth-century sense of the term, a record of daily events. Although Crusoe uses dated entries, he does not describe the events of a given day on that day. Crusoe notes in his journal how he constructed his table and chair, for example, yet he has just told the reader in the memoir section that he did not start keeping his record until he had made himself the wherewithal for sitting and writing. Crusoe's use of tenses and more particularly of adverbial phrases of time supports the assumption that he is writing about his first weeks on the island from a later perspective: He repeatedly refers to time as though it were time past, employing phrases like "that day" and "the next [day]"[34] instead of "today," "tomorrow."

The reader is at first led to believe that Crusoe wrote the journal retrospectively but nevertheless while he was marooned on the island, for according to Crusoe's own testimony he began writing after he made himself a chair and a table and stopped when his ink supply failed him. But in the course of the record inconsistencies appear that contradict this interpretation. Defoe's narrative does not sustain the fiction of a precise time of writing. Crusoe repeatedly interrupts his journal with commentaries he could only have written after he left the island. The latter part of the journal is interspersed with ever-lengthier sections of what are clearly memoir, distinguishable as such either because Crusoe throws in a phrase like "but to return to my Journal" (p. 79), or inasmuch as he refers to his readers – readers he could not have expected ever to have had while he was marooned on the island. The journal finally dissolves into the memoir without a clear break or demarcation.

As a narrative medium, a special device for conveying material in a manner that could not be borne by the normal flow of retrospective narrative, Crusoe's journal does not appear to have much purpose. The *fact* that Crusoe keeps a journal seems to be important, however. Before the journal insert begins, Defoe's enthusiasm for the idea shines through Crusoe's words: "I began to keep my Journal, of which I shall here give you the Copy (tho' in it will be told all these Particulars over again) as long as it lasted" (p. 69). The journal, we gather, will be transcribed at all costs, even at the risk of boring the reader. But as Crusoe's increasingly frequent and extensive lapses into memoir style attest, Defoe apparently decided in the course of writing that the diary form was an awkward choice. Several pages later, when it is time to describe the building of the wall, Crusoe, or Defoe, is evidently tired of reiterating events in journal form, for Crusoe writes: "This Wall being describ'd before, I purposely omit what was said in the Journal" (p. 76).

The importance of the diary as a fact, contrasted to its simultaneous lack of importance as a narrative structure, suggests that Defoe introduced it primarily as a signal. In this regard it is illuminating to consider Defoe's other probable source for the journal, Puritan autobiographical literature. According to the code of religiously meaningful actions a Puritan can perform, the commencement of a journal, a sitting down to reflect and a taking of accounts, signifies that a process of spiritual betterment is under way. This is the case in *Robinson Crusoe* as well. Whereas in the seventy pages of narrative that precede the journal Defoe treats the reader to practically none of the passages of pious moralizing for which the novel is celebrated, the journal itself is full of such passages, and it also contains the entire story of Crusoe's religious awakening, his repentance of his past life of sin and seagoing, and his conversion to an unwavering belief in the unfailing goodness and mercy of Providence. It is this particular sequence in Crusoe's story that corresponds to the stereotypical pattern of Puritan conversion as it is found in Puritan autobiographies.[35] Defoe makes the impression of hurrying toward these events in Crusoe's journal.

Crusoe's first step on the path of repentance is made when he notices that corn has sprung up near his habitation. In great joy he begins to speculate on the possibility that a divine miracle has taken place. He backslides, however, when he recalls that he himself must have carelessly thrown the grains of corn onto the ground. Two subsequent warnings, a violent earthquake and a storm, fail to move his hardened heart. At length God's wrath strikes Crusoe in the form of a terrible ague. In his fever he has an awful dream of a man descending in a flame from a cloud. Terrified, Crusoe utters the first prayer he has spoken in many years. As he recovers physically from his sickness, he also mends the state of his soul. Heaven – so Crusoe interprets – causes him to open the Bible he saved and brought ashore from the sinking wreck. The first words he sees are "Call on me . . . and I will deliver" (p. 94). Later, when he repents of his sins and prays for forgiveness, the true meaning of the biblical words becomes clear: He will not be delivered from the island, as he first hoped, but – much more important – he will be delivered of his guilt. With this recognition his conversion is complete. Directly after the conversion, Crusoe abandons the fiction of the journal and begins to summarize, and it is not long before his ink supply conveniently starts to fail him.

Interestingly, Crusoe's curious lapses into retrospection occur primarily within the context of the account of the spiritually significant events. It is in the section describing the steps leading to conversion that Defoe seems least able to maintain the fiction that Crusoe is writing a day-to-day diary. After recounting the first incident, the springing up of the corn, Crusoe notes, "But to return to my journal" (p. 79). The next incident, Crusoe's dream, is followed by another "But I return to my Journal" (p. 91). The third major spiritual event, the opening of the Bible, is likewise apparently told from the perspective of the memoir, since Crusoe finishes it with the words: "To this Hour, I'm partly of the Opinion, that I slept all the next Day and Night, and 'till almost Three that Day after; for otherwise I knew not how I should lose a Day out of my Reckoning in the Days of the Week, as it appear'd some Years after I had done" (p. 94). And Crusoe ends the story of the conversion on this note: "And I add this Part here, to hint to whoever shall read it, that whenever they come to a true Sense of things, they will find Deliverance from Sin a much greater Blessing, than Deliverance from Affliction. – But leaving this Part, I return to my Journal" (p. 97).

It is as if Defoe can only tell the story of the conversion from a certain temporal remove. If we look at one of the central sections in which Crusoe's soul-searching before conversion is reproduced, we will see that it is entirely in the past tense:

> *As I sat here, some such Thoughts as these occurred to me.*
> What is this Earth and Sea of which I have seen so much, whence is it produc'd, and what am I, and all the other Creatures, wild and tame, humane and brutal, whence are we?
> Sure we are all made by some secret Power, who form'd the Earth and Sea, and Air and Sky; and who is that?
> *Then it follow'd most naturally,* It is God that has made it all: Well, *but*

then it came on strangely, if God has made all these Things, he guides and governs them all, and all Things that concern them; for the Power that could make all Things, must certainly have Power to guide and direct them.

If so, nothing can happen in the great Circuit of his Works, either without his Knowledge or Appointment.

And if nothing happens without his Knowledge, he knows that I am here, and am in this dreadful Condition; and if nothing happens without his Appointment, he has appointed all this to befal me.

Nothing occur'd to my Thought to contradict any of these Conclusions; and therefore it rested upon me with the greater Force, that it must needs be, that God has appointed all this to befal me. [p. 92; italics mine]

Crusoe's moral conflicts, seemingly the ideal stuff for a diary, are related as matters of the past; instead of writing his speculations directly into the journal, that is, omitting the parts I have italicized, as a modern author would have him do, he soberly reproduces his qualms of conscience at a later date.

Defoe's failure to establish a direct mind-to-pen connection in Crusoe's journal cannot be explained historically, as the consequence of a lack of acquaintance with a narrative technique sufficiently advanced for reproducing a character's thoughts with immediacy, since there existed in the early eighteenth century a literary device designed precisely to accommodate this function: the letter. Epistolary novels were translated from the French and published in England and also written by Aphra Behn and others before Defoe wrote Crusoe's journal. It is probable, however, that Defoe stood so entirely under the influence of the stylistic conventions of Puritan autobiography that it did not strike him as appropriate to modify them into a narrative style more suited to the journal form. Epistolary novels were about love affairs and consequently could not be considered as models for serious religious allegory. If Defoe had merely presented the reader with what Crusoe experienced and wrote in his diary from day to day, the resulting narration would have undermined the essential teleological pattern of Christian spiritual autobiography and subverted the didactic purpose to which Defoe makes Crusoe relate the story of his conversion in the first place.[36] The affected subject of the conversion cannot discern the full truth of the process, extract its moral benefit, and pass this on to readers in the most stirring colors until he has had the time to gain considerable perspective on the events. There would have been ways for Defoe to have presented the imperative didactic message without muddling the fiction of the journal; he could have left the journal intact and had Crusoe add the interpretation afterward, for example; but as it is, he sacrifices technical consistency in narration to the advantage of having Crusoe draw the appropriate moral on the spot and thereby duplicates precisely the manner of Puritan autobiographers. Immediacy and psychological realism are subordinated to didactic intent.

Defoe's *Robinson Crusoe* inspired hundreds of imitations in England and on the Continent,[37] but Crusoe's journal was not one of the features of the original that was copied. Robinson's literary descendants tend to pay lip service at best to the idea of journal keeping: The narrator of *The Hermit: Or, the Unparalleled Sufferings and Surprising Adventures of Mr. Philip Quarll* (1727) pointedly announces that he does "not pretend to take a methodical Journal"[38] of his voyage, and the heroine of another imitation, Charles Dibdin's *Hannah Hewit, or, the Female Crusoe* (1792), remarks that if she were to enumerate all her employments, her "history would appear little better than a journal."[39] Michel Tournier does use a journal in his recent Robinson novel *Vendredi, ou les Limbes du Pacifique* (1967), which he constructs as a meditation on the destructive but, more profoundly, constructive effects of solitude on the individual, but in eighteenth-century English literature there is only one work that could be seen to owe its inspiration to the journal in *Robinson Crusoe*. This is a short fictitious diary that appeared in 1728 under the title *Authentick Relation Of The Many Hardships and Sufferings of A Dutch Sailor*. Unlike *Robinson Crusoe*, however, the *Authentick Relation* is not an optimistic tale of self-reliance and survival in the wilderness, but a morbid account of an abandoned sailor's helplessness, increasing debilitation, and death. The diarist, marooned by his commodore for crimes of sodomy on the island of Ascension, slowly dies of exposure, hunger, and thirst while apparitions of evil spirits taunt him with his former crimes and torment him with increasing fury. The anonymous author takes elaborate pains to deceive the reader into believing that the work is a genuine journal.[40] It is a psychologically realistic, day-to-day account of the sailor's sufferings, in which the narrator frequently writes his thoughts directly into the diary in the present tense: "The 7th, my wood is all gone; so that I am forced to eat raw flesh and salted foods. I cannot live long; and I hope the Lord will have mercy on my soul! The 8th, drank my own urine, and eat raw flesh." In 1730, two years later, another version of the same story appeared under a different title: *The Just Vengeance of Heaven Exemplify'd. In A Journal Lately Found by Captain Mawson, (Commander of the Ship Compton) On the Island of Ascension*. This version, which contains a suggestive engraving of a skeleton stretched out on the rocks of an island with a scroll entitled "A Journal" lying at his side (see the frontispiece to this volume), "puritanizes" the style of the original and thereby destroys its verisimilitude. The diarist, who is becoming physically feebler by the moment, "improves" his record with many pious reflections; he extracts the last drop of moral meaning from his own exemplum. Whereas in

Robinson Crusoe timely repentance is rewarded by heavenly mercy, the diarist of the pamphlet is punished relentlessly for his crime of sodomy, although he repeatedly cries out his penitence and prays to God to forgive him. A later critic, appalled at the harsh moral message of the work, wrote in condemnation:

> I am amazed . . . at the Impiety of some of these Imitators, who dare to ascribe the Products of their own Fancy to the Leadings of Divine Providence, and even from Fictions, to argue the Reality of the Superintendence of the Almighty over human Affairs, while they know they are writing Falsehoods in his Presence.[41]

While sea journals and logs have been widely imitated in fiction – Poe's "Ms. Found in a Bottle" (1833) and *The Narrative of Arthur Gordon Pym* (1838), Pierre Loti's exotic travel novels like *Aziyadé* (1879), and Malcom Lowry's *Through the Panama* (1961) are only a few examples of the many sea–adventure stories written in part or entirely in journal form – the Puritan diary has few fictional descendants. The Protestant diary influenced diary novels mainly indirectly, as the ancestor of the intimate diary, which in turn influenced the production of diary fiction. Protestant journals themselves were dull affairs and for that obvious reason were scarcely imitated in fiction. It was only in Germany, where the tradition of Pietist diaries was strong and where the publication of Johann Caspar Lavater's *Geheimes Tagebuch* (1771–3) caused a sensation, that one finds traits of the Protestant journals seriously imitated in novels. Otherwise, the influence of the Protestant journals makes itself most strongly felt in the fictive diarists' statements of motivation. Even in fictive journals of an entirely different type, it is sometimes suggested that the journal is to be a record of conduct. In the "Journal" in Richardson's *Pamela* (1740), for instance, which is in fact a continuation of Pamela's letters to her parents and has nothing in common with a religious diary, an incongruous Protestant motivation is suggested: The narrator says that Pamela wrote her account "Journal-wise," not only "to amuse and employ her Time," but so that she "might afterwards thankfully look back upon the Dangers she had escaped, when they should be happily over-blown, as in time she hoped they would be; and that then she might examine, and either approve of, or repent of, her own Conduct in them."[42] Likewise, in Moritz August von Thümmel's rococo travel diary novel *Reise in die mittäglichen Provinzen von Frankreich* (1791–1805), the diarist perceives his journal as an outlet for sentiment, as "the intimate friend to whom I pour out my heart," yet when an ignorant little French girl asks him what a diary is, he defines it in Protestant terms, as "an account of profits and expenses – of time – of our sentiments and our errors."[43]

8

Letter-Journal Novels and the
Influence of Richardson

"I see what you think of me," said he gravely – "I shall make but a poor figure in your journal to-morrow."

"My journal! . . . But, perhaps, I keep no journal."

"Perhaps you are not sitting in this room, and I am not sitting by you. These are points in which a doubt is equally possible. Not keep a journal! How are your absent cousins to understand the tenour of your life in Bath without one? How are the civilities and compliments of every day to be related as they ought to be, unless noted down every evening in a journal? How are your various dresses to be remembered, and the particular state of your complexion, and curl of your hair to be described in all their diversities, without having constant recourse to a journal? My dear madam, I am not so ignorant of young ladies' ways as you wish to believe me."

Jane Austen, *Northanger Abbey* (1818)

Full-length novels written entirely in journal form did not begin to appear until the second half of the eighteenth century. These first diary novels are all of a single type, the type that originated in Samuel Richardson's *Pamela:* They are letter journals. Unlike later diary novels, which uphold the fiction that what the diarist writes is meant for his eyes alone, letter-journal novels are addressed to a recipient who is usually also a confidant. The use of the word "journal" to describe what we today would call "letters" has its precedent in contemporary nonfictional literature. Jonathan Swift referred to the letters he wrote during a sojourn in London from 1710 to 1713 to his companion Esther Johnson and her friend Rebecca Dingly as "journals,"[44] and when Thomas Sheridan edited and published the correspondence in 1784, he gave it the title *Journal to Stella.* Laurence Sterne started to write a similar journal, which he described as "a Diary of the miserable feelings of a person separated from a Lady for whose society he languish'd,"[45] to his friend Eliza Draper when she left London for India in 1767. These works, and their fictional counterparts, are called "journals" instead of merely "letters" because, in accordance with the eighteenth-century meaning of the word "journal," their authors wrote with the intention of conveying a circumstantial record of the events of each day. The journal for the friend was an ongoing account of the diarist's life, from which the writer pledged to omit no detail. Thus, Hermione of *Hermione, or the Orphan Sisters* (1791), one of the English letter-journal novels, promises her correspondent Sophie that she will "write as you desire, minutely and sincerely, every event of my life, in the same style of journalizing which we have continued so long."[46] Mary Montague in Susannah Gunning's novel *Memoirs of Mary* (1793) writes letters from court to her grandmother, but she also sends a "journal" that in part covers the same period of time. The letters are written in a hurry so that Lady Auberry can receive immediate news of her newly departed granddaughter, while the journal is intended to keep a more detailed account.[47]

Typically, the journals are sent periodically in packages to their recipients. Rebecca Dingly urges Swift to "make your journals shorter, and send them oftener."[48] The correspondent and bosom friend of the heroine in Frances Sheridan's letter-journal novel *Memoirs of Miss Sidney Bidulph* (1761–7) observes that even after she moved to Vienna, Sidney, who remained in England, "kept up the method we had agreed on of communicating every thing that happened, even to trivial matters," and that this procedure "encreased the bulk of the packets I used to receive from her to a prodigious size."[49]

The letter-journal novel is the first important type of the diary novel, and it is also a variation on one of the main novel genres of the eighteenth century, the epistolary novel. Historically, the letter-journal novel can be considered the transitional type between the two forms.[50] While the great epistolary novels written in the period of the genre's expansion were multivoice constructions involving several correspondents, single-voice epistolary novels, including those explicitly called "journals," were written mainly in the epistolary novel's declining phase. In England, for example, most letter-journal novels were written in the decade of the 1790s, the period when the volume of production had already passed its peak and the genre was on the decline.

Like the epistolary novel in the eighteenth century, the letter-journal novel started as an English fashion and spread later to the Continent. The majority of novels that employ the device copy the style of Richardson. The volume of production of epistolary novels, as Frank Gees Black shows in *The Epistolary Novel in the Late Eighteenth Century,* rose sharply in the mid-1760s and peaked from 1767 to 1788. Most of the novels written in this period of greatest popularity and until the end of the century imitated the sentimental manner of Richardson.[51] Richardson set the precedent for fictive letter journals with *Pamela:* When Pamela is abducted on her would-be seducer's orders and held captive in an old, lonely mansion in the country, she continues to write to her parents, but her communications are called a "journal" because she has no way of sending them and can only hope that her parents will receive them someday.

The structural relatedness of the epistolary novel to the diary novel has been widely remarked.[52] The epistolary novel and the diary novel are both forms that are anchored in the fiction of periodic writing, and consequently series of letters, like diary entries, are particularly suited to the description of events that took place in the recent or immediate past and to the expression of present thoughts and feelings. Richardson speaks of "writing to the moment" and energetically defends the advantages of the mode in the 1759 preface to *Clarissa:* "Much more lively and affecting . . . must be the style of those who write in the height of a *present* distress; the mind tortured by the pangs of uncertainty (the Events then hidden in the womb of Fate): than the dry, narrative, unanimated style of a person relating difficulties and dangers surmounted, can be." The narrative ideal expressed here diverges considerably from the didactic goal of *Robinson Crusoe.*

Of course, the epistolary form has possibilities that are closed to the diary novel.[53] In novels that include epistolary exchanges between several characters, the letters may be events in their own right rather than just records of events; they can play a part in the plot by crossing, not arriving, or similarly failing their intended purpose. But more important, epistolary novels with several correspondents take a sharp turn away from simple first-person narration in the direction of the drama.[54] Since there are several speakers, the reader is encouraged to analyze and compare the respective merits and motivations of the characters rather than merely to champion the cause of the main character. Thus in *Clarissa,* our first inclination is to sympathize with the heroine, but when the seducer Lovelace begins to get equal time by writing increasingly frequent letters to his confidant, we begin to question whether he really is as villainous as Clarissa's reports of his misdeeds led us to imagine. Situations of even greater complexity can be created if the author decides to multiply the number of fictive readers, or recipients of letters. If a correspondent communicates with several different characters, his own voice can be broken into contrasting expressions of his personality. An author can portray an insincere character with ease in a multivoice epistolary novel, whereas in a diary novel the credibility of the single speaker is much more difficult to undermine.

The epistolary novel with only a single correspondent is the type most similar to the diary novel. The sole difference in this case is that in the epistolary novel there is a fictive reader, whereas in the diary novel the fictive reader is missing. Yet here, too, there are gradations of similarity, for a fictive reader in a letter-journal novel may be more or less present. If a fictive reader is a character involved in the plot, he is likely to influence the style and content of the letters addressed to him. In the anonymously published *Lettres portugaises* (1669), for example, the nun who has been abandoned by her lover directs her letters to the faithless lover himself. One might be tempted to consider this early French epistolary novel, the *locus classicus* of psychological epistolary fiction, one of the first examples of the letter-journal form. We hear only the nun's voice; the novel, like the later *Werther* imitations, is plotless; the letters focus on expressing the nun's obsessive jealousy and despair. The work is diarylike in the modern sense of the word: The nun even admits at one point, "I write more for myself than for you; I seek only to comfort myself."[55] But both in the explicit emphasis on an exchange of letters, and in its expression of strong emotion rather than sentiment, this novel is quite unlike later Richardsonian letter journals. It shows the influence of Ovid's *Heroides,* verse epistles from women of mythical antiquity to their far-off lovers. Especially at the beginning, the lover's implied attitude of callousness seems to be a determining factor in the style, tone, and content of the nun's letters.

In contrast to this type of epistolary novel, the author of a single-voice epistolary novel can reduce the fictive reader to a nonpersonality, a mere ear for the reception of confidences, so that the existence of the addressee does not affect the content, quality, or tone of the letter writer's thoughts. In the letter-journal novels the fictive reader is always this ghostlike kind of confidant. The presence of such a reader does not restrict the sincerity of the letter writer's thoughts or make them markedly different from the thoughts a diarist would commit to paper, for in the eighteenth century, when the letter-journal novels were written, it was not implausible, but rather customary, that one should unbosom oneself with complete sincerity to a confidant. The fiction of secret writing, far from enhancing the sincerity of the utterances, would have had the opposite effect of casting suspicion on the character of the hero. For would an honest person have secret thoughts he can confide to no one? Is it possible for an upright individual not to have a single friend? For the sake of discretion one did not want to trumpet one's feelings abroad in society at large, but if the emotions were natural and not shameful there was no reason not to confide them to a friend. Thus Sidney's letter journal in the *Memoirs of Miss Sidney Bidulph* is allegedly entirely sincere: Sidney "revealed all the secrets of her heart" to "an intimate friend of hers, of her own sex" in her journal, which was "for her perusal only."[56] Hermione in *Hermione, or the Orphan Sisters* would likewise have us believe that her letter-journal withholds no secrets; she writes: "When I reflect how unreserved, how perfectly free from constraint, are my communications, I can scarce conceive how I possess the resolution to transmit them to writing. Indeed had not an early habit of confidence familiarized me to the idea of laying open my heart, I should never have found courage to risk the hazards of so long a journey as they must take before they reach your hands."[57]

Richardson advocated "writing to the moment"; and letter-journal novels signal sincerity, often explicitly. These factors would seem to lay the foundation for an uninhibited confession of intimate feelings and for an unmediated expression of thoughts, so that one would expect to find in the letter-journal novels the kind of self-expression in the present tense that for didactic reasons was conspicuously missing from the journal of Robinson Crusoe. But the emphasis in these works lies elsewhere. Not the present-tense expression of thoughts but, rather, the past-tense description of events predominates. The reason has to do with a complex of generic determinants, but it is ultimately traceable to the character type these novels almost invariably involve.

The diarist in a letter-journal novel is usually a young, virtuous woman. Her character is conventional rather than profound. One can expect her to be chaste, well bred, and reserved; she behaves herself irreproachably, and with the greatest delicacy; she abhors pretense and intrigue and, if given the choice, prefers the country to the court; she desires to marry the one man she loves, and she is sensitive, yet above all things obedient to the wishes of her parents; if her story takes her beyond her wedding, she proves a steadfast wife and a tender, self-sacrificing mother. Whether this story ends happily or not, the heroine's exemplary behavior in the face of adverse circumstances is always meant to inspire admiration. She is a character with whom the contemporary female reader can identify, whose cause she can embrace wholeheartedly, without the slightest moral misgiving. The thoughts and emotions of such a heroine naturally do not admit of much variation. The reader knows in advance what she will think and feel. It is not her thoughts that are of primary interest, consequently, but rather the events that befall her. Letter-journal novels typically have exceptionally convoluted, melodramatic plots. A heroine is seldom allowed to glide serenely and without difficulties toward the suitable and satisfactory match that represents the culmination of her career. Usually she starts out with a serious handicap—she is orphaned, impoverished, seduced, mismatched, or the like—and has to weather one adventure, or rather trial, after the next before the novel comes to its happy (or, less often, unhappy) conclusion.

Frances Sheridan's *Memoirs of Miss Sidney Bidulph* provides an example of such a plot. The main action, stripped of the subplots, is as follows: The heroine, Sidney, is eighteen years old when she begins her journal. The virtuous and wealthy Orlando Faulkland, who would make an ideal match, courts her; she is attracted to him and accepts his proposal of marriage with her mother's sanction. At the last moment before the wedding, Sidney's mother comes up with a hastily conceived, ill-considered moral objection to Faulkland. The dutiful Sidney suffers but does not argue, and to please her mother she marries a man she does not love. She proves as dutiful a wife as she was a daughter, although her husband humiliates her by having an affair with another woman and casts her out of his home on an unfounded suspicion that she is unfaithful. After his mistress leaves him, Sidney forgives him everything and takes him back, even though he has lost his entire fortune. She even sacrifices her own jointure to provide money for the family, so that when her husband dies, she is totally destitute. Faulkland still loves her and wants to marry her, but her delicacy forbids her to consider the idea. Instead she persuades her former fiancé to marry a woman he "wronged" and who bore his child. Later events prove that the woman is really a "rake in petticoats" who seduced Faulkland. Sidney meanwhile reaches the depths of misery. Her mother dies; her children get smallpox; and too proud to ask for financial help, she is reduced to selling her clothing for money. She succumbs to a "disorder of the spirit" and lies sick for an extended period, until a long-lost cousin and millionaire from the West Indies materializes and decides to reward her for her virtue by becoming her benefactor. Sidney uses her new wealth to do numerous good and selfless deeds. Finally, when Faulkland's adulterous wife dies, she agrees – with much hesitation and only after immense pressure is put on her from all sides – to marry her true love. Immediately after the wedding the dead wife turns out not to be dead after all. Faulkland commits suicide in horror, and Sidney, her happiness snatched from her grasp, withdraws to the countryside to live in retirement.

In the eighteenth century the fiction of the journal lends itself admirably to this kind of attention to the plot, for the word "journal" implies that a complete account will be given. It often happens that some other person continues the journal while the diarist is unable to do so because of sickness, an excess of grief, or the like. In the *Memoirs of Miss Sidney Bidulph*, Patty, the maid, keeps the journal on several occasions: when Sidney, her mistress, is too bored to write, when her husband is on his deathbed, and when, ruined financially and treated badly by her relatives, she is prostrated by depression. In Moritz August von Thüm-mel's *Reise in die mittäglichen Provinzen von Frankreich* (1791–1805), like-wise, a friend picks up the pen when the diarist Wilhelm succumbs to the effects of a bad fish he ate at a Marseille banquet.

The "sincerity" that is signaled in a letter-journal novel, the "secrets of the soul" that are promised, are thus in fact indiscreet incidents rather than feelings. The "confidential material" consists of what hap-pens *outwardly* to the diarist: She confides to her friend the faithlessness of a lover or husband, the unreasonableness of a parent, reduction to poverty, or a slandered reputation. This is not to say that feelings were unimportant; they are essential in these sentimental novels, but they are contained in, implicit in, the highly melodramatic course of events. The character's thoughts, her responses to any given situation, are predict-able because her character is predetermined by convention. It is barely necessary for her to do more than give an account of her situation for the reader to know the precise degree of her delight or exactly what agonies she must be suffering. In a novel with this type of virtuous heroine, a stock situation calls forth a stock response. The "sincerity" of the heroine in a letter-journal novel of the sentimental type is thus strictly limited. It implies simply that she will give a complete and honest account of her adventures. It does not mean that she will bring the hidden depths of her soul to light, for these depths do not exist. Furthermore, although such a heroine certainly can be said to collect experience, she normally undergoes no psychological development whatsoever.

The character of a letter-journal novel heroine is so conventionalized that first person narration sometimes seems to be an obstruction. In the *Memoirs of Miss Sidney Bidulph,* for example, Sidney, who is supposed to be a model of steadfastness in the face of misfortune, can only impart essential information about her husband's neglect to her confidant (and the reader) obliquely. It will not do to have Sidney indulge in com-plaints, but the reader must nevertheless somehow be told that she has every right to lament her hard luck. The following passage illustrates Frances Sheridan's technique:

> *Mr. Arnold adds cruelty to* – but let it be so; *far be reproaches or complaints from my lips;* to you only, my second self, shall I utter them; to you I am bound by solemn promise, and reciprocal confidence, to disclose the inmost secrets of my soul, and with you they are as safe as in my own breast.
>
> I am once more composed, and determined on my behaviour. *I have not a doubt remaining of Mr. Arnold's infidelity; but let me not aggravate my own griefs, nor to a vicious world justify my husband's conduct, by bringing any reproach on my own.* The *silent sufferings* of the injured must, to a

mind not ungenerous, be a sharper rebuke than it is in the power of language to inflict.

But this is not all: *I must endeavour, if possible, to skreen Mr. Arnold from censure.*[58]

By declaring that she will suffer in silence, Sidney manages in one breath to tell her confidant that her husband is unfaithful and to enhance the reader's impression of her fortitude. By ostentatiously refraining from reproaches, she indicates that the harshest condemnation is in order. In later first-person narratives with unreliable narrators, the reader is encouraged to suspect that the narrator is giving a distorted account; the hero's story, his self-assessment, is juxtaposed with the true story that emerges between the lines. In the *Memoirs of Miss Sidney Bidulph,* in contrast, the heroine is neither insincere nor self-deluding but merely too virtuous for her own story. What emerges between the lines is not a more complete understanding of her personality, which is self-evident from the beginning, but rather the correct moral assessment of her husband's treachery. The reader's task is to interpret the heroine's heroic restraint in the light of what she knows of her character and to supply the appropriate outraged response. Letter-journal novels are at their most interesting at such moments, where there is a discrepancy between the true story and what the heroine is allowed to tell, between the woman's natural reactions and the understatement or exaggeration she imparts to her confidant. When an author uses this kind of counterpoint, the single-voice narrative begins to take on some of the sophistication of the multivoice epistolary novel.

Because the heroine's character is so conventionalized, one encounters in the letter-journal novels few expressions of feelings that do not have their specific cause, much less introspection for its own sake. When the heroine transcribes her thoughts, these thoughts are almost invariably dependent on events. They are either reactions to past events, or speculations about possible future events. They are also connected to events in the narrative situation. Let us look at a sequence in *Pamela.* Pamela is relating in her journal to her parents how her emissary, Mr. Williams, was attacked by rogues while riding, and how Mrs. Jewkes, her overseer, reacted gleefully to the news. The horror of her situation provokes Pamela to decide, in mid-letter, to run away. She steals down to the garden, and all seems to be perfect for an escape. She goes in again to record this fact in her letter, and she also records her resolve to go down and really run away. But the next sentence of her letter explains that she was foiled by the appearance of a bull. She writes:

Do you think there are such things as Witches and Spirits? If there be, I believe in my Heart, Mrs. Jewkes has got this Bull of her Side. But

yet, what could I do without Money or a Friend? – O this wicked
Woman! to trick me so! Every thing, Man, Woman, and Beast, is in a
plot against your poor Pamela, I think! – Then I know not one Step of
the Way, nor how far to any House or Cottage; and whether I could
gain Protection, if I got to a House: And now the Robbers are abroad,
too, I may run into as great Danger, as I want to escape from; nay,
greater much, if these promising Appearances hold: And sure my
Master cannot be so black as that they should not! – What can I do? – I
have a good mind to try for it once more; but then I may be pursued
and taken; and it will be worse for me; and this wicked Woman will
beat me, and take my Shoes away, and lock me up.

But, after all, if my Master should mean *well,* he can't be angry at
my Fears, if I *should* escape; and nobody can blame me; and I can more
easily be induced with you, when all my Apprehensions are over, to
consider his Proposal of Mr. Williams, than I could here; and he
pretends, as you have read in his Letter, he will leave me to my
Choice: Why then should I be afraid? I will go down again, I think!
But yet my Heart misgives me, because of the Difficulties before me,
in escaping; and being so poor and friendless! – O good God! The
Preserver of the Innocent! direct me what to do![59]

Then Pamela tries to escape once more, and fails, and records her
failure in her letter. In the above passage, Pamela's thoughts are situa-
tional: They are dependent on action and attached to action. She thinks
her thoughts because she wants to escape and has just failed in an
attempt to do so. She records her frustration at meeting the bull in the
garden; she considers what might have happened if she had succeeded
in escaping; she wonders what she should do next; she takes into account what the outcome of an unsuccessful escape attempt might be;
she reflects how advantageous it would be if she really did manage to
run away; she worries, and asks God what to do. The passage conveys
a mental state of agitation and even desperation, but Pamela is agitated
for the sole reason that she is in the middle of a risky and perilous
situation.

The passage from *Pamela* is an excellent example of "writing to the
moment." Pamela writes her momentary thoughts directly into the diary
in the present tense. But the immediacy brings with it a narrative situation that is problematical and strained. Pamela "thinks" at such length in
the present tense because she is in the middle of a dilemma the outcome
of which she cannot foresee. Because the present-tense thoughts are
completely dependent on events, Richardson is obliged to slide the
events forward into present time as well. If Pamela were to describe the
events *post festum* in her journal, her agitation would be superfluous, and
the number of thoughts to be recorded in the present tense would be
greatly reduced. Richardson's immediacy results here in one of the im-

plausible epistolary situations critics are fond of pointing out. If a letter-writing woman is made to record the climactic events of her life and her powerful feelings about them with as little temporal postponement as possible for the greatest possible effect, the result is often a situation of wild improbability, for it is precisely at such moments that it seems least likely that she should sit "scribbling" at her desk. Pamela is presumably trying seriously to escape and should be devoting all her energies to that endeavor, but she keeps running back upstairs to add a few more sentences to her letter. To make sense of the situation, the reader has to overlook momentarily that Pamela is writing a letter and imagine that she is simply thinking. Her thoughts are basically just that – thoughts; they resemble an interior monologue much more closely than anything anyone would write in a letter.

The problem present-tense thought transcription causes in *Pamela* is a problem for letter-journal novels in general. These novels usually avoid tension by keeping away from present-tense writing and, instead, describing both events and feelings in the past tense. Events can best be recounted once they are over, and since thoughts are subordinate to events, the narrator's reactions are also reported more easily in the past tense. The heroine's agitation, which implicitly extends into the time of writing, is conveyed by an exclamatory style and by word choice rather than by present-tense writing.

Later letter-journal novelists who use the present tense do not improve on the Richardsonian model, with the exception of Sophie La Roche in *Geschichte des Fräuleins von Sternheim*. This work is a Richardson imitation, although the main character, Sophie von Sternheim, is neither a Pamela nor a Clarissa but, rather, an Enlightenment heroine. Sophie prefers the simplicity of country ways to court life and intrigues, loves philosophy, and desires to do good by helping the poor, establishing schools for girls, and the like. Her type will dominate in German women's novels throughout the first half of the nineteenth century. Preserving her virtue is only a secondary obsession of Sophie's, but nevertheless she is seduced, in the Richardsonian tradition, and her seducer, like Pamela's, has her abducted and held captive in a remote spot in the country. Sophie La Roche avoids narrative tension in the journal Fräulein von Sternheim keeps during her captivity by scrupulously dividing Sophie's initial present-tense lamentations from her later account of the events that have befallen her. This separation succeeds because the journal is placed in a third-person context; an omniscient narrator informs the reader of Sophie's abduction before the journal begins, so that the reader knows the reason for the heroine's pathetic and despairing outburst in the first pages of her journal.

The diary, then, like the letter, is seemingly a form that is ideally suited to the transcription of thoughts in the present tense. Yet the first novels that employed the journal fiction did not use it primarily for that purpose. In the letter-journal novels, as in Robinson Crusoe's journal, other generic determinants blocked or counteracted the possibility of present-tense thought transcription. Crusoe must play his own exegete; consequently, writing time is distanced from the events leading to the conversion and Crusoe's mental turmoil is put in perspective. In *Pamela* and its successors, in contrast, present-tense thoughts would be desirable. But the preeminence of the plot interferes with present-tense thought transcription. It was not until novels began to be written in which character depiction took precedence over intrigue that present-tense thought transcription became one of the main functions of the diary form in fiction.

9

Wertherian Diary Novels

The next major step in the development of the diary novel took place in Germany. It is possible to pinpoint a seminal work that is responsible for the development and marks the turning point: Johann Wolfgang von Goethe's *Die Leiden des jungen Werthers*. Except for letter journals and letter travel journals, no diary novels were written before the publication of *Werther* in 1774. (Foreign translations quickly followed the publication of the original: The first French translation appeared in 1776; the first English translation was published in 1779.) *Werther* itself is not a diary novel but a single-correspondent epistolary novel with a silent recipient. It is thus structured like a letter journal, although the word *Tagebuch* is never used to describe it. But otherwise *Werther* has little in common with the Richardsonian letter-journal novels. The flow of letters from Werther to Wilhelm, interrupted only by occasional letters to Lotte and the editor's closing narrative, is not plot-oriented like the voluminous "packets" that constitute the Richardsonian letter-journal novel but, rather, is character-centered; and *Werther* is written in an entirely different style. The novel resembles an intimate journal much more closely than the similarly constructed novels that preceded it. Letter-journal novels in the manner of Richardson continued to be written after the publication of *Werther*, especially in England; but the first diary novels of the secret, intimate type were written in Germany and France, and they were largely fashioned after the model of *Werther*.

Wertherian diary novels copy certain plot motifs from Goethe's novel, the most obvious being the unhappy love story and the suicide; they use the character type of the sensitive, problematic, suffering hero; or they adopt what has fittingly been called the "Wahnsinnsstil" of Empfindsamkeit.[60]

Thus Johann Martin Miller's best-selling *Siegwart, eine Klostergeschichte* (1776) and Lorenz von Westenrieder's *Das Leben des guten*

Jünglings Engelhof (1781–2), novels that are usually recognized as *Werther* imitations (though not slavish ones), contain diaries written in the sentimental manner of *Werther*. The hero of Karl Philipp Moritz's *Anton Reiser* (1785–94) keeps a diary of his emotions, which he realizes are identical to those of Werther when Goethe's work appears later in the same year: "In that very year *The Sorrows of Young Werther* had appeared, and it meshed, in part, with all the ideas and feelings he had at the time – about loneliness, a sense of nature, a patriarchal way of life, that life is a dream."[61] Johann Gottfried von Pahl's *Herwart, der Eifersüchtige* (1797), the diary of a jealous husband who finally commits suicide, shows the influence of *Werther*. *Ramiros Tagebuch, Aus alten Papieren eines Freundes des Grafen Donamar, hrsg. von Feodor Adrianow* (1804, by Friedrich Bouterwek) is closely modeled on *Werther*. Ramiro falls in love with a married woman and, like Werther, goes through the three stages of falling in love, attempted renunciation, and a relapse that leads to the crisis and death, although he lets himself be shot in a duel instead of shooting himself. French diary novels indebted to *Werther* include Madame de Souza's didactic and sentimental novella *Charles et Marie* (1802), where an "altar to Werther"[62] stands in the garden; Souza's hero, Charles, has the conservative moral outlook of a model youth, however, and wins his Marie in the end after surmounting several pseudo-obstacles. Charles Nodier's youthful diary novella *Le Peintre de Saltzbourg* (1803) is more faithful to the spirit of the original. The hero, whose anguish at finding his true love married to someone else augments his general mood of disillusionment and *mal du siècle*, finally meets his death, which is possibly a suicide, wandering aimlessly in the mountains in the wintertime. Nodier later recognized his debt to *Werther* and other German works, calling his novella a "pastiche" of German novels.[63]

Quite apart from these eighteenth- and early-nineteenth-century Wertheresque diary novels, it is difficult to overestimate the influence of *Werther* on the diary novel in general.[64] Particularly in Germany throughout the so-called *Biedermeierzeit* (1815–48), diary novels were written that echo *Werther* in one or more respects. Many of these novels do not aspire to be anything more than entertainment, but some are meant as serious representations of characters who suffer from what is felt to be the malaise of the times.

August Kuhn's "Blätter aus Edmunds Tagebuche" (1822) is an example of a trivial adaptation; its appearance in a volume entitled *Mimosen: Erzählungen für gebildete Frauen* speaks for its tone as well as its quality. Kuhn picks up the Wertherian themes of a misconducted passion and a wrecked life, which the hero ends by putting a bullet through his breast. The story is trimmed to fit the requirements of sentimental women's literature: All the participants in the silly plot are noble.

F. A. Märcker's *Julius. Eine Lebensgeschichte aus der Zeit* (1829) is a more serious work that presents a portrait of the protagonist through his letters and diary leaves. The alienated, anguished, gifted hero is an updated Werther, who more than anything else wants a sense of purpose, a goal, an original life. He laments that everything great seems already to have been done by others, and chafes at the smallness of his age. His restiveness and artistic ambitions cause him to lose his beloved to another, more responsible man. His friends leave or die; he finally loses faith in his genius, wastes away with depression, and dies.

Freiherr Ferdinand Leopold Karl von Biedenfeld's "Aus den Papieren eines Selbstmörders" (1837) is likewise intended seriously; the hero, an unstable Wertherian type who expresses himself in an excessive, melodramatic style, "suffered and died from an illness of our time that is very widespread and has many varieties."[65] A poor young man in a big city, the diarist is possessed by unbounded desire: He is determined to be a genius and a celebrated novelist, thirsts for material success, wants a glorious career as a political journalist, and falls in love with a young woman not least because she is a rich banker's daughter. This sensitive social climber, who has much in common with Balzac's famous though later Lucien de Rubempré, is of course destined to lose his illusions, and he finally commits suicide.

Adolph Weisser's *Hinterlassene Papiere eines geistlichen Selbstmörders* (1841) is a diary novel whose protagonist, a depressive, lonely, impressionable neo-Werther, adores nature, beauty, and Greece, hates the confining institutions and morality of society, and has the misfortune to be a Catholic priest. The reader watches the guilt-ridden hero topple from one violent emotion to the next and listens to him react, in an almost unbelievably overblown style, first to a rapturous Platonic attachment and then to a passionate and sensuous love affair before he finally falls prey to persecution mania and ends his life by drinking poison out of his chalice. No injustice is done to this exceptionally sloppily constructed novel by calling it the nadir of the *Werther* trend.

Not all diary novels in the manner of *Werther* have male protagonists. The convent-and-death-bound diarist in Miller's *Siegwart* is a woman, and a number of Romantic and post-Romantic diary novels tell the stories of women. The heroines are unhappy, but they rarely commit suicide. Wertherlike outbursts of strong feelings and despair tend to be combined with the typical love-and-renunciation and/or marriage plots of eighteenth-century epistolary novels. Karl Gutzkow's *Wally, die Zweiflerin* (1835), a third-person novel that contains a diary, is an exception: It is chiefly the heroine's suicide that calls *Werther* to mind.

Despite its initially cynical, modern tone, the novel slides toward Romanticism in the third book, where Wally's *Tagebuch* is printed. When Wally's lover abandons her, the originally soulless, frivolous, animal-like heroine loses her orientation and begins to torment herself with atheistic doubts, which she records in a diary. Wally's despair and the formal construction of the diary (the editor embeds in his own narrative the last diary leaves that Wally writes continuously on the day of her suicide) are Wertherian echoes.

The influence of *Werther* persists even in diary and part-diary novels of the late nineteenth and early twentieth centuries. André Gide, for instance, who revised his own diary into his first novel *Les Cahiers d'André Walter* (1891), renamed his hero Walter after having read *Werther*.[66] The love story with which the slim plot opens is autobiographical and the problem of subduing the desires of the flesh is wholly Gide's, but the continuation of the fable, the beloved Emmanuèle's marriage to another man, her death, and Walter's own death are Wertherian. Reinhard Goering's *Jung Schuk* (1913), the tragedy of a medical student in letters and diary leaves, is *Werther*-like. The moods of the hero Gustav alternate between exaltation and despair; like Werther, he designates himself as a wanderer and defends the idea of suicide; he becomes enmeshed in a love affair that ends badly; and he is finally overcome by a revulsion for life and self that leads him to commit suicide. Hans Carossa's *Dr. Bürgers Ende* (1913), the diary of a melancholy doctor, also recalls *Werther*: After the doctor's ideal beloved, who is also his patient, dies, the diarist drinks poison. Joseph Goebbels's youthful novel *Michael: Ein deutsches Schicksal in Tagebuchblättern*, a work that the Germanist and onetime student of Friedrich Gundolf's wrote in the early 1920s and finally managed to publish in 1929 when he was well known for other reasons, is written throughout in an exalted, exclamatory style typical of poor Werther imitations and contains certain echoes of *Werther*, particularly in the description of the circumstances surrounding Michael's death. To judge from his ominously prophetic tone, Goebbels probably directly imitated the currently fashionable style of messianic Expressionism, even though its political message must have been uncongenial to him. He ends the nationalistic, anti-Semitic, rabidly antiintellectual work on this note: "I have made myself anew: the conscious, proud and free German human being, who wants to win the future!"[67] Maurice Rostand's diary novel *Le Second Werther* (1927), is, as the title announces, closely modeled on *Werther*. Rostand copies details like the commenting editor and the last letters to Lotte and Albert. We are obviously meant to sympathize with the hero of "cette misérable histoire,"[68] whose fate is even more cruel than Werther's: His fiancée elopes with his best friend. Yet the decadent fin-de-siècle diary novels left their mark on this work; the hero, who mesmerizes himself by contemplating his own unfitness for life, is less like Werther himself than like the diarists of the 1890s in his hypersensitivity, tendency to self-analysis, and neurotic dependence on those close to him.

Why did the epistolary novel *Werther* provide the impetus for the first modern diary novels, and why did it have such a lasting influence on the genre as a whole? The reason has to do, on the one hand, with the immense popularity the work enjoyed and, on the other, with its similarity to a fictive diary. It is revealing that a number of contemporary critics argue that *Werther* itself is, or ought to have been, a diary novel. Gerhard Storz, for example, contends that *Werther* is essentially a diary novel: "These letters contain . . . confession, self-portraiture, an outpouring of emotions. What is dashed off under dates is essentially diary entries, not letters. . . . Essentially and actually, then, Goethe's *Werther* is a diary novel."[69] And Arno Schmidt, a twentieth-century writer who was especially fascinated by eighteenth-century forms, objects that Goethe made a mistake in not calling *Werther* a diary: "In *Werther,* then, we have a case of a great artist having made an absolute mistake in choosing his form; for we hear only Werther. . . . *Werther* is a diary novel; quite simply!"[70]

There is no denying that the tone of *Werther* approximates one we today associate only with diaries. In arguing that *Werther* is or should have been a diary, however, these critics overlook the position of the novel in the history of narrative fiction. If we accept *Werther*'s affinity to the intimate diary unquestioningly, we wish out of sight the problematic question of how Wertherian functions actually were transferred onto the diary form. Historically, the form of Goethe's work can be explained in terms of the development of the epistolary novel: It stands in the tradition of the sentimental novels in letters started by Richardson and continued by Rousseau. The form of *Werther* can be seen as the final step in a line of development where the plot was reduced and the expression of feeling through the subject expanded, and where, correspondingly, the form was simplified from a multivocal construction to something more closely approaching a monologue.[71] Moreover, it should be stressed that a pre-Wertherian tradition of the diary novel from which Goethe might have derived inspiration does not exist. If *Werther* had been a fictional *journal intime,* it would have been the first in Western European literature.

We have seen in the case of the Richardsonian letter-journal novels that the correspondence, the act of communication, functioned as a guarantee of the sincerity of the letter writer. The same postulate holds true for *Werther* as well. If Goethe had written *Werther* as a diary novel, not only the advantage of using the correspondent Wilhelm as a foil but, more important, the significance of what one critic describes as Werther's "progress from speaking to not being able to speak, from conversation to the reading aloud of expressive texts, from dialogue to monologue and finally to silence"[72] would have been lost. Within a frame of reference in which the ability to communicate was perceived as natural, Werther's speechlessness is a sign that his breakdown is imminent.

In the age of *Empfindsamkeit* when *Werther* was written, intimate letters, whose effusive style often far exceeded that of *Werther* itself, were the vogue.[73] The popularity of letters persisted well into the first half of the nineteenth century, especially in Germany.[74] As the eighteenth century drew to a close, however, the secret personal diary increasingly joined the letter as a medium for subjective self-expression. Alain Girard, a historian of the French *journal intime,* dates the beginnings of the genre roughly around 1800,[75] and Wolfgang Schmeisser's study of the German pre-Romantic and Romantic diary indicates approximately the same dating for Germany.[76] Goethe's remarks on diaries in the novella "Die guten Weiber" (1800), however, lead one to believe that diary keeping was already fashionable twenty years earlier; he writes, "Twenty years ago, diaries were more in fashion, and many a good child truly believed it had a treasure when it recorded its states of mind every day."[77] Ludwig Tieck's parody of 1798, the novella "Ein Tagebuch," lends support to Goethe's dating; the diarist refers to the Herrnhuter and the modish spinning out of "false emotions."[78]

The transition from the letter to the secret diary in fiction mirrors the historical overlapping of their nonfiction counterparts. The diary form was not adopted suddenly, but rather in gradual and tentative stages. The tradition of the epistolary novel was firmly established, and it exerted a considerable pull on the first fictive diaries written in the immediate wake of *Werther*. These novels adopt the new form, as it were, hesitatingly. Sophie's diary in *Siegwart,* for example, is letterlike: It is "a kind of diary, which was addressed to him [Siegwart]," and nearly every sentence is addressed to "Thou." It is a secret diary only because its contents are incommunicable: Sophie writes of her unnoticed, unrequited love for Siegwart, which she of course cannot confess to anyone, least of all Siegwart, during her lifetime. "I must not speak,"[79] she writes hopelessly. Siegwart is to receive the diary only after Sophie's misery is terminated by a hoped-for early death. In Pahl's *Herwart, der Eifersüchtige,* the diary form likewise appears to be used because the protagonist's thoughts are incommunicable. Since Herwart is obsessively jealous of his wife and is also terrified that others might secretly be making fun of him for being a cuckold, letters are a logical impossibility.

The greatest obstacle to copying the real model of the secret intimate journal in fiction appears to have been an unwillingness to eliminate the fictive reader. In the earliest examples of confessional diary fiction there is a marked tendency to retain the fiction of a confidant, if only as a shadow figure, as a point of orientation. Thus, Anton Reiser's diary is called "a kind of diary . . . in the form of a letter to his friend,"[80] even though it has no features of the personal letter. The youthful Reiser writes an extremely stylized, literary proclamation of his miserable state of mind. Charles of Madame de Souza's *Charles et Marie* likewise clarifies his use of the journal form for the reader by comparing his diary with a confidence related to a friend. He declares to a fictive confidant who is introduced at the outset, but never reappears, that he will write *as if* to him: "Every day I noted down the different sentiments I felt. *I thought you would read this journal,* and I said to myself: My friend will be a second conscience for me; *I will address myself to him or speak to myself with equal sincerity.*"[81] Even two decades later, when the fiction of a secret journal should have presented no obstacle to the reader's imagination, the idea of the confidant is retained. Mrs. Opie's *Madeline, A Tale* (1822) is an intimate journal, *"the history of a weak woman's heart,"* replete with *"secret details."*[82] Yet Madeline keeps her journal at a friend's suggestion and even intends that her friend should read it someday:

> When those whom we love and revere are far removed from us, there is a melancholy satisfaction in fulfilling their wishes, and endeavoring to act according to their judgment: therefore, my dear and ever-regretted Mrs. St. Leger, I will comply with your request, that I should keep a journal of my feelings, my actions, and the unimportant events of my obscure but quiet life. Some day or other it will no doubt reach your hands.[83]

The lonely, friendless, invalid diarist in Medora Byron's *Bachelor's Journal* (1815) finds it similarly difficult to write without a correspondent, and therefore dedicates his diary to the girls of England, imaginary future readers whom he sees before his mind's eye as he writes.

Thus, even in the early nineteenth century the diary form was not completely taken for granted in fiction. While a novelist could write a novel in letters without further ado, the authors of diary novels frequently felt called upon to explain, or let their protagonists explain, their unconventional choice of form. Authors writing around 1800 tended to try to avert the possible misconception that the journal to follow was a traditionally conceived pedagogical or religious instrument devoid of sentimental interest. Novels that adopted the fiction of the intimate diary had to contend with a changing real model; it was not yet entirely self-evident that "diary" implied that an uninhibited confession of the secret life and emotions of the diarist, and not a methodical, moralizing record of virtues, vices, and petty events, was in store. In his quasi-fictional "Tagebuch," which he wrote in 1774 after *Werther* appeared but did not publish, Jakob Michael Reinhold Lenz still tries to record the events of every day. Bouterwek in *Ramiros Tagebuch,* writing thirty years later, makes a point of having the hero distinguish the sentimental journal he plans to write from a religious diary. Ramiro declares that his diary will not be "about my virtues and vices, . . . but, rather, about the peculiar events of my inner life."[84] His diary is not a form of daily self-discipline, he asserts, but rather a record of the interesting changes that take place in his inner life: "Why, after all, give a pedantic account of every day? When something happens in me that is worth recording, then it is time to aid memory with the pen."[85] Even as late as 1822, Edmund of Kuhn's "Blätter aus Edmunds Tagebuche" finds it necessary to clarify what he proposes to do in his diary. Lest the title give the reader an incorrect impression, Edmund makes explicit in his first diary entry that his journal, unlike the diary his parents obliged him to keep when he was an adolescent, will be a secret and therefore sincere record of his actions and feelings: "Now I am alone in the world; I can record my views, feelings, and the unvarnished representation of my actions all the more uninhibitedly in the diary I am beginning today and that only God sees besides me."[86]

Diary novels in the manner of *Werther* differ markedly from the letter-journal novels in several respects. First, a novel in the manner of *Werther* involves a particular character type as the protagonist: a labile, moody idealist, usually a young man. He is capable of a great range of emotions, "from worries to excesses, and from sweet melancholy to ruinous passion,"[87] as Werther says of himself, and is particularly susceptible to emotional extremes. In *Werther* itself and in several of the earlier imitations, the hero's ultimate aspiration is self-transcendence, a mystic and ecstatic union with a pantheistically conceived universe. In other works the hero seeks self-realization, but it can be said of every Wertherian hero that he desires something, be it pragmatic or intangible, that is out of reach. Consequently, he is liable to cruel disillusionment when he is forced to recognize the actual poverty of life, his own limitations as an individual, and the inflexibility of his social surroundings. A monist by inclination, he is ultimately destined to perceive duality all around him and to be destroyed by it. He eagerly and passionately seeks his happiness and, unable to find it, tends to term himself a *wanderer,* which is his negative self-image. The microcosmic counterpart of mystic union, and the goal of the wanderer, is the domestic idyll, the quiet simple life, a home, a wife, children. The hero who desires self-transcendence is prone to think wistfully of the simplicity of life in Homeric times, of the innocence of children, of times when man was an integrated and happy participant in universal life. The unity the Wertherian hero desires is symbolized by his love for a woman. The fulfillment of his love would represent the attainment of unity, yet just as the universe closes itself to him, the woman proves unattainable. The symbolic unattainable woman figures in nearly every Wertherian diary novel.

The Wertherian hero typically delights in nature, but when he is unhappy his picture of the universe changes like a mirror image of himself. Instead of an all-embracing, God-filled nature, he sees nature as a destroyer, a great graveyard. A man's life seems like a second compared to eternity, an ephemeral bubble on the ocean of existence. He has no use for worldly occupations or a career. A social system based on class and rank, the conventions of social intercourse, relationships sought in the interest of self-advancement rather than friendship repel him. As a rule he is a seeker of sincerity and authentic life. It is rare that the Wertherian hero engages in what René Girard and Lucien Goldmann have called a degraded search for authentic values. Instead the social structure strikes him as false, empty, senseless, and so totally divorced from the true values of life as to be unreal; and when he describes society, he is apt to draw on the *topoi* of the world as a stage and its inhabitants as marionettes or masks. Work generally impresses him as a waste of time. He devotes much of his energy to speculation about life, death, and man's place in the universe.

The Wertherian hero dies young and usually commits suicide. In this respect the post-Romantic novels are more faithful to the original than the early *Werther* imitations, which tend to avoid the controversial finale. (The suicide of the atypically wrongheaded hero in Pahl's *Herwart, der Eifersüchtige,* written in 1797, is meant strictly as a "cautionary example.")[88] The hero's suicide (or voluntary death) is half an escape from the unbearable reality of his existence, half the triumph of his conviction that in death he will attain the unity he failed to find in life.

Unlike the heroines of the letter journals, the Wertherian character has depth. Werther's famous statement "I return into myself, and find a world"[89] is the premise according to which the character of the hero in Wertherian novels is conceived. The structural device of periodic writing takes on a new function: Whereas in the letter journals it enables the heroine breathlessly to tell her friend the latest news, in the Wertherian novels it permits the hero to reveal the complexity of his character. The successive diary entries present the spectrum of the hero's changing moods. It must be qualified that in the Wertherian diary novels, the hero's character is frequently flattened. The more trivial the work, the more the idealistic and sensitive character is taken for granted, just as the virtuous heroine was taken for granted in trivial letter-journal novels, and the emphasis shifts from the presentation of the poetic spirit who cannot survive his encounter with a prosaic reality onto the unhappy love story, which is often given new, melodramatic twists. In *Ramiros Tagebuch,* for example, Ramiro's married beloved has a tyrannical and unjust husband. In Nodier's *Le Peintre de Saltzbourg* the husband of the diarist's true love is tragically in love with someone else, and the wretched spouses are married to each other only because of a dying mother's last wish.

Correspondingly, the many nuances of mood one finds in *Werther* itself are often leveled to – or, more correctly, intensified into – their extremes. Yet the very tendency toward representing extreme emotional states makes it clear that the interest in these novels lies in psychological portraiture, in showing the depths and nuances of the hero's feelings. The passages in which the hero gives expression to his strong emotions are the truly engaging ones, the parts the reader waits for; the novels were written for their sake and are constructed around them. The plots of these novels are usually skimpy, mere excuses to give the protagonist an opportunity to express his feelings extensively. The hero never has adventures in the sense that a letter-journal heroine does. As the fictive editor of Rostand's *Le Second Werther* suggests in a melodramatic metaphor, the Wertherian tragedy unfolds far from the *theatrum mundi;* he hears in the hero's voice "the melody of the last human heart" sounding above a cruel and frivolous orchestral background.[90] The fable in these novels is aimed directly at the tragic denouement. It is indicative that the Wertherian diary novel is generally written over a very short period of time, the period prior to the crisis (*Werther* itself with its eighteen months is considerably longer than most imitations). Letter-journal novels, in contrast, often go on for many years. Thus, in the Wertherian diary novels problematical characters replace the problematical plots of the Richardsonian letter-journal novels.

It follows from the preeminence of the depiction of moods and emotions in these works that thoughts are not – as they are in Richardsonian letter-journal novels – dependent on events. The events in a Wertherian diary novel are relatively unimportant, mere adhesive segments to hold together the endless string of emotions and reflections that pour from the diarist's pen. The diarist's thoughts are independent and not reactive. There is often no apparent reason for the protagonist's moods. If anything, the events could be said to be dependent on thoughts: The function of the events in the narrative is mainly to enable the hero to meet the tragic fate for which his character destines him. Stated differently, the Wertherian hero records nothing that does not intimately concern him and have a significant impact on his sensibility. Epic, objective descriptions have no place in these stories. What the hero describes is filtered through his subjective lens and colored by his momentary mood. The occasional nature descriptions – the happy spring landscapes, the dismal bleak wintry wastes, the crashing storms – are generally merely projections of the protagonist's feelings onto the outside world.

The heroine of a letter-journal novel writes in a primarily *descriptive* style. The Wertherian hero, in contrast, writes in a style that can be called *expressive*. That is, he is concerned to express how he feels, rather than to describe events and his reactions to them. It is in the Wertherian diary novels that one first sees the collapse of the narrative triangle and its effects. The diarist, the subject, has become the absolute focus of attention, and he in turn devotes himself to expressing his momentary state of mind. No obstacle stands in the way of the present-tense transcription of thoughts. Indeed, the Wertherian hero is a very versatile master of the present tense. There are many ways of noting one's feelings and thoughts in the present tense, depending on the subject's mental distance from its object. To name one extreme, one can dash down one's thoughts as they occur to one spontaneously, so that, as in the passage from *Pamela* printed above or in interior monologue, the writing follows the thought processes themselves. To name the other extreme, one can present the fruits of extensive and distanced analysis, so that the text sounds like a set of conclusions. The Wertherian diarist generally steers a course between these extremes. He may graph his fleeting sensations, and he may record what he perceives to be absolute truths, but typically – and there is a typically Wertherian style – he seeks to express his *essential* state of mind at the time of writing. Let us look by way of example at how some Wertherian heroes express the despair they feel:

> 1. Lieber Wilhelm, ich bin in einem Zustande, in dem jene Unglüklichen müssen gewesen seyn, von denen man glaubte, sie würden von einem bösen Geiste umher getrieben. Manchmal ergreift mich's, es ist nicht Angst, nicht Begier! es ist ein inneres unbekanntes Toben, das meine Brust zu zerreissen droht, das mir die Gurgel zupreßt! Wehe! Wehe! und dann schweif ich umher in den furchtbaren nächtlichen Scenen dieser menschenfeindlichen Jahrszeit. [*Die Leiden des jungen Werthers*][91]

> [Dear Wilhelm, I am in a state in which those unfortunate ones must have been of whom it was believed that they were driven about by an evil spirit. Sometimes it seizes me; it is not fear, not desire! it is an inner unknown raging, which threatens to rend to pieces my breast, which presses on my throat! Alas! Alas! And then I wander about in the terrible nocturnal landscapes of this season, which is inimical to man.]

2. Alles ist graus, und fürchterlich, und tod um mich. Die Menschen –
ich scheue sie alle. Die Natur – sie scheint meiner zu spotten. Die
Treulosigkeit dieses einen stellt mir die erstern alle als treulos dar; und
indem mich die Schönheit der letztern zu einem Genusse einladet,
dessen ich unfähig bin, so sehe ich mich durch sie geäfft. Ich wandle
unstät und flüchtig umher, und suche Ruhe und Trost, und hasche
nach dem Schatten. [*Herwart, der Eifersüchtige*]⁹²

[Everything around me is horrible, and awful, and dead. People – I
avoid them all. Nature – it seems to mock me. The latter's faithlessness
represents all the former to me as faithless; and inasmuch as the latter's
beauty invites me to a pleasure of which I am incapable, I see myself
made its sport. I wander about, restless and fugitive, and seek quiet
and comfort, and grasp at shadows.]

3. Die Haare meines Haupts stechen mich, wie eben so viele Nadeln,
auf meinem Scheitel. Mein Hirn siedet inwendig, und von außen
spannt mich die Haut. Meine Augen fallen lichtlos in den Kopf hinein,
und verlieren sich. Die krächzen, wann sie sich bewegen, und laufen
über von Thränen. Mein Mund fällt schlaf nach der Seite, und bewegt
sich selten nur, wenn ein gewaltsamer Seufzer tief vom Herzen ihn
aufzwingt, daß er schluchze. So sinket mein Kopf hinunter an mein
Herz, das deßen nicht achtet. [*Leben des guten Jünglings Engelhof*]⁹³

[The hairs on my head stick me, like so many needles, on my crown.
My brain seethes inside; and outside the skin becomes taut. My eyes
fall into my head sightlessly and lose themselves. They croak when
they move and run over with tears. My mouth falls slackly to one
side, and moves only seldom, only when a mighty sigh deep from the
heart forces it open, so that it sobs. Thus my head sinks down on my
heart, which does not regard it.]

4. Entsagung! Tönt es in meiner Brust wie ein dumpfer Ruf aus dem
Grabe. Und mir ist, als sah ich mich schon hingestreckt unter den
Todten, den Lebendig-Todten, deren Herzen nicht mehr schlagen
dürfen; deren bleichen lippen kein Ach! mehr entschwebt; deren letzte
Hoffnung erloschen ist; deren kalter Wunsch kein Ziel mehr hat, als
Ruhe. [*Ramiros Tagebuch*]⁹⁴

[Renunciation! It sounds in my heart like a hollow call from the grave.
And I feel as if I saw myself already stretched out among the dead, the
living dead, whose hearts may no longer beat; whose pale lips no
"Ach" escapes; whose last hope is snuffed out; whose cold wish has no
further goal but peace.]

These passages have neither the accretive, expanding quality of the
interior monologue, in which minute mental vibrations are strung out
in a potentially endless associative chain, nor the compact formulation
of final statements pronounced after an analysis has been made. In fact,

it is not relevant to measure the style on a scale of the writers' temporal closeness or distance from their thoughts, for what counts is their emotional distance from them. While they write, these heroes' sense of the intensity of their being miserable is immense. What they write has the force of an outcry. The outcry itself is a standard feature of the style ("Wehe!" "Ach!"), as are sentence fragments, inversions, apostrophes, and repetitions. If the diarists' choice of formulation in the passages appears less than readily obvious, it is because they wish to suggest that the intensity of their feelings is inexpressible in everyday prose (Werther writes, "I don't know how I should express myself");[95] they must have recourse to figurative language in order to communicate the abysses of their despair. The stylistic devices, the metaphors ("Geist," "Grab," "Schatten," "schweifen," "wandeln," "Herz" and other references to the body, etc.) are a kind of code[96] that signals the intensity of the diarist's feeling. The style of *Werther* was contagious and became extremely widespread.[97] The narrator of *Anton Reiser,* for instance, observes that after Reiser read *Werther,* he could not free himself from the influence of its style and its ideas for years to come:

> The too often repeated rereading of *Werther* considerably retarded his expression as well as his power of thought, for the turns of phrase and even the ideas in this writer became so familiar to him through frequent repetition that he often thought them his own, and even many years later he had to fight against memories of *Werther* when drafting his essays. This was the case with many young writers who were educated since that time.[98]

Critics have remarked that Goethe's Werther undergoes no development as a character. Hans-Egon Hass, for example, demonstrates at length that Werther's "being" is determined from the outset and is only unfolded, but not altered, by the love story and the course of events.[99] The heroes of Wertherian diary novels are as a rule similarly static. Their characters are complex, but they do not change; they have depth but no flexibility. With few exceptions the novels do not present psychological studies of their characters in the modern sense of the case study. Correspondingly, the ideal reader of these novels is not asked to view the narrator as a psychological exhibit. The role prescribed to the reader is and can only be one of pure sympathy. For the Wertherian hero is not only wholly sincere; his desires are authentic, and his fate is tragic. Herbert Schöffler writes of *Die Leiden des jungen Werthers:* "The 'Sorrows of Young Werther' is the first tragedy without guilt, without a principle of evil. No villain lays the hero low. A new, much deeper tragedy is attained, the tragedy of a wholly new era."[100] Whether one finds the cause of the tragedy in the relaxation of Christian dogma in the eighteenth century and its final consequence, the impossibility of a sure belief in the existence of God, as Schöffler himself does, or in the rise of a restrictive bourgeois society that hindered the free development of the individual personality, as does Lukács,[101] Werther's malaise is genuine and justifiable, and it lays claim to universality. The editor of *Werther* tells us in the introduction: "You cannot deny his mind and character your admiration and love, and his fate your tears."[102] In *Werther* the reader is not meant to identify with the recipient of the letters, Wilhelm, who is presumably a more rational temperament than Werther and is critical of him. In the all-diary novels there is not even this implicit source of criticism. The role prescribed to the reader is one of unquestioning belief and sympathy.

10

The Diary Novel in the Nineteenth Century

It is well known that the epistolary novel enjoyed a tremendous volume of production until the end of the eighteenth century and then began to decline, until by approximately 1830 it had all but disappeared from the literary scene. Considering the mimetic origins of the genre, it is not farfetched to suppose that one of the reasons for its decline is that the real model on which it was based began to vanish. In other words, the intimate letter itself became passé. In the course of the nineteenth century it became less and less natural to confide the secrets of one's heart to a friend. In the meantime a new genre, the secret journal, began to displace the letter in its function. Those of *Werther*'s late epigones who chose the diary form for their novels had an obvious reason for doing so: Whereas letters appeared more and more out-of-date as a device for reporting sincere thoughts, the diary itself increasingly accommodated the same function.

The explanation usually given for the decline of the epistolary novel is that new novel types for which the epistolary form was not suited arose and became popular. In England, for example, Gothic and then historical novels began to corner the literary market starting around 1789.[103] The slow-moving, eddying epistolary form would have been a hindrance in a Gothic romance, in which suspense and shock effect were of vital importance. A correspondence, suited to the presentation of personal matters and reflections, was not an ideal form for unfolding the broad panorama of factual detail and actions required by the historical novel either. With the beginnings and spread of realism and the increasing dominance of third-person narration, an epistolary novel became more and more of a rarity. The counterepistolary trends affected the development of the diary novel as well. The climate during periods of realism and naturalism was extremely unfavorable to the production of novels in a form whose advantage lies in facilitating the portrayal of a single person's mental world in depth but which is weak when it comes to conveying an objective picture of reality, creating a milieu, showing the interaction of many characters over an extended period of time, or even rendering an entire biography. Intimate diaries were written in increasing numbers throughout the nineteenth century; but the diary novel, after its promising beginning in Germany, went into a sharp decline. Some novels were written wholly or partially in the form of diaries, but compared to the production in Germany in the wake of *Werther,* there were few of them; they were outside the mainstream of the novel and, with a few exceptions, were largely undistinguished.

Eugène Sue's *Arthur* (1838) illustrates how a broadly based plot and the depiction of manners can interfere, in practice, with the realization of the intimate journal fiction. *Arthur* is the first novel Sue wrote for the *feuilleton,* then newly born. Sue signed a contract for the projected novel under the title *Journal d'un inconnu,* and two installments appeared under that name. At the beginning, the fictive editor repeatedly refers to Arthur's manuscript as a "journal." Yet the novel turns into a memoir with journal excerpts and a short final journal section. If Sue changed his mind in the course of writing and decided to write most of the novel in memoir form, it is probably because he realized that the novel's serial publication called for an emphasis on plot and adventure instead of on a subtle exploration of character. The narrator, Arthur, is the type of torn soul, the divided personality, the *enfant du siècle* for which the journal form seems uniquely suited. But Sue uses the hero's fatal combination of traits – on the one hand great idealism, passion, and generosity, on the other black suspiciousness – primarily to shape and relate a series of melodramatic episodes. Arthur's fatal flaw is not developed but, rather, is translated into a sequence of romances and ruptures. His character, fixed once and for all, is the constant element in an episodic, far-flung plot. Plainly, a day-to-day time scheme would have encumbered rather than aided narration. The reader would have found it perplexing and tiresome to watch the hero react, on a day-to-day basis, to adventures that repeat the same pattern. Retrospective telescoping serves Sue's purposes better.

Some diary fiction written in the nineteenth century simply continues trends already present in eighteenth-century fiction. For example, there is the women's trivial heartthrob literature, which is an extension on a subliterary level of patterns found in the eighteenth-century epistolary novel. An innocent, virtuous, often noble young heroine is placed in a standard predicament, and pours out her heart in her diary so that the reader's tears can flow. A favorite theme is the woman seduced and abandoned, which we find, for example, in Rosalie's diary in Amalia Schoppe's *Die Verwaisten* (1825) and Mrs. Opie's *Madeline. A Tale*

(1822), the "history of a weak woman's heart." Sentimental tragedies of renunciation are also popular. In works such as Fanny Tarnow's "Paulinens Jugendjahre" (1830) and "Blätter aus Theresens Tagebuch" (1830), Karl Herloßsohn's "Schwester Anna und ihr Tagebuch" (1846), and Octave Feuillet's *Journal d'une femme* (1878), the heroine renounces the man she loves out of a refined sense of moral scrupulousness; she suffers unspeakably in order to triumph morally. It is taken for granted that marriage to the right man would mean ultimate happiness for the heroine. A number of women's diary novels are frankly didactic: They use the form to display a model woman who embodies all feminine virtues, and then reward this paragon with a happy marriage. In J. Selten's *Luise, oder Was ein Mädchen durch Sittsamkeit, Selbstprüfung und Fleiß werden kann* (1830), an indigestible diary novel for young girls, readers are reminded that a woman should be virtuous, modest, chaste, and obedient to parents and husband. She should be a scrupulous housekeeper; she should get up early, not waste the day reading novels, and if at all possible take an interest in charity work. In Henriette Hanke's *Der Braut Tagebuch* (1842), the message is the same: Woman's truest nature fulfills itself in her role as wife and mother.

The most interesting of these didactic novels is Marie Nathusius's *Tagebuch eines armen Fräuleins* (1853). The work was popular enough to be reprinted over and over, even in the early twentieth century, or the era of women's emancipation movements. The heroine, a paragon of all womanly virtues, makes good despite poverty and adverse circumstances on account of her virtuous character, her consistently serene and cheerful disposition, her industrious habits, her Christian principles, and her forgiving nature. To support her family, she takes on a position as a governess with a noble household. At first she gets a cold reception at the castle, but she soon wins everyone's heart. With her loving care she transforms her youngest ward, a gloomy and distrustful girl, into a happy child; she converts some members of the family to churchgoing; she starts projects in the village, visiting the sick, cooking for the poor, and making Christmas presents. Finally she gets her fairy-tale reward: The chatelain makes her his wife. She ends her diary on the following pious note: "I wish to be a very humble housewife, a gentlewoman, like the one who kneels, praying, in the picture on the altar, just as gentle and devoted and pious and faithful. Help me be this, you my dear lord."

Fredrika Bremer's *Diary* (1843) is the only women's diary novel that stands out as more progressive. Albeit within the framework of romantic melodrama, the diarist presents a feminist argument against marriage. As a character, however, Bremer's heroine is no different from the virtuous heroines of lofty ideals, moderate conduct, and unselfish motivations found in other contemporary women's diary fiction. Bremer finds no reward for her heroine other than the traditional one; in the end, despite her earlier pronouncements, the diarist announces her engagement. The justification for this finale is that the man she will marry has high principles and orphan children, for whom she will be a mother.

More interesting than these women's novels are works that similarly use the diary form for its immediacy but extend it into new contexts. Victor Hugo's youthful novel *Le Dernier jour d'un condamné* (1829), for example, the journal of a prisoner condemned to die, was written as a political statement against the death penalty. The journal is designed to show in the most vivid and pathetic colors the sufferings of a man awaiting death. Hugo makes the story as heartrending as possible: We hear of a widowed mother, a wife, and a child the prisoner leaves behind, the horrible jeering of the crowd, and so on, and the style is if anything more melodramatic than that of the *Werther* imitations. The pathos climaxes when the prisoner mounts the steps to the guillotine and, still writing, hallucinates a last-minute reprieve. Similar journals of condemned prisoners, possibly written in imitation of Hugo, are August Lewald's "Aus dem Tagebuch eines Guillotinirten" (1831) and L. Schubar's *Memoiren eines Verurtheilten* (1842).

Other journal fiction, for example Hermann Conradi's "Sein erstes Buch" (1888) and Upton Sinclair's youthful novel *The Journal of Arthur Stirling* (1903), make use of the diary's immediacy to show the sufferings of struggling and unrecognized young artists. *Arthur Stirling,* a partially autobiographical work, is, like Hugo's *Le Dernier jour d'un condamné,* not meant as a psychological study of the protagonist but, rather, uses the intimate journal to present the sufferings of an exemplary character in the face of adverse conditions. The callousness of the publishing world in a capitalist society is largely responsible for the hero's anguish. Stirling, a young poet given to exalted moods, finally commits suicide after a year of waiting, on the brink of starvation, for the acceptance of his blank-verse tragedy. The novel's leitmotif is freedom: Citing Emerson, Carlyle, and Nietzsche, the poet dreams of the freedom to realize one's personal vision, to create without suffering material hardship.

In a few instances the diary form is used to portray typically nineteenth-century character types. For example, part of Lermontov's *Hero of Our Time* (1840) consists of Pečorin's diary. Pečorin, the "hero of our time," is a bored, ruthless, enigmatic character who plays the role of a dynamic force, the embodiment of fate, in the lives of others. As a young officer in the Caucasus, he steals a horse to win a girl, but then loses interest in her and is seemingly indifferent when she is killed for his crime. He wins the heart of a princess and then leaves her; and he purposely kills a rival in a duel. He says of himself, "I have a restless imagination and an insatiable heart. Nothing satisfies me; I get used to suffering as easily as I do to enjoyment, and my life becomes more empty every day."[104] Lermontov, whose purpose is to illuminate the psychology of his Byronic hero, presents Pečorin from various points of view: through the eyes of an old soldier, in action, and finally through his intimate diary. If Pečorin keeps a diary, it is because he has, in his own view, one of those split personalities given to cold reflection as well as action that will reappear over and over in nineteenth-century literature. He writes, "In me there are two men: the one lives, in the fullest sense of the word; the other reasons and criticizes him" (p. 211).

The fictive editor of the diary says, "As I read the diary I felt convinced of the writer's sincerity, so mercilessly has he laid bare his own weaknesses and vices" (p. 93). In fact, the diary is not sincere at all in the sense of being confessional or honestly self-analytical, although Pečorin candidly reveals his thorough badness. Pečorin does not analyze, but rather presents himself; he does not criticize himself, much less repent, but rather recounts the stories in which he played a major role, paying much attention to detail and showing as much interest in what others said and his opinion of them as in himself and his own reactions. Ostensibly, Lermontov is drawing ever closer circles around Pečorin and approaching him the closest in his intimate diary. In fact, there is no great difference between Pečorin as we see him in action, the opinion others have of him, and his own self-assessment. All of them add up to the same thing, but none of them quite reveals the mystery of Pečorin's personality. He remains something of an enigma in his badness and boredom. Lermontov breaks with tradition in writing a diary that does not present a privileged point of view. Pečorin is not self-deluding, but he also has no particular truth claim to insights about himself.

If Pečorin is fascinating and inscrutable, the diarist in Kierkegaard's "Diary of a Seducer," which the Danish philosopher included in *Either/ Or* (1843) as part of the papers of the aestheticist "A," is a deeper, more complicated, more diabolical, and more calculating nature, who plays with others for sheer aesthetic pleasure. The process of seduction – laying his nets, making his calculations, watching the young girl fall into his trap – is a source of extreme pleasure to him. Like an expert game player, he begins by giving himself the worst odds; he chooses a girl he doesn't know, one he sees on the street. In his diary he ponders the best moves. He relishes the prospect of savoring the girl's transparent, naïve emotions as they blossom, and also enjoys reflecting on his own emotions and reactions, as his going home to record them in his diary attests. For he is not only the amoral, ruthless, demonic seducer; he is also the aesthetician, the expert, one who repeats, refines, anticipates, and compares. He enjoys the literary resonance of his adventure: The girl's name (Cordelia) reminds him of *Lear,* and it pleases him to compare himself with a Mephistopheles without a Faust. Befittingly, he has made a pact with himself or, as he says, "with the aesthetic." He writes, "Has the interesting always been preserved? Yes . . ."[105]

Lermontov's and Kierkegaard's diarists are fascinating but repellent. Their empty hearts and their hunger for sensations inspire their amoral actions, while a streak of cold reflectiveness in their characters, combined with self-fascination, motivates them to keep diaries. All glamour and enigma are stripped from the characters of the diarists in Turgenev's "Diary of a Superfluous Man" (1850) and Dostoevskij's *Notes from Underground* (1864)—whose title parodistically echoes Gogol''s "Diary of a Madman". These narrators are dissatisfied, hyperconscious, self-criticizing anti-heroes. They prefigure the discontented diarists of novels of the 1880s and 1890s who keep diaries compulsively, as an expression of their overdeveloped habits of reflection, and take perverse pleasure in inflicting anguish on themselves by writing.

The narrator of "The Diary of a Superfluous Man," the thirty-year-old Čulkaturin, is motivated to write because he thinks he is about to die. He starts telling the story of his life but breaks off, finding his life too ordinary for the telling. Instead, he decides to describe his character, and he immediately pounces on the adjective "superfluous." Superfluity, he announces, is his principal characteristic. To prove his point, he tells of an incident, a three-week fantasy of being in love with the daughter of a functionary in the village where he was once stationed. The girl, Liza, neither reciprocated nor as much as guessed his feelings. Instead, she fell in love with another newcomer in town, a charming prince. Tortured by rage and jealousy, the narrator insulted the prince and dueled him. He thus turned himself into a universal object of scorn and hatred in the village. After the prince abandoned the girl, she married not the diarist but another man as mediocre as himself.

The diarist's motivations for telling this story are left extraordinarily opaque. In deciding to write, he may be reacting to the shock of finding out he is going to die and resisting the doctor's verdict by taking some form of action. He may want to pull himself together, to recollect, to relive certain parts of his past, to draw a balance before dying. Asking himself the same question, why he is writing, when he begins, the diarist answers, "What does it matter?"[106] But why, in the last days before his death, does he decide to revive the memory of the most painful incident of his life? He himself does not understand, in retrospect, why he chose this theme. At the end of his diary he reproaches himself for having wasted his precious time, and then echoes, "What does it matter?" (p. 93).

His writing – his decision to start a diary, his drifting to a painful memory, his self-condemnation, his later regret of his choice of subject, and his final resigned indifference – can be seen to reflect or, better, repeat a pattern of behavior that emerges in his story as well. Čulkaturin suffers from a split between the head and the heart similar to Pečorin's. He is preoccupied with himself and hence hyperconscious of other people's presumed assessment of him; he tends to misjudge situations, and to read nonexistent sympathies or aversion (mainly, snubs) into other people's behavior; he seethes with unexpressed feelings and is maladroit in company; he is given to impulsive actions that he will later regret. In his later analysis of himself, however, he is rational and merciless in pronouncing judgment; in reflection he becomes superior, enlightened, detached.

His writing is an expression of the same conflicting tendencies in his personality. He begins his diary impulsively. As his last entries make clear, in spite of his dismissive attitude toward himself he cares intensely about himself and his life and dreads dying. His writing at once expresses his self-hatred and represents a defense. In condemning himself as a superfluous man he punishes himself; but he also distances himself from himself and asserts his intellectual control and the superiority of his judgment. His rhetoric is often that of one who is writing for an audience. He may be insignificant and mediocre, he seems to be saying, but he is also his own best critic. At the end, he is overwhelmed with regrets. He has once again mismanaged something; he has written the wrong story. He compensates, however, by proceeding to a higher-level insight. He excuses himself with a "what does it matter," with the resigned observation that his actions are of no import anyway.

It is perhaps possible to understand "The Diary of a Superfluous Man" as a work that is meant to recall *Werther,* especially since Turgenev admired Goethe and was well acquainted with his works.[107] Čulkaturin's story is in many respects parallel and in many respects antithetical to Werther's. Čulkaturin is not an unhappy soul in a happy world but a bungler in a predictably cruel world. He loses his woman not to her fiancé but first to a dashing prince and then to a mediocrity like himself. If Werther is the tragic hero at the center of his story, Čulkaturin is on the peripheries, even of the major events of his life; he regards the center in fascination but with each level of reflection draws another invisible circle between himself and it. Werther spontaneously pours out his feelings from day to day; Čulkaturin returns to his memories long after the fact. Werther's suicide is the direct expression of his passion. Čulkaturin, an egotist, is inspired to write by the anticipation of his natural death, which has nothing to do with his disappointed passion. The main indication that the reader is meant to recall the idealistic Romantic hero when reading the diary of the unglamorous, self-doubting nineteenth-century anti-hero comes at the end of the book. Čulkaturin writes, "Farewell Liza!" (p. 95). He thus echoes Werther's last words: "Lotte! Lotte farewell! farewell!" But Čulkaturin adds, "I wrote those two words, and almost laughed aloud. This exclamation strikes me as taken out of a book. It's as though I were writing a sentimental novel and ending up a despairing letter . . ."

If Turgenev is the first author to make a connection between diary keeping and tormenting self-reflection, in *Notes from Underground*, Dostoevskij creates the self-conscious narrator par excellence. The fictive editor presents the Underground Man as the nineteenth-century type, the representative of the current generation. The work is divided into two parts. The first is a diarylike series of notes that begins with a self-description, or rather a self-accusation and self-defense, and then drifts into a polemic against utopias. The second part is a reminiscence, which the narrator calls a "novella," about an encounter with a prostitute named Liza; the narrator tells how he senselessly hurt her feelings and destroyed their relationship.

Dostoevskij's hero certainly has all the faults of Turgenev's hero: He is excessively conscious of others' opinions of him and hence awkward in company; he is given to impulsive actions that he later regrets; his writing expresses the mixed motivations of self-accusation and self-justification. But Dostoevskij's hero takes these problems to an extreme. If Čulkaturin insults and duels a prince because he imagines the prince ignores him at a ball, Dostoevskij's hero does nothing when an officer at a billiard table simply picks him up and moves him out of the way; he broods on revenge for years afterward, and finally hits on the solution of bumping the officer on the Nevskij. If Čulkaturin needs the recognition of others, Dostoevskij's hero needs to feel superior to others. He realizes that he is dependent on and yet cannot stand the real world. He manages to destroy his relations with everyone he comes near. Turgenev's hero regrets never having lived; Dostoevskij's hero realizes that he is incapable of living.

Dostoevskij's hero's personality is explicit rather than submerged. Unlike Turgenev's Čulkaturin, the Underground Man is not a mystery, for he anticipates every interpretation of himself; he compulsively raises the lamp of his consciousness to illuminate the dark corners of his personality, and he is always a step ahead of himself in dissecting and doubting his own motivations. Writing about himself is clearly part of, and testifies to, his "illness." He declares that he wants to try to experiment whether one can be completely frank with oneself, yet he himself

calls attention to the fact that he writes as if for readers. All the poig-
nancy connected with approaching death is removed. We are merely
confronted with the spectacle of a character writhing under his own
lamp. Dostoevskij especially stresses the moment of masochistic enjoyment: The narrator claims to despise himself, yet he recognizes that he
takes pleasure in contemplating his degradation.

The diaries by Lermontov, Kierkegaard, Turgenev, and Dostoevskij
all radically question a direct link between the diary and sincere self-
expression. The reader is not meant to sympathize with these men of
empty hearts and overactive intellects. The character types themselves
belie the concept of sincerity, and the act of writing becomes an ambiguous enterprise, apparently the product of conflicting motivations.
For the demonic, amoral heroes the diary serves primarily as a mirror
of their vanity, and for Čulkaturin and the Underground Man as an
instrument of self-torture. The diarists reflect too much, and leave too
many questions open, for us to believe that they are in possession of the
whole truth about themselves.

In addition to these works there were a few attempts in the nineteenth century to integrate the diary form with realism, to use the form
to give a portrait of a typical character and his milieu. Works that
present the aspirations and difficulties of honest, hardworking people
and give a picture of village life include Heinrich Zschokke's "Das
Neujahrsgeschenk. (Aus den Tagebüchern des armen Pfarr-Vikars von
Wiltshire)" (1819); Steen Steensen Blicher's "The Journal of a Parish
Clerk" (1824); Gustav Nieritz's *Jacob Sturm, oder: Tagebuch eines Dorfschulmeisters* (1847); and Otto Ernst's *Überwunden. Aus den Aufzeichnungen eines Schulmeisters* (1908).

Adalbert Stifter's "Feldblumen" (1840) and Wilhelm Raabe's *Die
Chronik der Sperlingsgasse* (1857) are two works that use the diary form
specifically for its episodic quality, in order to present a sequence of
brief, charming scenes. Both works explicitly draw on the analogy to
the visual arts. "Feldblumen" is one of Stifter's earliest novellas; the
fanciful style and the chapter headings ("Primel," "Veilchen," etc.)
testify to the influence of Jean Paul. The novella's charm lies in its
cheerful outlook on life and in its exquisitely wrought style. The narrator, a painter, has an idealistic, humanitarian nature; his optimistic temperament colors the entire story, which is mainly about his love affair
with the ideal woman, a paragon of beauty, intelligence, and learning.
In addition, he gives a delightful portrait of Viennese life; we are shown
the parks, the countryside, the soirées, the balls, the charming and
witty companions, the beautiful women, the mildly eccentric artists.
The diary form was presumably chosen for its immediacy. The painter,
who is especially generous in recording his appreciations of what he

sees, gives us his impressions while he is still dazzled by them. Stifter himself did landscape painting; particularly in the landscape descriptions, writing seems to imitate painting in the composition and the coloring of the scenes.

Die Chronik der Sperlingsgasse is Raabe's first novel, which he wrote as a student in Berlin. The narrator, an old man, is inspired to write a "book of pictures," a chronicle of the Berlin street (the Sperlingsgasse) where he has lived since his student days. The purpose is to chase away the melancholy fantasies of old age with the bright leaves of his memories. The work is a diary and a memoir in one: The author intersperses the story of his present winter with memories of life and friends that reach fifty years back. One sunny "picture" from the past serves to brighten one day of the present. Time seems almost spatialized into images. The narrator tells of his foster child with her pet canaries and her romances, of excursions in the woods and adventures in the marketplace, of the changing neighbors in the Sperlingsgasse. Yet for all its diversity, the book gives the impression of great continuity, a continuity that has to do with the novel's unified, sentimental world view, which is shared by all the characters and reflected in the old man's appreciative imagination, with the little world of the Sperlingsgasse and its environs, with reappearing friends, and with the old man's own associations and reminiscences.

As diary keeping in its various forms became more and more widespread and fashionable, writers of fiction increasingly used the form with satiric or humorous intent. We have already seen that Addison and other eighteenth-century writers used the form to poke fun at the fictive diarist's mode of life and opinions, and that in the nineteenth century, authors like Thackeray and the Grossmiths wrote similar satiric diary fiction. Diary keeping itself was likewise parodied very early. Writers make fun of the diary as a shapeless, endless form; they note that it serves as a receptacle for gossip; diary keeping is seen to encourage self-indulgence and self-importance. Ludwig Tieck's "Ein Tagebuch" (1798) is an example of an early parody. The diarist, who finds that his life resembles bad fiction, rejoices that his form does not force him to compensate for his creator's lack of skill. He writes, "I'm very pleased that I'm not in the miserable situation of having to write a coherent book," and "Such a style as I'm writing here is permissible only in a diary."[108]

Fictive diaries about travel adventures tend to use the form humorously or satirically. These novels were written starting in the late eighteenth century; the earliest are letter journals, the later one diaries. They draw on three models: travel journals, which were written for publication as early as the sixteenth century and appeared in print more and more frequently in the seventeenth and eighteenth centuries; imaginary voyage literature, which was often written in the form of letters; and Laurence Sterne's *Sentimental Journey* (1768), the single work that had the greatest influence on travel-journal novels. *A Sentimental Journey* was widely imitated in England, received an enthusiastic response in France, and, immediately translated into German as "Eine empfindsame Reise," became a cult book that gave a period of German literary history — *Empfindsamkeit* — its name.[109] Sterne's work itself is neither in epistolary nor in diary form; it consists of short pieces, written from a retrospective point of view, about the narrator Yorick's adventures in France. Several of the works in which its influence is felt, however, notably Moritz August von Thümmel's *Reise in die mittäglichen Provinzen von Frankreich* (1791–1805) and Jean Paul's "Des Luftschiffers Gianozzo Seebuch" (1801) are written as diaries.

Yorick's adventures are all but bodiless: He emphasizes the touching, evanescent moment and the quaint small detail. He writes allusively, rather than presenting a straightforward account, and undercuts his own sentimentality with irony. The travel-journal novels are anecdotal in the tradition of Sterne. The adventures they recount tend to be more substantial than Yorick's, however, and the narrators more heavy-handed; irony often becomes satire. Mainly we hear how travelers fall afoul of bizarre foreign customs. The diarist in Frederick Marryat's *Diary of a Blasé* (1836) is bemused by Belgian humor, while the diarist in Jerome K. Jerome's late work "The Diary of a Pilgrimage" (1891) is baffled by German beds. The naïve young German hero of Achim von Arnim's "Die Verkleidungen des französischen Hofmeisters und seines deutschen Zöglings" (1824) is astonished by the finesse of the French; his compatriot in Franz Freiherr von Gaudy's *Aus dem Tagebuch eines wandernden Schneidergesellen* (1836) is horrified by the deceitfulness of the Italians; and as we find out from George Sand's diary novel *La Daniella* (1857), a travel journal with a love intrigue, French travelers fare no better with their Italian neighbors.

The travel-journal novels tend to draw heavily on the authors' own travel experiences. Some are barely fictionalized accounts that focus on the places visited and the people encountered rather than on the fictitious voyager himself. The journal form in such works is little more than a convenient frame to hold together anecdotes. Sometimes the journal fiction fades into a mere device to link independent stories; an extreme but not unusual case is E. T. A. Hoffman's *Fantasiestücke in Callot's Manier. Blätter aus dem Tagebuche eines reisenden Enthusiasten* (1814–15), where the formula "leaves from the journal" simply means a collection of tales. The "traveler" in such works is a shadow figure who plays no role at all in the stories.

At their best these travel-journal novels are masterpieces of the pica-resque. Moritz August von Thümmel's seven-volume rococo novel *Reise in die mittäglichen Provinzen von Frankreich* is an outstanding ex-ample. The work, which Thümmel based on his own travels in France in 1772 and 1774–7, presents a potpourri of anecdotes, descriptions and appreciations of sights, and even "pink pages," written in an ornate style and interspersed with poems and songs. The witty, ironic, and worldly narrator, Wilhelm, writes with a light touch and excels in contrasting high expectations with disappointing reality. The main ob-ject of his satire is the church with its dark superstitions, ignorant priests, and corruption. Yet the rationalist does not lack his own brand of frivolity; we hear of convivial banquets, idyllic sojourns in small villages in the French countryside, and flirtations with beautiful but devious young girls.

In these travel-journal novels, the form itself often gets swept into the general atmosphere of satire. The narrator in Anna B. Jameson's *Diary of an Ennuyée* (1826), for example, begins:

> What young lady, travelling for the first time on the continent, does not write a "Diary?" No sooner have we stept on the shores of France – . . . forth steps from its case the morocco bound diary, . . . wherein we are to record and preserve all the striking, profound, and original observations – the classical reminiscences – threadbare rap-tures – the poetical effusions – . . . which must necessarily suggest themselves while posting from Paris to Naples. Verbiage, emptiness, and affectation![110]

Thümmel already parodies the "fictive document" convention of the eighteenth-century novel. The journal in the *Reise* is not merely a "me-dium" but becomes a kind of picaresque hero in its own right: Wilhelm nearly forgets it in a bust of Rousseau, its hiding place in superstitious, Catholic Avignon; he considers selling it to make some more money for his trip; he allegedly destroys it in his fever; it is confiscated by the French police, who in their simplicity think one of his odes is a laundry list; he chops pages with politically compromising secrets into small triangles but saves them in his powder bag. Thümmel also satirizes the confessional tradition he pretends to write in with a *mise en abîme,* a pope's diary with a description of an orgy, and after a friend tells the diarist his work is immoral, he decides to take his cue from Rousseau and withhold it for twenty years before publication.

Fictive diaries also appear, humoristically, in mystery stories. In Wilkie Collins's *Moonstone* (1868), for example, a work composed of fictive documents written by witnesses to events surrounding the moonstone's disappearance, Collins satirizes both the form and the diarist with the diary of the pious busybody Miss Clack. As a child, Miss Clack learned to fold her clothes, write in her "little diary," and say her prayers before she went to bed. She observes, "I have continued to fold my clothes, and to keep my little diary." Of her present diary, she says, "Everything was entered (thanks to my early training) day by day as it happened; and everything, down to the smallest particular, shall be told here. My sacred regard for truth is (thank God) far above my respect for persons."[111]

The first-person account is a useful device in narratives where the author wants to withhold information and thereby prolong suspense. The reader is given a partial view of the situation, yet is left as mystified as the character himself about the true solution. Bram Stoker's *Dracula* (1897) is a celebrated example of a work that uses multiple diaries to unfold the story. Journals kept by Count Dracula's victims and others reveal the vampire's devious plan to purchase an English estate, his sinister voyage from Transylvania and melodramatic arrival on English soil, his nightly visits to Lucy Westenraa's room, and finally his attacks on Mina Harker, his flight back to Transylvania, and the successful campaign to annihilate him by driving a stake into his heart. The diary technique serves at once to heighten the claustrophobic atmosphere of mystery and impending horror and to enhance the humorous effects. Stoker does not miss the opportunity to poke fun at the convention of the "authentic document." At the end of the novel, Jonathan Harker takes the records out of the safe seven years after Dracula's death and muses, "In all the mass of material of which the record is composed, there is hardly one authentic document; nothing but a mass of typewriting, except the later note-books of Mina and Seward and myself, and Van Helsing's memorandum. We could hardly ask any one, even did we wish to, to accept these as proofs of so wild a story."[112]

PART III

The Diary Novel in the Late Nineteenth and Early Twentieth Centuries

The Publication of the *Journaux Intimes* and the Fin-de-siècle Diary Novel

The diary novel did not begin to come back into vogue until the period one critic calls that of the "crisis of the novel,"[1] the period that began with the attacks on Naturalism in France in the early 1880s. The form gained a new foothold, in other words, precisely in the period from approximately 1885 to World War I when the non-epic genres, the theater and especially poetry, dominated and when of the epic genres the short story was preferred to the novel. The revival of the diary form in fiction started in France first and then spread to other European countries. There are various presumable reasons for the renewal of interest in the diary novel, one of the most important of which is that intimate journals, which had become a significant confessional genre particularly in nineteenth-century France and were also written contemporaneously throughout continental Europe, began to be published in considerable numbers starting in the 1880s.

Diaries had been published all over Europe long before the last decades of the nineteenth century; in England, for instance, to name two important examples, John Evelyn's diary was published in 1818 and Samuel Pepys's was deciphered and published in 1825. In the course of the nineteenth century, more and more diaries written in past centuries were unearthed and published, often by historical societies, for what was felt to be their historical interest, while extracts of more closely contemporary diaries were printed as sources of biographical information or for the sake of the memorabilia or thoughts they contained. In the 1880s and 1890s in France, however, a wave of publications of the personal, private diaries of near contemporaries, of recently deceased figures of the immediate past, was initiated. These works naturally aroused great interest. The major works were Henri-Frédéric Amiel's *Fragments d'un journal intime* (1882–84), Jules Michelet's *Mon journal* (1888), Eugène Delacroix's *Journal* (1893), and Benjamin Constant's *Journal intime de B. Constant et lettres à sa famille et à ses amis* (1895). It is noteworthy that these intimate journals were published *as diaries* rather than as extracts, thoughts, testimonials, or sources of historical or biographical information. Something like a consciousness of a diary as a genre had come into being. With these publications, the intimate diary became an established public fact. In 1898 a first article appeared that considered the diary as a literary genre, Richard M. Meyer's "Zur Entwicklungsgeschichte des Tagebuchs."[2]

What made the intimate diaries particularly interesting was that they afforded a uniquely privileged insight into the personal lives of other individuals. They contained extensive day-to-day records of the lives, thoughts, and feelings of persons who thought they were writing for themselves only or at most for the eyes of an intimate friend and therefore – it could be presumed – expressed themselves with complete sincerity. The nineteenth-century "intimists," as their historian Alain Girard calls them, did not write their diaries with an eye to their eventual publication.[3] If it crossed their minds that others might publish their journals after their death, as it apparently did Amiel's, the potential literary value of the journal was nevertheless not uppermost in their minds during the act of composition. It was not until after these early intimate diaries were published that writers started to regard the intimate diary as a publishable literary genre and, like Gide, to write "sincerely" for the public.[4]

One cannot go so far as to say that the diary novels written from the 1880s on conformed to a single type, reducible to a pattern of imitation of the *journaux intimes*. The statistical increase in their production can probably be attributed to influence only in the widest sense, that is, the publication of the *journaux intimes* brought about an awareness of the diary as a usable form for fiction. Nevertheless, what I find to be the central and avant-garde use of the diary form in fiction around the turn of the century is related to the *journal intime* as a specific type of the diary, in the sense that the interest in the *journaux intimes* and the production of diary novels were both manifestations of the same contemporary trend: an interest in psychology that began with the publication of Taine's *De l'Intelligence* and Ribot's *La Psychologie anglaise contemporaine* in 1870 and increased as the discoveries of experimental psychology and pathology in the 1880s and 1890s became known.[5] The intimate journals, which their authors regarded as the place for describing, investigating, and expressing their selves, are documents of considerable psychological interest. Alain Girard finds that self-centeredness is what all the *journaux intimes* have in common. If the diarist writes about other people, he concentrates on their relationship to himself. The journals contain relatively few descriptions, anecdotes, or portraits. The diarists are often, though not necessarily, introspective in the sense of being self-analytical; but they are all introverted. They have a sense of possessing an interior world, rich in possibilities and worthy of exploration. Girard writes that "interiority dominates in them."[6]

By far the most influential intimate journal was that of the Genevan scholar Henri-Frédéric Amiel. The "great wave" of journal publication, as Girard shows, began with the publication of Amiel's diary in 1882–4; it was Amiel's journal that was most responsible for increasing public consciousness of the intimate diary as a genre and that had the greatest effect on the use of the diary form in fiction.[7] Amiel's mammoth record, regularly kept for forty-three years and 16,900 pages long, is the intimate journal *par excellence* and the acme of the tendencies toward introversion, introspection, and the expression of *mal du siècle* that are to a greater or lesser extent present in all the nineteenth-century intimate diaries.

In the extremely selective version of the diary that Amiel's friend Edmond Schérer published in 1882–4 and that, revised slightly in 1887, went into fourteen French editions before World War I, a number of motifs recur that, when assembled, present an exceptionally vivid and unambiguous portrait of the character type the author embodies. Repeatedly, Amiel regretfully notes his propensity to reflect, to analyze and dissect the objects of his consciousness. He thinks the habit of mind – to which his motivation to keep a journal from adolescence until death can surely be attributed – is destructive: It reduces his capacity for spontaneous action and feeling, impairs his self-confidence, makes him timid and hesitant, vitiates his will, and prevents him from leading a normal, active life. "Whence comes this timidity? From the excessive development of reflection, which has practically reduced to nothing spontaneity, élan, instinct, and by the same token audacity and confidence" (July 27, 1855). He also describes this negative habit of mind as "doubt": his unhappiness "comes from doubting thought, oneself, men, and life; from a doubt that enervates the will and deprives one of power, that makes one forget God, that makes one neglect prayer, duty; from the restless and corrosive doubt that makes existence impossible and sneers at all hope" (July 14, 1859). In particular he blames his compulsion to reflect and his inclination to doubt for paralyzing his ability to act. After questioning out of existence any instinctive sense he may have had of what is right, he finally decides that it is better not to act at all: "When I have to act, I see only causes for error and repentance everywhere, hidden menaces and masked grief" (July 27, 1855). His passivity, his "growing incapacity for practical action" (June 17, 1857) is one of his most consistent worries, for which he repeatedly tries to find philosophical justifications. He in fact dislikes practical life: "Practical life makes me recoil" (April 6, 1851). He shrinks from reality generally because it is too overdetermined and too definite: "Reality, the present, the irremediable, and necessity repulse or even frighten me" (April 6, 1851). Reality leaves him bored and apathetic: "I oscillate between apathy and boredom" (April 26, 1852). He prefers to operate with possibilities, to play off what is against what might be. Turning away from everyday life, he is filled with "longing for what is unknown and far away" (April 26, 1852). Consequently dissatisfaction is, for him, an inescapable state of being: "The promised land is where one is not" (February 10, 1853); "For me, what might be spoils what exists" (April 6, 1851). The opposite side of this coin is that, having rejected reality in favor of imaginative possibility and relinquished action in favor of reflection, he worries that he has abjured life entirely. "Tomorrow you will disappear, ephemeral being, without having lived" (July 22, 1870), he accuses himself, and he complains, "What has interposed itself between you and real life? What sheet of glass, so to speak, has deprived you of joy, possession, and contact with objects, leaving you only with a glance?" (August 18, 1873). "The glance" is all that is left to this spectator rather than participant in life: "My privilege is to be an onlooker in the drama of my life" (November 8, 1852). As a consequence of his problems, Amiel considers himself an unusual and paradoxical person: "What a singular nature, and what a bizarre propensity! . . . Contradiction and mystery!" (July 21, 1856).

The 1882–4 edition of the journal reveals other sides of Amiel that do not merely reinforce the syndrome of overconsciousness, doubt, passivity, and disgust; but it was precisely these negative and problematical aspects of the diarist that the contemporary audience found significant and appealing. Amiel was felt to be the modern type and to incorporate the modern malaise. His character has a considerable coincidental similarity to that of the hyperconscious anti-hero of Dostoevskij's *Notes from Underground* (1864). Paul Bourget, who wrote an article on Amiel for his *Essais de psychologie contemporaine* in 1884, pronounced:

> He will remain famous as he has become famous, first because of the inexorable sincerity of his confession, and also because he presents us with a perfect example of a certain type of the modern spirit. This superior, paralyzed man, capable of the most daring speculation and unskilled at the least daily task, at once exalted and uncertain, frenetic and cowardly, this Protestant Hamlet, sick with hesitation and tragic scruples like the other, represents one of the innumerable cases of the conflict between intelligence and volition. He embodies with a surprising intensity this sickness of the age, which seemed cured around 1840 and is reappearing today in different forms.[8]

12

Overreflectedness

Amiel's journal had a direct influence on the young André Gide, who started keeping his journal in 1886, several months after his teacher gave him Amiel's diary to read. Gide's first novel, *Les Cahiers d'André Walter* (1891), which he wrote in the form of a diary, contains leaves from this early journal.[9] The discovery of his Swiss compatriot Amiel's journal also almost certainly caused the young Edouard Rod to change the form of his first novel of consequence, *La Course à la mort* (1885), from a third-person narrative to a diary.[10] *La Course à la mort* is worth examining in some detail, because it is one of the earliest examples of diary novels that reflect traits of Amiel's journal and because it incorporates these traits in an exceptionally compact and exemplary way.

La Course à la mort is undoubtedly one of the gloomiest novels ever written. The nameless hero is an Amiel deprived of his idealism, moral sense, and intellectual curiosity and dyed to the darkest hue of Schopenhauerian pessimism. Like Amiel, he finds that he is crippled by an overactive consciousness. He compulsively doubts and questions everything; he is bored and disgusted with life and with himself; he is inactive and convinced that in the face of universal uncertainty, all action is useless; and he is haunted by the fear that he will never participate in real life or have any genuine experiences. He observes that nothing ever happened to him, or if it did, he never noticed it. "The events immediately changed into sensations, which an immediate and unconscious analysis hastened to decompose,"[11] he writes. Indeed, during the twenty-two months during which he writes the journal, almost nothing does happen to him. The novel has no plot and little action. It is a portrait of the hero composed exclusively of his self-analyses and his pessimistic judgments on life. In 1890 Rod, by then a professor of comparative literature at the University of Geneva, explained that he came to write *La Course à la mort* as a reaction against Naturalism. He had originally been a disciple of Zola's, but around 1880 he began to feel "disgust at descriptions, at their minuteness, at their uselessness" and to consider writing a novel that concerned itself solely with the inner life of a character:

> I thought . . . of replacing [descriptions] by the study of a person's intimate self, and, through an excessive and very natural reaction, I began to dream of a novel liberated from what I called "contingent circumstances," an exclusively interior novel that took place within the heart. It was then that I wrote *La Course à la mort,* the book that cost me the most effort to write and the one I shall always remain most attached to.[12]

In particular the hero of *La Course à la mort* longs for love, for a grand passion with its joys and sufferings. But he cannot bring himself to describe as such his ambiguous feelings for the only available candidate for his affections, a certain Cécile N. What he wants from love is to be able to forget himself, to shut off his consciousness and feel "my heart beat with great irregular blows."[13] But he watches all his emotions too closely. He is simply incapable of feeling:

> I am tired of a life that nothing nourishes, I am exhausted like torrents in summer, I am thirsted like dry grass. My nerves tense in a desire that touches on the unknown; my panting thought darkens in an anguished hope, the image it invokes crosses it like a lightning flash, grows, imposes itself on it, and is quite close to me, holds me in the drunkenness of its gaze: it is almost forgetfulness, almost love. . . . And everything passes! [pp. 107–8]

After Cécile N. dies, he realizes that he adores her: "Above all, I love her, I love her as never before!" (p. 276). Otherwise, he notes with chagrin that the most real emotions he has are in dreams or caused by works of art. Life itself fills him only with the sensation of dull repetition. He dreams of escaping Paris, which he loathes, and traveling to the South Seas, but when he does take a trip to the Rhineland, where he remembers having spent happy days as a student, he decides that he carries his misery around with him and cannot revert to the naïveté of youth that made him find Germany beautiful. "I am even disgusted at what I do not know, or rather, I have the too lively feeling that disgust is at the heart and the root of everything" (p. 135), he writes. A rotten core lies at the center of everything. When he returns to historical and philosophical studies, he finds throughout world literature only evidence to support his pessimism. He reasons that progress is a fallacy, for man's capacity for suffering grows with his intellect and his sensibility. He concludes, "Humanity is moving toward definitive, triumphant, universal, absolute misery" (p. 162). In particular, he is convinced of the decadence of European culture, which he describes as a too complicated edifice that is crumbling irreparably and destined to topple. He dismisses socialism as a chimera because human nature can never be satisfied.

Another important diary novel of the period that is thematically similar to Amiel's journal is the Norwegian Arne Garborg's *Trætte mænd* (1891), a work that Garborg, who normally wrote in Landsmål, composed in Dano-Norwegian to show what type of person his overselfconscious, bored, vacillating fin-de-siècle hero is. The work resembles Rod's novel and is even more strikingly similar in its themes to *Notes from Underground*.[14] *Trætte mænd,* in fact, captures the tone of a real, unabridged intimate diary more closely than *La Course à la mort,* for the diarist, Gabriel Gram, about whose public life the reader learns next to nothing, writes genuinely as if for himself; he omits connections, repeats himself over and over again, obsessively returns to his main preoccupations, and notes all his headaches, bouts of insomnia, and symptoms, which he thinks indicate incipient delirium tremens. Few concessions are made to orient the reader in this murky four-year record of the intimate secrets of a tortured consciousness, for which the diarist, convinced that the Oslo society in which he lives consists of impenetrable façades and that communication with his neighbors is impossible, feels he has no other outlet.

If Gram has the undislodgeable feeling that all sorts of filth and secret vices bubble beneath the surface of society and that every kind of monster lurks under men's masks, these observations certainly apply to the pessimistic and suspicious diarist himself. A more complex personality than the one-sidedly pessimistic hero of *La Course à la mort,* Gram suffers from what might be called, before Freud named these psychic agencies, a clash between the superego and the id. An idealist of puritanical moral standards, he yearns for "higher things," for ethereal love and friendship. Sex, especially female sexuality, disgusts him, as he insists rather too often. He is attracted to the philosophy of self-denial, Buddhism. At the end of the novel he flees the "sewer" of the world by embracing Catholicism and thus follows the example of Joris-Karl Huysmans's decadent hero Des Esseintes in *A rebours* (1884), who ultimately hopes for deliverance through religious belief. Yet Gram is fascinated by the tabooed topics of sexuality and irrational forces; he longs to unleash elemental passions. He has both sadistic and masochistic torture fantasies and periodically entertains thoughts of killing himself. He speculates on hypnotism, magnetism, and spiritism, and even tries to become a medium. Gram's vacillation is less the logical outcome of his nihilistic convictions than of his psychological conflicts. His rambling diary both feeds on and sustains his inner struggle. Like Dostoevskij's Underground Man, he is fascinated by his contradictions and takes pleasure in his malaise, while anything that suggests the straight line of progress, like utopian socialism or women's emancipation, is anathema to him. He prefers the painful titillation of spiraling from self-indulgence to self-observation and self-disgust.

La Course à la mort and *Trætte mænd* are not only thematically similar to Amiel's journal, but also similar to it in style. Amiel, Rod, and Garborg write in the present tense a great deal, and they all use the present tense in a manner that could be described as "absolute" or "gnomic." That is, their narrators express themselves in statements that represent their cognitive conclusions about themselves and the world. These statements border on aphorism and lay a corresponding claim to absolute validity. The style mirrors the diarists' reflective mental habits. It makes these novels quite different from the Wertherian diary novels. Whereas the Wertherian diarists tend to write expressively, seeking to convey in words the intensity of their emotions, the fin-de-siècle heroes tend to speak of themselves in absolute pronouncements from which they are emotionally detached. Theirs is the style of the analytical, distancing consciousness; indeed, expressions of feeling would be out of place, for these diarists are, as they complain, incapable of feeling.

There are many similarities between the fin-de-siècle diary novels and the Wertherian diary novels. In both, the character of the problematical diarist is central; in both, there is only a minimal plot; and both tend to use the diary for the purpose of present-tense thought transcription. But there are also essential differences. The heroes of both types are miserable, but in the fin-de-siècle diary novel the characteristic reason for the misery is self-consciousness. Consequently it is the protagonist's character itself rather than circumstances that blocks the possibility of his happiness. "My own heart is my only enemy,"[15] Rod's hero says. One symptom of the difference is that whereas the Wertherian hero loves a woman he cannot have, the fin-de-siècle diarist decides not to approach a woman he could have because he cannot make up his mind that he loves her. Rod's hero manages only a peculiar love-hate relationship to Cécile N.; likewise the protagonist of *Trætte mænd,* who thinks about love incessantly and wishes he could be swept off his feet, fails to muster an unambiguous passion for the woman he is attracted to. He complains, "Nothing à la Romeo. Nothing à la Werther. It is a painful, sick, divided love, a moment of dissolution in my life; senses and soul are captured and bound, yet my consciousness is cold, clear, and mocking."[16] The fin-de-siècle diarist typically longs for life, for sensations that will penetrate the protective plate of his consciousness and relieve his ennui, and not for the peaceful simplicity of the domestic idyll the Wertherian hero dreams of. In Edouard Rod's second diary novel *Le Sens de la vie* (1889), a companion piece to *La Course à la mort* whose initially bored, skeptical, self-analytic hero is cured of his *mal du siècle* and gradually turns into a well-adjusted person, the diarist's breakthrough is symbolized by his acceptance of a simple domestic existence with a wife and child.

The experience the fin-de-siècle hero typically desires most is love. The hero of Hugues Le Roux's diary novel *Gladys* (1894) goes about inducing a grand passion in himself in an artificial, almost scientific way; the woman he seduces is the incidental means, not the end. The diarist of Paul Bourget's part-diary novel *Le Fantôme* (1901) is another "of these souls avid for sensation" who is possessed by "this passion for passion, this love of love."[17] The desire for sensation is also expressed in a longing to travel to far-flung, exotic places. While the Wertherian hero, the metaphysical wanderer, looked for a quiet haven, the fin-de-siècle hero dreams of excitement and adventure. The hero of the Swedish writer Hjalmar Söderberg's diary novel *Doctor Glas* (1905), for instance, using travel as a metaphor, writes that he wants to jump "aboard the first ship to come sailing by laden with action."[18] The decadent diarist in Jean Lorrain's *Monsieur de Phocas* (1901), the duc de Fréneuse, whom nothing bores more than his parental estate, is tempted by the sumptuous beauty of Venice, the Moorish dancers of Constantinople, and the holy golden city of Benares. But although this wealthy young nobleman has the financial means and the leisure to satisfy his every desire, he has to admit that it is in vain to "collect emotions":

> Avid for sensations and analyses, I informed myself through them as though they were anatomical sections, and none gave me the expected vibration, precisely because, lying in ambush in my nervousness as in a swamp, I spied out this vibration, and because there is no knowing voluptuousness, but rather an unconscious and healthy joy, and because I willfully spoiled my life by poking at it with instruments instead of living it.[19]

In both of these works the diarists' desire for sensation drives them to extraordinary lengths. Söderberg's Doctor Glas finally poisons a patient he detests in order to liberate the man's young wife. The duc de Fréneuse becomes enraptured with the gaze of moribund eyes, which he pursues in opium soirées, houses of child prostitution, and sinister Oriental cults. Finally he too commits murder, forcing the diabolical artist friend who goaded him on to depravity to swallow the contents of his poisoned emerald ring.

Love affairs, travel, and adventures are merely external stimuli, and some diarists reason that if the cause of their misery is consciousness, then the solution must lie within themselves as well, specifically in the area of the self that consciousness represses, the unconscious. For the diarist in Hermann Hesse's short prose piece "Tagebuch 1900" (1901), the unconscious is the "soul," a sort of mysterious reservoir where the truest part of the self lies hidden. He writes: "O this soul, this lovely, dark, homelike, dangerous sea! While I tirelessly scan, caress, question, and storm its shimmering surface, it again and again occasionally washes up before me, from bottomless depths, some strangely colored mystery, as if to mock me."[20] The unconscious cannot be tapped at will, but it is turbulent and dangerous when its passions are accidentally unleashed. Max Brod uses similar categories in his diary novel *Ausflüge ins Dunkelrote* (1909). The diarist, who is initially a hopelessly "violet" (unimpassioned, fashionably witty) individual, finally takes a plunge into the "dark red" zone of elemental passion.

The decadent diarists inspired parodies. For example, Otto Julius Bierbaum satirizes the color code, which is traceable to Max Dauthendey's volume of experimental poetry *Ultra Violett* of 1893, in the story "Emil der Verstiegene," written in the same year. Nothing that exists on earth is refined enough for the diarist Emil, a sensitive young plant who speaks in enraptured tones of the glory of pure vowels and finally kills his poetic career by marrying a fat girl and becoming happy. A similar prosaic note ends Frank Wedekind's parody "Ich langweile mich" (1906); the bored diarist's cat gives birth to kittens in a drawer containing his "symbolic manuscripts." André Gide's *Paludes* (1895) is usually considered a satire on Symbolist and decadent circles. Gide presents the diary of a poet who is writing, at a snail-like pace, the diary of a celibate living in a tower surrounded by a swamp, also called *Paludes*. The poet's work is intended to symbolize the horrors of life's daily repetitions; Gide's work illustrates them. Franziska, Gräfin zu Reventlow's *Herrn Dames Aufzeichnungen* (1913) is a more extensive satire of the decadent life-style. This roman à clef focuses on the Stefan George circle in Munich. The diarist, Dame, whose name indicates fashionable psychological conflict trivially and succinctly, plays the observer; he records his mystification at violet ties, spiritism, the cult of ancient Greece, Rome, heathenism, and Germanism that erupts into wild orgies at *Fasching,* and at the cult words "Substanz," "Erlebnis," and "Geste."

In the Wertherian diary novels, the fiction of the diary signaled sincerity. It continues to do so in the late-nineteenth- and early-twentieth-century diary novels, but a second significance overshadows the implication that the diarist will be sincere, namely the idea of a destructive self-consciousness tearing at itself from day to day. Given the conception that reflection is a pernicious act, diary writing takes on pejorative connotations. A self-conscious person exacerbates his misery by committing his reflections to paper, and by keeping a diary he turns self-observance into a ritual. The hero of *La Course à la mort* announces his intention to keep a diary almost with a sense of shame, as though he were touching forbidden fruit: "I at first resisted the temptation to take notes on this intimate drama: my impressions become feebler when I write them down."[21] A person who keeps a journal could not be farther removed from the felicity of naïve self-abandonment. The view that daily writing is a dubious habit is quite the opposite of the Puritan conception of diary keeping as a healthy, commendable, order-producing activity. In *Robinson Crusoe,* the commencement of a journal is an indication that Crusoe is on the road to spiritual betterment; but in a scheme of things in which diary keeping is considered a malady, it is the cessation of writing that is a positive sign. The self-questioning millionaire of Valéry Larbaud's *A. O. Barnabooth* (1913) and the melancholy moralist of Rudolf Huch's *Max Gebhard* (1907), for instance, both give up their diaries when they decide to marry their housekeepers and settle down; and when the diarist of *La Course à la mort* finally musters up enough energy to retire to an idyllic spot in the Siebengebirge and gradually begins to forget himself and take joy in the things around him, he begins to write less and less and to forget to date his entries. Whereas in *Die Leiden des jungen Werthers* the lapses in Werther's correspondence toward the end of the novel presage the impending calamity, in *La Course à la mort* the diarist's increasing neglect of his journal signals the opposite, that his malaise is finally on the way to being cured.

13

Psychological Fiction and Pathological States

The new uses novelists found for the fiction of the diary from the 1880s on can be seen in the context of one of the dominant preoccupations of the fin-de-siècle, psychology. A reawakened sense of the importance and centrality of the self left its imprint on all the literary movements of the period in one way or another, from Symbolism to the new directions in the novel. Schopenhauer's ideas were enthusiastically received, especially after Théodule Ribot published his *La Philosophie de Schopenhauer* in 1874,[22] and they reinforced beliefs about the nature of reality and the role of the self with which readers of Taine's *De l'Intelligence* were already acquainted: that the world we know by experience is not the real world, that all we can know is what is in our own minds, and that we in fact create reality as we perceive it. At the same time that the self was declared to be the world, the ontology of the self as a stable entity was questioned. In *De l'Intelligence,* Taine maintained that the self consists of a succession of states of consciousness and is thus temporally discontinuous. Jean-Martin Charcot and then Pierre Janet supervised research on hysteria at the Salpêtrière that led to the exploration of the idea of the unconscious. The split personality was discovered; Ribot and other psychologists concluded that the self is multiple.[23] For the novel, one consequence of the new understanding of the self was that the doctrines of Naturalism fell into discredit. It was not surprising that especially the younger generation of novelists started to feel the "disgust at descriptions" Rod speaks of and to consider an emphasis on hereditary and environmental determinism misplaced, while the mental world of the individual appeared a far worthier subject of investigation. Michel Raimond shows in *La Crise du roman* that after 1885 point of view in the novel became an issue; most writers came out strongly in favor of point of view and against panoramic descriptions presented by an omniscient narrator.

First-person narration is naturally a useful tool for depicting the reality of an individual mind. Not all writers objected, as Henry James did, to "the terrible *fluidity* of self-revelation."[24] The diary form offered the additional advantage of an intermittent time structure. As an accretion of small, separate segments, the journal is an ideal form for projecting the impression of a discontinuous, self-contradictory, fragmented consciousness. Rod for one was certainly aware of these possibilities of the form. The diarist of *Le Sens de la vie,* who in fact undergoes a profound (and foreseeable) change in the course of writing, complains that he has lost all contact with his past selves and in the future will have no way of regaining access to his self of the present moment:

> I lost that self on the way, that self whose appearance I have nearly preserved and of whose blood not a globule remains in my blood, who almost had my face and who is dead, just as the self that succeeded it will soon die in its turn, until the heterogeneous collection of these successive and confused beings who form my personality finally disappears. . . . I feel myself flowing like the water of a river, like the sand of a clepsydra; I know that I will no more recognize myself in tomorrow than I recognized my self of today in the night before.[25]

Rainer Maria Rilke's *Die Aufzeichnungen des Malte Laurids Brigge* (1910) is perhaps the most successful example of a novel in which the fiction of unchronological "notes" reinforces the theme of the precarious ontology of the self, which is both the prey of foreign forces and susceptible to convulsions from within.

The periodic structure of the diary also makes the form useful for depicting, with a maximum of immediacy, the change in a protagonist's views or psychic condition over the course of time. A favorite use is to show the development of a pathological state. Guy de Maupassant uses the diary form in two short stories, "Un Fou" (1885) and the final version of "Le Horla" (1886), to this end. "Un Fou" is the diary of an eminent and respected judge, found after his death, in which he records how he is seized with a desire to kill and to see blood flow. He slaughters a bird, a child, and a man with impunity because of his high position, and gloatingly sends a man to death for the last crime. The fiction of the diary is appropriate, since the judge has no other option for keeping a record of his illegal deeds. Like Nikolaj Gogol' in "The Diary of a Madman" (1835), Maupassant explicitly labels the journal as that of a lunatic; the reader knows what to expect, and the sympathetic attitude with which we might otherwise approach the diary is automatically canceled. This is not the case in the far more interesting and complex "Le Horla." The diary shows how an initially sane man becomes a pathological case, but the reader is not told that this is so; the diarist is so firmly in the grip of his delusions that he sounds deceptively reasonable, and the reader, given no outside point of view, has to decide for himself whether the diarist is going insane and subject to paranoid hallucinations or whether, as he himself claims, he is gradually falling prey to an invisible Brazilian vampire. In either case the "Horla" makes the narrator feel depressed, drinks his milk and water at night, tries to suffocate him in his sleep, and finally begins to control his will and his thoughts so he is powerless to run away. Hoping to kill the Horla, the narrator finally burns down his own house. Maupassant originally wrote "Le Horla" as a first-person retrospective oral description enclosed in a third-person frame; the immediacy and horror are greatly increased in the final day-to-day version.

Around the turn of the century a good deal of diary fiction appeared that, like Maupassant's two stories, involves diarists who are madmen or criminals, or both. There are a few nineteenth-century prototypes; the best known is Gogol's "Diary of a Madman." Around the turn of the century mental illness became fashionable, however, so that the fictive diaries of pathologically disturbed characters came to represent a significant proportion of diary fiction generally. This fiction falls roughly into two types, each of which is represented by one of Maupassant's two tales. First, there are case studies, like "Un Fou"; and second, there are diaries with unreliable narrators, like "Le Horla."

The case studies predominate. In these stories the interest is genuinely psychological. As in "Un Fou" and "The Diary of a Madman," the purpose is to show, by presenting the intimate journal of a murderer or a clearly labeled madman, the development of a pathological state "from the inside." Thus the diarist in Bourget's *Le Fantôme* chronicles the progress of an obsession and its dire results: The diarist, who cannot free himself from the memory of the ecstasy he enjoyed with a mistress now long dead, meets the woman's look-alike daughter and in a trance-like compulsive action proposes to the unwitting girl and marries her. Bourget, who always stayed *au courant* of the latest psychological theories, dwells on the phenomenon of déjà-vu, which had recently been the subject of considerable research.[26] Madness likewise plays a part in the second notebook of Gide's *Les Cahiers d'André Walter*. Walter, who is writing a novel about a hero who goes mad, goes mad himself, to the accompaniment of insomnia, nightmares, waking visions, and presentiments of catastrophe. Paul Adam's short story "L'Inéluctable" (1897) is the diary of a murderer who kills compulsively, against his own resolution to the contrary. Lorrain's *Monsieur de Phocas* is the story of an obsession that leads to a murder; hallucinations abound, and the narrator, who definitely has sadistic, indeed vampiristic, tendencies, speculates that he might have a split personality. In this work, however, the day-to-day structure of the diary is not used to show the progression of a pathological mental state or in fact character development at all; Fréneuse's character remains fairly static. Instead, Lorrain uses the form to create a prismatic sequence of separately titled sketches, some of which with their heavy embroidery of imagery resemble prose poems.

The Prague writer Paul Adler's *Nämlich* (1915) is, in contrast, the diary of a madman with a clinically plausible disorder. It is remarkable in that three-quarters of its ninety-five pages are devoted to incoherent and largely impenetrable lunatic ravings. The first expository pages of the diary, which the diarist, a violinist at the local opera, writes while still in possession of his faculties, and the final episode, where Adler reveals that the hero has been committed to an asylum, serve as points of orientation. In the middle, after the diarist deteriorates from a drinking habit to hearing bells to believing his mother and faithless wife are plotting against him, he stumbles from one murky hallucination to the next. His imaginings crystallize into the typical patterns found in case studies: He supposes that he is in direct communication with Christ (or God), believes that he himself is Christ or the Father, and records conversations with biblical and historical figures. Heinrich Schaefer's *Gefangenschaft* (1918), a full-length book and an Expressionist period piece, and Arnold Ulitz's "Der geträumte Thron. Aus den Aufzeichnungen eines Kronprätendenten" (1916), the diary of a man who believes he has been chosen as the future king of Poland, are similarly unambiguous madmen's diaries.

Other authors present the fictitious diary of a mentally disturbed or criminal character less for the sake of clinical realism or sensationalism than to illustrate some particular psycho-political or theoretical issue. The best of these works is Hjalmar Söderberg's *Doctor Glas,* which caused a scandal when it was published in 1905 because it seemed to sympathize with murder for ethical reasons. The work is a psychological novel, even though the diarist, a Stockholm doctor who murders a patient's husband, seems to have his psychic life so firmly in his grip that the analyst-reader finds little that calls for additional clarification. Superficially, Dr. Glas is an extremely rational person, a man who is dispassionately self-analytical, inspects his own motivations, has clearly formulated opinions, and acts prudently rather than out of impulse or even conviction. He articulates his motivations for murder clearly and objectively: He hopes to do his patient Helga Gregorius a favor by killing her husband, the repulsive Pastor Gregorius, who pesters her to fulfill her marital "duties," so that she can be with the man she loves, the handsome Klas Recke. He thus kills rationally, altruistically, morally. He performs the murder as quickly, painlessly, and safely as possible, by giving the pastor a cyanide pill.

One could easily read the novel as a work without hidden depth, where the author agrees with the narrator (the character of Glas has been judged a self-portrait of the author), and that therefore really is a plea for ethical murder. According to this reading, the function of the diary form would merely be to give an "inside" view of the considerations that led to the murder, to shed light on a necessarily secret story. But is this all? The novel is not focused exclusively enough on the murder to justify such an interpretation. Instead, it presents a diversified and rather appealing psychological portrait of the narrator, and it ends not with the crime but with Glas's reactions, or rather lack of reactions to it. At the beginning of the novel he is bored and longs for action, and at the end he relapses into boredom, alienation, and a sense that life has passed him by.

Yet this psychological dimension, which, credibly, gives Glas a personal as well as an ethical motivation for the crime, also seems extraordinarily well illuminated. Glas notes, "One of the basic instincts of my being, it is, never to suffer in myself anything half-conscious, half-clear, whenever it lies in my power to bring it out into the light of day, hold it up, see what it is."[27] He analyzes his own unconscious motivations with such dispassionate thoroughness that there seems to be nothing left for us to read "between the lines." Thus the murder is preceded by two dreams that Glas himself analyzes as wish-fulfillment fantasies, dreams in which Glas kills Gregorius and Helga appears to him naked. Glas precedes his extensive interpretation of the second dream with the Freudian insight that dreams often reveal hidden wishes: "And now I come to think of it more clearly – many a time has a dream taught me something about myself, often revealed to me wishes I did not *wish* to wish, desires of which I did not wish to take daylight cognizance" (p. 90). He comes to the obvious conclusion that he is in love with Helga Gregorius. Clearly, we conclude, murder is for the doctor a means to possessing her – both by eliminating her husband and by *winning* this perfect, unattainable woman by action, by performing a great deed.

Is a reading that puts the doctor's motivations into question more than he himself does possible? The doctor's blind spot has to do with his one peculiarity, the fact that he is a virgin at thirty-three and finds sex disgusting. From the beginning, starting with his thoughts on abortion, Glas identifies murder not with crime but with purification. With his Gabriel Gram–like revulsion toward sex, he seems to see murder as a kind of cure: If sex sullies the world, murder purifies it. It is revealing that Glas thinks only in terms of "clean," hygienic murders. Yet the curve of Glas's emotions before, during, and after the murder is strikingly similar to the curve of the sexual act. His "affair" with Helga, which is both preceded and followed by a sense of emptiness, climaxes – but in murder, not possession. Glas's sexual appetite is at its height directly before the murder and becomes less after it. After the crime, the doctor mixes the leaves of his diary, the record of the killing, among his gynecology notes. One might say that murder becomes, for him, a substitute for sexual fulfillment, a release of sexual energy. Murder, in a complicated fashion, is at once his mode of revenge on those who have sex, his own substitute gratification, and a solution that seems to permit "love" – which he identifies with "action."

Gustav Meyrink's short story "Eine Suggestion" (1904), another murderer's diary, is interesting because it questions the idea of writing in order to rid oneself of unpleasant memories. The topic recalls Freud's and Breuer's theories on the cathartic effect of speech, published ten years earlier in *Studies on Hysteria*. To suppress his guilt feelings and expunge all memory of the poisonings from his mind, and, at the same time, to keep the crimes an absolute secret, Meyrink's diarist begins writing a diary in code. He tries to suggest forgetfulness to himself, giving himself the command "I don't want to think of it anymore! I don't want to! I don't, don't, don't want to think of it anymore! Do you hear? You shall not think about it anymore!"[28] Where Breuer brought Anna O.'s repressed traumatic memories to consciousness under hypnosis, Meyrink's diarist attempts single-handedly to repress the memory of his crime, playing the role of hypnotist as well as subject himself. And while for Anna O. speaking is an instrument of expulsion and thus of forgetting, writing for the diarist serves rather to engrave the traumatic killings in his memory. Diary keeping backfires: Writing proves as treacherous a remedy here as it was a dangerous pastime in the diary novels with overconscious protagonists. Writing in cipher places an additional burden on the diarist's overwrought fantasy. Finally, tortured by dreams and hallucinations of the dead victims, he goes mad. He ends his misadventure by translating the entire diary out of code and deciding to confide his story to a doctor.

Toward the end of and immediately after World War I, the war itself becomes the motivation for madness. Hans Siemsen's story *Auch ich, auch du. Aufzeichnungen eines Irren* (1919) is the diary of an insane asylum inmate who has been driven crazy by war atrocities and war guilt. In Andreas Latzko's novella "Der Kamerad – ein Tagebuch" (1918) the author makes use of the madman's diary as a didactic device. The narrator, the inmate of a mental ward, is a profoundly sane antimilitarist who understandably suffered shock after having attended a soldier with a blown-off face. Despite the subtitle, the testimony is not, strictly speaking, a day-to-day journal. The word *Tagebuch* is used, presumably, to convey the idea of sincerity and also, possibly, to allude to the tradition of madmen's diaries. The story is a heartfelt and moving condemnation of a misplaced patriotism that leads to aggression, of the horrors of warfare, and of the barely comprehensible facility with which so-called sane war enthusiasts forget these horrors.

The fiction with unreliable narrators presents the issue of unreliability, which will take on complex forms in fiction such as Gide's *La Symphonie pastorale,* in the simplest possible fashion. The presupposition is that there is a real story behind the story as told by the narrator. The reader is meant to respond to the question, To what extent does the tale the diarist tells correspond to the real story? There are two possibilities: Either the diarist is sane and is therefore to be believed, or he is crazy and must be discredited. The evidence that counterbalances the narrator's story is usually just the reader's own common sense. When the narrator tells an incredible tale, the author does not have to integrate conflicting voices into the text or introduce signals that undermine the account the hero gives. The interpretation that the narrator is crazy naturalizes the story. The possibility that he is in his right mind, on the other hand, gives us license to savor, for a moment, the idea that the fantastic can come true. The object of the stories is to tease the reader; a tug-of-war is meant to take place within his own responses. Will he let himself be seduced by the story? Will he fall under the sway of the narrator's emotive immediacy and wonder, against his better judgment, whether he is really being threatened by a vampire, bewitched by a sorceress, or the like, or not?

Thus, Hanns Heinz Ewers's story "Aus dem Tagebuch eines Orangenbaumes" (1908), the diary of an inmate of an insane asylum who is in the firm grip of a delusion that he is successfully completing a transformation into an orange tree, is similar to Maupassant's "Le Horla," inasmuch as it remains completely unclear which portions of the narrator's beguilingly "plausible" tale, if any, we should believe. Was the narrator – as he would have the psychiatrist he is writing the diary for believe – "bewitched" by an enchantress-mistress who can make men believe they are trees, or does his madness have another, unstated cause? Karl Hans Strobl's vampire story "Das Grabmal auf dem Père Lachaise" (1917) likewise poses the question whether the diarist is really the victim of a vampire, as the narrator eventually surmises, or whether months of solitary confinement in a mausoleum have driven him insane. In this story there are strong reasons to prefer the fantastic reading to a purely psychological one. The dead woman in whose tomb the narrator is staying, in the hope of receiving a substantial monetary prize, probably really is a vampire who dupes the naïve and excessively self-confident diarist, who had resolved to annihilate her, into murdering his wife instead. In having a vampire victim tell his story in a diary,

Strobl is probably following the model of Bram Stoker's celebrated novel *Dracula* (1897).

The self-analytical and psychological diary fiction written in the late nineteenth and early twentieth centuries completes the breakdown of the reader role of identification, which we already saw in such nineteenth-century works as Turgenev's "Diary of a Superfluous Man," Kierkegaard's "Diary of a Seducer," and Dostoevskij's *Notes from Underground,* that was characteristic of the Wertherian diary novels. The self in these novels becomes the world, but at the same time it is reduced. Discontinuous over time and subdivided within itself, it is no longer, strictly speaking, an identity. Consequently the reader cannot identify with it – at least not in any unproblematical sense. In the era of psychology the reader comes to the text armed with the knowledge that just because a person may be sincere, he is nevertheless probably not to be trusted. The heroes who suffer from the malaise of the times, the self-conscious, self-questioning, self-disliking heroes of Rod's and Garborg's novels, are, unlike Werther, neither likable nor tragic. Of course, they represent a philosophical type, and the reader is thus meant to identify with them, but with a jolt: in spite of himself rather than automatically. In the case of the pathological heroes, the reader role of nonidentification or unwilling identification is naturally much more pronounced. The reader must distance himself from a first-person narrator who is plainly unreliable, that is, insane, regardless of the immediacy and pathos with which he writes. He is forced into a stance of analysis: He becomes the psychiatrist listening to a patient rather than the confidant listening to a friend. Diary novels with insane diarists work at cross-purposes, like detective stories: The reader is supposed to be carried away by the thrill, but at the same time must preserve his detachment in order to solve the mystery.

Toward stream of consciousness

Its first-person perspective and day-to-day structure make the diary form an extremely convenient frame for the psychological novel. When the novelist's aim is not to depict a painfully self-conscious hero, however, but rather the mental world and psychological development of a normal or pathological protagonist, the fiction of writing the diary brings with it tends to be something of a hindrance. One wants to show what the character thinks, not what he writes. A tendency to slip into interior monologue, into a thought and not a written style, is observable in many of the diary novels of the period. In Bourget's *Le Fantôme,* for instance, the diarist sits alone in a hotel room and writes down what is in effect the train of his thought; in an associative sequence he thinks about his marriage, his past, and his own character; he registers the sky and sea outside in passing; and he finally decides as a result of his meditations to return home to his wife.[29] One often has the sense that what the writers really need is a convention for reproducing the flow of the thought processes, and that the diary form is an only partially satisfactory stopgap.

From the point of view of the history of the diary form as one narrative device among others, it is interesting that one of the first writers to use the stream-of-consciousness technique, Arthur Schnitzler, wrote five short stories in diary form before he discovered Dujardin's *Les Lauriers sont coupés* and applied the method of the "monologue intérieur" in his celebrated novella *Leutnant Gustl* in 1900.[30] In three of the stories in particular he uses the form to show psychological development: "Der Andere" (1889), "Blumen" (1894), and "Die Frau des Weisen" (1897).[31] All of these stories concern the genesis and development of an obsession.

Although Schnitzler makes the fiction of the diary explicit in all the stories, in none of them is the idea of a written record necessary or even convincing. The diarists do not express themselves in a "written" style. Instead, the narration follows their thought processes, translating what one critic calls the "prespeech level" of consciousness into language in a way characteristic of the stream-of-consciousness technique.[32] A comparison of passages from "Der Andere," "Blumen," and *Leutnant Gustl* shows how close the style in the two diary stories comes to the style of the interior monologue:

> Welch eine Nacht ist das! Ich kann nicht schlafen! . . . Es ist kaum Mitternacht vorüber . . . Ich will doch jetzt hin . . . was soll ich hier, in meiner Wohnung tun . . . Ein paar Stunden nur, und die Tollheit ist wieder vorüber . . . Wie klar wird alles sein . . . Aber bis dahin! . . . Nun, es sind ja nur Stunden . . . ["Der Andere"]

> [What a night it is! I can't sleep! Midnight is scarcely past . . . I want to go there right now. . . . What should I do here, in my apartment . . . Only a few hours, and the madness will pass . . . How clear everything will be . . . But till then! Well, it's only a matter of hours.]

> Da bin ich nun den ganzen Nachmittag in den Straßen herumspaziert, auf die stiller weißer Schnee langsam herunterschwebte, – und bin nun zu Hause, und die Lampe brennt, und die Zigarre ist angezündet, und die Bücher liegen da, und alles ist bereit, daß ich mich so recht behaglich fühlen könnte . . . Aber es ist ganz vergeblich, und ich muß immer nur an dasselbe denken.
> War sie nicht längst für mich gestorben? . . . ja, tot, oder gar, wie ich mit dem kindischen Pathos der Betrogenen dachte, "schlimmer als tot"? . . . . Und nun, seit ich weiß, daß sie nicht "schlimmer als tot"

ist, nein, einfach tot, so wie die vielen anderen, die draußen liegen, tief unter der Erde, immer, immer, wenn der Frühling da ist, und wenn der schwüle Sommer kommt, und wenn der Schnee fällt wie heute . . . so ohne jede Hoffnung des Wiederkommens – seither weiß ich, daß sie auch für mich um keinen Augenblick früher gestorben ist als für die anderen Menschen. Schmerz? Nein. ["Blumen"]

[Well, so I've been walking around all afternoon in the streets, on which still white snow slowly floated down, – and now I'm at home, and the lamp is burning, and the cigar is lit, and the books are lying there, and everything is ready so I might feel comfortable . . . But it's quite useless; I always have to think of the same thing.

Hadn't she long since died for me? . . . yes, dead, or even, as I thought with the childish pathos of those deceived, "worse than dead"? . . . And now, since I know that she isn't "worse than dead," no, simply dead, like the many others that lie outside, deep below the earth, always, always, when the spring is there, and when the sultry summer comes, and when the snow falls like today . . . without any hope of returning – since then I know that she didn't die a single moment earlier for me than for other people. Pain? No.]

Warum schaut mich denn der Herr dort an der Säule so an? – hat der am End' was gehört? . . . Ich werd' ihn fragen . . . Fragen? – Ich bin ja verrückt! – Wie schau' ich denn aus? – Merkt man mir was an? – Ich muß ganz blaß sein. – Wo ist der Hund? . . . Ich muß ihn umbringen! Fort ist er . . . Überhaupt schon ganz leer . . . Wo ist denn mein Mantel? ["Leutnant Gustl"][33]

[How come the gentleman by the pillar over there is staring at me like that? – did he hear something after all? . . . I'll ask him . . . Ask? – I must be crazy! – Do I look funny? – Can people tell anything from the way I look? – I must be very pale. – Where is the scoundrel? . . . I have to kill him! He's gone . . . No one here at all . . . Where's my coat?]

The "written" messages in "Der Andere" and "Blumen" reproduce a kind of reflective daydreaming, the kind one might indulge in while sitting at one's desk. Stream of consciousness ("Gustl") liberates the thinker from his desk; Schnitzler shows Gustl's reactions as he is leaving a concert hall. But otherwise the two kinds of writing are quite similar. Like the "thought" passage, the diary passages follow the diarists' associative trains of thought and show their momentary emotions. They lack the logical organization of an expository style. They too make frequent use of the ellipsis for punctuation. The diarist of "Blumen" absorbs his perceptions of the things around him (the lamp, the cigar, the books) into his meditation like Gustl (the gentleman), and, like Gustl, he often "thinks" by posing questions to himself.

It is probably not an exaggeration to assert that considering the increasing dominance of psychology in the novel, and especially as far as the objective of reproducing thought processes is concerned, the interior monologue represented a technical advance over the diary and displaced it. James Joyce, like Schnitzler a self-proclaimed disciple of Dujardin's, also used the diary form before he developed the stream-of-consciousness technique in *Ulysses;* Stephen Dedalus's journal at the end of *A Portrait of the Artist as a Young Man* (1916) has been called Joyce's first interior monologue,[34] although the style is considerably more journal-like than that of Schnitzler's stories. Peter Brang states that although the diary fiction has persisted into contemporary Russian literature, its potential expansion has been limited by the widespread acceptance of other devices, specifically *style indirect libre* and the interior monologue.[35] One could state the case differently: The development of better techniques for psychological fiction has caused writers to choose the diary form to thematize the act of writing.

Nevertheless, the diary form does serve a purpose in the psychological novel that the stream-of-consciousness technique does not fulfill equally well. In Schnitzler's novellas the fiction of writing is unnecessary, but the periodicity of the diary, the possibility of acquainting the reader with the protagonist's thoughts at spaced intervals, is essential. The obsessions that are the subject of the case studies must have time to develop; we have to be able to observe the "patient" from time to time. In "Blumen" a period of several months is required for the flowers to take their uncanny hold on the diarist. Furthermore, Schnitzler is concerned to show the development only of one particular aspect of a character's thought. It is hard to imagine how these novellas could have been written in the stream-of-consciousness style, since that technique conventionally aims at reproducing the total flow of a character's consciousness over an uninterrupted and necessarily brief period of time.

After the autonomous interior monologue was developed and first-person narration was thus liberated from the convention of writing, one finds a curious mélange of styles. The first decades of the twentieth century witness, within the frame of the psychological novel, the emergence of what might be called "quasi-diary fiction" – a kind of first-person fiction similar to diary fiction, particularly inasmuch as it maintains a clearly periodic narrative scheme, yet fundamentally different because there are no explicit references to writing. Such fiction is characterized by the use of the present tense, both the kinds of the present tense appropriate to the diary (constative statements of interiority, expressives, etc.), and those inappropriate to it (the historical present, interior monologue, constative punctual statements). Thus, Johannes R. Becher uses periodic first-person narration in his novella "Das kleine Leben" (1914), with all the present-tense forms one might expect to find, with a stretch of the imagination, in a fictive diary. But it seems unlikely that his uneducated, disoriented, labile *Lumpenproletariat* narrator is actually writing. Other examples of works that adopt every feature of the diary except for the fiction of writing are Heinrich Nowak's *Die Sonnenseuche* (1920), Robert Zellermeyer's "Erscheinung" (in *Die Gefährten*, 1921), and Hermann Meister's "Das weiße Herz" (1925). In all of these stories the purpose is to show psychological change or fluctuation over a period of time.

14

Unreliable Narration:
André Gide

As we saw in the last chapter, unreliability in narration is based on some evident discrepancy between the "discourse" and the "story," or in other words, between the story as the narrator recounts it, and the story itself. An unreliable narrator, then, is a person who deceives himself, or wishes to deceive us, in his interpretation of events. We have seen that the simplest way to present an unreliable narrator is to create one who is a patent lunatic. In such a case the reader is given two options, either to believe the narrator, or to classify him as mad. The reader who suspects that the narrator is unreliable may base his judgment on evidence external to the story, on his knowledge of human nature, for example, or on a certain conception of sanity the narrator does not live up to. Alternately, the text itself may contain signals that suggest that the narrator's discourse is inauthentic. In any event, the reader is invited to read against the grain, to discern a discrepancy between the narrator's voice and some ulterior underlying truth.

Theoretically, any first-person narrator – indeed, any narrating voice – can be undermined or fashioned into an unreliable source. But the more exposure we are given to a narrating voice, the more vulnerable the voice becomes. The fictional autobiographer who all but vanishes from the story, who retreats to a vantage point of enlightened authority, who narrates his life from the consistent, atemporal perspective of hindsight, presents few surfaces for attack. In epistolary and diary fiction, in contrast, we are exposed to a narrating voice over a considerable period of time. We hear someone who is close to events, whose fragility has ample time to become apparent. In epistolary and diary fiction, moreover, time stretches out before the narrator. The future that awaits the hero, as evidenced by the pages of the book that await the reader, is a future the narrator himself cannot predict. These forms are thus especially well suited to the presentation of unreliable narrators.

In the diary novel we hear only a single voice, and the diarist is probably writing secretly, for himself. The narrator does not have the letter writer's obvious opportunity for displaying his insincerity; he cannot address different versions of the same story to different readers. How can an author undermine a diarist? There are various ways to introduce other points of view in the diary novel. A fictive editor can "publish" the diary and write an introduction, telling the reader what to think. The trouble with this device is that the editor's opinions easily can get drowned out before long by the single, insistent voice of the diarist. The diary may be followed by a postscript, but such an after-word of course does not affect the reader's spontaneous, first-reading response to the text. Other characters' points of view may be inserted into the diary in different ways: The diarist can be made to report a conversation verbatim, for example, or to copy a letter into his journal.

The diarist is also capable of discrediting himself without the contrast another character's voice provides. An author who wishes to maneuver his protagonist into this position has to rely on the reactions of the actual reader (i.e., the ideal reader actualized). He allows the diarist to report but misperceive events whose significance and outcome are clear from the standpoint of common sense. In the typical instance, the reader watches the diarist walk unwittingly into certain disaster. Our knowledge of narrative conventions and our expectation of a certain plot structure, too, may lead us to disbelieve what the diarist says. In Rudolf Huch's *Max Gebhard* (1907), for example, we surmise that the hero will not make himself miserable by marrying a woman he no longer loves, despite – or perhaps because of – his mounting guilt feelings. In Jacques Chardonne's *Eva ou le Journal interrompu* (1930) the narrator's initial protestations that his marriage is blissfully happy arouse our suspicions; blissfully happy marriages do not make novels. The reader is allowed to know, or suspect, more than the diarist; a second point of view is created *ex nihilo,* that is, out of the actual reading situation.

This kind of dramatic irony creates a play between two time levels. The reader is freed from the perpetual level of the diarist's present tense and given a glimpse into his future. Two kinds of time exist simultaneously and jar on each other: "real" but unwritten time that has its certain telos (i.e., the time in which the reader's superior consciousness moves), and the deluded, narrated time of the diarist's consciousness, which projects a false telos onto the future. Eventually the two kinds of time collide and the diarist's time disintegrates under the impact of real time. At the moment of his disillusionment, the continuity of the diarist's belief is destroyed. He experiences a *dédoublement* and comes as close to being two people as a single person can: A newly born, knowing self looks in dismay at the disappearing, precatastrophic self. The present self is really a tragically heightened version of the reader himself: The diarist now knows all that the reader knew. At the moment of recognition the two points of view become one again.

Finally, it is also possible for unreliability to be based on ellipsis, on *inadequate* narration on the part of the narrator. Thus in *Max Gebhard* the narrator simply leaves out pertinent material. He reflects on himself and on every conceivable topic – the legal profession and the law, aesthetics, Nietzsche, Goethe, the transmigration of souls, and anti-Semitism – but as far as events are concerned, he pushes the unstated to the utmost. The reader is left to infer most of the plot from the narrator's reactions to incidents he does not bother to describe. The mimetic diary obviously lends itself particularly well to such a technique – for what real-life diarist leaves us with a complete account? The reader is left to read between the lines, to piece together a whole story out of the diarist's jottings.

My main purpose in this chapter will be to examine Gide's diary novella *La Symphonie pastorale* (1919) as an example of unreliable narration, but a more complicated example, in which the author creates an initial contrast between the narrator's report and a real account of events and then undermines this binary system in order to arrive at a sophisticated questioning of the ideas of truth and illusion. Before we look at this novella, however, it will be useful to consider its context among Gide's other works, both as a text in diary form and as one that takes self-deception as its theme.

André Gide is the first major writer of the twentieth century to use the journal form extensively and persistently in his work. Inspired by reading Amiel, he began to keep an intimate journal at the age of twenty. This project became his celebrated *Journal,* a mammoth work that covers a period of sixty years, from 1889 to 1949, and that Gide published in three major installments, in 1939, 1944, and 1950. Gide was thus the chief representative of a new generation of intimists who, writing in an era when the publication of intimate journals was becoming common, could not forget that they were potentially composing their own for posterity. With their journals, these writers stand between the nineteenth-century intimists like Amiel and Michelet, who wrote for themselves, and later writers like Max Frisch, who started his journal as a conscious literary enterprise.

Besides keeping a journal, Gide used the diary form in a number of novels. Here again, he was aware of what other novelists, for example, Rod, had already done with the form.[36] *Les Cahiers d'André Walter* (1891), Gide's first novel, is in diary form; the satire *Paludes* (1895) is a journal in a journal; and brief journals figure in *La Porte étroite* (1909) and *Les Caves du Vatican* (1914). After writing *La Symphonie pastorale,* Gide continued his experimentation in *Les Faux-Monnayeurs* (1926), in which he juxtaposes Edouard's journal with third-person narrative. Finally, in 1929, he wrote *L'Ecole des femmes,* the diary of a naïve and then undeceived wife.

Gide became acquainted with the journal at a time when it was no longer regarded as the vehicle of an unproblematic sincerity but, rather, as a site of conflict, specifically a conflict between spontaneity and reflection, and hence also writing. In the first years Gide expresses precisely these tensions in his journal. He perceives his two guiding ideals as *morality* and *sincerity* – both values traditionally associated with the journal. Morality implies devising rules for oneself; the young writer formulates, and carefully enumerates, rules of conduct by which he will live his life. Sincerity implies authenticity, being rather than seeming. Here lies the seed of conflict, for from the standpoint of sincerity, morality appears suspect. Gide finds that the reflectedness of morality prevents him from being spontaneously true to himself; the intention, the desire, to be sincere cancels out the sincerity in advance. He writes, "I am torn by a conflict between the rules of morality and the rules of sincerity. Morality consists in substituting for the natural creature (the old Adam) a fiction that you prefer. But then you are no longer sincere. The old Adam is the sincere man."[37]

One could argue that the journal is a spontaneous and therefore sincere form; but Gide, quite in keeping with the prejudices of the age, connects writing with analysis. He notes, "The emotion would lose its bloom of sincere spontaneity if I analyzed it for the purpose of my writing" (p. 4). Keeping the journal appears to him to further morality, order, and reflection, while the enterprise of sitting down to write takes on the aspect of "composition," of literariness. In his most important and extensive passage on the subject, he condemns his journal:

> That constant analysis of one's thoughts, that lack of action, those rules of conduct are the most tiresome, insipid, and almost incomprehensible things in the world when one has got beyond them. I could never get back into certain of these moods, which nevertheless I know to have been sincere. . . . The desire to compose the pages of this journal deprives them of all worth, even that of sincerity. They do not really mean anything, never being well enough written to have a literary value. In short, all of them take for granted a future fame or celebrity that will confer an interest upon them. And that is utterly base.
> . . . how dull these marvelous seaweeds become when you take them out of water. [p. 28]

In *Paludes* Gide draws the conclusions of this condemnation by putting ironic distance between journal keeping and the idea of sincerity.

In later years the issues of sincerity and morality vanish from the

Journal. An entry of 1909 shows that the value Gide attached in his youth to sincerity has paled; he writes, "The word *sincerity* is one of those that are becoming harder for me to understand" (p. 242). Nevertheless, Gide's early preoccupation with morality, sincerity, and the seduction of words, especially as they relate to journal keeping, are of interest for an interpretation of *La Symphonie pastorale,* whose original conception dates back to the same period, because morality, sincerity, and language are its central themes. Moreover, the tension between sincerity and morality that Gide perceives in the 1890s will persist in his work under different names, while the preoccupation with oppositions will eventually modulate into an interest in the nature of such divisions. Gide will become interested in different ways of expressing and modifying them. Thus in *Les Nourritures terrestres* (1896), the work that represents a crucial vitalistic breakthrough for Gide, the tension continues; here the terms are conceived as sensualism versus conventional morality. In *Les Caves du Vatican* (1914), Gide examines a spectrum of oppositions that can be subsumed under the headings "reality" and "illusion." In *Les Faux-Monnayeurs* (1926), he articulates a theory of the novel in terms of the representation of reality versus artistic stylization, abstractions, and the use of convention.[38] Critics usually try to place *La Symphonie pastorale* in a biographical context, citing events of 1916–19 in order to explain why Gide returned twenty-five years later to a conception of the early 1890s. But the novella can also be placed in an intellectual and artistic context; with its theme of truth and illusion it engages ideas that can be traced back through Gide's entire oeuvre. Since these ideas are particularly prominent in the works of fiction Gide wrote both directly before and after *La Symphonie pastorale,* that is, in *Les Caves du Vatican* and *Les Faux-Monnayeurs,* and since the three works can be understood as a progression in which Gide not only explores and questions the validity of lines of division but also, increasingly, experiments with formal techniques for doing so, it will be useful to consider the novella against the background of the earlier *sotie* and the later novel, where Gide also uses the diary form.

In *Les Caves du Vatican* Gide explores the question of reality and illusion, or of the different kinds of systems we construct for dealing with reality, on the level of theme. Reality and illusion appear in various metamorphoses: as empirical science versus Catholicism, as the probabilities of human psychology versus the imaginative constructs permissible in belles lettres, and as the facts of reality versus the fabrications of a confidence artist. Each of the five main characters designated by the five chapters represents a different way of looking at the question. Four of the five impose arbitrary and inflexible lines of division between the real and the imaginary and thereby become comic figures.

Only the fascinating central figure, Lafcadio, the perpetrator of the *acte gratuit* or unmotivated crime, manages to fuse conventionality with contingency. A bastard or "half son," he has one foot in the world of the nobility and the other in the underworld; his hermaphroditic beauty attracts men and women alike; Gide lets him appear at spatial border-lines and points of temporal change (we first see him in a doorway, and in the last scene he looks out of a window at dawn). Lafcadio acts inconsistently, in accordance with no particular set of principles. He rescues two children from a burning building, for example, but later kills a stranger by pushing him off a train because he sees a light before he can count to twelve. His mode of action resembles play: It is not precisely sheer invention, and it does not accord with the rules of the real world either. The novel reflects Gide's fascination with a figure who does not accept the traditional distinctions or invent, with any seriousness, any of his own.

In *Les Faux-Monnayeurs,* which in Gide's original conception was to be narrated by Lafcadio, Gide articulates the question of the dividing line, which here figures most generally as the distinction between real life and fiction or representation, in various ways on the level of theme.[39] But his innovation is to let the novel's formal structure itself pose the question of the dividing line. Gide's most obvious device is the *mise en abîme:* He creates in *Les Faux-Monnayeurs* a mirror of his own actual writing situa-tion. The main character in the novel is a novelist who is writing a novel about a novelist. While writing *Les Faux-Monnayeurs,* Gide kept a journal that he published under the title of *Journal des faux-monnayeurs.* Edouard, Gide's fictive novelist, likewise keeps a journal, which is printed as part of *Les Faux-Monnayeurs,* alternating with sections of third-person narrative. In the *Journal des faux-monnayeurs,* Gide records his ideas for the novel; Edouard likewise says that his journal "contains a running criticism of my novel."[40] Gide observes that *Les Faux-Monnayeurs* has two focuses: "On one side, the event, the fact, the external datum; on the other side, the very effort of the novelist to make a book out of it all."[41] Edouard echoes that his novel will be about his main character's struggle "between what reality offers him and what he himself desires to make of it."[42]

Gide complicates this *mise en abîme* by giving Edouard's novel the title *Les Faux-Monnayeurs.* We are thus meant to entertain the idea that Edouard wrote the novel we are reading, the third-person sections as well as the journal. Gide poses the question of the dividing line through form by giving the title of his novel a double reference and asking us to wonder about its status. *Les Faux-Monnayeurs* itself, with its proposed dual status, crosses the border between "inside" and "outside," be-tween the real-life frame and the fictional construction.

The question of the authorship of *Les Faux-Monnayeurs* is the first of a series of such questions the novel poses, questions Gide invariably fails to answer; his purpose is, rather, to trigger a chain of reflections in the reader. By using the economical means of stating through form, he does not have to present an argument explicitly; rather, the reader supplies it himself, after the initial, irresolvable question is asked.

Thus if we do decide to accept the idea that Edouard is the author of *Les Faux-Monnayeurs,* we are left to reflect to what extent *Les Faux-Monnayeurs* realizes the subject Edouard proposes for it, the theme of "the rivalry between the real world and the representation of it which we make to ourselves" (p. 205). Both the conventions of narrative and Gide's own simultaneous composition of a journal and a novel suggest that we are to interpret the relation of the two kinds of narration, the third-person narrative and the journal, as one of more versus less real. The question is, which is which? One might argue that Edouard's journal, like Gide's journal, is more "real" than the rest of the text, for the novelist is more real than his novel, and the narrative in which he plans the novel is consequently more "real" than the novel itself. But one can also argue that the third-person sections are of superior "reality." The opening section of the novel is third-person narrative; Edouard is introduced as a character in it. According to novelistic convention, a frame is more real than what it contains.

The question of superior reality proves undecidable. The appeal to the novelistic convention of the frame falls flat by the end of the novel; if the third-person narrative promises to be a frame, it does not keep its promise, for the book closes with the journal, not the third-person narrative. How and where, moreover, are the third-person sections "dictated by reality" (p. 188), as Edouard says his novel will be? What exactly does that mean, "dictated by reality"? The novel's focus of interest may drift, as does a real person's attention; the novel may lack a novelistic structure and closure. But can one completely eliminate novelistic conventions in a novel? One might ask where Edouard gets his insights into the thoughts of other characters, and where he gets their letters that he prints – do they give them to him, does he steal them, or does he make them up? Authorial omniscience itself is a novelistic convention.

As critics have remarked, the book's title, *Les Faux-Monnayeurs,* succinctly expresses the problem of reality and its representation in the novel.[43] When Edouard chose the title, he vaguely had in mind popular novelists who market the false coin of borrowed ideas. But then, ironically, after all Edouard's talk of the difficulties of making fiction conform to reality, there is a real counterfeiting incident in the novel. The incident of passing false coin reproduces in its structure the method Edouard envisages for his novel. Counterfeiting involves a dialectic between the false and the real; it means putting something imaginary into circulation and getting something real in exchange. The boys spend false money and get real change for it. Edouard likewise hopes to cross the border between fiction and real life by getting real characters to finish his stories for him. He puts this theory into practice with one of the boys who is responsible for circulating the false coin by showing him a passage from his novel that he has based on his real-life conversation with the boy's mother, in order to provoke his response. But the young adept sees through the old counterfeiter's trick at once and refuses to finish his story for him.

The equivalence Gide establishes between writing fiction and minting coin gives us an insight into his theory of artistic representation. Not just counterfeit money but money itself is a representation. In the novel, too, "reality" is an empty term. One can speak, at best, of "reality" and "invention" as hypothetical opposites, standing for "better" or "worse" representations, acceptable currency versus other kinds. The question we are left to ask ourselves is, which is which: whether the representation that rings truest is not simply the one that is most conventional.

In *Les Faux-Monnayeurs,* Gide uses different kinds of narration to express the differences between the real and the fictional and the gradations between them, and to question the sense of such distinctions. *La Symphonie pastorale* expresses similar tensions, but here Gide operates within the narrow framework of first-person narration. He achieves an effect comparable to that of the novel by making his narrator unreliable. To do so, he plays on different connotations of the diary form: Whereas in *Les Faux-Monnayeurs* he uses the diary for its connotations of closeness to reality, in *La Symphonie pastorale* he uses it for its connotations of sincerity.

Before we start to discuss *La Symphonie pastorale,* it should be pointed out that an interpretation of the work as an unreliable narration is by no means uncontested among Gide's critics. Rather, it is an issue of hottest dispute. The interpretation of this novella presents difficulties because of biographical evidence, of which there is, as almost always in Gide's case, almost too much. The reader who reads only the text readily concludes that the narrator is a dangerous hypocrite, an unreliable narrator not endorsed by the author. But the biographical circumstances surrounding the composition of the work have been interpreted as a reason for understanding the pastor as a figure who, if he does not actually have Gide's wholehearted support, at least is a kind of tragic hero. Thus critics have tended to focus their energies on explaining the biographical evidence in such a way that it accords with their reading of the text, or else to focus them on interpreting the text so that it supports what is seen to be an incontrovertible connection between Gide's state of mind in 1918 and anything he might have written at the time.

The argument based on biographical evidence is roughly this: Although the project for a novella about a blind girl goes back to 1893, and although Gide claimed that in writing the book he was merely completing "the last of my youthful projects," he actually wrote it at a time when his central preoccupation was his relationship with the sixteen-year-old Marc Allégret, and when his relations with his wife, as a consequence, very much deteriorated. Between the composition of the first and second notebooks he spent his summer vacation in England with Marc, and during his absence Madeleine Gide burned his letters – events that had the effect of putting a great strain on his marriage.[44] Thus, it is argued, Gide must have identified with the pastor, especially since the pastor's Bible reinterpretation closely resembles the philosophy of joy Gide himself propounded in *Numquid et tu . . . ?*(1916). Marc stands behind the figure of Gertrude in the novella (she is called "Marceline" at the beginning of the manuscript),[45] and Amélie can only be seen as a "brutal caricature" of Madeleine Gide.[46] The work, then, is really "an act of self-justification on Gide's part";[47] the catastrophe is the fault not of the pastor but of his son Jacques, who exerts a pernicious influence on Gertrude with his preaching from Saint Paul.[48]

Other critics – the majority – prefer a reading based on textual evidence and argue that the pastor can be identified with Gide only insofar as all his protagonists are versions of himself, that is, not in any simple sense.[49] They call to their support Gide's own pronouncements on the work. Several years after publication Gide called the work "the criticism of a kind of lying to oneself."[50] If the pastor represents Gide's ideas, he represents them in a caricatured, dangerous form. Gide wrote of the pastor many years later, in 1945:

> Through him, yet more than to seek to express my own thought, I painted the reef toward which my own doctrine could lead when this ethic is no longer severely controlled by a critical, constantly watchful spirit that is not indulgent or complaisant toward itself. Here (in the pastor's case) the indispensable critical spirit is completely lacking.[51]

The work is, then, like so many of Gide's other works, at least partially self-critical. Critics reconcile their reading of the text with views held by Gide since *Les Nourritures terrestres,* with *Numquid et tu . . . ?,* and with the biographical facts by arguing that Gide supports the pastor's idea of a utopia, which is a constant element in his thought, and whose "real destroyer . . . is conventional religion."[52] He condemns the pastor not for immorality but for hypocrisy.

Facts about Gide's life, it seems to me, should be kept in the background of a reading. We have no sure method for applying biographical
evidence in the reading of a text; we also have no certain means for
asserting that a text stands in a particular determinate relation to an
author's frame of mind at the time of writing. In the particular case of
La Symphonie pastorale, the evidence is conflicting and inadequate; and
we also do not know what Gide's plan for the novella was at any given
time. To be sure, the novella can be interpreted as a tragedy rather than
as a condemnation of the pastor. But this reading does not cancel out
the possibility that Gide created a narrator who is insincere and unreliable. The text speaks strongly for the pastor's unreliability; if Gide
intended us to read otherwise, we would be forced to conclude that the
text is a poor realization of his idea.

In the novella, Gide shows us the most pernicious effects of the
pastor's utopian ideas. His choice of a pastor for his protagonist is not
fortuitous; the specific mode of the pastor's fall, his passion for a six-
teen- or seventeen-year-old girl, is rendered the more ironic considering
his profession, his initially conservative moral ethic, and his sincere
belief that he is impervious to superficial beauty. His reinterpretation of
the Bible is manifestly guided by his passion; there is no real intellectual
moment behind his religion of joy. Overtly it is the tragic ending,
Gertrude's suicide, that testifies to the pastor's error. This catastrophe,
however, is the revelation, the symbol, of an error on which the pastor's religion of joy was constructed.

Within the more general truth of representation that Gide will propose, the most powerful truth in the novella is located in sense perception, particularly in the sense of sight. The pastor's passion is triggered
by vision. Gertrude initially reciprocates the pastor's passion, evidently,
because she cannot see – in particular, because she cannot see his face.
When an operation is finally successfully performed on her eyes, she
suddenly *sees* the truth: "When I saw Jacques, I suddenly realized it was
not you I loved – but him. He had your face."[53] She also sees the misery
on the face of the pastor's wife, Amélie, and recognizes that through
her affections, she was in part responsible for her misery.

The pastor's tragic error is to construct a fantasy of a perfectly harmonious world that can only stand as long as Gertrude is deprived of
her most important sense. He resolutely ignores intrusions of reality
that to an increasing degree contradict his precarious utopian construction. God's first words in creating the world were "Let there be light."
The pastor, in contrast, creates a world whose initial premise is the
inability to see. The edifice he builds is valid only if one is literally
blind, as Gertrude is, or spiritually blind, as the pastor is, to the dishar-
mony around one. His self-elevation as an interpreter of the Bible can

be regarded as part of an act of hybris, a misguided attempt to improve on God's world and create the world anew. His mode of presenting his role in the finding and raising of Gertrude reveals a tendency to mimic the Creation story. In his account of how he found Gertrude, which he gives, fittingly, in seven diary entries, he mythologizes both his role and the find, superimposing fairy-tale and missionary-tale motifs onto the adventure. He emphasizes how he brought light to darkness; bearing a lantern, he intrepidly ventures into the unknown, the darkness of souls, the mysterious darkness where, normally, "none of my pastoral duties take me" (p. 142). After bringing Gertrude back, he begins to create a paradise for the new human being – replacing a natural visible world for the blind girl with a world of words. Gide plays the deceptiveness of words off against the truth of vision. With his words, the pastor teaches Gertrude that the world is joyous, happy, beautiful, and harmonious. His seemingly ingenious pedagogical device of explaining the colors to her by analogy with the sounds emitted by different instruments in a symphony creates an impression of synesthesia that Gertrude herself willingly adopts. Black and white, in his explanation, are not opposites but combinations of all the other colors. The pastor persistently blurs distinctions with his use of words, applying Christian vocabulary to the profane (for example, he speaks of "consecrating" time to Gertrude and of *amour* – Christian, but also secular, love). Of course, the reader cannot help but hear an ironic undertone in the pastor's "naïve" use of double meanings. While the pastor is attempting to blur distinctions, to create a "pastoral symphony," the narrative itself upholds these distinctions.

The pastor writes his journal in two notebooks. In the first, he records the story up to this point retrospectively, writing in seven entries from February 10 to March 12. He begins the second notebook after a hiatus of a month and a half, in which he completes the retrospective narration up to the present and then continues on a day-to-day basis, writing from April 25 to May 30. The two notebooks reveal two different levels of self-deception.

In the first notebook, the pastor deceives himself about his feelings for Gertrude and his motivations for spending so much time with her. He reveals himself only very gradually as an unreliable narrator. It is only by the end of the notebook that signs of unreliability outweigh the impression of extraordinary probity he makes on us at the beginning and paradoxically manages to sustain. It is primarily when we reread, therefore, and particularly after we have read the second notebook as well, that we interpret his disarming locutions in an ironic light – his self-deprecating comments about his faults as a historian, for example, his admission of lapses in memory, his sincere reluctance to support his arguments with Holy Writ, and his apparent forthrightness about his negative and uncharitable emotions.

To justify our interpretation of the pastor of the first notebook as unreliable, we are not obliged to recur to appeals to common sense or moral arguments. Gide validates our reading by having the pastor himself reach the same conclusion at the beginning of the second notebook. In the first entry, the pastor recognizes what he has failed to acknowledge for so long, that he is in love with Gertrude. He wonders how he has managed to deceive himself about the nature of his feelings for so long: "Now that I dare call by its name the feeling that so long lay unacknowledged in my heart, it seems almost incomprehensible that I should have mistaken it until this very day – incomprehensible that . . . I could still have doubted that I loved her" (p. 201).[54] The reader, however, has been a step ahead of the pastor – though not much more than a step – in discerning the truth. The art of unreliability lies precisely in giving the reader a slight temporal advantage. The narrative carries suspense and points forward to the moment when the reader's suspicions will be confirmed; and the reader's appetite for this confirmation sharpens his attentiveness to the text.

How does Gide communicate with the reader over the pastor's head?[55] He uses four principal techniques. First and most important, he lets the pastor quote a second, dissenting voice, that of his wife. Amélie's reproaches that the pastor is neglecting his family are credible, and in the climactic scene with Jacques, where Amélie all but tells the pastor in so many words that he is in love with Gertrude, her accusations become particularly compelling. More and more, Amélie's transparent innuendos support the reader's interpretation of the pastor's motivations.

Second, Gide has the pastor record, seemingly in all innocence, facts – loaded facts that lead us to suspect that he is attracted to Gertrude in a more than pastorly way. The principal fact of this kind is Gertrude's beauty.

Third, Gide lets the pastor write revealing turns of phrase that say more than he intends; and he lets him misunderstand events whose significance is plain. The reader thus knows, although the pastor does not, that he is jealous of Jacques. For example, in the entry of February 28, the pastor says that two years ago during Christmas vacation, his son Jacques started helping him teach Gertrude, and notes, "At first I was glad to be helped in this respect" (p. 167), without going into further detail. Why "at first"? The unreliability of the narrator and also his self-delusion over the course of at least the last eight months become painfully clear in the scene where he finds Jacques helping Gertrude with her harmonium practice in the chapel, a scene that erupts in his refusal to countenance Jacques's proposal of marriage. The reader can only conclude that the pastor, muddy about his reasons for forbidding the marriage, possessive without recognizing it, understanding only what he wants to understand, was then already in love with Gertrude. After Jacques complies with his order to leave for vacation, the pastor persuades himself that his son's love was not serious. He fails to understand his wife's veiled warning and imposes a different construction on her comments – that she, too, is opposed to Jacques's marriage with Gertrude. It is alarming that the present, narrating pastor submits no analysis of his behavior but remains as unenlightened as ever as to the state of his feelings.

Finally, Gide shows us the pastor's preoccupations through the rhythm of his writing. These preoccupations become particularly clear in retrospect, after we have reconstructed a framework of not explicitly stated events – a second, fuller chronology that allows us to evaluate the significance not only of what the pastor says but also of his omissions. One omission has to do with the fact of writing itself. Why does the pastor begin writing a *retrospective* account of his relationship with Gertrude exactly when he does, on February 10; and why does he break off on March 12? He himself gives the reason that he is snowed in and has time on his hands. A better explanation might be that the snow prevents him from seeing Gertrude. If we read carefully, we discover that the pastor had lodged her away from the family to prevent her from seeing Jacques, and that this situation has existed since August; until snowfalls made the roads impassable, however, the pastor himself visited her. His obsession with the girl takes the form of writing when he cannot see her in person. He stops writing precisely when the snow melts.

In the first notebook, Gide sets up a binary system by which the narrator's account stands in contrast with the account the reader gradually pieces together. In the second notebook, an odd permutation occurs. As we recall, at the beginning of the second notebook the pastor arrives at precisely the insight the reader had on completing the first notebook: He realizes he is in love with Gertrude. He thus develops into a voice that confirms his own previous unreliability. The story of the first notebook momentarily becomes the discourse. The two levels seem to merge: The degree of deludedness that separated the pastor, the writer, from the reader, effectively vanishes. At this moment, however, a new opposition is set up, one that involves replacing the cognitive standard of correctness of the first notebook with a moral one: The pastor's love for Gertrude is now recognized as *morally* questionable.

One would expect that the result of this insight would be that the pastor would alter his conduct in accordance with the moral principles he has always upheld. One would expect that he would continue his journal in the interest of self-correction; that he would put the journal to its traditional Protestant use, that of putting one's spiritual life in order. Instead, it becomes clear that his unconscious aim in writing the second notebook is less self-correction than self-justification. Rather than reflect on himself, he begins a vast reinterpretation of his ethical principles, the motive of which is to construct a world that will accommodate his desire. He no longer deceives himself merely about his feelings; rather, armed now with the "truth" that he loves Gertrude, he lets his passion shape his thinking and gives his illusions free rein. Instead of revising his desire so that it conforms to the fixed moral standards that structure his existence, he reconstructs the very foundation of his world so that it will support the figure of passion he has traced on it. The ultimate result is that his passion in turn shapes the outcome of the story.

The figure for the merging of levels, and also for the sleight of hand that permits the reversal, is reading. If the pastor resumes writing after a hiatus of six weeks, it is because he has become his own reader in the meantime. The identification of the pastor with the reader is an important one. In the first notebook a hierarchical relation is set up between reality and text, whereby the authority, the person empowered to pronounce judgment on the deficient text, is the reader. In the second notebook Gide parodies the power and authority of the reader. If the pastor follows his correct reading of his own journal with action that belies all insight, it is because he becomes a reader for a second time. This time the text is the New Testament. The change from criteria of knowledge to criteria of morality brings with it a reversal of the authority of the text, in this case the Bible, vis-à-vis the world of human thought and conduct. Obviously, the pastor should bring his deficient conduct into conformity with the standard of conduct the Bible represents. Instead, he overthrows the authority of the Bible and interprets Christ's words in such a way that they sustain his passion.

In the first notebook, the pastor declares that he considers it wrong to justify his conduct by referring to the authority of the Bible, a declaration that supports our initial impression of him as a model of moral probity. He writes, "I never think it becoming to allege the authority of the Holy Book as an excuse for my conduct" (p. 150). Inasmuch as the pastor supports his actions with quotations from the Bible in the first notebook, his interpretation of these quotations is quite orthodox. The chief quotation he uses is "I have brought back the lost sheep" (p. 149).

In the second notebook, in contrast, the pastor embarks on extremely dubious interpretations of certain biblical passages. Directly after he comes to the critical recognition that he is in love with Gertrude, instead of reflecting on this startling insight, he embarks on what seems at first to be wholly a digressive rereading of the New Testament. "Gertrude's religious instruction has led me to reread the Gospels with a fresh eye" (p. 204), he begins. It has often been pointed out that the pastor's reading of the Bible bears a close relation to *Numquid et tu . . . ?*, Gide's own attempt at biblical exegesis that he wrote between 1916 and 1919 and first published anonymously in 1922.[56] Gide, like the pastor, emphasizes believing in the words of Christ and announces that the secret of the Gospels is joy. Gide puts passages that he himself wrote into the mouth of the pastor verbatim. Yet critics tend to understand such borrowings as self-critical; Gide himself said that the work warns against the dangers of "the free interpretation of the Scriptures."[57]

The most glaring example of the pastor's tendency not only to choose but also grossly to misinterpret biblical passages to suit himself is his treatment of one of the first passages he cites, a verse from John. The pastor writes, "Et cette parole du Christ s'est dressée lumineusement devant moi. 'Si vous étiez aveugles, vous n'auriez point de péché'" (p. 107). ("And these words of Christ's stood out before my eyes in letters of light: 'If ye were blind ye should have no sin'" [p. 206].) Christ is referring to the Pharisees, who willfully and perversely persist in misinterpreting Christ's miracle. The Pharisees claim to see and to understand, whereas in fact they understand wrongly: They are spiritually blind. "If ye were blind," said Jesus, "ye should have no sin: but now ye say, We see; therefore your sin remaineth" (John 9:41). If the Pharisees admitted their spiritual blindness, they would not be guilty. Ironically, the biblical quotation the pastor chooses, if correctly interpreted, would apply directly to himself: The pastor, who has just recognized his love for Gertrude but is about to make a sophistical argument excusing his passion, is just such a Pharisee.

In *Numquid et tu . . . ?*, Gide quotes the passage in its entirety and interprets it in a way that shows that he thinks it is directed against those who doubt (presumably, the Pharisees, who doubt Christ's miracle).[58] The pastor arrives at an entirely different reading of the passage, one that all but reverses the sense. First, he amputates the quotation so that it appears to imply that blindness is equivalent to lack of sin. Then he continues, "Le péché, c'est ce qui obscurcit l'âme, c'est ce qui s'oppose à sa joie" ("Sin is that which darkens the soul – which prevents its joy"). Here the pastor introduces a new concept – joy – that does not figure in the original. The purpose of his proposition, which does not follow from Christ's words, is to establish an opposition between sin and joy. The pastor's justification for considering his desire free from sin is that it brings him happiness; happiness, for him, becomes the goal relative to which every means is excused.[59]

The pastor continues, "Le parfait bonheur de Gertrude, qui rayonne de tout son être, vient de ce qu'elle ne connaît point le péché. Il n'y a en elle que de la clarté, de l'amour" ("Gertrude's perfect happiness, which shines forth from her whole being, comes from the fact that she does not know sin. There is nothing in her but light and love"). The biblical passage establishes what could be seen as a "natural" derivative connection between the literal and metaphoric senses of blindness and sight. Christ's miracle is to make the blind man see. The miracle stands for bringing the man to faith, for the man (unlike the Pharisees) says, "Lord, I believe" (John 9:38). Thus, literal blindness stands for spiritual blindness, and sight is a metaphor for spiritual illumination. The pastor juggles these relations, however, and arrives at exactly the opposite equation: Real blindness (represented by Gertrude) signifies spiritual light. Christ made the blind man see, but it is in the pastor's interest to keep Gertrude blind. "Is she not happy as she is?" (p. 208), he will ask, rhetorically. Blindness, the pastor has intimated thus far in his interpretation of Christ's words, is equivalent to lack of sin. Sin, he reasons, is opposed to joy. Now he can set up an equation between blindness and happiness. Gertrude's blindness makes her happy. The nefarious implication is that for Gertrude, sight, insight, and knowledge would destroy her happiness. Implicitly it would also destroy his own. The possibility that Gertrude could be operated on and gain her sight fills the pastor with dread.

The effect of the pastor's reinterpretation of the Bible is to put into question the binary system on which the first notebook was based and also the discreteness of the levels of truth and illusion. First, Gide makes us reconsider what we were initially willing to accept as a fixed relation between discourse and story by experimentally reversing the priority of reality over the text he sets up in the first notebook. At the same time he makes us question the value of recognizing the "truth" of the story of the first notebook. The pastor takes this "truth," which from a pastorly point of view must appear morally wrong, and modifies his principles to accommodate it. The truth of the first notebook becomes the illusion of the second.

Second, by proposing that the new standard of truth against which to measure delusion is a book (the Bible), Gide questions the idea of unmediated access to the "truth." As Jacques and the pastor's exchange of quotations shows, the Bible is not luminously and unambiguously clear in its interpretation; nor is it, as the pastor's reinterpretation shows, unsusceptible to distortion. The susceptibility of the pastor's text to interpretation in the first notebook – the power granted to the reader – makes the susceptibility of the Bible to interpretation all too credible. By the same measure, the reader must admit that his access to

the "true story" of the first notebook was based on an act of interpretation similar to the pastor's exegesis of the Bible. As in *Les Faux-
Monnayeurs,* Gide seems to be making the point that reality, or "the
truth," is available to us only through our representation – that it is, like
a text, subject to interpretation.

Gide questions the discreteness of the levels of truth and illusion in
another way as well in *La Symphonie pastorale.* In the second notebook,
when the narrative shifts into the present, the categories of discourse
and story begin to merge. Gide exploits the flexibility of the diary form
to juxtapose two different kinds of narration, retrospective and day-to-
day narration. In the retrospective part the pastor's self-justificatory
discourse merely has the status of a commentary on the past, so that
this discourse is subordinate to a set of events that has already taken
place. But in the day-to-day part his views take on the status of a
present event, and they also represent a taking of position that potentially will affect the future. By the end of the novella, far from simply
commenting on the story, the discourse, as the representative of the
pastor's passion, actually provokes the story. For the pastor's delusions
ultimately bring about the catastrophe of Gertrude's suicide.

Thus the structure of irony on which the first notebook was based – a
structure that depends on contrasting the reading of an event with a set
of assumptions that are incorrigible – is undermined. Not only the hierarchical relation but also the very separation into two discrete levels is
questioned. The irony of the novella takes on wider dimensions. It is
not just the irony of the pastor's self-deception. If it were, we would
see the path of this self-deception clearly traced against an unalterable
background. In the first notebook such a background gradually
emerges – the background of the correct reading of the pastor's motivations. In the second notebook irony itself, which depends on contrast,
is ironized. As in *Les Faux-Monnayeurs,* Gide shows that to assume that
there are "facts" in the context of human lives is to oversimplify. It is
not the "facts" themselves that are powerful but the passions and interests that generate them. These passions also influence our understanding or misunderstanding of "the facts": Like a text, a configuration of
events comes alive only at the moment of interpretation; and such an
interpretation is conditioned by interest and passion.

Thus in *La Symphonie pastorale* Gide attempts, by using the journal
form alone, to do something not unlike what he achieved with much
more elaborate means in *Les Faux-Monnayeurs.* In both texts he experiments with formal techniques for expressing the play between reality
and illusion. In *Les Faux-Monnayeurs* he lets two narrative forms, Edouard's journal and the third-person narrative, suggest pairs of contraries;
and he questions the validity of the oppositions by making the text

self-reflexive and leaving the status of its various parts undecidable. In *La Symphonie pastorale* he achieves a similar effect by creating a discrepancy between the narrator's discourse and his story. The flexible temporal structure of the journal enables him both to sustain the dualities and put them into question. In the first, retrospective notebook, an unacknowledged parti pris, which reveals itself in slips as well as in the actual choice of incidents and shaping of the narrative, makes clear that the narrator is blind to his own biography. In the second part the repressed voice, now acknowledged, speaks. But here Gide shifts to a periodic scheme of writing; events are related from day to day as they happen. The new, "true" voice cannot see into the future; it is blind to the catastrophe that its misinterpretations will provoke. The catastrophe reinstates the dualities in a revised or reflected form, but not before Gide has questioned them by reversing the order of priority between the discourse and the story and by allowing these categories, both of which are in fact generated by the pastor's passion, to merge. Reading (as well as speaking and writing) becomes the symbol for the interpenetration of levels. Once again Gide points to the power inherent in representation and interpretation. Whether "reality" is supposed to have priority over the text or the text priority over human conduct, it is in fact the pastor, the writer-reader, who seizes power. He distorts what he touches with his exegeses and attempts to create the world anew with his words.

15

Reliable Narration: Rainer Maria Rilke's *Die Aufzeichnungen des Malte Laurids Brigge*

In a period characterized by an interest in psychology, when novelists were attracted by the possibility of portraying characters' unconscious motivations and adopted techniques like unreliable narration to do so, it is interesting to find some diary novels that depart from the pattern. Such novels include not only works that use first-person discourse expressively in the mode of *Werther* but also such works as Rilke's *Die Aufzeichnungen des Malte Laurids Brigge* (1910), Elisabeth Janstein's *Die Kurve* (1920), and, later, Sartre's *La Nausée* (1938), a work that has often been compared to Rilke's novel.[60] These works shift away from portraying a psychologically conceived self. The protagonists' experiences, their writing, are not meant to reflect back on their own personalities. Rather, their experiences become exemplary; they take on a suprapersonal validity. What the writers seek is the expression of a vision – a vision that breaks through conventional patterns of perception and is thus also beyond the reach of everyday language, a vision of the indescribable, where no writing subject, first-person narrator or otherwise, is automatically privileged. The journals are meant as a mirror of things as they *really* are, with perceptual barriers removed.

Because the protagonists, in their exemplary function, are no longer writing strictly about themselves, the choice of first-person narration, of the diary, no longer has to do either with an assertion of privileged insight into the self or with implied self-deception. The diarist does not write "secretly," because he does not want anyone to know, but rather keeps a private journal, we can presume, because he thinks what he is writing is of interest only to himself. The protagonist's diary is thus not meant as a problematical statement of interiority, nor are emotive expressions of feeling, although they are present, of central importance. Instead, the choice of the first person appeals to the idea of poetic or prophetic vision. Within the conventions of this appeal the first-person voice establishes the writing's claim to authority; for a visionary's insights are authoritative only as long as they do not become common-place, accepted, and spoken by authorities. Rilke's Malte and Sartre's Roquentin, as lonely, alienated present-day city dwellers, show that prophetic vision is something still possible and accessible in the twenti-eth century.

Writing becomes superficially problematical in these novels, as is only natural in the age of language crisis; but it is not the central problem in the narrative. The language of the diary itself is not ques-tioned. It drifts toward the different truth claim of poetry. Roland Barthes writes in *Mythologies,* "Contemporary poetry is a *regressive semi-ological system.* . . . Poetry . . . attempts to regain an infra-signification, a pre-semiological state of language."[61] The changes that Malte and Roquentin believe are taking place are outside semiological communica-tion systems, and most particularly beyond the reach of "description" or "mastery by language"; but they can nevertheless be evoked by figurative language, by the leap of metaphor and the collisions of cat-achresis. However much these works explicitly cast doubt on the effi-cacy of language, implicitly they support a belief in the power of poetic language.

The purpose in this chapter will be to discuss Rilke's *Die Aufzeich-nungen des Malte Laurids Brigge* as an example of a novel that presents a vision, in order to show how Rilke goes about presenting it and, yet more important, what techniques he uses for establishing the authority of his protagonist's discourse. *La Nausée* could serve equally well as an example, but since its interpretation is relatively clear, with critics largely in agreement except on issues like the status of the end, it seems more profitable to concentrate here on Rilke's more complex, less explicit, less widely known work. It is worth noting that Sartre's principal technique for presenting his protagonist's vision, like Rilke's, involves metaphor. But Sartre's underlying presuppositions are differ-ent, and he therefore uses his technique to a different effect. Whereas Rilke engages the notion of a transcendent reality and suggests that things can be viewed in a new, truer relation, Sartre advances the yet more problematical hypothesis that we can see reality "naked," stripped of all the ordering fictions we have superimposed on it. Rilke's metaphors are designed to render manifest what is normally unperceived; they therefore yield crisp, particularizing images. Sartre's metaphors, in contrast, are meant to unveil the undifferentiated chaos of "existence," to show things "without their names." They thus tend to blur distinctions, to reduce things to amorphousness.

Die Aufzeichnungen des Malte Laurids Brigge is an autobiographical work, although Rilke insisted after he finished the novel in 1910 that he had separated himself from Malte and that Malte had become a character on his own.[62] Malte is Rilke's age when Rilke was in Paris (twenty-eight), and a number of the Paris incidents are Rilke's own, as documented by letters to Lou Andreas-Salomé in 1902 and Clara Rilke in 1907. Rilke, who had hitherto been a prolific and fast writer, always stressed how difficult, if not torturous, writing *Malte* had been for him. He started writing the novel in February 1904 in Rome, put it aside until the fall of 1908, and finished it in January 1910.[63] Later, he referred to it as "this difficult, difficult book,"[64] called it an "indescribable caesura" and a "watershed" in his life,[65] and was still complaining in 1915 that he was having trouble beginning anything new after it.[66]

Existing drafts of *Die Aufzeichnungen* show that before putting the novel in its final, notebook form, Rilke began it as a story narrated by a person who lived for a while with the central character, "der Schweigsame" ("the silent one"). He then revised this beginning, changing it into a third-person narrative in which Malte starts to reminisce to a friend in Paris, in front of a fire, about an incident in his childhood. Rilke's French translator, Maurice Betz, gives further information. Rilke told Betz that he began writing a series of dialogues between a young man and a girl; the young man speaks of a Danish poet, Malte, who lived in Paris and died young. Eventually, Rilke "interrupted the dialogue and began to write Malte's own diary."[67] According to Betz, the person of Sigbjørn Obstfelder had served as one of the inspirations for the character of Malte. Werner Kohlschmidt shows that there are numerous parallels between Rilke's techniques and Obstfelder's in his diary novel, *En præsts dagbog* (1900). It thus seems probable that Rilke was influenced in the choice of his form by Obstfelder.[68]

In a letter of April 11, 1910, to the Gräfin Manon zu Solms-Laubach, Rilke, wondering whether it will be possible for readers to reconstruct "a whole existence" out of Malte's papers, comments: "What the book comprises is, to be sure, nothing complete. It is as if one had found disordered papers in a drawer and simply didn't find any more for the moment and had to make do." This comment seems directed at explaining the inherent limitations (and possibilities) of the notebook form rather than at denying the existence of an artistic order in *Malte*. The work may seem unstructured on first reading, but it has an overt chronological structure (the fragments are ordered in the order in which they were written) as well as a more subtle structure of thematic associations. Ulrich Fülleborn, with reason, calls *Malte* a prose poem and finds that it is constructed according to the same principles as Rilke's lyric cycles.[69]

At the beginning of *Die Aufzeichnungen*, Malte tells us that he is beginning to change. The change has to do with the way he sees things,

with his vision, vision understood here as a metaphor both for understanding and for the creative "re-seeing" of the artist. Rilke's preoccupation with "Schauen" is familiar from *Ewald Tragy,* his essays on the
Worpswede artists and Rodin, poems in *Das Buch der Bilder,* especially
"Eingang," and the *Neue Gedichte.* Malte announces at the outset, "I am
learning to see."[70] Thereafter, he returns only occasionally to the topic
in an explicit fashion. What the narrative presents is not Malte's analysis
of the continuing process of his "learning to see" but, rather, evidence
that indicates that the process is continuing and that at the same time
illuminates the subject for the reader by taking it onto a higher, suprapersonal plane. The theme is present or latent in the oblique forms of
statement – metaphors, anecdotes, parables – that overshadow, increasingly, Malte's own story. It is one of the central themes of *Die Aufzeichnungen.* As we shall see, one of the central metaphors with which
Rilke illustrates the theme of vision is the mirror. One of my purposes
will be to show that Rilke also realizes this metaphor in actual techniques he uses in the novel. Mirroring, which is important for the
theme of artistic creation, also informs the novel's construction.

Seeing in *Malte* is closely connected to the question of self-
development and personal strength. In the first book of the novel,
which is devoted largely to reminiscences of childhood, Malte's lack
of strength is thematized. In the episode of Christine Brahe's ghost,
the first story in a series of Malte's recollections of childhood, Malte
succinctly formulates what will prove one of his chief terrors; it is
being reduced to "an empty place." This reduction of the self to
nothing is the result of insufficient personal strength. It has to do with
an incapacity to defend oneself against adverse circumstances, like ill-
nesses; to withstand impressions that threaten to flood the self from
without; or to control one's own runaway imagination, which magni-
fies these fears and risks interrupting the continuity of the self from
within. Repeatedly, Malte shudders at the idea that he might be invaded by a force so alarming and pernicious that it seems external,
like the "Big Thing" of his childhood, some thing that will disrespect
the boundaries of his self and turn him inside out, like the fever that
scatters his memories unceremoniously all over the bed. He is fascinated by other people who seem prone to the same kind of mischance;
he identifies, for example, with a man who has Saint Vitus's dance,
whom he sees twitching helplessly down the Boulevard St. Michel.
One of the functions of the theme of the "Fortgeworfene," or "beg-
gars," in Book I is to objectify for Malte his sense of his own spiritual
poverty.

Rilke often articulates the theme of helplessness, which is caused by the self's passivity, by using metaphors of vision that concern seeing versus being seen. In the terrifying mirror episode, for example, Malte, as a child, succumbs to a distorted mirror image of himself. In describing the power play, Rilke transforms visual reproduction into verbal domination. When Malte dons a costume and steps before the dim attic mirror, the mirror, which is made of green glass bits and thus gives a distorted image, is often reluctant to repeat ("did not want . . . to repeat promptly what had been said to it" [p. 91]). But on one occasion it takes advantage of young Malte's confusion to seize the upper hand suddenly and "dictate an image." In Kleist's well-known "Marionetten-theater" essay, the beautiful youth loses his grace before the mirror and becomes little more than the mirror image's mirror image. Here, the relation between the berobed, masked Malte and his mirror image is likewise reversed, but much more violently and abruptly. "Now the mirror was the stronger, and I was the mirror" (p. 95), Malte writes. Malte is obliterated: "I simply ceased to exist." The metaphor is realized concretely when Malte loses consciousness after a headlong dash down the attic stairs. Just as the Brahes' immense dining hall reduces Malte to an empty place, the mirror, an object, turns Malte, the passive human subject, into a mirror.

Malte the narrator, who is preoccupied with the right way to live, projects a punishment fantasy onto the childhood adventure. The mirror, normally docile and able only to repeat, revenges itself on Malte for not possessing the inner strength necessary to withstand the complete covering up of his surface. It becomes a malevolent eye that takes advantage of the falseness of Malte's image to falsify him completely. In the novel's terms artistic vision means seeing "Wirkliches" – penetrating to the essential nature of things rather than perceiving only their superficial appearance. The mirror parodies the young Malte's fatal fascination with appearances and wreaks the consequences of his shortcoming on him with a vengeance: Like a bad poet, the mirror seizes on Malte's garish outward appearance and obliterates his real essence.

In the second book, the theme of seeing and being seen modulates gradually into the theme of loving and being loved. Just as it is deadly to be seen, it is deadly to be loved, and conversely, the ability to love, like the ability to see, is an assertion of power. The only safe love is unrequited or "intransitive" love, and its only sure object is God, for "one need not fear that he will return one's love" (XI, 937). Beginning with the episode of Malte's father's death, where Malte observes that his father's pierced heart closed "like an eye," Rilke begins, ingeniously, to combine the metaphors of vision with the theme of love, to establish an equivalence between the heart and the eye. The loving heart is like a lamp that burns eternally: "To be loved means to be consumed.

To love is to give light with inexhaustible oil" (p. 209). A heart that loves is like an eye or refracting lens that can distort its object or cause a conflagration with its heat. Thus, Malte notes that Christ, with his love, stops many people on their way to loving God: "The lens of his vigorously refracting heart once again assembles their already parallel heart-rays" (p. 209).

The novel's final section, the parable of the Prodigal Son, brings together the themes of vision, love, and personal strength. In his re-telling, Rilke turns the biblical story of the father's compassion and forgiveness into an allegory of the son's triumphant transcendence of his family's love and his transformation into one capable of loving. Driven to leave home by the sheer necessity of escaping the oppressive love of his family, the son learns in his *Wanderjahre* how to love without consuming or harming his object. He finally begins "the long love to God, . . . that silent, aimless labor" (p. 214).

Rilke originally treated the theme of the Prodigal Son in a poem of 1906, "Der Auszug des verlorenen Sohnes" ("The Departure of the Prodigal Son"). In the poem, the metaphor of vision predominates. The son runs away from the false images of himself that surround him in his parental home, from a setting that "like the water in old wells,/mirrors us tremblingly and destroys the image." In the *Malte Laurids Brigge* version, the theme of vision is subordinate to the theme of love; it comes up only occasionally in an overt fashion, in the win-dow of the house that "fixed you in the eye" (XI, 940) and the dogs that look at one expectantly. The son's return, however, which be-comes the most significant part of the story, has implications for the theme of vision as well as for the theme of love. In the course of his patient love to God, who does not answer, the son acquires steadiness and "inward composure" (p. 215). His return shows that he has over-come the danger of being a passive object, whether of love or of vision. When he goes home, his family recognizes him, but he is able to withstand their love because he now has an identity that can no longer be altered by the gaze of others. He realizes that his family's love "had nothing to do with him" (p. 216).

The theme of gaining power, which is identified toward the end of the novel with love of God, is elaborated earlier in terms of vision as well. The concept of seeing, by which we can understand artistic vi-sion, is not simply the opposite of being seen, as loving is the opposite of being loved. Malte's references to vision and their implications be-come clearer if one considers the second, discarded beginning to *Malte*. In this earlier version, the episode of the appearance of Christine Brahe's ghost begins the book and it is given explicit significance by Malte: It is "the key . . . to all the future doors of my life" (XI, 951).

Malte explains that the episode contains a lesson, the most important lesson of his life, albeit one he has not yet mastered. This all-important lesson is "not to get up when they enter and pass by, the ones that actually should not come, the inexplicable ones" (XI, 952). He adds that his father managed this feat, though not as admirably as his grandfather. In the final version too, his grandfather, now specified as his maternal grandfather Brahe, is not even slightly disturbed by the ghost's entrance but can regard the apparition with equanimity. His father, in contrast, rushes out of the room. But later Malte's father manages to stay seated and lift his wineglass. "Staying seated" in the face of the otherworldly – maintaining one's composure, having the presence of mind to proceed with familiar actions – plainly involves a kind of personal strength.

Rilke introduces the motif of the mirror into this concept of power as well. Malte admires his delicate, wall-eyed little cousin Erik for his poise in the face of his dead ancestors. Erik manifests his strength by bringing a mirror to the family portrait gallery. Hoping to find a picture of Christine Brahe in the gallery (not the ghost herself!), Malte encounters Erik, who tells him her picture is not there. Portraiture betokens death; Erik himself dies soon after his portrait is painted. Because the ghost of Christine Brahe walks, her portrait is not in the gallery. Little Erik announces categorically: "Either one is there . . . and in that case one is not here: or one is here, and cannot be in there" (p. 103). But Erik has brought a mirror to the gallery, for as he says, "she wants to see herself" (p. 102). The ghost – the otherworldly, the invisible – wishes to see itself; and little Erik has the strength of mind to bring her a mirror.

In the final section of Book I, the description of the "La Dame à la Licorne" tapestries that Rilke had seen at the Cluny museum, Rilke returns to the theme of mirroring. The last tapestry, the concluding image of Book I, presumably has the greatest significance – even though Rilke probably did not rearrange the order of the tapestries, as critics have asserted.[71] The tapestry shows a "festival" without guests, and without expectations. It represents a scene of presence and completion ("es ist alles da"), and of eternity ("alles für immer"). The woman who figures in all the tapestries is seated, and the unicorn is on her lap. Rilke closes the description with these words: "It is a mirror, the thing she holds. See: she is showing the unicorn its image – " (p. 113).

The mirror here can be seen to represent artistic vision. It has the important connotation of *reproducing* the object; it makes visible what *is* there rather than what is not. If it gives a reversed or inverted picture, this is consonant with Rilke's suggestion, in a letter of 1910, that art is inversion. Rilke writes: "Art . . . is the most passionate inversion of the world, the path of return from the infinite, on which all honest things come toward one. Now one sees them in their entirety, their face approaches, their motions become perceptible in detail."[72] The mirror image in Rilke's conception is consistent with Rilke's theory of art that creation is a form of seeing, not imagining. Rilke, a supremely imaginative poet, did not have an exaggerated respect for invention. For him, the significant artistic act consisted in seeing what is there but is normally not perceived. In "Eingang" ("Prelude") (1900), the first poem in *Das Buch der Bilder,* the magical act by which the "Du" becomes a demigod consists in lifting and moving a tree, in extending the boundary of the comprehensible world before the transcendent and incomprehensible begins. The imaginative act consists in expanding the world (or multiplying its significances). It does not consist in inventing it; the tree is a natural object. It is revealing that in his monograph and other statements on Rodin, Rilke makes clear that he most admires Rodin for his "vision." He also consistently emphasizes that Rodin did not invent. He writes in the monograph, "He gave no room to his fantasy; he did not invent."[73]

Thus he who holds up a mirror captures what *is* there, not a fantasy of his own. Yet what the mirror reproduces in the tapestry in *Malte Laurids Brigge* is a mythical beast, a phenomenon no more real than Christine Brahe's ghost. It makes visible what the unicorn, as well as the other manifestations of the otherworldly in the novel, represents: What is there but is, to the normal and unpoetic eye, invisible. Holding up the mirror is a symbol of power, the power to which Malte aspires: the ability to see creatively, in other words, to see correctly, and yet to see beyond the constrictions of perception that has become automatic. The power of the artist, then, is the power not to become the one in the mirror (a symbol of weakness) but, rather, to make present, make visible, what others cannot see.

That artistic power consists for Malte in making visible what is normally invisible is documented by the sections on Ibsen and on Malte's maternal grandfather, Count Brahe.[74] In both sections, the visual metaphor is connected to the verbal arts. According to Malte, Ibsen's achievement was to search for "equivalents among the visible for the inwardly seen" (p. 76), to put on stage visible representations of minute psychic processes. As for Brahe, Malte tells us that he possessed the rare gift, which has died out in the present day, of being able to tell stories. He dictates his memoirs to Abelone. Impatient at her inability to spell a name (which suggests to him an attenuation of the vivid image he sees before him), he cries: "Will they *see* at all, what I am saying?" (p. 132). Later he demands of Abelone whether she sees the figure he is describing, and she remembers "that she had seen him." Malte tells us that the count himself disregards such conventional temporal distinctions as those between past, present, and future, and simply regards everything as present, including his long-dead relatives. The count's childhood, Malte says, lay before his inward eye "as in a clear northern summer night" (p. 131).

Both Ibsen and Brahe can be considered as Malte's models. This conclusion is supported explicitly by Rilke's statements in a letter of November 10, 1925, to his Polish translator, Witold Hulewicz:

> Just as Ibsen, for example (let's say Ibsen, for who knows whether he really felt that way . . . ?), just as a dramatist of yesterday searches for visible proofs for the event that has become invisible in us, the young M. L. Brigge also feels the need to make graspable for himself, by means of appearances and images, a life that continuously withdraws into the invisible.

He adds, "Malte is not for nothing the grandchild of old Count Brahe, who held everything, past things like future things, simply to be 'present.'" Malte's tendency in Book II to retell historical legends and thereby to make the past present shows that he is following in the footsteps of Count Brahe.

Does Malte himself succeed? This question might be examined from two different points of view: that of Malte as a character in the novel, and that of Malte as the narrator of *Die Aufzeichnungen*. As a character, Malte in a sense sees clearly from the outset, as his marvelous images testify; but he lacks the strength necessary to remain steadfast in the face of his vision. While his imposing grandfather Brahe disregarded temporal discontinuity and thought of death as "a trifling incident which he utterly ignored" (p. 35), Malte himself is afraid of discontinuity and terrified of the final and inevitable break, death. He expresses his terror in the description of a man he sees dying in a *crémerie;* with horror, he sees the world, the world of familiar objects surrounding him, become unintelligible to the dying man. After this episode, Malte begins to think about possible forms of continuity. He considers the continuity implicit in the blood of a family, in the successive generations of his noble line; but he rejects this form of continuity as a personal solution. When his father's heart is pierced and the wound closes like an eye, Malte concludes that the line of the Brigges has ended. A certain traditional view of things, handed from father to son, is no longer possible. Malte comes to prefer continuity in his own lived experience, memory, as a solution. It is perhaps for this reason that he begins telling stories of his own childhood. According to Malte, the memories that constitute our strength are those that we have forgotten and return to us, those that are transformed into our experience and become part of us. They represent a concentrated fullness that cannot easily be dispersed by some momentary uneasiness that lays bare an "empty place." It is only from such experience ("Erfahrung") that poetry can be written: "Not till they have turned to blood within us, to glance and gesture, nameless and no longer to be distinguished from ourselves – not till then can it happen that in a most rare hour the first word of a verse arises in their midst and goes forth from them" (p. 27).

The overt turning point in Malte's quest to attain strength comes with the episode of the blind newspaper seller. It is the only episode in the second book, aside from the story of the medical student, where Malte, who has become more and more absorbed in retelling historical legends, returns to his own experiences in Paris. Formerly, Malte had hurried by this blind newspaper seller, not wanting to look at him. Rather than look at him, he tried to imagine him: "I was busy picturing him to myself; I undertook the task of imagining him" (p. 177). On this occasion, however, he really looks at him: "I determined to intimidate and suppress the increasing skill of my imagination through the external reality" (p. 178).

It is extremely significant that the man is blind. As we have seen, to invite another to return one's gaze, to demand recognition from others and verification of one's own self from one's surroundings, is a sign of weakness. "Mirroring" in the eyes of others can reinforce, but also profoundly alter or even obliterate the self. Malte is most terrified by people who cannot look back at him at all, because they seem to inhabit another reality. They seem to testify both to the existence of that other reality, and to the nonexistence of Malte's. Malte writes of the dying man in the *crémerie*, for example, "a moment more and everything will have lost its meaning, and that table and the cup, and the chair to which he clings, all the near and the commonplace, will have become unintelligible, strange and heavy" (p. 51). Malte's reaction to this man is the same as his father's the first time Christine Brahe's ghost appears – he rushes out of the room.

A blind man is the epitome of someone who cannot return the viewer's gaze, and it is perhaps on this account that the blind newspaper seller is a particular object of terror for Malte. Malte's achievement, seeing the blind man rather than imagining him, becomes more significant when one uncovers the hidden reference: Looking at a blind man is like looking at God. The references to the divinity in the episode of the blind newspaper seller begin when Malte tries to imagine the blind man. He writes:

> I had to make him as one does a dead man, of whom there remain no proofs, no components; who has to be achieved entirely inwardly. I know now that it helped me a little to think of those many demounted

> Christs of striated ivory that lie about in every antiquary's shop. The thought of some Pieta came and went. [p. 177]

Malte, then, tries to imagine someone who is as if long since dead, whose former existence only shabby old replicas recall. When Malte finally looks at the blind man, the Christian references continue: "It must have been a Sunday" (p. 178), and there is a church, a garden, and "almost Roman" alleys. The conclusion of the episode makes the parallel between the blind man and God clearer still. Malte begins with a play on words; he writes, "My God, it struck me with vehemence, so indeed you *are*" (p. 179). One tends to read "mein Gott" initially as an ejaculation, but later it seems more like an apostrophe. Thus the blind newspaper seller, whom Malte compares to a "Zeiger," or pointer, a hand of a clock face, is a figure for God: not the old God, who is dead and for whom no more proofs exist, but a God who is inherent in present-day reality, who manifests his goodness in details like the blind man's new hat and Sunday tie.[75] By looking at the blind man, Malte finally discerns a positive moment in the seamy, repulsive, ominous side of Parisian reality and acknowledges by the same measure a transcendent reality. He holds – to apply the specular metaphor – a mirror up to God.

Malte is a poet, and one of the central themes of *Die Aufzeichnungen* is artistic vision. The self-referential nature of the novel suggests that the question of vision be examined not only from the standpoint of the main character but also from the standpoint of Rilke's achievement in the work. Several critics have evaluated the novel in the terms it itself sets up, taking the artistic achievement of *Die Aufzeichnungen* as evidence for Malte's success or failure as a poet.[76] I too would like to consider Malte's (or Rilke's) achievement in its own terms, by examining, specifically, the realization of the mirror metaphor as a figure for artistic creation in techniques Rilke uses for the novel. The question of Malte's success is now whether he, as an artist, succeeds in "making visible the invisible," and if so, how? My purpose is not primarily to judge Malte's own success or failure as a poet but to show how Rilke's metaphor, and the techniques he uses to realize it, affect our reading of the novel and, more generally, to assess their relevance for a theory of first-person narrative.

The mirror, conceived as Malte conceives it – as the mirror held up to the invisible – can be seen to stand for a turn from a descriptive or referential mode of representation to a metaphoric or figurative mode. As we have seen, Malte's mirror image is precisely *not* the mirror image of realism. It is also not a mere insubstantial copy of an object that is in itself substantial. Instead, in Rilke's concept, a dialectic interchange takes place between the mirror image and the mirrored object. An object takes on reality only as an object of perception, only inasmuch as it is visible or capable of being represented, and a representation, such as a mirror image, testifies to the object's reality. It is in this sense that the mirror comes to stand for artistic power in *Malte*. With its central theme of vision, and also in the poetic techniques Rilke employs, *Die Aufzeichnungen des Malte Laurids Brigge* stands closest to the poem cycles Rilke wrote in roughly the same period, from 1903 to 1908, the *Neue Gedichte* and the *Neue Gedichte, Anderer Teil*. The mirror motif emerges prominently for the first time in his writings in a group of poems written in 1907–8. The idea in these poems – "Quai du Rosaire," "Dame vor dem Spiegel" ("Lady Before the Mirror"), "Venezianischer Morgen" ("Venetian Morning") – is that an exchange takes place between a real object or scene and its mirror image. "Reality" or importance is displaced onto the mirror image, but the mirror image returns its strength to the mirrored object and enriches it. This exchange between the real and the imaginary is sometimes seen as an erotic encounter that culminates, or would logically culminate, in the fusion of the mirror image with the object. In "Dame vor dem Spiegel," for instance, the woman drinks from her image: "She drinks what a lover would drink in his transport."[77]

The idea of an erotic encounter between the real and the imaginary allows Rilke to develop a kind of metaphor that I shall call a narrative conceit. A poem presents a sequence of events in such a way that point for point a second sequence of events, involving a different subject, is suggested. For example, in "Dame vor dem Spiegel" the overt subject is a woman who is dressing (or undressing) in the evening in front of a mirror. The poem suggests, however, that the woman brews and drinks a potion. In "Die Flamingos" ("The Flamingos") the same technique is employed even more daringly. Overtly, Rilke describes flamingos as they emerge from the water, stand on the grass, and, disturbed by noise from the aviary, stalk off. But this sequence is set in the terms of an autoerotic and voyeuristic fantasy. The fantasy, difficult to ascribe to the birds themselves, can be naturalized by referring it to the human beings who figure in a comparison in the first stanza, to the "you" and the man who speaks of his girl friend. By using such words as "blühend" ("blooming"), "Beet" ("bed"), "Weiche" ("softness," "groin"), and "Neid" ("envy") to describe the birds – words that suggest a human erotic context and a woman, Rilke implies a sequence that involves the girl friend as an erotic object. The overt subject and the object of comparison, the flamingos and the human lovers, are "mirrors" of each other; they interact so that our perception of both is put into a new light.

Rilke uses a similar, narrative technique of metaphor in *Malte*. Whereas in the poems the actual subject is usually placed in the foreground and the object of comparison presented through allusion, in *Malte*, Rilke tends to suppress the actual subject of the comparison, which is often an abstract idea, and to let only the vehicle figure in the episode. The metaphors set in motion a dialectical interaction between an unnamed idea, which nevertheless informs the whole sequence of images, and represented events in such a way that the idea figures as the absent subject of the metaphor. Particularly where the unnamed subject is an abstract idea, the result tends to border on allegory, but even here an allegorical reading would do injustice to the richness and surrealistic quality of the imagery. Rilke shifts the emphasis too energetically from the subject onto the vehicle, which takes on a life of its own. For example, in the episode of the woman who loses her face, Rilke starts with the familiar metaphor of the mask for social role or identity, but suppresses the "proper" concept and substitutes the word "face" for mask. He begins, "There are quantities of human beings, but there are many more faces, for each person has several" (p. 15). Everything that is subsequently said about faces reflects back on the unnamed subject, social roles, or on the ability to change one's outward personality. Rilke finishes:

> But the woman, the woman; she had completely collapsed into herself, forward into her hands. . . .
> The woman startled and pulled away too quickly out of herself, too violently, so that her face remained in her two hands. I could see it lying in them, its hollow form. It cost me indescribable effort to stay with those hands and not to look at what had torn itself out of them. I shuddered to see a face from the inside, but still I was much more afraid of the naked flayed head without a face. [p. 16]

One could say that the concluding scene shows how a person can be startled into "dropping her mask" – but it would do injustice to the terror inspired by the image of the woman's face coming off in her hands, and leaving a head without a face, to consider it merely a further commentary on identity and role. Rilke's image is too extravagant to be reduced to allegory.

The technique of narrative metaphor with a suppressed subject is not only used in *Die Aufzeichnungen* as a method for commenting, in semi-allegorical fashion, on abstract concepts. It is also often used to "objectify" psychic states. Examples include Malte's two fevers, the fever that renders small objects around him dangerous and the childhood fever that forces things out of him that he cannot cram back in (pp. 60–1, 86). Fear is objectified in the episode of the self chased by the heart: "Your heart drives you out of yourself, your heart pursues you, and you stand almost outside yourself and cannot get back again" (p. 69). Anxious apathy is suggested by the dining hall at Urnekloster that sucks all the images out of the young Malte and leaves him empty (p. 31). The dilapidated wall of the torn-down house that so terrifies Malte because he "recognizes" it (pp. 46–8) is clearly a mirror of Malte's own spiritual poverty, and his consequent susceptibility to being invaded or permeated by outside forces. In the case of psychic states, the implication is that there *is* no proper expression. Here the narrative metaphor functions as a kind of catachresis.

As we have seen in the examples from the *Neue Gedichte*, "Dame vor dem Spiegel" and "Die Flamingos," this metaphoric technique can be used in a *narrative* context involving a sequence of events. A radical step would be to let one sequence of events substitute fully for another, as an extended catachresis for a transcendent subject. Alternately, a single subject can be illuminated through a series of such vehicles, as if a series of "mirrors" were held up to an object. This concept of metaphoric mirroring is more satisfactory for elucidating Rilke's technique in *Malte* than the concept of leitmotif, for the idea of leitmotif does not imply the interaction that is prominent in any conception of metaphor.[78] Thus in *Malte*, the topic of making visible the invisible is illuminated by a number of triumphant figures: Erik, the woman in the tapestry, Ibsen, Malte's grandfather Brahe. The theme of being controlled by a strange and pernicious force within oneself appears in the stories of the "Big Thing," the man with Saint Vitus's dance, and Charles the Bold's unruly blood. The question of identity and role is adumbrated by the house without a facade, the woman without a face, and the story of Charles the Bold, whose cheek was torn off by the ice. The subject of leaving home or breaking with tradition and expectations is reflected in a number of stories: Malte's own, the account of the young girls in the museum, and the parable of the Prodigal Son, which is a mirror of many of the book's themes and stories.

One could also assert that Rilke expands the technique into one that informs the whole narrative. *Malte* is a first-person narrative that is structured like a metaphor—where Malte himself, the first-person narrator, figures as the "absent" subject of his book or, more precisely, as the "unnamed" subject of metaphor. In the second version of the beginning of *Malte*, Rilke indicates that Malte is an exemplary character by making him, so to speak, the vehicle of a metaphor that points to absent lives. The narrator sees many faces in Malte's face; when he sees Malte's face illuminated by the flickering flames of a fire,

> It was shown to him what possibilities lay in this face: the masks of many great and peculiar destinies stepped out of its forms and sank

back again into the depths of an unknown life. There were traits of splendor and circumstance in these masks, but in the unfinished and quick change of their expression, hard, closed, refusing lines also appeared. [XI, 952–3]

In the final version of *Malte,* subject and vehicle are reversed. The "great and peculiar destinies" are present and step in front of an account of Malte himself, which is submerged. But they reflect back on Malte himself and his concerns. The result is a situation of figural dialectic, where there is no clear subject.

Rilke explained to his Polish translator, Hulewicz, that the historical figures Malte treats in the second part of the book should be understood not for their own sakes but as "vocables of his distress."[79] It is significant that the themes of strength and weakness occur more and more often in the retellings of historical legends. Immediately after Malte, in an explicit reversal, comes to a different and more positive formulation about death – death, which seems so incomprehensible and so completely against us, might be "*our own* force, all our own force that is still too great for us" (p. 145) – he tells a story of strength in the face of death: The poet Felix Arvers, who "hated the approximate," postponed dying in order to correct a nun's mispronunciation. The Nikolai Kusmitsch story is a burlesque, a parody of weakness in the face of reality. In the story of the weak-willed student whose eyelid keeps dropping shut, Malte helps by offering his own will. The solitary who achieves self-containment despite the taunts and temptations of the world clearly mirrors Malte. The tale of Grisha Otrepjow, the false tsar, tells of a man who had the will and the strength to become what he wanted, while the complementary tale of Charles the Bold is about succumbing to a greater force. Finally, Malte speaks of Venice, the city that exists by force of will.

Rilke's technique of metaphoric mirroring allows us to reassess his use of the notebook form in *Die Aufzeichnungen.* At first glance the novel violates the convention of "naturalness" we have come to associate with the diary novel. It strikes us as artificial and literary, both in the poetic texture of the writing and because of the frequent disconnectedness or independence of the fragments from their context. Rilke seemingly chose the diary form for its formal proximity to the prose poem cycle; he appears to waver between the two genres, striking an uneasy compromise between separate sketches and the portrait of an eccentric character. But once we have recognized that the "notes" represent variations on mutually mirroring themes and are presented in the chronological sequence of Malte's composition, the sense behind Rilke's fusion of prose poem and diary becomes clearer. For the presence of a character – the author of a "diary" – grounds the relatedness of the themes, while the progression of and within the themes in turn reveals the character. Malte's subjectivity is the focal point that draws the separate sketches into relation. If we are inclined to accept and even to seek out a connectedness between seemingly disparate subjects, it is because all of them are presented as products of a single imagination, which, presumably, projects its own coherence onto the objects of its interest. Malte's fragmentary writings can, in turn, be read as moments of insight in his quest for a greater coherence. Thus the fusion of genres, prose poem and diary, suggests to the reader a process of conversion by which Rilke's most far-flung subjects are the expression of Malte's deepest and most personal subjectivity, while the progressive choice of subjects bears witness to Malte's personal progress as a character and even as a poet. Rilke's "digressions" testify to Malte's ability to draw into relation increasingly remote areas of experience. The final entry, the parable of the Prodigal Son, can be, and often has been, taken as a kind of oblique summary of Malte's progress thus far that indicates the point he has reached at the termination of *Die Aufzeichnungen*. The parable tells as a literal story of departure, voyage, and return what Malte accomplishes psychically: As the Prodigal Son goes back to "redo" his childhood, for example, Malte recalls to memory his own.[80]

But Rilke's oblique, metaphorical technique could also be interpreted in terms of the authority Malte wins as a first-person narrator. The exemplary quality of Malte's experiences, the "guarantee" of the truth of his visions, hinges on the metaphor of the mirror. Malte gains authority as a first-person narrator by turning from self-description to oblique self-presentation, and from referential to figurative language. He derives his authority from the implicit ability to hold up the mirror away from himself—to show the invisible its face. In doing so he turns the mirror of representation away from the self. The questionable enterprise of self-objectification is done away with. There is a striking absence of anything resembling self-portraiture in *Malte*. When Malte does talk about himself, for example, his childhood, he describes universal experience. He tends to use the impersonal *man*, not *ich*, in such passages (e.g., in the description of birthdays [pp. 128–9]). Moods are generally evoked through "objective correlatives." Malte's excitement at unrolling his mother's laces is an example of an experience many children share, and it is made yet more accessible through the comparison of these laces to landscapes.

In conclusion we can say that Rilke replaces the dialectic between the portraitist and his portrait, which is destined to fail, with a successful dialectic between the subject and the vehicle of metaphor. Instead of establishing a relation between an original and a copy, he initiates a quest for a subject whose attainment is constantly deferred.

Malte's anecdotes, his stories of absent lives, are like a series of mirrors that reflect back on himself. These reflecting anecdotes do not entangle Malte in criteria of consistency and completeness. Rather, they suggest expansion, diffusion, a halo of significations, the infinite reflections of facing mirrors. Metaphor in this expanded sense is one of the techniques Rilke uses to lend credibility to his narrator's discourse, engage our sympathy for his self-presentation, and suggest to us a nonpsychological reading of the text. The whole narrative could be conceived as a catachresis for the self, for which there exists no proper expression. It could also be seen, with its mutually reflecting themes, as a hall of mirrors.

Women Writers

Around the turn of the century a number of diary novels with women protagonists were written by women novelists. Female diarists are, of course, not new in the history of the diary novel; inasmuch as diary fiction is a direct descendant of epistolary fiction, it could rather be said that heroines have been prominent since the genre's beginnings. Richardson established patterns that the transitional letter-journal novels adopted and the sentimental nineteenth-century diary novels continued. But the prevalence of women in diary fiction around 1900 reflects contemporary diary-keeping customs more directly than it relates to this tradition. Around the turn of the century, diary keeping became more and more of a commonplace activity for middle-class women.

Women were encouraged to keep journals for wholly traditional reasons, which go back to diary keeping as a religious exercise and have little to do with the sophisticated, "modern" view of the diary that the publication of such intimate journals as Amiel's inspired. The middle-class woman with time on her hands can console and amuse herself by keeping a diary, and confiding in a diary offers a prudent substitute for potentially dangerous confidences made to a friend. Diary keeping is the modern form of the Catholic confessional and Protestant self-scrutiny. Reflection can only improve, not hurt, a woman; the idea, which recurred in contemporary fiction involving men, that diary keeping might be pernicious, is alluded to only infrequently and not taken seriously. The statement of motivation found in Marcelle Tinayre's *Madeleine au miroir* (1912) is typical for early-twentieth-century women's diary fiction and illustrates why a woman of the period might decide to write a diary: "To fix the reflections of life that pass through the mirror of my woman's thought, to collect impressions, opinions, images – is it not an excellent remedy for boredom, a diversion from annoyance, a useful examination of conscience?"[81]

The most interesting of these novels are those that take women's problems as their specific focus. Nearly all such novels were written in German. One can seek the reasons in the contemporaneous late flowering of the German women's rights movement. In the 1890s German feminists intensified their efforts to gain recognition for the problems of women; the Bund Deutscher Frauenvereine (Federation of German Women's Associations), founded in 1894, began under the leadership of the radical Verein Frauenwohl to campaign for goals like the abolition of prostitution and finally for female suffrage.[82] At the same time, women authors began to write novels that explored women's problems. There is an evident connection between the advent of political feminism in Germany and the so-called *Frauenroman* movement. In the 1890s writers like Gabriele Reuter, Helene Böhlau, and Klara Viebig began to write novels that treated such questions as young girls' struggles against their parental home, women's independence and careers, and unwanted pregnancy.[83]

The women's novels written in diary form appear not to have been influenced by the few women's intimate journals that had appeared in print. The most widely read intimate journal written by a woman was Marie Bashkirtseff's *Journal* (1887; translated into German 1897), which tells the story of an emancipated woman, a precocious, self-fascinated, extremely ambitious young Russian artist who took painting lessons in Paris and died of tuberculosis at the age of twenty-three. But Bashkirtseff, a noblewoman and rich, was not a victim of society; rather, she was a victim of failing health and a narcissistic ambition that exceeded her genius. The work does not have a feminist message, although in the last year of her life Marie Bashkirtseff reflects on what being female meant for her career: "Born a woman, I exhausted my energy in tirades against fate, and eccentricities."[84]

The diary novels written by women around the turn of the century also bear very little resemblance to the attempts of contemporary male authors to represent the female psyche in fictional diaries, such as the diary fiction of Marcel Prévost or Peter Nansen. Peter Nansen's *The Diary of Julie* (1893), for example, the story of the nineteen-year-old daughter of a Copenhagen professor, is an excellent psychological portrait of a bored and self-possessed though naïve young girl, but it nevertheless relies on contemporary clichés about women. Julie starts the affair because she longs for a "strong hand"; she sets out merely to have a fling but of course falls in love with her dishonorably intentioned lover and finally wants to marry him. Marcel Prévost, whose main theme was feminine psychology, wrote a number of diary novels with women protagonists; in these works too we find a sensitive representation of women's problems, but despite Prévost's growing feminist leanings the novels tend to be reactionary in their message.[85] Thus one of the better novels, *Le Jardin secret* (1897), the diary of a married woman of about forty who discovers that her husband is leading a double life, shows a revolution, or more precisely a counterrevolution, in the heroine's attitude: At first she thinks of Ibsen, George Sand, and her own girlhood aspirations to become a poet, and she considers getting a divorce. Then she repenetrates her own hidden life and finds that it is in desire if not in practice a mirror of her husband's. Even an imperfect marriage is better than solitude, she decides; she will try to preserve her own marriage even if it means closing her eyes to her husband's infidelities. Her final solution is to try to perfect herself as a wife rather than reform her husband.

What the German women's diary novels written around the turn of the century have in common is an interest in the problems of women in a society that overlooks their needs, resists their ambitions, and severely restricts their opportunities. Like the male heroes of diary novels written in the same period, the women are discontented, but their problems are political, in the widest sense, rather than existential. We are shown young women's hopes, expectations, and desires, and are told how reality fails to live up to them. The central themes are the "women's problems" of marriage, divorce, pregnancy, and prostitution, as well as the question of education and careers for women. Whether a novel has an explicitly feminist message or not, whether the heroine is an articulate advocate of women's rights or an overburdened housewife, the authors always raise the larger questions of women's opportunities and women's roles.

In the eighteenth-century letter journals and in women's diary fiction written in the first half of the nineteenth century, heroines of conventionally virtuous character were called on to respond to bizarre turns of fate. In the women's diary novels written around 1900, in contrast, women of distinct personality and imagination find themselves in stock situations. The authors show how the personality and promise of a complex heroine run aground on her drearily predictable story. We see women in the same typical situations, for which their intelligence, originality, and resourcefulness prove no match. First, there is the married woman, who manages to stay within the framework of bourgeois society only at the price of conformism and subservience and who, perpetually under her husband's heel, suffers intellectual and spiritual deprivation. Second, there is the divorced woman, a social outcast. Third, there is the liberated single woman, the artist or student who has broken with conventions; this type is usually presented as the most enviable female model. Finally, there is the woman who, forced to earn a living, does not enjoy bourgeois security in any of its forms; she is a prostitute or – what amounts to approximately the same thing – a struggling actress. If the heroine represents one type, the others are usually introduced as minor characters.

In his novel *Wunschloses Unglück* (*A Sorrow Beyond Dreams,* 1972), a biography of his mother, Peter Handke considers the difficulty of writing about women's lives and decides to write about his mother by juxtaposing "formulas," applicable to all women's lives, to "descriptions" of his mother's life in its particularity. He writes: "I compare, sentence by sentence, the stock of formulas applicable to the biography of women with my mother's particular life; the actual work of writing follows from the agreements and contradictions between them."[86] For women writers in the late nineteenth and early twentieth centuries, the diary form offered a solution for juxtaposing the formulaic with the particular, for showing the impact of formulaic situations and stock catastrophes on a heroine's sensibilities. The plot is the formula, while the reactions the heroine records in her diary are the individual part of her story.

Elsa Asenijeff's *Tagebuchblätter einer Emancipierten* (1902) is an explicitly feminist work. The diarist is a twenty-six-year-old woman who has reflected on the issue of women's place in society and has well-formulated feminist views. At the beginning of the novel she has already broken with bourgeois society. She is divorced: "Am I ever glad that I'm finally divorced – whew!"[87] she writes. She scorns the idea of remarriage and has taken the symbolically progressive step of enrolling as a student at the university.[88] The diarist thinks that the norms and institutions of contemporary bourgeois society, in particular marriage, deprive women of all intellectual freedom and systematically obstruct their chances for self-realization. She programatically condemns the male-oriented social structure she lives in and women's traditional subordinate role in it, and calls for revolt: "Either-or. Either we stay the way we've been – nothing but the exciters of man – that give him joy and suffering. Or – we get rid of all that and look for what is really in the depths of our nature."[89] The diarist's aim, then, is not to encourage women to aspire to traditional male roles. Instead she believes with many feminists of her day that women are fundamentally different from men; what is imperative is their intellectual liberation and their self-discovery as women. Her diary purports to be a record of her own search for herself, but it is in fact an indictment of the society that causes such a search inevitably to fail.

The diarist uses the diary chiefly to express her views and to comment on the stories of other characters. Women trapped in miserable marriages and women whose grand passions are disintegrating into banality provide fuel for her fire. Very little happens to the diarist herself, and she undergoes little or no psychological development; her problems at the end are exactly the same as they were at the beginning and in the middle of her record. The novel's plotless, analytical and self-analytical mode makes it a feminist counterpart to novels like Rod's *La Course à la mort* or Garborg's *Trætte mænd*. The diarist's values in fact belie her contention that women are essentially different from men. Precisely like the male malcontents, Asenijeff's diarist is disgusted by the banality and falsehood of society; she finds that everyday life lacks the stuff of greatness; she responds to the deficiencies in her environment with typical turn-of-the-century ennui; she even wonders whether overconsciousness, the curse of the tired generation, is not at fault in preventing her from having "real experiences" and achieving inner harmony. She longs for a grand passion; she dreams of perfect communication with a kindred spirit of the opposite sex. But she perceives a suffocating social tradition and male stereotypes of women to be the main obstacles that prevent her from achieving her goals. Men, she insists, see women either as wives and mothers or as objects of sexual conquest. Her one attempt to achieve the kind of perfect relationship she desires is frustrated because the man who is the object of her strictly Platonic affections boasts to other men of having conquered her. To her great bitterness, she finds no way of retaliating; a lawyer laughs at her when she asks about pressing charges.

Gabriele Reuter's *Ellen von der Weiden* (1900) is a more successful novel, in which the social and feminist criticism is suggested rather than explicitly articulated. Reuter, an established writer who was labeled a feminist after the appearance of her first successful novel, *Aus guter Familie* (1895), addresses herself to the problems a woman has during and after her marriage. The diarist is an artist's daughter, a spirited, intelligent, forthright young woman who finds herself increasingly bored and restricted by her marriage to a complacent, authoritarian Berlin doctor. Her diary serves at once as an outlet for her complaints and for her sincere and repeatedly reiterated resolve to conform to her husband's wishes. Passionate, enthusiastic, and temperamental, she falls in love with a painter whose brilliance and sensitivity compare favorably with her husband's stuffiness. Too honest, or too naïve, to hide her attraction, she declares her love to her husband, even though she has nothing but a few kisses on a walk one night to confess. The consequences are disastrous: Her husband insists that she break off all communication with her admirer. She complies, but her husband's mood blackens as time passes; he suspects the child she is pregnant with might not be his own and finally demands a divorce in which she will accept the guilt. She acquiesces and suffers "disgrace," with the inevitable loss of social status. Still in love with the artist, who fails to contact her, pregnant by her husband, whom she does not love, she falls into a state of depression and apathy.

The novel's message, that there is no place for an intelligent woman in contemporary society, emerges in the juxtaposition of the inexorable curve of the plot, which shows how social realities determine the heroine's fate, with Ellen's zigzagging emotions and reactions. Ellen is not given to theorizing, and she herself does not articulate what is typical about her story, much less espouse any particular feminist platform. She does not see her fate politically or think in terms of rights or reforms, but rather remains essentially bourgeois in her attitudes and values. She rejects the idea of getting together with other divorced women, for example, and finds a personal solution to her problems in her love for her child. She expresses her views and feelings, which are often inconsistent, but invariably insightful and honest, rather than analyzing or propounding them. Gabriele Reuter lets minor characters, like Ellen's father, articulate the truisms that have made Ellen a victim: Women are dependent on men for their social status; since they are valued for their youth and beauty, they often marry prematurely; once married, they are obligated to make radical compromises in their personal freedom and adopt an attitude of docility, while their husbands, under no comparable pressure to please their spouses, lack any similar incentive to limit their egotistical demands. Unlike a man, a woman cannot afford to cede to a moment of passion without serious consequences. In society's view, it is the woman's responsibility to preserve the marriage. If the marriage ends in divorce, it is inevitably the woman who suffers.

Margarete Böhme's *Tagebuch einer Verlorenen* (1905), the diary of a prostitute, was one of the best-selling diary novels ever published. By 1917 it had gone into 330 printings. In 1929, Georg Wilhelm Pabst made a movie of it. To judge from the many similar *Tagebuch* titles published in the years directly following – *Tagebuch einer anderen Verlorenen* (1906), *Das Tagebuch eines Glücklich-Verheirateten* (1906), *Aus dem Tagebuch einer Sünderin* (1906), *Aus dem Tagebuch eines Schwachen* (1907), *Tagebuch einer männlichen Braut* (1907), *Tagebuch eines Modells* (1907), to name but a few – it started a fashion for diary fiction with an erotic slant, whose other early model was Octave Mirbeau's *Le Journal d'une femme de chambre* (1900), the diary of a snobbish, gossipy, resentful Parisian domestic who writes a backstairs exposé of her bourgeois employers.

The heroine of *Tagebuch einer Verlorenen,* Thymian, is a bourgeois girl who "falls" by becoming an unwed mother at age fifteen. If the book was immediately popular, it is probably because it combined two subjects: the first, the piquant subject of prostitution and female sexuality, which was politically fashionable at precisely that time because of efforts made by the umbrella organization for women's rights groups, the Federation of German Women's Associations, to abolish legalized prostitution; the second, a similarly fashionable indictment of bourgeois morality and the double standard. The novel is a case study with a realistic plot, authentic milieus, and a lively style. The author insists on the fiction of the "authentic document": She alleges that a real prostitute gave her the diary to publish. This fiction is not at all implausible; the work could almost be taken for a real diary except at the end, when Thymian falls into the cliché role of the "noble prostitute." Thymian's style, for example, becomes slangier and slangier as she slides more and more deeply into prostitution.

The work's message is that as present-day society is constituted, a girl who becomes an unwed mother, though through no fault of her own, has only three options for her life: an unpleasant, degrading marriage to the seducer; spinsterhood; or life as a courtesan. If she chooses the latter, like Thymian, she will never be able to return to bourgeois society. But the life of the "honest woman" who marries is not enviable either; Thymian's father philanders while his wife is dying of tuberculosis. In bourgeois society the woman is always a victim. Thymian notes, "The world belongs to men; we women are only tolerated means to an end."[90] Thymian decides she would rather die than marry the servant who seduced her. She is sent to a reform institution after giving birth to her child, which is given up for adoption against her will, but after considerable deliberation about the choices open to her, she runs away and becomes a demimondaine. She becomes the mistress of a man who supports her; when this situation falls apart she moves to Berlin and establishes herself as a "language teacher," or, in other words, as a prostitute. She makes many attempts to return and become an honest woman – when she comes into an inheritance, she begins doing good deeds, helping former friends and poor people – but she cannot reinstate herself in society, for every time she emerges from her withdrawal someone recognizes her as a former prostitute. No "decent people" want to associate with her. She becomes increasingly lonely, depressed, and suicidal. Her psychological maladjustment is supported by realistic details: for example, she goes through a phase of compulsive buying. Finally she dies of tuberculosis at the age of thirty-one.

Helene von Mühlau's *Nach dem dritten Kind. Aus dem Tagebuch einer Offiziersfrau* (1911) is another novel that concerns the problem of unwanted pregnancy. Financial worries lead the heroine, a conventional housewife and mother, into misadventure – she ends a fourth pregnancy with an illegal abortion and is subsequently blackmailed by the abortionist's son. Feminism enters this novel only indirectly when the heroine, Rose, compares her lot with that of her younger sister, a happy, self-supporting, unmarried art student. Rose is constantly afraid that her sensitive, easily irritable husband will fall out of love with her because she is busy from morning to night with three children and is forced to neglect her intellectual interests, artistic talents, and appearance. She characteristically blames herself for having burdened him with supporting a family and living with a dull household routine.

Emmy Hennings's second novel, *Das Brandmal.Ein Tagebuch* (1920), finally, is one of the most interesting early-twentieth-century diary novels written by a woman, although it does not have an overt political message. Hennings is perhaps better known as the companion and then the wife of the Dadaist Hugo Ball, with whom she helped found the Cabaret Voltaire in 1916, than for the novels and volumes of poetry she published starting in 1913. Before she met Ball, she was an aspiring actress. In her autobiography *Das flüchtige Spiel: Wege und Umwege einer Frau,* she describes how she drifted around Europe, taking on odd jobs for short periods of time. She was committed less to making a career onstage than to a bohemian way of life; she says she could imagine no other form of existence in her early twenties.[91] Many of the adventures in *Das Brandmal,* the story of a young would-be actress named Dagny, duplicate episodes in Hennings's autobiography. Like Hennings herself, Dagny takes a job at a wine tavern as an *Animierdame* (B-girl), but she is dismissed for encouraging a customer to abstain from drinking alcohol; penniless, she peddles a room deodorant from door to door; she gets a job in a revue when a former actress's mother dies; she visits the body of a dancer in a morgue; finally she gets an engagement at a huge Budapest variété, the "Royal Orpheum."

Whereas the autobiography gives the impression that Hennings greatly enjoyed her adventures, the novel emphasizes the pathetic aspects of such an existence. In contrast to Hennings herself, Dagny is not married when she starts to drift. Rather, she is totally destitute. She is forced into one degrading situation after another: She is obliged to sell her hair and her clothing; she sleeps on park benches; finally she becomes a prostitute. Advertisements for *Das Brandmal* declare the book is "ein neues *Tagebuch einer Verlorenen.*" The second of the novel's three parts concerns Dagny's life in a brothel. Finally, after taking a series of minor acting jobs in various cities, Dagny falls ill and dies.

Many of Dagny's stories are characterized by realistic particularity and grotesqueness of detail and a stranger-than-fiction quality that set them apart from the stereotypical events we have come to expect from fiction about women, though the general direction of the plot, Dagny's disintegration, and the tragic ending are inevitabilities we anticipate from the outset. Yet the emphasis is on Dagny's reactions rather than the events themselves. Hennings has Dagny tell the stories in order to show how she feels – alienated, laughed at, outcast, lonely. Dagny expresses her reactions during the events rather than her reflections afterward; the technicalities of the writing situation are thus, as in many diary novels of the same period, frequently ignored.

Every novelist who writes in diary form has to find a technique for integrating storytelling with self-expression. Here, the narrator speaks as if in two different, alternating voices, a "storytelling voice" and a "confessional voice." A peculiar tension is created, one that ultimately produces the portrait of a fascinating character. Dagny tells the grotesque stories in her "storytelling voice" – in a pert, deadpan manner that suggests the precocious worldly wisdom of the picaro or the equanimity of a woman who has seen it all. This part of her personality motivates some of her actions; it is clearly Dagny's picaro personality, for example, that goes to the Anatomy to try to sell her body for three hundred German marks. The "confessional voice" reveals a vulnerable and childlike person. Dagny expresses herself with the extraordinary intensity of someone whose emotional demands on life remain perpetually unfulfilled. Often her intensity borders on religious fervor; Hennings converted to Catholicism after a serious illness, and the bohemian Dagny, too, is a deeply religious person. She is sensitive, open to impressions and to injury, and nonjudgmental and compassionate, often to the point of sentimentality. She often complains of being confused, of being too close to things. She longs for affection and for a home. She has a vivid imagination; for example, she recounts a nightmarish allegory of time reminiscent of the fantasies of Rilke's Malte Laurids Brigge. The spirit represented by the confessional voice makes Dagny open, guileless, and uncalculating. She never loses her unaffected generosity and her innocence. In this role she has the reader's complete sympathy, even though she makes no attempt to stop drifting and thus to escape victimization.

Diary novels by and about women were written in France, too, but before Geneviève Gennari wrote *Journal d'une bourgeoise* (1959), a widow's diary about the difficult life of a single older woman, and Simone de Beauvoir chose the journal form for the novella *La Femme rompue* (1967), the story of a middle-aged woman deserted by her husband, very few of these works touched on feminist issues or represented women as victims. In the era of the revival of the diary novel, French feminism was neither new nor particularly opposed. Starting in the 1880s women slowly began to be accorded legal rights, in particular the right to higher education, and especially after 1910 the political climate in France was generally favorable to women's rights and even the issue of female suffrage. The French suffragettes took pride in maintaining a moderate tone.[92] Marcelle Tinayre's *Madeleine au miroir, journal d'une femme* (1912), for example, is a series of reflections on different issues of everyday life that addresses itself to a certain extent to the lives and problems of women, but it is politically an extremely moderate work. Speaking of the English suffragettes, the diarist—no doubt expressing the sentiments of most readers—accords sympathy to the idea that women should have the right to vote but disapproves strongly of the suffragettes' methods, and concludes, "The gesture of the suffragettes is not lovely, because it is not feminine."[93] Léontine Zanta's *La Science et l'amour* (1921) is the only French diary novel of the period whose diarist considers herself a feminist. The diarist, a young intellectual and student of philosophy at the Sorbonne during World War I, is highly conscious of belonging to a "new generation of women" who will necessarily take men's places in society after the war. Her *crise de conscience* concerns what she sees as a choice for women between affective and intellectual life. Her religiousness reflects the fact that at the time, the French women's rights movement was very much confused by the support of the Catholic church.[94]

One might conjecture that the diary is a particularly attractive form for women's fiction because, as a flexible, open, and nonteleological structure, it complements the nonautobiographical quality of women's lives and the traditionally dependent, accommodating female role. A diary can be written in snatches and with little concentration; it is adaptable to the housewife's interrupted day. In diary fiction written from 1900 to 1920, it is primarily the confessional implications of the diary that attract women novelists. But some contemporary women writers see fragmentary, open forms like the diary as the readiest possibility for finding a new women's voice. Sara Lennox, citing the views of Christa Wolf, Irmtraud Morgner, and Christa Reinig, notes that "a narrative which takes the form of a series of short, only tenuously connected texts corresponds to the shape of most women's lives, which consist of a series of interruptions" and speaks in favor of "experimental literary forms to depict the deformations of the female psyche as it has been constructed by patriarchy."[95] As we will see in greater detail in a later chapter, Doris Lessing in her novel *The Golden Notebook* makes use of precisely these features of the diary, its fragmentary quality and its implications of fragmentization, to capture the quality of her heroine's life.

PART IV

The Contemporary Diary Novel

17

The Diary Novel in the Twentieth Century

The publication of nineteenth-century intimate journals had a positive effect on the production of diaries of all kinds. Secret diary keeping became an encouraged adolescent exercise; a confirmation candidate could expect to receive a blank volume so labeled as a present.[1] At the same time, professional writers began to look upon the diary as a promising literary form and to write diaries with an eye to a wider audience. One need think only of such well-known twentieth-century literary diaries as those of André Gide, Hans Carossa, Julien Green, Ernst Jünger, and Max Frisch; many other writers followed suit.[2]

As early as 1898, Richard Meyer observed that "vast quantities of intimate records" were in print.[3] Especially after World War I, the publication statistics for literature of all kinds written in the form of diaries, from pseudointimate journals to collections of travel and war impressions and factual reports on every subject, shot upward. Peter Boerner in *Tagebuch* describes the situation in the twentieth century as an "overflow in production."[4] Something similar can be said of the diary novel. There is a sharp numerical increase in publication figures starting after World War I. Furthermore, whereas it is not clear whether before the war the authors of diary fiction were aware that they were writing in a tradition, there are abundant indications, from subtitles to the mention of the form in works of literary criticism, that the diary novel had become a consciously accepted genre by the 1920s. In 1921, for example, Will Vesper published a novel, *Die Wanderung des Herrn Ulrich von Hutten,* with the subtitle "Ein Tagebuch-Roman"; in the same year a pedagogue wrote an article on the advantages of having schoolchildren write fictive diaries in composition classes; and three years later a literary critic mentioned diary fiction for the first time in a work on narrative theory.[5]

At the beginning of his *Diary in Exile* of 1935 Leon Trotsky wrote, "The diary is not a literary form I am especially fond of; at the moment

I would prefer the daily newspaper. But there is none available. . . .
The advantage of a diary – alas, the only one – lies precisely in the fact
that it leaves one free from any literary requirements or prescriptions."[6]
What Trotsky saw as the diary's "only advantage," its formal elasticity,
has proved to be a crucial advantage for the continuing popularity of
the journal as a private and a literary form and thus also for the life of
the diary novel. The *journal intime* may be passé, at least as an avant-
garde literary mode; but a diary is under no obligation to incorporate
the sort of subject matter characteristic of intimate journals. Lacking
rules that restrict its style, topics, and length, the literary diary is a form
that requires a minimum of conformity and hence allows for a maximum of self-expression.

A diary can be produced with comparatively little effort. Expressed
negatively, almost any piece of writing that is too formless and chaotic
to deserve another name can be termed a "journal." "Readers . . . will
be delighted to meet this charming personality again, even in diary
form," writes *The Times Literary Supplement* in mixed praise of Dorothy E. Stevenson's *Mrs. Tim Carries On* in 1941. "In a conventional
novel this would be deadly enough: in the diary form, it is disastrous,"
the *New York Times Book Review* comments of Wallace Graves's *Trixie*
in 1970. One recent critic, in a judgment premature for a work written
in 1938, even registers surprise that Sartre uses "one of the most hack-
neyed of forms" in *La Nausée*.[7]

The diary is a democratic form that anyone can write, but the modern trend of mass participation in literature is not the only reason why
the genre has become so widespread. It is one of the few literary forms
that has stood to gain by the modern disaffection with the traditional
means of expression. The belief that chaos underlies our perception and
the notion that, as Nietzsche put it, a "movable army of metaphors,
metonymies, and anthropomorphisms"[8] masks rather than reveals the
truth of that chaos, has become a commonplace in the twentieth century. The devaluation of linguistic currency was accompanied by a
distrust of any art form that imposes an order. Hofmannsthal's Lord
Chandos writes, "I have completely lost the ability to think or speak
about anything in a coherent way. I had the sensation that everything
fell into pieces, and that those pieces fell into yet more pieces."[9]

The diary is a loose form. It is not cohesive; it consists of pieces. The
only order implicit in it is the successiveness of narration itself. The
diary is not even bound to the front-to-back organization of the book:
Rilke, for example, asks us to read *Die Aufzeichnungen des Malte Laurids
Brigge* "as if one had found disordered papers in a drawer."[10] If an
author chooses to suppress the kinds of content that collaborate with
the sequential implications of narrative, such as individual biography, in

favor of kinds that do not, there is no reason why the diary cannot be converted into a collage of fragments or a random-order construction that can be opened and read anywhere. While neither specifically mimetic of what is perceived to be the modern environment, as, for example, a Futurist text is, nor intrinsically expressive of convictions of chaos, as a Dada poem is, the diary as a form is, nevertheless, adequate to a speed-dominated and lotterylike reality in the sense that speed, change, and contingency do not make it appear automatically obsolete. Because its mode is one of linear temporal succession, it does not seem to impose distorting structures on the natural order of experience. It has no end: Consequently it is never "finished," either as a text or as a work of art.

While the diary reflects what is conceived to be contemporary conditions in a negative way, by not actively misrepresenting them, it also makes possible the expression of an individual experience that is unable to identify meaningfully with social reality. Its author can retreat to the limited but safe ground of the first person singular. The "I" of the diary is not the "I" of the storyteller, which according to Walter Benjamin carries the authority of experience and has counsel to impart.[11] The self of the diary is "just me." The reduction in stature of the first person singular was already evident in psychological novels of the late nineteenth century. A diary entry communicates an implicitly relative single opinion, and a fleeting opinion at that. The diarist can jot down his ephemeral thoughts spontaneously, with a minimum of contrivance and reflection. He can be as inconsistent as he wishes. Peter Weiss's persona in his autobiographical novel *Fluchtpunkt* expresses succinctly the appeal the journal has for contemporary writers:

> I could not see my work as an independent mechanism, my work was part of my everyday life. I could not imagine isolated works of art, only immediate expressions of the present, of a continuous change and revaluation, and because of this, for me, there was only a diary, notes, sketches, the various stages of a picture, perhaps mingled with improvisations of a musical or dramatic nature, but never this crude chunk of a novel, a rounded picture.[12]

The possibilities the diary form offers are open to the diary novel as well. Strictly speaking, the diary novel has more possibilities than the real journal, since the aims of a fiction need not be restricted to those of its nonfiction counterpart. We have seen how the diary novel can be used as a vehicle for dramatic irony, a function that of course holds no interest whatsoever for a real diary writer. Starting with an exceptionally straightforward form involving a single point of view and simple present-time succession, an author can devise a more complicated structure with a second point of view based on insight into the future. The two different points of view in the ironic diary novel – the reader sees farther into the future than the diarist, even though he reads no more than what the diarist writes from day to day – are similar to the two points of view in autobiography, in which the present writing self who sees the outcome is juxtaposed to the self being written on who sees only as far as he has lived. In fictive autobiographies, the tension between told time and the time of the telling can become the point of the story. In Italo Svevo's *Confessions of Zeno,* for example, the first-person narrator, far from taking himself for granted as a confident authority on the subject of his own life, broods irresolutely on the insufficiencies of his excessively teleological memory, which is unable to capture the past without falsifying it. Because the diary is basically oriented on the present, inherent temporal inconsistencies are less obvious than in autobiography. But on closer examination, the diary actually presents a much more complex structure of temporal difference than the autobiography. A real diary that concentrates on the past would be an anomaly, but a diary novel can intentionally focus on past events to achieve a polarization of past and present time similar to that possible in autobiography. Furthermore, the diary represents not really a continuous present, but, rather, a sequence of discrete present moments. A temporal difference exists between the units of time or entries. This difference allows an author to set up particularly complicated kinds of temporal tension between the present and the present-becoming-past.

A complication of the point of view in an all-diary novel is harder to achieve. The diarist's "I" presents a limited perspective, even if the diarist should be schizophrenic. The diary is not a form suited to presenting different independent views of the same thing, as Nathalie Sarraute, for example, presents multiple views of the same furniture in *Le Planétarium.* At best the diary can filter second points of view through the uniform lens of the diarist's perception. However, precisely because the diary is a narrative full of built-in breaks, it can accommodate many different kinds of material, including hearsay from different quarters. Like a frame narrative – an example would be Chaucer's *Canterbury Tales,* in which the pilgrim Chaucer's views of the tellers of the tales differ from those of the company themselves – the diary as a form for communicating hearsay can leave unresolved the question of whether the first or the secondary narrators are to be believed.

It is not possible to generalize about the use of the diary form in fiction after World War I. There are many different kinds of diary novels. Each period has its reasons for favoring or neglecting particular narrative strategies. The advantages the diary form traditionally offered do not correspond to the goals of post–World War II novels that aspire to being avant-garde. As we have seen, a fictional text written in the form of a diary can lay a special kind of claim to authority by pretending that it is an authentic document. Considering that separate categories for fiction and nonfiction are being questioned particularly today, however, a legitimation for fiction that gives it the trappings of "fact" would be more than superfluous. The fiction of the diary is also a useful vehicle for depicting a character and, if desired, for presenting a psychological study of the fictive diarist. Before *style indirect libre* came into general use and before the interior monologue and the stream-of-consciousness technique were invented, the diary was a convenient means of acquainting the reader with what a character thinks privately. It was more plausible than a "stage monologue" in which the omniscient narrator pretends to overhear his character, less reductive than a thought report, and more self-evidently veracious than a letter. But the present-day novelist has a wealth of techniques for thought transcription at his disposal, and the diary no longer presents itself as an especially felicitous solution. After the stream-of-consciousness novel was invented, the diary form became outdated as a tool for depicting the psychological processes. One could say, however, that in contemporary fiction it is the psychological novel itself rather than the diary form that is out-of-date. As Lionel Trilling remarks, "Only a little effort of honesty is needed for us to recognize how bored we are by the detailed exposition of the psychological processes when we meet it in contemporary fiction."[13]

In twentieth-century prose fiction the diary is often used, as it were, anachronistically. Many present-day diary novels retain functions inherited from fiction of the pre–World War I period that derive from an understanding of the diary as a confessional mode. Some such works, written by well-known authors, have received recognition. One such is George Bernanos's *Le Journal d'un curé de campagne* (1936), the intimate journal of an idealistic, dying priest. Another is Saul Bellow's *Dangling Man* (1944), a diary that records the growing malaise and ill-temper of an unemployed man waiting to hear from the draft board.

Diary novels that are genuinely novels of their time and do not still trade atavistically on the credit of the *journal intime,* however, tend to use the diary form as a device. This use requires some explanation. In the broadest sense, the phenomenon relates to and can be accounted for in terms of what can be called an expressive use of literary form. This term was coined by Yvor Winters, who used it in an exclusively pejorative sense to denote a tendency among modern writers to express the chaos of modern life by using a chaotic form. In distinction to Winters, I mean by expressive form an economy by which a form is used to generate meaning (not necessarily a sense of chaos). The form may reinforce in a more than redundant way a statement already made in the work, or it may make a statement not made elsewhere or even contradict another textual voice. Two types of formal expressiveness, in particular, play an important role in the modern diary novel. The first has to do with the form's connotations; the second, with its structure.

Every literary form takes on connotations. An increasing potential for expressivity is typical of genres generally; forms take on the connotations of functions with which they have been frequently or familiarly associated. One finds in the history of genres an increasing tendency to play on such intertextual resonance. A writer can evoke connotations just by choosing a form, and indeed, it becomes difficult to use an old form innocently.

Mimetic fictional forms present a special case. Because their history is linked to that of the nonfictional model, these forms not only acquire self-reference but also automatically have a second field of reference. From the beginning the nonfictional model provides connotations, and it continues to supply new ones as it itself changes. Thus connotations borrowed from real models have been part of the fictive diary from the outset: In the journal in *Robinson Crusoe,* Defoe calls on the notion of the conversion familiar from Puritan autobiographical writing, and the letter-journal novels offer the circumstantial detail implied by an understanding of the journal as an account of daily events. Initially such connotations tended to be used straightforwardly, in accordance with the overt purpose of the work. Later in the history of the genre, when certain connotations had become clichéd attributes of the form, they could be used with detachment and sophistication, for example, to arouse expectations that were then disappointed or at cross-purposes with other elements in the book. In the *Werther* imitations, as we have seen, the reader's expectations of sincerity, aroused by the journal form, are met by the heroes' actual sincerity. Gide in *La Symphonie pastorale,* in contrast, uses the journal's connotations of sincerity ironically, in order to debunk them, by creating a protagonist who is patently insincere.

A particularly interesting example of a twentieth-century diary novel in which the author uses the connotations of the form at cross-purposes with the narrator's initial stated intent is Evgenij Zamjatin's *We* (1920). In this utopian satire the connotations of the diary affect the diarist's personal development and thus also the nature of the text he produces. At the beginning the narrator is a perfectly well-adjusted citizen of a totalitarian socialist state. As a "number," rather than a person, he starts to keep an impersonal, public record of the United State. Little by little he changes from a brainwashed "number" to a self-conscious, rebellious individual with independent ideas, desires, and dissatisfactions, and his record concurrently becomes more and more a record of his own thoughts and feelings, that is, a private diary. Writing what is in effect a diary seems instrumental in changing the diarist's self-conception; the form, with its connotations of individualism and secrecy, helps provoke his breakthrough to self-consciousness.

The type of formal expressiveness that is most characteristic of twentieth-century diary fiction is a self-conscious use of the fiction of writing. Here it is not a question of drawing on the diary's traditional connotations; rather, writers perceive that a traditional aspect of the form, namely writing, holds new implications. In order to understand this use, we must remember that the convention of the written document in the first-person novel outlived the functions that motivated its origins. From its beginnings and well into the eighteenth century, the fiction of writing served the essential purpose of explaining the existence of the work and attesting to its plausibility as an object in the real world. By convention, the novel's origins and mode of self-presentation were not left in an unspecified relation to the world of experience but were elaborately integrated into it. The origins of the narrator's text could supposedly be traced to the framework of the real world, and the work's mode of presentation was consonant with that claim. The published book purported to be a mere reproduction or transcription of an anterior document that in turn contained the description of real events the narrator had witnessed himself. The fiction of writing was an essential, in fact *the* essential, part of the mimetic gesture. In the course of the eighteenth century, then, the genuine-document fiction was used in an increasingly perfunctory manner, or in elaborately playful ways. These signs, along with such others as the adoption of the fictive-narrator convention in third-person fiction, testify that any serious attempt to legitimate the novel as "history" was already outmoded. The novel disengaged itself more and more from a direct responsibility to reality and substituted for it an obligation to a category of "fiction," which in turn had its recognized status in the real world.

For a time, in the last decade of the nineteenth century, the fiction of writing was an appendage without a purpose. Authors who wanted to use the periodic form of the diary to show the psychological development of a character actually found themselves encumbered by the fiction that the protagonist was writing down his thoughts. Later authors retained the periodic time scheme and the first person but dropped the fiction of writing. Where the imitation of real genres was no longer important, and where novelists had at their disposition techniques of representation that had no counterparts outside of fiction, the constitutive elements of the diary form could be pulled apart; authors could drop the "diary" designation and use whatever elements they pleased. What had been borrowed as a package when the formal mimesis of real models had been an operative criterion for legitimizing fiction – the diary type, the form, the connotations, and the fiction of writing – could be plucked apart and regarded as a set of separately usable techniques.

Where the fiction of writing was no longer an obligatory convention in first-person fiction, it became a device that called attention to itself. Authors began to use it with a deliberate end in view, often to thematize writing or representation generally or to call attention to the problems involved in self-representation. Writing as a form of verbal representation acquired interest at a time when the project of representation began to be examined with increasing attentiveness, and when its forms and means were subjected to close scrutiny. The "language crisis" at the turn of the century questioned the adequacy of verbal representation, and at the same time, first-person discourse became suspect from an epistemological point of view. Where novelistic conventions existed that were meant to disappear like glass before the workings of a character's conscious or unconscious mind, namely *style indirect libre* and stream of consciousness, writers could use the fiction of writing to draw attention to the self's attempts to represent itself.

A number of twentieth-century authors have used the fictive diary to question more or less pointedly the traditional claims and purposes of writing. In some such works, the idea of the diary itself is incidental; writers are interested in the form primarily for the sake of the fiction of writing. Thus in the first book of *Molloy* (1951), termed a "diary" by the narrator,[14] and in the periodically written *Malone Dies* (1951), Samuel Beckett uses the fiction of writing in a gently parodistic way, that is, without a sharply focused contrasting level of truth. The fiction of a document written from day to day intensifies the absurdity and claustrophobic quality of the reports, in which the angle of vision is strictly limited. Malone ostensibly writes for the purpose of putting order into his life, an order that nowhere becomes apparent. "I did not want to write," writes Malone, "but I had to resign myself to it in the end. It is in order to know where I have got to." Later he writes, "My notes have a curious tendency . . . to annihilate all they purport to record."[15] Language at best introduces an order Malone himself mistrusts. His "inventory," for example, seemingly a straightforward genre, backfires because he cannot decide which of his possessions are his. Beckett painfully stresses the awkwardness of the writing situation: Malone first drops his exercise-book, then loses his pencil.

Peter Weiss in *Der Schatten des Körpers des Kutschers* (1960) thematizes more boldly the implications of language as a means of representation. The narrator writes in a loose journal form, although the document is nowhere termed a "diary" (*Tagebuch*); the narrator calls his writing *Aufzeichnungen* ("notes"). The narrator, a twentieth-century male Pamela who is convinced of the uselessness of any activity he might pursue, starts to record in minute detail what he sees around him, starting with his observations from the seat of a toilet and ending with a description of the coachman's and the housekeeper's shadows as they make love. His record is remarkable for its attempt to be "objective." The narrator describes only the surface of things, without venturing any kind of interpretation, summary, or evaluation, so that the book reads like an attempt to translate a film recorded by a bizarrely placed camera into language. As the narrator says, his text consists of "rows of words that I form according to what I see and hear."[16] This experiment in depriving language of its conventional representational privileges, such as recourse to the past, association, and synthesis, and making it mimic film, is interesting to the reader mainly for the shock value of its tedium. In the shadow scene, the comic high point of the book, the narrator parodies the attempt to render surfaces without depth, to record perceptions without ulterior signification. Shortly afterward, discouraged and apathetic, he abandons the narrative in mid-sentence.

Other writers emphasize the connotations of the journal as well as the fiction of writing in order to thematize representation. Gide set a precedent for this use in *Les Faux-Monnayeurs* (1926). As we have seen, he uses the journal for its connotations of closeness to reality, and he focuses on the question of representation by using the device of the self-reflexive work of fiction. Other writers have similarly used the journal for its connotations of closeness to reality in novels about novelists in order to make a statement about representation.[17] Malcolm Lowry, for example, sets himself a goal similar to Gide's, that of questioning the line of demarcation between fiction and perceived reality, in his all-diary novel *Through the Panama* (written 1949-57; posthumously published). His novelist-protagonist, Sigbjørn Wilderness, who is incapable of looking at anything without having literary associations, keeps a journal of his trip through the Panama Canal. Its contents begin to duplicate the plot of his projected novel, and they simultaneously become a pastiche of the voyage symbolism of centuries of literature. Of negligible value as a piece of descriptive literature, the journal serves rather as a point of transaction between the narrator's obsession with his literary predecessors and his own future projects. Literature swallows up experience; with the journal Lowry debunks the idea of an original, unmediated perception of reality and its representation in language.

James Merrill uses the same techniques to examine the same questions in *The (Diblos) Notebook* (1965) but arrives at different conclusions. The fictive novelist returns to the Greek island of Diblos after an absence of seven years to write a novel about the past. To his mind the projected novel, conceived as a story about another person, contrasts unfavorably with his journal, in which he records his own current experiences and perceptions. Essentially preoccupied with himself, he despairs at ever being able to understand someone else's motivations; the "real story" of the past keeps interfering with his attempts to recast it as fiction; and recent impressions keep intruding, suggesting new interpretations of old facts. In his journal he jots down his drafts for the novel, complete with crossings-out, and he also expresses his frustration with the project. He concludes that writing fiction is nothing but an evasion of self-knowledge. Writing at a time when questioning the means of representation had become a commonplace apologetic gesture in continental fiction, Merrill appproaches his subject with typically Anglo-Saxon preoccupations. In his view language does not create pre-fabricated perceptions; instead, the subjectively perceived fact prevails over any attempt to create fiction.

Finally, Françoise Sagan uses a structure that is similar to Merrill's in her novel *Des Bleus à l'âme* (1972). She begins by alternating sharply demarcated segments of a writer's diary and a novel but then starts to merge the two so that her novel becomes more lifelike and her writer's fantasies more novelistic. Thus, like Merrill, she suggests to the reader that setting up a strict differentiation between "fact" and "fiction" is arbitrary if not impossible. But she ends her work on a note that is far different from any struck by Merrill: She has her novelist write herself into her own novel, begin an affair with the protagonist, and then bid her fictional characters adieu. This ending leaves the reader with a sense of the ambiguity of such a step: To what extent is it desirable, to what extent inevitable? To what extent does it dictate and to what extent is it dictated by the end of the novel? But the close at least testifies to Sagan's defiant will to affirm that the most seductive solution to the novelist's problems is making fictions.

Other twentieth-century writers play with the diary's structure, instead of with its connotations, in order to express meaning. In order to distinguish this second kind of expressive form from formal expressiveness based on connotations, let us compare a literary form to a game – say, bridge. Bridge has certain connotations: It is known as a popular game in the United States, as a game that demands skill as well as luck, as a way of passing or wasting time, and so forth. But bridge also implies a set of rules, rules that both limit the moves players can make and suggest strategies for playing the best game. Players expect the individual moves in a given game to fall within a range determined by the rules, and they also develop a notion of a "good" game.

A literary form can likewise be seen to represent a set of rules. Readers expect an author who chooses a particular literary form to stick to the rules, and the rules in turn suggest more or less expedient ways of playing the game. If an author breaks the rules signaled by the form or makes peculiar moves, the reader's attention is alerted by the uncustomary procedure. The odd use of form demands an explanation. It acts as a signal to the reader to search for meaning. Within the context of a known formal structure, an irregular move can generate a meaning that is not explicitly stated. A classic example of such a case is found in Goethe's poem "Locken, haltet mich gefangen" in the *West-östlicher Divan*. The *a b a b* rhyme scheme leads the reader to question Goethe's choice of the name "Hatem" as a rhyme word for "Morgenröthe," and to substitute a name that rhymes – "Goethe."

The fictive diary offers a set of rules, namely, a day-to-day time scheme, the first-person voice, and the fiction of writing. Within the context of other forms available for telling stories, these rules suggest certain logical moves, or in other words, the diary form presents itself to the novelist as a particularly appropriate way to tell certain kinds of stories. Most obviously, the diary form seems well suited to an autobiographical story with a focus on the present. If this "logical" potential of the form was not initially realized, the reason has to do with the history of mimetic fictional forms: When such genres came into being, the mimetic imperative both imposed a shape and placed restrictions on contemporary fiction and interfered with a full realization of the form's potential. But later, in the same process by which the elements that formed the mimetic package were gradually disengaged from one another, writers began to see the diary form as an empty structure with an abstract potential. This potential could be realized in a mimetically plausible manner, or it could be manipulated to more complicated artistic ends. Authors began to use the diary form less mimetically and more dextrously and inventively.

In the following sections I shall discuss three diary novels that use the diary form in an experimental fashion. The authors break with the traditions of the diary novel. They do not use the form either mimetically or in accordance with its manifest logic, but play a different sort of game with it, in order to accomplish an ulterior expressive end. The three novels, Max Frisch's *Stiller* (1954), Michel Butor's *L'Emploi du temps* (1956), and Doris Lessing's *Golden Notebook* (1962), are representative of the kinds of manipulation to which the diary form lends itself most readily. As I have indicated, the formal attributes that hold the greatest appeal for present-day authors of real journals, discontinuity (or the fragmentary character of the diary) and open-endedness, are among those that can be exploited most promisingly, and the aspects that are the most obviously susceptible to deformation are the diary's temporal structure and its single point of view. Thus, *Stiller* uses the journal form to present different views of an absent person; *L'Emploi du temps* records changing perceptions of a receding past; and *The Golden Notebook* juxtaposes segments of several diaries written by the same person to depict different aspects of an experience.

If form is used expressively, it may be because the author believes that the statement to be made eludes more direct modes of communication. This is so in the case of the three novels chosen as examples. All three novels are written against a background of a distrust of language; all of them emanate from the assumption that words obfuscate rather than express the truth of experience (although Michel Butor transcends his starting point, as will be shown.) Coincidentally, the three novels all use the diary form to confirm the fact of inexpressibility rather than to capture the inexpressible object. If from the reader's point of view the finished novels do in fact succeed in capturing their object, this is a purely unofficial success; the works actively proclaim its theoretical impossibility. The novels complement one another interestingly, for in spite of their superficial differences they are, as will be shown, at base similar both in their choice of theme and in their use of the diary form. All three novels use the diary to present multiple, mutually relativizing (and therefore "endless") versions of a central focal object, whether this is a person as in *Stiller,* a past period of time as in *L'Emploi du temps,* or a sequence of experiences as in *The Golden Notebook.* In each novel this focal object is in one way or another absent, and in one way or another it is shown to be irretrievable. In each novel, therefore, the diary's formal open-endedness finally comes to symbolize its material and metaphysical empty center.

18

Max Frisch: *Stiller*

Max Frisch is a twentieth-century writer who has made the diary form particularly his own. Not only is his most acclaimed novel, *Stiller* (1954), written in journal form: Frisch has published two literary journals, *Tagebuch 1946–1949* and *Tagebuch 1966–1971;* the last pages of his next novel after *Stiller, Homo Faber* (1957), are a diary;[18] and his latest novel, *Mein Name sei Gantenbein* (1964), is a diarylike *récit.* "The diary form is a peculiarity of the writer who bears my name," Frisch states in an interview with Horst Bienek published in 1962.[19] He claims that for him the use of the form is a kind of necessity, like the necessity of having a pointed nose: "Imagine that a man has a pointed nose, and you ask him on behalf of the readers: where does your preference for a pointed nose come from? In a word: I don't have a preference for a pointed nose. I don't have a choice—I have my nose."

Max Frisch's predilection for the journal form has a theoretical foundation not dissimilar to the one that Peter Weiss's persona in *Fluchtpunkt* expresses. Frisch's views on language and artistic expression, such as those that run through his first literary journal, *Tagebuch 1946–1949,* are not strikingly innovative. They are interesting rather because they are entirely typical of twentieth-century theories of literature yet at the same time are deeply and originally felt. Several critics have dealt with the subject of Frisch and the diary form in detail.[20] It is unnecessary, therefore, to give more than a short summary of Frisch's theory of artistic expression here.

Frisch's ideas are based on a conventional twentieth-century disbelief in the ability of language to say anything worth knowing. Words cannot reveal the truth. Instead, the truth is somewhere between the words: It is "the inexpressible." Not only words but all self-affirming orderings are untrustworthy. Art should therefore optimally be a continuous negation of the illusion it creates, a "process of alienation." Open forms, in particular the fragment and the sketch, serve this purpose best: "It is conceivable that a late-born generation, such as we presumably are, has particular need of the sketch, so that the polished, complete forms we have inherited, which no longer bring new births, do not freeze and kill us." Finished, monumental works of art are out of place in our time: "The attitude of most of our contemporaries . . . is, I think, one of questioning, and as long as we lack a complete answer, the form of the question can only be provisional. Perhaps the only face the question can wear with decency is the fragment." Interestingly, Frisch comes to see artistic form – as opposed to the "substance" of words – as the most promising element with which to approach the truth. He who would express "the inexpressible" resembles a sculptor who chisels through a lump of "sayable" material to get at the statue beneath and is always in danger of destroying the object of his quest. According to Frisch the surface of the statue – the form – is the closest one can come to the truth: "This surface of everything it is finally possible to express, which would have to be one with the surface of the mystery, this immaterial surface that exists only in the mind and not in nature, where there is no dividing line between mountain and sky, either – perhaps that is what is meant by form?"[21]

Max Frisch's novel *Stiller* is a kind of object lesson for his theory of fiction. It is a masterpiece of saying through form. Friedrich Dürrenmatt, who wrote an essay on the novel's craftsmanship, rightly concluded that its form was "a brilliant idea." "The uniqueness lies in the form," wrote Dürrenmatt. "The form is an exact mirror of the problem."[22] This is not to say that the form is convincing in the sense of being realistic. The circumstances under which the diary is written and its style and content are extremely unlikely. For that matter, the plot of *Stiller* is improbable too. Both the form and the plot are metaphors for an abstraction. The form is a concise metaphor; the story, an extended one. In the discussion that follows, we shall see how Frisch uses the diary form expressively, what he uses it to express, and how such expression relates to and manipulates the code of generic characteristics we have come to expect from diaries and diary novels.

Stiller is the diary of a man who is imprisoned by Swiss authorities on the suspicion that he might be a certain Anatol Stiller, a Swiss sculptor who disappeared from the country six years earlier. Why Stiller is wanted by the police is at first unclear. It is hinted that he might have been involved in a spying incident, but later the diarist finds out that the extent of his misdemeanor was to neglect to register his absence with the police and pay his taxes. The imprisoned suspect insists that he is not Stiller, but James Larkin White, an American. His defense attorney, Bohnenblust, an unsympathetic upholder of law, order, and literalism, asks him to write the story of his life to provide proof of his identity as White for the court. This is the pretext that permits the self-styled White to fill seven notebooks with a heterogeneous assortment of material, including accounts of day-to-day events, stories about his alleged past, retellings of his visitors' conversations, reflections, and yarns. All of these fragments have to do, directly or indirectly, with two subjects: the mysterious Anatol Stiller and the problem of personal identity. Most of the prisoner's visitors, for example, are persons who knew Anatol Stiller intimately. Stiller's wife, the ballerina Julika; his lover, Sibylle; and Sibylle's husband, Rolf, who happens to be the prisoner's public prosecutor, all either come to the cell or are visited by the prisoner on bail, and they tell him their stories of Stiller and what he meant to them. The diarist records the minutes of these meetings, presumably with a good deal of editorial license. The reports of the visitors' accounts take up most of Books 2, 4, and 6. In the other notebooks and interspersed with accounts of the visits the diarist reflects on his own identity.[23] Especially at the beginning the prisoner appears to be having an existential identity crisis. "I am an unhappy, insignificant, unimportant person," he writes.[24] He says relatively little to confirm his identity as James Larkin White – he legitimates his claim to being an American chiefly by insisting that he has an insatiable thirst for whiskey – but he vehemently denies that he is Stiller. In the course of the diary the prisoner's reflections on the question of identity become increasingly frequent and detailed. The reader is given increasing reason to believe that the diarist knows more about Stiller than he wants to admit. In the final notebook, the prisoner acknowledges implicitly not that he is but that he *was* Stiller. The question of identity turns out really to be a question of tense. The prisoner was Stiller six years ago, but no one thinks of asking him that; and he is not, to his way of thinking, Stiller anymore.

The reflections on identity are the key to understanding the novel. Everything else – the multiple, differing views of an absent person and the tall tales – are oblique illustrations of this central theme. In fact, as we shall see, the entire apparatus of the suspense story exists solely for the sake of illustrating the premise that a person's identity is something that cannot be taken for granted. The ploy of mistaken identity requires, of course, that the reader play the game. For example, he has to believe conversations that break off at the crucial point before a genuine confrontation between "White" and a visitor who is convinced that White is Stiller can take place. The diary form, which allows the prisoner to terminate a description of a scene whenever he sees fit, aids these foreshortenings. In addition, Frisch uses a device that makes it easy for the reader to accept White's idiosyncratic manner of presentation. It is possible to read the novel with few second thoughts because

Stiller/White's style conforms to a well-known literary convention, that of the stranger-satirist who sees the author's world with new eyes and describes it with a kind of high unseriousness. Before it becomes clear that the book is about the problem of identity itself and not about a particular case of mistaken identity, it is quite possible to believe that the prisoner is really an American tourist who finds it preposterous that he has been put in jail in a foreign country on charges of being someone else, yet is interested to see how the adventure will run its course and therefore puts up with imprisonment with good-humored irony. The convention of the sincere diary does not play a role at first: The journal is not a private document, after all, but a testimony written for the court; and a spoof designed to annoy the literal-minded Swiss officials is, therefore, in order. *Stiller* is a perfect double-take book. On second reading, when it is clear from the outset that Stiller is Stiller, the convention of the sincere diary appears in an interesting light. Strictly speaking, Stiller is being very sincere, in the sense of being true to his new self.

Frisch's novel maintains one other point of connection to the tradition of the diary novel. So that the exigency of his identity crisis may gain our credence, Stiller is meant to have our whole sympathy, and to that purpose Frisch tailored his character so generously that almost any reader who is interested enough in the novel to read through it can identify with him without effort. Stiller's self-portrait at the end of the fifth notebook is a description of *Homo psychologicus* in the twentieth century, a mirror Frisch holds up to the reader:

> His personality is vague; hence a tendency to radicalism. His intelligence is average, but in no way trained; he prefers to rely on sudden brainstorms and neglects his intelligence, for intelligence puts one before decisions. Sometimes he reproaches himself for cowardice; then he makes decisions he later can't stick to. He is a moralist, like most everybody who doesn't accept himself. . . . He has a great deal of imagination. He suffers from the classical inferiority anxiety that comes from making exaggerated demands on himself, and he considers his fundamental sense of owing something as his depth – possibly even as religious feeling. He is a pleasant person, charming, and doesn't get into arguments. When he can't get by with charm, he withdraws into melancholy. He would like to be genuine. . . . He constantly lives in anticipation. He loves to leave everything in a state of suspense. He is one of the people who, no matter where they may be, can't help thinking how nice it might be someplace else. He flees the here-and-now, at least inwardly. [pp. 191–2]

Stiller's public prosecutor, who writes an afterword to the diary and frequently functions as the ideal reader of Frisch's novel, tells us that the central figure is meant to be representative. "I don't see Stiller as an exception," he suggests; "I see some of my acquaintances and myself in him" (p. 243). Novels written in diary form, as we have seen, have tended to have as their protagonist the social misfit, the creative malcontent, or the sensitive brooder. Despite the intricacies to which Frisch has subjected the diary form in *Stiller,* the novel can be seen as a late instance in this pattern of generic absorption. In this most general sense its form, the journal, stands in peculiarly conventional relation to its theme and its aims.

As a novel that exists, so to speak, in two versions – a first-reading version that is White's account of mistaken identity, and a second-reading version that constitutes a philosophy of identity objectified in the story of Stiller's identity crisis – *Stiller* can also be seen to have a formal structure that fulfills two purposes at once. First, the diary is a technical device that permits the story to unfold, that enables Frisch to carry the tightrope exercise of balancing two senses of his narrative through to the finish. Until the tension breaks in the seventh notebook, and it becomes clear that the prisoner's diary has been the ironic yet nevertheless genuine confession of Stiller himself, Frisch's novel points toward the future: It is more anticipatory than reflective. By allowing anticipation to be combined with reflection, the diary form is, in fact, essential to this novel's plot, for another type of narrative would not have been able to sustain the device of mistaken identity that turns Stiller's identity crisis into a drama. A retrospective first-person narration, for example, would have failed by obliging Stiller to say that once upon a time he had pretended not to be himself. The diary form works because it permits the narrator to write periodically from his present level of experience. It is imperative that the central episode in Stiller's story, the period of mistaken identity from arrest to the conviction, unfold in the present tense. The reader must not be allowed to see farther than the prisoner himself could reasonably be expected to see. It is equally necessary that the work present itself as a written document; thus the reader is never allowed to know more than the diarist wants him to, and for a very long time, Stiller holds his audience captive with periphrasis. A nondocumentary first-person narrative in the present tense written, for example, as an interior monologue or in stream-of-consciousness style would have fatally impaired Frisch's pivotal paradox, the paradox the diary form, with its fiction that Stiller is presenting his writings and not his thoughts, can so gracefully sustain: that Stiller is simultaneously dishonest and sincere on the subject of his own identity. The journal form is able to create a continuous dialectic between the diarist's asseverations that he is White on the one hand and the evidence that he is Stiller on the other, so that as the proofs of identity acccumulate, the obvious truth the diarist tenaciously refuses to make explicit, that a person's reality cannot be reduced to his name, dawns gradually on the reader.

Stiller's form is more than an ingenious way of accommodating the plot. Frisch manipulates the diary in such a way that the novel's formal construction becomes the reflection of the complex of problems surrounding the theme of identity that the work expresses. On this second level, the diary is not a technique but a signifying structure; it constitutes a kind of second logical proof for Frisch's philosophy of identity. It should be stressed that this function does not become apparent until the end of the novel. The theme of identity does not crystallize in the reader's understanding until the end of the book, and it becomes evident only in retrospect that each separate facet of the narrative, but particularly the novel's formal structure, has been contributing to it sub rosa. I shall follow this chronological sequence of understanding, therefore; before showing how the construction of *Stiller* mirrors the theme, I shall give an interpretative summary of Frisch's main ideas about identity as they are presented in the novel.

The assumption is made in the novel – by the prisoner, by the public prosecutor who writes the afterword, and also by the Frisch of that period[25] – that there is such a thing as a true self, a center that corresponds neither to the image others have of one nor, in the probable course of events, to one's own self-image. Living in accordance with one's true identity is equated, mystically, with living a "real" life.[26] Stiller writes, "It's hard to say what makes a life a real life. I call it reality, but what does that mean? You could also say it means that a person becomes identical with himself" (p. 51). Ideally, the passage of time merely unfolds the individual's true identity. "Where are we going?" asks Novalis's Heinrich von Ofterdingen. "Always homeward," his companion answers. This is the relation Frisch draws in *Stiller* as well. The richest and most authentic course of life is an inward voyage. Frisch speculates on the relationship of the passage of time to the self in *Tagebuch 1946–1949*:

> Time does not change us. It merely unfolds us. . . . It is only a magic device designed to stretch our being out and make it visible, by dissecting life, an omnipresence of all possibilities, and laying it out in a series. Only thus does life appear to be transformation. Again and again, therefore, we are forced to conjecture that time, the succession, is not essential, but only apparent. It is an aid to our imagination, a process of unrolling that shows us in succession things that are in fact interlocked, a simultaneity we nevertheless cannot perceive as such, just as we cannot perceive the colors of light if its rays are not refracted and dissected.[27]

In *Stiller* as well, the true self is understood as an infinite generator, whose potential is spun out into versions by time.

The composition of the true self is not explicitly defined in *Stiller*, but it has something to do with the emotions, which are conceived to be an immutable core of identity beneath consciousness that consciousness can under no circumstances wish out of existence. In an allegorical story of a trip to Genoa, the public prosecutor compares the feelings with a package of flesh-colored cloth. He relates how in an unguarded moment he purchased this cloth from a swindling native peddler and then spent the rest of his stay trying to get rid of it again. The cloth is ugly and in the worst taste; as a package it is obstructive. Rolf finds no buyers and no takers. He cannot even lose the package on the street without someone returning it to him. His pride, his self-image are finally at stake in the task of disposing of the despised fabric. Finally he throws it in a public toilet. In the same way, it is implied, every contemporary intellectual tries vainly to suppress his cumbersome feelings.

In conformity with the philosophy we observed in late-nineteenth-century diary novels, the villain that prevents the individual from becoming himself in *Stiller* is his own consciousness. In Frisch's novel, however, "consciousness" is conceived as a kind of superego: It registers the norms and expectations of society and sets a standard for the self that reflects these conventions. Failing to take cognizance of the true self beneath, consciousness designs for the self a false image concocted out of the way it would like to be seen and the way it thinks it really is seen. If consciousness catches sight of the inclinations of the true self, it smothers them as if they were something indecent. The public prosecutor explains that there is "a discrepancy between our intellectual and our emotional niveau" (p. 242). The more subtle and aesthetically refined the consciousness, the more devious its routes to escape the feelings:

> We kill our primitive and thus unworthy feelings, so far as possible, thereby running the risk of killing our emotional life altogether. Or we simply give our unworthy feelings other names. We lie about them. We label them according to the wishes of our consciousness. The more agile our consciousness, the better read, the more numerous and noble are our back doors, the more ingenious our self-deception. A person can entertain himself like that excellently for a lifetime, but he doesn't reach life that way; instead, he inevitably reaches self-alienation.

One cannot think one's way to life: The intellectual is the prime victim of the dissociation of sensibility, the individual whose self-image most thoroughly distorts his true self. Stiller once caught a glimpse of his true self years earlier when he fought in the Spanish Civil War and failed to shoot two enemy soldiers. His response is to create increasingly elaborate and self-praising fictions to cover his failure, so that his "act of cowardice" becomes the false silent center in his life.

The self-image may be a falsification, but at least it is liable to perpetual revision. The image other people make of one is, in contrast, a hopelessly static reification. A subject is every other subject's object: Unless other people happen to be in love with us, they turn us into grotesque still lifes that are composed mainly of what we mean for their own self-images. Consequently, the images others have of us in no way make up a unified picture. When Stiller/White meets his younger brother Wilfried, they reminisce about their respective mothers, who of course were one and the same person. Stiller reports:

> His mother was very strict, it seems, mine not at all. . . . [My mother] never would have had the heart to be so strict. . . . His mother said: Now pull yourself together, if you want to be a proper boy! My mother said: Leave the boy in peace, now! My mother was convinced that I would somehow succeed in life. Wilfried never had any such experience; his mother was worried that nothing good would ever come of Wilfried. . . . He hadn't been a talented child, he explained; he hadn't even learned to play the piano. My mother, I know, saved on cleaning and ironing women, and cleaned and ironed herself so she could pay for my flute lessons every month; for I was considered talented. How funny the two mothers were! [pp. 245–6]

In the quasi-religious vocabulary of the novel, which echoes that of the *Tagebuch 1946–1949,* image making is a form of sacrilege. As Julika says, "Thou shalt not make unto thee any graven image!" (p. 113).[28] Making an image is a sort of murder that can genuinely harm the person on whom it is practiced. Frisch writes in *Tagebuch 1946–1949:*

> Some hard and fast opinion of our friends, of our parents, of our educators – it too burdens many of us like an old oracle. . . . We too are the authors of other people; we are, in a secret way, responsible for the face they show us. . . . We think we are the mirror and only seldom suspect to what degree the other is really a mirror of the set image we have created, our product, our victim.[29]

The theme of murder recurs repeatedly in the novel. Stiller speaks of having "murdered" his wife: The fact is that he could not accept her frigidity and lack of emotional responsiveness and was perpetually trying to change her, to remake her in an image that was more congenial to his own image of himself. His conduct toward her is similar to his treatment of a certain cat he was asked to take care of during a stay in California. Like Julika, the cat has an unshakable sense of self. It does not need Stiller, but it expects him, since he is there, to treat it with consideration and not to try to reform its ways. The cat knows that its place is in the house. Stiller, who hates cats, tries to make the animal understand that its place is out of doors. It howls on the window ledge. Stiller finally nearly kills it. This makes him feel guilty; his wife also made him feel guilty. Stiller speaks of the other "murders" he has committed, mimicking the big-time criminal for his gullible warden, Knobel. At least one of these fabulations is more than just a wish-fulfillment dream: Stiller "kills" a client who once refused to pay for a sculpture, Direktor Schmitz, by reifying him, by thinking of him summarily as a "hair-oil gangster" (p. 33). Stiller's former profession as a sculptor or maker of images, his rejection of his profession, and a final scene in which he destroys all the sculpture in his atelier can be seen as an allegory of his progress toward freeing himself from automatic patterns of perception.[30]

The central symbol of the falsifying image is the name. Names, imposed on us initially by other people, symbolize the extent to which our identity is determined – or, as Frisch suggests, menaced – by others. According to Stiller, a name, which accumulates connotations and re-calls them automatically, represents the ultimate reduction of a human being. He complains: "Everything works like a machine: up above the name drops in, the supposed name, and right away, down below, the form of behavior belonging to it comes out, all set, ready for use, the cliché of a human relationship" (p. 184). As a consequence of the deadly force of names, Stiller refuses to let himself be identified as Stiller. The disorderly conduct that leads to Stiller/White's imprisonment is a sym-bolic act of refusal to being reduced to an image. Stiller hits a Swiss customs official who "asserted with an air of legally protected arro-gance that they'd tell me, all right, who I really was" (p. 10). The prison to which he is then sent can be understood as the prison of the role in which society is trying to confine him.

Living a role or roles is seen in the novel to be a loss of self. In the vicious circle of role-playing, the individual, caught in the dialectic of self-consciousness well known since Hegel, imitates the image others make of him by living up to the expectations set by social norms. The more perfect this imitation is, the more the individual actually becomes what he imitates. The image of the other becomes a self-image and the true self is effaced. "It is a question of imitating, not becoming," cries the Roman actor Genest in Jean Rotrou's play *Saint Genest*,[31] as he notices he is actually turning into his stage role of a Christian martyr. Stiller similarly concludes: "One would have to be capable of passing through their confusion without defiance, playing a part without ever confusing oneself with it. But for that I would have to have a fixed point" (p. 183). To secure the "fixed point," however, a Kleistian advanced stage of consciousness must be reached. The ideas in the novel are largely inherited from Romanticism. Even a kind of Roman-tic transcendence is implied: In the mystical-religious terminology of the novel the last step in personal development, autonomy, means replacing the other, the people in whose regard our identity constitutes itself, by God. In this ideal stage the center of the circle is simultaneously outside its circumference. On the other hand, nothing is condemned so heartily as the Romantic cult of the genius. The public prosecutor and Stiller consider with disapproval the lines from *Faust II*, "I love him who desires the impossible," and conclude that only a demonic figure could have spoken them. Frisch leaves it to the reader to figure out that a friendly character – Manto – speaks them, foreshadowing Faust's success in finding Helena.

In the seventh notebook the journal is revealed to be the elaborately sincere first-person diary of Anatol Stiller, but until then it appears that Frisch has undertaken to modify the conventional function of the form in an unusual way. He shifts the emphasis off the narrator and onto someone else (the mysterious Stiller) and puts even more distance between the diarist and his subject matter by having White report hearsay from third parties on the subject of the mysterious Stiller. In short, Frisch temporarily pulls the first-person narrative apart so that it takes on the aspect of a third-person narrative. At first, the diary proper, the first-person record of White's days in prison, seems to be just a sort of empty clothes rack on which the substance of the story – evidence on Stiller's character from a multitude of sources and large chunks of information about Stiller's past – can be hung. Since the authorities believe White to be Stiller and repeatedly force him into situations in which he has to confront Stiller's shadow, the prisoner has abundant opportunities to gather information: He encounters the Stiller of six years past as a husband, a brother, a friend, a lover, a dental patient, an artist. The longest accounts come from three chief informants, who in fact tend to talk obsessively about themselves but in whose lives Stiller played a central role. In Book 2, Julika comes to the prison and tells the story of her marriage to Stiller at length; in Book 4, the public prosecutor tells White about his wife's affair with a stranger he never met called Stiller; and in Book 6, Sibylle, his wife, recounts her version of the affair with Stiller. White's decision to present these accounts as "minutes" – "I want . . . to try to do nothing in these notebooks but keep a record" (p. 70), he writes – is understandable, considering that he is a total stranger to Stiller and his circle. The long accounts of the visitors' conversations strike the reader as the optimal way for the prisoner to record his adventure. White's minutes are not an actual transcription of the conversations, however. Instead, in each instance he writes a narrative that adopts the point of view of the visitor, and sprinkles it liberally with distancing phrases to indicate that the opinions expressed about Stiller are not his own. In the first pages of the Julika narrative, we thus encounter phrases like (italics mine): "*Als Fremder hat man den Eindruck*"

("*As a stranger, one has the impression*") (p. 69), "Ihre Ehe in jenen ersten Jahren *soll* wundervoll *gewesen sein*" ("Their marriage in those first years was wonderful, *I gather*") (p. 70), "Er nahm es *offenbar* als Niederlage seiner Männlichkeit, wenn die schöne Balleteuse, vielleicht nur etwas ehrlicher als andere Mädchen, nicht in Empfindung zerschmolz unter seinem Kuß" ("He *apparently* took it as a defeat to his masculinity when the beautiful ballerina didn't melt at his kiss") (p. 77), "Stiller hatte es immer weniger, *scheint es, dieses* Verständnis für seine Frau" ("Stiller, *it appears,* had *this* understanding for his wife less and less") (p. 78), "Es war *wohl* nicht zuletzt dieses Lächeln, was die arme Julika immer weitertrieb" ("It was not least this smile, *probably,* that drove Julika further and further") (p. 79). This is a brilliantly ambiguous style; even on second reading it is not easy to tell when Stiller is summarizing what he actually hears, and when he is drawing on his own subjectively colored memory. Since White, as is to be expected, has his own impressions of each visitor – he writes of Julika, for instance, "Any reasonably experienced man – which Stiller, apparently, was not – would have immediately recognized in this fascinating little person a case of extreme frigidity" (p. 67) – it is quite plausible that he can draw conclusions about what Stiller and his relationships with others must have been like by balancing his perceptions against the visitor's story.

To all appearances, therefore, the diarist White is zeroing in on another person who is unknown to him. In *Stiller,* as in a detective story, the mosaic of hearsay gradually becomes complete, so that we think we and the diarist are finding out more and more about the absent focal point of the novel, Stiller. In fact the evidence becomes overcomplete. It is not that the witnesses are not convincing; on the contrary, each of them is sympathetic and highly credible. But the views we get of Stiller are different, subjective, and therefore at best partially trustworthy. They are, in short, viewpoints of Stiller and not Stiller himself. Our prey has materialized, but in a suspicious multiplicity of versions. Then White is revealed to be Stiller, and Frisch lets his far-flung construction snap back into the limits of a traditional intimate diary. But in the process of expansion something has happened to the narrative that makes impossible an about-face contraction into an unambiguous first-person account of Stiller on Stiller. When we discover that White is Stiller, we realize that we have been receiving the descriptions of Stiller through a double filter: We have seen Stiller as Stiller saw the way other people saw him. Frisch has manipulated point of view in such a way that the novel's form itself comes to illustrate the substance of the reflections about identity and role-playing. The circle of image making and the role-constituting force of other people's images closes in the concrete instance of the narrative's structure. The center remains empty. By coming closer and closer to the real Stiller, we were actually getting farther and farther away from him. The object of our pursuit has dissolved into reflections of reflections. The suspense story of mistaken identity becomes a metaphor for the paradox of the infinite self: The more exposure one has to another person, the more confidently one presumes to give him a final, and falsifying, label.

The novel performs the same sort of disappearing trick in another way as well. By using the device of mistaken identity Frisch forces the reader to accept a starting position that involves the assumption that a person can be identified by a name. The reader is obliged to wonder whether the prisoner is identical with the lost Stiller and therefore is deluded into believing that this is the central question of the novel. At about the same time that the evidence speaks overwhelmingly for the case of identity, in the seventh book, it becomes apparent that it is immaterial whether the prisoner is Stiller or not. The answer to the question gets the reader nowhere; it keeps him tied to the surface of conventional, falsifying perception.

In *Stiller,* Frisch thus replaces the genre-indicated convention of the public versus the private self with the idea of the actual, alienated self versus the true self. He artificially widens this gap by splitting his character into two entirely different persons: White, the conceptualizing, conscious self, the man of words and "spokesman" for Stiller; and Stiller, the mystical and ungraspable true self whose name reflects his silence. In mid-twentieth century, the idea of a private and authentic self that can unfold and develop at a safe distance from its false public facade is questionable at best, but Frisch believes in it, and for him, Wittgenstein's famous dictum "What we cannot speak about we must consign to silence" holds true. In Frisch's view it is impossible to grasp the authentic self or represent it in language. The role Frisch assigns to the reader in quest of Stiller – where the reader stands for any "other person" – is that of Faust, or one who "desires the impossible." As the novel's disapproval of Manto's words suggests, the reader is not destined to find Stiller the way Faust finds Helena. Instead, the reader's attempt to grasp Stiller points to Faust's first, "mephistophelian" attempt to seize Helena: Faust's experiment led to an explosion, and Helena vanished. Likewise, Frisch implies, when an observer reaches out to grasp the desired object, when he tries to cross the magic border between representation (illusion) and mystical essence, the object of his quest dematerializes.

The remarkable achievement of Frisch's novel is that every aspect of it participates in the theme of identity and role by illustrating some facet of the problem and thereby reinforcing Frisch's central premises. If we momentarily look aside from the diary as an expressive form and consider it again as a technique, it becomes plain that the form is useful to Frisch not least by virtue of its elasticity. A journal is sufficiently stretchable so that Frisch can intersperse the primary plot with very different forms of statement. This diversity grants the reader a high degree of involvement in the text: He is constantly encouraged to solve the mystery, the mystery not just of the prisoner's identity but of the book's construction as well. He has the satisfaction of tying together what appear to be loose threads. At first the journal appears to be a catchall for the prisoner's random and unpredictable experiences, but the reader soon discovers that it is in fact a tightly organized interweaving of repetitions of and enlargements on a theme.

For example, the three yarns that Stiller invents to entertain Julika and his warden, Knobel, all prove to be variations on the theme of identity. The story of Isidor represents an ironic perversion of the idea of "always homeward." Isidor has a wife who always asks him where he has been, as if she knew precisely where he "is" at the moment of asking. Isidor joins the Foreign Legion; when he returns home after an absence of many years, his wife asks him, grotesquely, where he has been for so long. Isidor has presumably changed completely, but he never changes in the image-making eyes of his wife. In the same way Stiller, who has six years of America and a suicide attempt behind him, is still Stiller, a known and calculable entity, to his wife Julika when he returns home to Switzerland: "She simply doesn't believe that I could be anybody except her missing Stiller" (p. 45). The legend of Rip Van Winkle, borrowed from Washington Irving, is another story of a homecoming after a long absence. Van Winkle realizes that it is pointless to ask the townsfolk if anyone still knows him, since he himself is no longer the Rip Van Winkle the people knew twenty years before, if indeed he ever was. Stiller similarly returns home to Switzerland bearing little resemblance to the Stiller he was before and even less to the array of static personalities the memories of his friends hold up to him. Van Winkle's dream in the hills provides an oblique illumination of Stiller's reflections on a possible escape from repetition, the aspect of his former life and marriage that disturbs him most. Instead of creating a perpetually fascinating utopia for himself, Van Winkle spends twenty years of dream time setting up bowling pins over and over again. Likewise Stiller concludes that repetition is an inevitable, constitutive element in even the most intensely lived life. The story of the discovery of the Carlsbad Caverns is a parable of a descent into the unconscious. Two men named Jim explore the cave and, although they were best friends, one kills the other when it is a question of survival. The winner seems to be a "truer" self than the loser: He discovered the caverns (i.e., the existence of the subconscious) first, whereas the victim, a sort of superego or part of the self that has to be overcome, is afraid of the caves. The victim probably represents the old Anatol Stiller, since it is said that his real name is "verschollen" ("lost") (p. 130), the term used for Stiller.

Like Julika's Stiller, Rolf's Stiller, and Sibylle's Stiller, the heroes of the tall tales are versions of the central figure, highly reflected self-images he devises for himself. The device of pluralistic portraiting, which suggests that infinite sketches can be drawn and that no one version is absolutely valid, testifies to Frisch's belief that the truth cannot be expressed in words. Writing has a peculiar, oblique relationship to the truth, not unlike the relationship of the rainbow to the sun: It does not present its object, but rather represents it in a series of variations, just as the collage of other people's opinions, personal reflections, and symbolic stories that make up Stiller's diary represents Stiller in its self-questioning pluralism. The positive force of writing lies in the form into which it is arranged rather than the statements it propounds. Frisch writes in *Tagebuch 1946–1949*: "Form: when the unimaginable – existence – succeeds in making itself apparent?"[32] By permitting different versions of the central figure to collect around an empty center, by making possible a collection of admitted fictions, the structure of *Stiller* expresses the thesis of the novel by imitating it.

The clearest statements on identity and role come not from Stiller but from the public prosecutor, and in his afterword the lawyer applies his categories to Stiller's own process of development. There is a good deal of argument among critics about the status of the afterword. Some consider it to be the key to the interpretation of the novel, while others, especially those who are impressed by the novel's form, doubt that the public prosecutor has the last word. His is just another point of view, they argue, for if Frisch had wanted to tell the reader what to think, he would have introduced an omniscient narrator rather than appended a first-person narration.[33] If the public prosecutor is to be believed, his afterword is a letdown from the point of view of formal construction: Dürrenmatt finds that these final pages, which follow the journal proper, "are for one reason alone not a complete failure – they stand in the shadow of something successful, unique."[34] It is correct that nothing compels the reader to believe the public prosecutor's interpretation, even though it occupies the privileged position of the end of the book. The introduction of an omniscient narrator in this book would have been an unpardonable contradiction in terms. Frisch's choice of a first-person narrator, in contrast, precludes compulsory belief. The first-person form of the public prosecutor's narrative signals to the reader that this is "just another viewpoint." But this does not mean that it is not also the interpretation of the novel. We *may* believe it; and since it is coherent, eminently reasonable, and in accordance with Frisch's own theories, there is no reason for us not to do so.

The public prosecutor believes that the process of becoming identical with one's self consists of three stages: (1) self-recognition, (2) self-acceptance, and (3) autonomy, or not needing to convince others who one is. According to the public prosecutor, Stiller achieved the first stage of self-recognition when he perceived that his existence as a sculptor was a poor excuse for a life and disappeared from Switzerland; he completed the progression to the second stage while in prison; and by the time he is convicted and released he begins to move into the third stage of autonomy. The court sentenced him to play an outward role, that of being Stiller, but he accepts it as a necessary evil, a being-for-others that has nothing to do with his real self. The public prosecutor explains that precisely because Stiller has reached the final stage, he no longer keeps a diary, for he is sure of his identity and has no further need to convince other people.

Thus, Stiller's "falling silent," which Frisch underlines symbolically by replacing the diarist by another narrator, is to be understood positively. The act of discontinuing communication in this twentieth-century work has a value similar to that in Rod's *La Course à la mort* and thus the reverse function of the parallel situation in Goethe's *Werther*. Werther's lapse into silence suggested that he was no longer *able* to communicate and mirrored his increasing despair. Stiller's silence signals that he no longer *needs* to communicate and that he has attained his goal of finding his identity. The last words of the novel, "Stiller remained in Glion and lived alone" would, if one follows the public prosecutor's line of interpretation, complete a circle back to the motto from Kierkegaard's *Either/Or* on the title page of the novel: "Behold, for this reason it is so difficult to choose oneself; for in this choice absolute isolation is identical with the most profound continuity, because through this choice every possibility of becoming something else, or rather of rewriting oneself into something else, is completely ruled out."[35]

Particularly if we accept the public prosecutor's interpretation, a last function of the diary form becomes evident, one that again links *Stiller* with the tradition of the intimate journal. Stiller writes, "Writing is — communication with the inexpressible. The more exactly a person expresses himself, perhaps, the more the inexpressible appears in its purity, that is to say, the reality that oppresses and moves the writer" (p. 249). For Stiller, keeping a diary means coming closer and closer to the truth of his self. Since he writes from day to day, in installments that relate less to each other than to his momentary state of consciousness at the time of writing, he need not express himself in terms of a set perspective or self-image. And since writing, by definition, does not express the truth, Stiller regards every fragment he composes in the constructive light of a further refinement of falsification he has managed to clear out of his way. He writes, "I sometimes have the feeling that one might emerge from one's writing like a snake from its skin" (p. 249). Thus the discontinuity the diary form offers benefits Stiller's personal development. Concurrently, its continuity allows the reader to see that what was for Stiller a discontinuous series of sheddings was in fact a continuous inward voyage toward the true self. Frisch juxtaposes Stiller's past life and his account of the present, so that the reader sees the stages of his progress over a narrative period of three weeks in their relationship to a narrated past time of at least twelve years. The record of his days in prison is the frame for a kaleidoscopic assortment of hearsay evidence, parables, and incidents from Stiller's past, but it simultaneously constitutes the culmination of the strands it incorporates and makes possible a resolution.

19

Michel Butor:
L'Emploi du temps

Like Proust's *A la recherche du temps perdu*, Michel Butor's diary novel *L'Emploi du temps* (1956) is constructed around the premise that between the event and the consciousness that apprehends it there is a loss, and that this loss is to be made good by memory. Butor, who published an article on "Les 'moments' de Marcel Proust" (written 1950–5),[36] must surely have been aware of the thematic relation between his novel and that of his predecessor; and although the significance of Butor's work is by no means exhausted in the analogy to Proust, the reader is struck by the number of parallels between *L'Emploi du temps* and *A la recherche du temps perdu*.[37] The number of ways in which Butor picks up Proustian categories, only to infuse them with a content or a sense as different from Proust's as possible, is striking. Butor's seeker of things past, Jacques Revel, for example, is an infra-Marcel. He is an office worker without social, intellectual, or artistic pretensions who is employed for a year in an oppressive English industrial center named Bleston, where the weather is as dreary as the cuisine. Far from being dukes and duchesses, his friends are common citizens: a co-worker at the office, a barman trainee, a salesgirl in a stationery shop, her sister, a student at the university, and an alienated African. Whether or not Butor's choice of setting and milieu is understood as an intentional distancing from Proust, a demythologization or banalization of the glamour and magic of Proust's world, the spirit in which Revel undertakes his recollection of things past could hardly be more foreign to Marcel's "mémoire involontaire." Whereas Marcel's past presents itself to him unbidden, with the lavishness of a revelation, Revel sets out to extract the past's secrets from its depths forcibly and one by one, by a conscious act of memory, or, rather, a set of conscious acts, performed every evening after work. Revel conceives of his activity as a "dredging" of the past.[38] He considers it essential to reconstruct the facts, and to reconstruct them in chronological order: "I must take possession of all these events that I feel are swarming and organizing themselves behind the cloud trying to efface them, to evoke them one by one in their order" (p. 53), he writes. To further this enterprise he begins to write a retrospective chronicle of his year in Bleston in the form of a diary.

As Revel methodically brings the milestones of his stay in Bleston to light, the reader may find it difficult to appreciate why his past merits being recaptured at all. The round of Revel's days has not only been undistinguished by adventures; it has been intensely monotonous. The appalling sameness, in fact, is precisely what motivates Revel to want to reconstruct it. In the eighth month of his stay in Bleston, he feels that he has been cheated out of his time. Seven months have elapsed, yet when he thinks back on them, "All these weeks . . . are practically contracting into a single immense, dense, compact, confusing one" (p. 52). The past appears to consist of "always this same movement" (p. 52). It is a period of time devoid of distinct events, too homogeneous, and thus somehow abridged. It is furthermore receding rapidly into the fogs of the English winter, dissolving, leaving him empty-handed. In his state of confusion, it is not the spirit of the past but, rather, its letter that Revel wants to recapture.

Thus during the first month of writing, May, Revel carefully reconstructs the happenings of the first month of his stay in Bleston, October. During the second writing month, June, he writes about November, proceeding in chronological order as planned; but he also starts writing spontaneously about the events of the present. In July he covers the past month of December, also writes about July, and in addition considers it necessary to give an account of May, which he never recorded, since in May he spent all his time writing about October. He works backward from the already covered month of June, or in other words, covers May in reverse. In the fourth month of writing, August, a complex structure of remembering and revising starts to emerge. Revel writes about January and about August, but also, working backward from May, about April (in reverse), and for a second time about June, since he feels that while in medias res he did not have a proper perspective on events and failed to do justice to them. In September, the final month of writing, he writes about February, March, and September, and he redoes August (thus implicitly shedding new light on the months described in the section he wrote in August, or January, April, and June), as well as July (and implicitly December, May, and October).

Jacques Revel is confused and is struggling to achieve clarity. Like the Puritan diarists before him, he keeps a journal in the expectation that it will help him to create order. But the more order Revel introduces into his diary, the more chaotic Butor allows this document to become. The time scheme of the novel, which juxtaposes writing time and written-on time in configurations of increasing complexity, reveals Butor's strategy, which is to examine how memory works, not just from the point of view of the present but from within a moving present, by presenting a series of reconstructions of the past that are succeeded by reconstructions of the reconstructions and so forth. To accomplish his purpose, Butor chooses a limited, arbitrary temporal frame (the space of a year) and relentlessly performs an exercise on it. The novel is mathematically plotted out, as Georges Raillard has demonstrated in a helpful series of diagrams illustrating the time scheme.[39] *L'Emploi du temps* is a book that exists primarily in the abstract. The concrete story Butor unfurls within it has the status of a verb vis-à-vis its conjugation, from which it may not deviate.

Butor is a theorist of the novel as well as a writer of novels, and in an essay entitled "Recherches sur la technique du roman"[40] he devotes two pages to an analysis of the diary form as a technique for presenting temporality. After discussing the implications of a strict chronological sequence in narration, which would imply no past and no memory, he develops the possibility of a double chronological sequence in diary form, involving an account of a past period of time supplemented by notes about the present. As an example he cites the diary in Kierke-gaard's *Stages on Life's Way*. Presumably this work was the narrative model for *L'Emploi du temps*. Butor mentions other literary usages of the diary in his critical writings, including the diary at the end of Joyce's *Portrait of the Artist as a Young Man*,[41] and considering the numerous similarities between the novel and *La Nausée*, he must have had Sartre's novel in mind as well; but Kierkegaard's is the only work that uses the form specially as a device for looking back on the past. After describing the use of the diary in *Stages on Life's Way*, Butor speculates on the possibility of multiplying the chronologies in a diary: "Suppose the narrator keeps not just a double, but a quadruple journal; inevitably the reversals of chronology within the work would multiply."[42] This is a more or less exact description of what Butor himself does in *L'Emploi du temps*. With each chapter, or month, one more level of temporal reflection is added. In May the diarist Revel writes a simple account of a past period of time; in June a double diary of past and present time; in July a threefold diary involving past, writing-time past, and present; in August a fourfold diary involving past, writing-time past, past written on in writing-time past, and present; and in September a fivefold diary of past, writing-time past, past written on in writing-time past, past written on in writing-time past as written-on-past, and present. Revel's endeavor thus resembles trying to get to the bottom of a mirror that is facing another mirror. The past he reflects upon increases not only

additively, from the standpoint of a vanishing present, but also exponentially, for he has to incorporate past viewpoints in his present analysis of a yet more distant past.

What ulterior motive provoked Butor to devise this extraordinarily
complicated permutation on the diary form for *L'Emploi du temps?* Like
Stiller, L'Emploi du temps is a *roman à thèse,* and one that requires a
particularly elaborate formal structure to carry out its intentions. The
overt theme of the work is memory; at first, the novel seems to be,
above all, a parodistic reply to Proust. But, as I hope to show, the
theme of language in *L'Emploi du temps* is even more important than the
theme of memory. Butor exploits not only the diary's temporal structure but also the fiction of writing, the idea of formulation in words, in
order to demonstrate by example views on language that he expresses
in his theoretical essays.

L'Emploi du temps takes as its starting point a concern with temporal
loss and asks whether memory is capable of recovering lost time. In the
course of the narrative Butor shifts ground, however, and raises a second question: Is language efficacious as a medium of recovery? The
displacement of the first issue by the second can take place easily and
inconspicuously because both ideas, that of temporal loss and that of
language skepticism, relate to a traditional cognitive schema. This
schema assumes that the absolute is available to us only in a debased
version of itself; something authentic, original, and valuable is necessarily obscured, mediated, or succeeded by some lesser entity. Two years
after the appearance of *L'Emploi du temps,* Alain Robbe-Grillet, another
nouveau romancier, tried to expose and thereby to dispose of one version
of the schema by labeling it the "myth of depth."[43] The "myth" does in
fact often use the spatial dichotomy of depth versus surface to figure
various other dichotomies, including identity/role, unconscious/con-
sciousness, event/consciousness, reality/text, text/interpretation.

The myth has its temporal versions as well. One well-known temporal figure for the fiction of depth is the Paradise/after-the-Fall pattern,
which Rousseau and Romantic writers projected, in the form of a child-
hood/adulthood dualism, on the individual life-span. This version of
the fiction has a corollary that proves as important for Butor as it was
for his Proustian model, the fiction of the "moment": the moment of
the fall, the first moment of self-consciousness. The passage of time
does not erode slowly, and the fall is not a gradual processs of degen-
eration; instead, a single incident or moment effects the transformation
from one absolute state (the prelapsarian state of grace) to another (the
state after the Fall). The Christian redemptive structure of erring/re-
demption is the inverse of this temporal figure. It too incorporates the
fiction of the moment, in the form of conversion. Epiphanies and privi-

leged moments of all sorts likewise reflect the idea of the moment of conversion. The redemptive structure also appears in configurations that are both spatial and temporal and thus capable of recovering both past time and lost space. Proust's madeleine episode is an example of such a spatial and temporal instant: Tasting the madeleine redeems the loss between consciousness and past events in a vanished space.

In *L'Emploi du temps* Butor reaffirms two ideas the depth myth would confirm: that memory cannot recover the past and that language cannot represent reality adequately. But the novel is not a straightforward debunking either of memory or of language. Instead, in a mischievous yet emphatic fashion, it parts company with the tradition of language skepticism with which it would seem at first glance to be allied. Butor contrives to let the traditional answer – that language is an inadequate medium – pose a new question: Is language a medium at all?

Mediation implies a going back to an absent entity, a capturing of a metaphoric "center." In *L'Emploi du temps* this "center" is symbolized by February 29, which in the novel's terms is the "midpoint" of the year the narrator Revel is trying to recapture. February 29 thus stands synecdochically for the past and, in the question of recovery through language, for the referent of Revel's text. If Revel were to succeed in recovering February 29, he would succeed in recovering the past and his language would prove a medium adequate to its referent. February 29 thus also functions as this novel's version of the redemptive moment. Since Revel never reaches February 29, the redemptive moment never takes place. Butor thus rejects an optimistic solution to the loss proposed by the depth myth. As the least frequent day of the calendar, February 29 becomes the empty center of Revel's narrative. The date calls into question the very idea of referentiality by suggesting that the center is necessarily empty: The "originary referent" is not only inaccessible but absent altogether, and "depth" does not exist.

According to the narrative logic of *L'Emploi du temps,* Revel's recovery of February 29 should come at the end of the novel. By failing to reach February 29, Revel fails to complete his text. Butor not only collapses the dualism proposed by the depth myth but also replaces the notion of a vertical relation between text and referent with the notion of the book-to-be-continued, with a syntagmatic or "horizontal" relation between successive words. The empty center (a depth-myth metaphor) becomes an open end (in post–depth-myth terms). In the structure of the novel, language, by going back (to pursue the desired object), at the same time goes forward (in the process of the pursuit). If one inspects the failing process of mediation in *L'Emploi du temps* more closely, one discovers that it is really a process of successful transformation. That is, language unwrites the optimistic solutions to the depth myth and, in the same process, writes an argument for its own autonomy. Butor thus makes a sharp logical distinction between a narrative of the signified and a narrative of the signifier in *L'Emploi du temps*. Together, these levels constitute a single, chiastically structured text: Language is made to fail as a medium, but in failing, it simultaneously undermines its status as medium.

Butor's version of the diary form helps the text establish, and at the same time undermine, its claim to referentiality. The steps the literalistic Revel takes to ensure that a correct record of past events will be written preordain his self-defeat. By trying to recapture the past in a diary, which he grotesquely multiplies into a labyrinth of five overlapping chronologies in the course of composition, he merely succeeds in foundering in a tangle of rambling sentences. Autobiography would have afforded Revel a privileged atemporal present from which he could have surveyed, and possibly summarized, a clearly delimited past. But a diary by definition marches forward with the passage of time; it daily creates more past. A multiple retrospective diary compounds the difficulties: The past increases not just additively, from the standpoint of a vanishing present, but also exponentially, so that as Revel tries to do verbal justice to the amassing past points of view, a purely written past mounts behind him. Likewise, an ominous future stretches before him, one that will consist only of text.

Revel compensates for the confusions created by his form by briskly trying to create order of a different kind. He dramatizes his (understandable) sense of the recalcitrance of his material by turning description into battle. In a monumentalizing gesture designed to lend dignity to his trivial enterprise, he imagines that monolithic antagonists, space and time, oppose him in his struggle to wrest his year in Bleston from the city's fogs. He sees Bleston, whose ancient name was Belli Civitas, as an active, living foe whose dusts, fogs, rains, perpetual mists, and ill-lit streets conspire to frustrate his quest for clarity. The unconsidered assumption that something obdurately "other" opposes him is the first act of differentiation with which he probes his amorphous past, and the subject-object polarity is the first ordering principle to which his "description" succumbs.

In the course of Revel's writing, language itself takes over the task of subverting his descriptive enterprise. In describing the enmity the city and time bear him, the narrator establishes a set of related metaphors that run through the whole novel and give the prose its peculiar heavy, sonorous quality. The central metaphors themselves are not at all far-fetched; rather, they suggest themselves almost automatically in Bleston's appearance and Revel's own aims. They and their more fanciful offspring crystallize naturally around the antagonism Revel perceives between himself and space-time. Since light and fire are Revel's weapons in his struggle for clarity of vision, he sees himself as an arsonist who will set the city ablaze and finally as an alchemist who will turn Bleston's dusts to gold. Damp Bleston, in turn, becomes Circe, a hydra, an octopus, a squid disgorging ink, a monstrous tortoise, a viscous body of water trying to drown Revel, and the river Lethe. Time shares the watery properties of space: It is described as the lapping waves of the tide; as deep, opaque water; and at its worst as surging, pitchy, assaulting breakers. Thus the associative chains of language begin to supply the connections lacking in Revel's actual past. It soon becomes plain that the narrator is not a faithful scribe recording the facts, but a desperate exegete groping for a reading of reality that will be adequate to the facts as he perceives them. For example, grotesque animals like the tortoise lead to insects. Bleston is full of flies, and Revel becomes increasingly obsessed by flies as the emblem of Bleston's evil. His suspicion that James Jenkins is the would-be murderer of George Burton develops to a large extent because Jenkins's mother wears a ring with a fly preserved in a glass bubble; her father was the architect of the New Cathedral, where one niche is decorated with a stone frieze of flies; and Burton is disturbed by a fly buzzing around in his hospital room after the accident. It is not easy, however, to decide at exactly what point the descriptions of facts in Revel's diary become interpretations of facts; there is no clear line of demarcation, no single, irreversible point of change in the novel. On the contrary, every figure of speech can be traced back to an attribute that either Revel or Bleston quite obviously and naturally possesses, to the fundamental, abstract antagonism between self and other that the novel seems to ask the reader to accept as one of its self-evident premises.

The synthesizing principles behind Revel's interpretations of reality vary. The narrator often seizes on a well-known story that seems relevant to his own life in Bleston and that suggests a prefabricated interpretation to him. Since he is particularly impressed by the Theseus and Cain legends, his reading takes a mythological turn. In "Les Oeuvres d'art imaginaires chez Proust" (written in 1963), an article published in *Répertoire II*, Butor shows that *A la recherche du temps perdu* is filled with fictitious works of art that Proust devised to reflect the novel itself and carefully altered to match his changing plan for the work-to-be-mirrored.[44] Revel's Museum tapestries and the Old Cathedral windows are, similarly, "mirrors" of *L'Emploi du temps*, but in a different sense. They depict stories already familiar to the reader, and the narrator of the novel copies *them*, fancying himself a latter-day Theseus or Cain. Revel finds his mythological readings so seductive that he clings to them even when the turns of his own fortune belie all connection with the myths. Thus, when Rose and Lucien announce their engagement, Revel brushes aside the discrepancy between his own disaster and Theseus's success and revises the myth to suit himself: There is no Phaedra for Theseus-Revel but, rather, a "broken thread" (p. 277).

The "work of art in the work of art" that has the most insidious influence on Revel is Burton's detective novel *Le Meurtre de Bleston*. Whereas the ancient legends appeal to Revel mainly as coherent structures into which he can coordinate his own scattered and multiplying metaphors,[45] the detective novel antecedes and predetermines the vision of Bleston that shapes his prose. In the early days, when the city presents itself to him as a confused blur of strange districts and buildings, the detective story supplies Revel with a detailed verbal description of his surroundings. Relieved to have found this guide, he takes the linguistic mediation to be the thing itself. This process of literary preemption recalls Butor's categorical assertion in his essay "La Critique et l'invention" that our view of the world is formed by books:

> To a great degree, we know the universe through books, and especially novels. . . . In our representation, what we see with our eyes counts for little compared to what people tell us, and very soon the words we hear with our ears are very few in comparison to those which we read. Narrative compacts itself into enormous reserves, inside which, from time to time, we undertake small explorations.[46]

Le Meurtre de Bleston becomes the pre-text for Revel's own diary. Soon after Burton declares that "in the detective novel the story goes against the stream, or more exactly . . . it superimposes two temporal sequences, the days of the inquiry that start at the crime, and the days of the drama that lead up to it" (p. 251), Revel begins to juxtapose two temporal sequences in his diary. In the course of composition he improves on the model's method by adding more and more time levels. He also unconsciously copies the detective novel's plot. In his version of the murder mystery, Burton is the victim, while Revel assigns himself the central roles: He becomes not only the agent of murder, as befits the relationship of epigone to literary father, but also the detective. The befuddled Revel would like to emulate the detective, who in Burton's formulation is a master of insight and rhetoric: "His entire life is directed toward that tremendous moment in which the efficacy of his explanations, of his revelation, of the words by which he unveils and unmasks, . . . the efficacy of his speech actually leads to the destruction of the criminal" (p. 214).

In the final month of writing, Revel achieves a breakthrough that enables him to conclude his diary in the triumphant conviction that the power of his vision has finally overcome all obstacles. The turning point for Revel comes when he succeeds in transcending the pre-text and the models and devises an original method of interpretation. This new approach, into which the better part of all the models has been absorbed, is a figural method similar to that by which the Old Testament is perceived to prefigure the New Testament and works of medieval Christian art are understood to depict this biblical relationship allegorically, but here the method is expanded to the point that everything is seen to be a metaphor for everything else. Butor may well be parodying Proust's "essences." All Revel's methods tend toward linking disparate things, and this final grand synthesis is the apogee of that process. Like the metaphors and the myths, Revel's final method has its origins in "describable" aspects of Bleston, specifically the phenomena of duplication in space and repetition in time. The diarist records with a certain fascination that Bleston has two railroad stations, two amusement parks, two cathedrals (which in Revel's favorite detective novel are the setting for two murders), and two Bailey sisters who look alike. The corresponding temporal phenomenon is his weekly routine, its repetitiveness symbolized in the image of the Ferris wheel. Revel finds these symmetries so suggestive that he begins to inject additional, unnecessary duplications into his life, by buying, for example, two maps of Bleston and two copies of *Le Meurtre de Bleston*. As Georges Raillard points out, "The entire story is obsessed by the theme of doubling."[47] Finally Revel starts to perceive correspondences all around him. There is but a small step between seeing similarity in similar things and seeing similarity in different things, for who is to say where similarity ends and difference begins? Revel thus decides that the cities and places portrayed in documentaries shown at the News Theater are figures for one another, for Bleston, and for the "hieroglyphs" – another Proustian echo – of the tapestries and the Old Cathedral window. He is delighted to perceive that the skies of Rome, Crete, Petra, Baalbek, Timgad, and Sicily are uniformly blue and, better yet, that Rome burns like Theseus's Athens in the Museum tapetries and that those ancient fires are red like the blood in Cain's window and like the fires that have been mysteriously burning in Bleston. For Revel, spatial likeness implies temporal continuity. He is thus able to reduce the hitherto unique and unmanageable presence of Bleston to a comprehensible and relatively harmless final link in a historical chain of cities and to proclaim his own year in the town the glorious culmination of a vast and interconnected sequence of events.

It is hardly surprising that a methodological breakthrough of the proportions of Revel's final figural interpretation should result in the apotheosis of the critic and the transformation of the exegesis into scripture. Composing his diary increasingly in the style of a liturgical chant, stringing together comparisons and parenthetical references to past events in sentences that go on for pages at a time, Revel comes to regard the work as a piece of prophetic writing that will free captive Bleston through its reception by future readers. His sense of triumph at the end is the joy of a pure imaginative victory. Although he does not know it, he has succeeded, not in retrieving the past but, rather, in creating a coherent fiction that has eclipsed both the past itself and the necessity for making sense of it.

In imposing an order on the chaos of his experiences, his diary has become a novel. The various types of analogical processes Revel used to "describe" his year in Bleston have dissolved the intended referent into words, but they have also recomposed these words into a new entity: Revel's text. Four central metaphors mark the coincidence of the unsuccessful referential diary and the new novelistic creation. Like gears, they engage both the referent (Revel's year in Bleston) and the process of capturing (or, rather, overwhelming) it with writing. These double metaphors are crossover points in the chiastic structure of the novel. They mark the limits of the narrative as description and at the same time serve as points of departure for an understanding of narrative as creation. They are the labyrinth, the map, the act of weaving, and the mirror.

The labyrinth originates as a metaphor Revel creates to describe his difficulties with time and space. Bleston appears labyrinthine to Revel, and he does not hesitate to transfer this spatial metaphor to time ("the labyrinth of time and memory" [p. 429]). Revel's writing comes to play a central role in this labyrinth metaphor. It is because Revel believes that a written record of the past will help him that he begins his diary in the first place, and he comes to view writing as the thread that will extricate him from the maze. The dated entries represent the days of his year and compose the chain descending into the past and linking him with his starting point:

> The rope of words that uncoils in this pile and connects me directly to the moment on May 1 when I began to braid it, this rope of words is like Ariadne's thread, because I am in a labyrinth, because I am writing in order to find my way in it, all these lines being the marks with which I mark the passages I already know, the labyrinth of my days in Bleston, incomparably more perplexing than the Cretan palace, since it alters itself even as I explore it. [p. 274]

Although Revel sometimes suspects that his writing is double-crossing him, as readers have surmised all along, he always recovers his faith in the power of language to create meaning and salvage memories from time's obliteration. By the end of the novel he recognizes that his words have been his means to victory over the evil part of Bleston: "It is finally clear that I have in fact succeeded in inflicting this wound on you, that my writing is burning you" (p. 382), he concludes. Revel of course never reaches the center of the labyrinth (February 29) or the "end of the thread" of text; the text-thread itself becomes a labyrinth *without* a center to be reached.

Significantly, Revel decides to begin his diary immediately after he burns his map of Bleston. He chose the map as his first key to Bleston in the hope that it would solve problems that, at that early stage, he believed were simply geographical. He received it, symbolically, at the hands of Ariadne-Ann. But his first act after purchasing the map is to get lost. Map in hand, he embarks on one of those divagations in Bleston that symbolize spiritual confusion. The trouble with the map is that it is too impenetrably a part of the external world. It is not a key to the city but, rather, a replica of the city in miniature, the city's "ironic response to my efforts to take its census and to see it whole" (p. 151). Butor lets readers appreciate the map's uselessness for themselves: The map is printed after the title page, and it proves to be quite inapplicable to the oppressive atmosphere of lurking evil Revel creates in his diary. *Le Meurtre de Bleston,* which puts Revel's dislike for the city into words (the ambiguous title expresses Bleston's hostile, criminally tainted atmosphere and, if read as an objective genitive, also suggests that the city can be "murdered"), serves him much better in his quest to comprehend Bleston than the map, which is revealed to be the city's accomplice. By way of coping with the map's disturbing authority, Revel superimposes other, imaginary maps over it, maps that, as reflections of his own experience in Bleston, are subject to modification with time. He envisions "other lines, other points of interest, other references, other networks, other systems of distribution and organization – in a word, other maps which, though vague and fragmentary at first, are gradually growing more precise and more complete" (p. 151). His antimap becomes an increasingly imaginative construction, until it finally turns into a kind of graphic extension or illustration of Revel's written text. After Revel burns the map in rage, he realizes that he has committed a senseless, inexplicable act of hatred and that he must come to an understanding of his resentment. He himself regards his diary as the means by which he will achieve this clarification. But the moment at which he transfers his allegiance from the map to the blank page can also be seen as a symbolic abandonment of his attempts to understand objectively in favor of attempts to transform imaginatively the things that disturb him. It is a process that begins with submissive reconstruction, changes into a more active but still not wholly autonomous interpretation that depends on fictive models, and finally blossoms into active creation of his surroundings.

The same progression from passiveness to action is recorded in the development of the metaphor of weaving. Revel at first has the sensation that he is being trapped in some external and hideous pattern, as if Bleston had begun to weave a net around him from which he is powerless to disentangle himself: "I feel myself completely surrounded by a sort of still and silent terror, . . . as if something that concerned me were weaving itself around me, closing in on me, slowly taking on a hideous shape" (p. 178). In a later passage the image becomes more concrete; Revel feels that he is in the middle of a loom, as if the helpless victim of ill-intentioned Blestonian Parcae: "I feel all around me the threads of the warp invading the weft like a tide; soon my hands will be caught up in this cloth and I myself, imprisoned within this loom, unable to find the right lever to change the pattern" (pp. 318–9). But toward the end, when Revel has found out that he can subdue Bleston by metaphor and myth, he discovers the artistic implications of the image and begins to depict himself as the weaver. He will, in his remaining days in Bleston, try to "reduce as best I can the gaps in this exploratory description, which, like a son of Cain's, I have been composing, forging, and weaving, ever since that murder in effigy, the burning of your map, Bleston" (p. 387). As the sons of Cain, father of the arts, weave textiles, Revel weaves his text[48] from the "thread" of his writing, both in the sense of writing a diary that moves like a shuttle forward with the passing days and backward to capture time (p. 396) and in the sense of weaving metaphors into myths, which capture and tame the space of the evil city of Bleston. Bleston will be re-created in and by his text. "Caught in the net of this cloth I am weaving, you will pursue a reading of yourself" (p. 394), he informs the vanquished city.

Inasmuch as Revel weaves his text, his endeavor becomes a fabrication. Inasmuch as Revel reflects on events, his text becomes a mirror. It is one of his fundamental errors to forget that the word "reflection" has more than one meaning.[49] The image of the mirror is central in his final figural interpretation: He designates as "mirrors" objects that appear to encapsulate the essence of a series of similar happenings in the past. The red clouds in a film on the burning of Rome at the News Theater are, for example, "bad mirrors, crude mirrors, dim mirrors that are tarnished, dull, and rough, through which, however, a whole series of red reflections succeeded in reaching us, the entire long, smoky, crackling, howling old intermittent red glow" (p. 333). In a similarly metaphorical sense, Revel decides to call his text a mirror with which he will catch Bleston:

> As for the whiteness of this sheet on which I am writing, . . . it is still
> a thick coat of paint . . .; but this thick coat of paint that my pen

scratches, like the point of a knife, that my pen scales like the flame of a blowtorch, covers a mirror, a mirror that reveals to me little by little, through all these cracks my sentences represent, my own face, lost in a gangue of muddy sweat, my own face, whose kernel of hyaline quartz my miseries and my rancor gradually wash, my own face and yours behind it, Bleston, yours ravaged by inner conflict, yours that will shine through more and more clearly, to the point that nothing will be seen of me except the glitter of the iris around the pupils and teeth around the tongue, yours which will finally be consumed in its amplified incandescence. [pp. 404–5]

The blank page, still a part of Bleston, is covered with paint. Revel imagines that he will scratch off the paint with his writing or, taking up the image of fire again, burn clarity into the page. But his description of the process of capture, though innocently meant, is surely to be understood ironically. The first thing that appears in the mirror is Revel's own face. "My own face," he intones three times, before mentioning Bleston. Bleston is *behind* the face of the solipsist; it shines *through* the face; it is brought into focus by Revel, who never completely disappears behind it. The mirror of the text consists primarily of Revel's reflection and only secondarily of his reflection on the subject of Bleston.

The end of *L'Emploi du temps* brings a certain confusion. It is unclear whether the novel ends on the positive note of Revel's triumph or the negative note of Butor's irony. On the one hand, the book superficially has a happy ending, and it is difficult not to believe an end. There is no one in the novel to contradict Revel or to put Revel's ultimate self-satisfaction into perspective, no editor to cap the diary with an analytic afterword. On the other hand, our common sense offsets the diarist's "I" and tends cautiously to discount his triumph; it suspects the presence of some "spirit of the story," as Wolfgang Kayser called it, that is not in unison with the narrator. We recall that the first person singular only represents a single point of view and that, even though that view is the only one we are provided with, if we insist on believing it we might be falling into the trap of a literary habit. We recall what Butor, who is highly conscious of the implications of the use of personal pronouns, has to say about the first person singular: "The 'he' leaves us outside, the 'I' lets us enter the inside, though it risks being a closed interior like the darkroom in which a photographer develops his negatives. The character cannot tell us what he knows about himself."[50] Has Revel succeeded, or has he failed, and if he has failed, in doing what? In his stated purpose of reconstructing the past correctly, Revel has obviously failed, as many critics have pointed out, and his failure is symbolized by his omitting to close the technical, temporal gap between his arrival in Bleston and the time he

starts keeping the diary.[51] As his exegesis becomes more grandly syn-
thetic, he becomes increasingly unconcerned with retelling the bare
facts of the past, so that in the last month of writing, September, he
rushes carelessly through a description of February and backward
through a description of March and at the end of the diary leaves an
open question concerning the midpoint of his year, February 29.

But as a poetic creation, Revel's work has succeeded. In Butor's view
it is impossible under any circumstances for human beings to pierce
through the wall of literature surrounding their perception to an unmediated reality. Consequently, a new, original text can be seen to fill a
gap, or inadequacy, in the huge library that constitutes our world,
where, as the shadowy substructure of the real world changes, new
gaps are continuously forming. Butor writes in his essay "La Critique
et l'invention,"

> The library gives us the world, but it gives us a false world; from time
> to time fissures are produced, reality revolts against books, and by the
> intermediary of our eyes, by the intermediary of language or of certain
> books, an outside makes a sign to us and gives us the feeling of being
> closed in. . . . The actual invention in its limited truth fills the gap that
> opens in the immense library.[52]

Thus when Revel writes toward the end of the novel, "I see you now,
Bleston streets" (p. 397), this proclamation of insight so similar to
Roquentin's "suddenly, I have seen," near the close of *La Nausée,* indeed registers a breakthrough to a new and potentially productive way
of seeing – for Revel's new comprehension, faulty as it is, goes beyond,
or in Butor's metaphor, "fills a gap between," the inadequate readings
of Bleston suggested to him by other fictions.

Revel's perplexing final dream of the New Cathedral illustrates the
problem of evaluating the end of the novel. The dream is a strange
mixture of grotesquerie and exaltation in which the church comes to
life, expands, and envelops the city and its inhabitants like a huge
breathing organism, while over the transept a great jeweled mechanical
fly flaps its wings, only to be replaced at last by a mysterious new
building that Revel can just catch a glimpse of before it disappears into
thickening fog. Is this bizarre transfiguration an inspired vision of a
utopian future, which would correspond to Revel's sentiments at the
end of the novel, or is it a premonition of an ultimate reign of terror
and an indication that Revel has finally gone mad? On closer analysis
this problematical cathedral is, and can only be, the one fictional work
of art in the novel that is a symbol for *L'Emploi du temps* itself, in the
sense of Butor's interpretation of Proust's work-in-the-work.[53] Furthermore, if *L'Emploi du temps* is to be understood as a reply to *A la*

recherche du temps perdu, it is worth noting that to Butor the cathedral in Proust's last volume symbolizes Proust's unfinished, unfinishable novel.[54] Revel records his dream of the cathedral directly after he announces that he will capture Bleston in his text as in a mirror. The vision of the cathedral is a symbolic *mise en abîme* of that ambitious and ambiguous scheme. As we know, Revel's pretext, the model he uses and then transcends, was *Le Meurtre de Bleston.* In Revel's view the principal flaw in the detective novel is the author's evaluation of the New Cathedral. George Burton sees only the splendors of the Old Cathedral and considers the New Cathedral a monstrous, tasteless pastiche. Revel develops a taste for the more recent building, however, and indeed judges it a masterpiece. Marveling that the author of the detective novel could be so blind, he writes in praise of the edifice:

> Even though I recognized that there was something very far from plagiarism in this bizarre construction, I had been made to feel that a spirit of surprising audacity had violently distorted the traditional themes, ornaments, and details, thereby achieving an imperfect, even crippled work of art, but one rich with a profound, irrefutable dream, a secret seminal power, and a pathetic appeal toward freer and better successes. [p. 175]

If *Le Meurtre de Bleston,* the pre-text, is equated with the Old Cathedral, then Revel's own text, an improved version of Burton's, is symbolized by the New Cathedral. In describing the New Cathedral, Revel actually supplies us with an evaluation of *L'Emploi du temps* itself. The novel is admittedly a bizarre and imperfect edifice, but it is daring, imaginative, and full of promise. At the end of the dream, the shadowy building that replaces the New Cathedral is the next metatext, which arises out of the insufficiencies of *L'Emploi du temps* and covers it in the expanding library of the world.

Butor hides a key to the interpretation of *L'Emploi du temps* in the New Cathedral: "Two rood-screens that touch" (p. 174) cast a shadowy X on the middle of the transept. In *Le Meurtre de Bleston,* Burton had placed the corpse – that is, the mystery to be solved – under this X. The X symbolizes the chiastic structure of *L'Emploi du temps.* Like a detective novel, *L'Emploi du temps* is "constructed against the stream" (p. 178); its various temporal series move backward and forward and converge on the mystery of February 29, the missing date that symbolizes the elusive point of change, or the threshold where the referential diary with its empty center meets the open-ended novel-to-be-continued. Revel's memory of the original murder under the X in *Le Meurtre de Bleston* – "the book produced an optical illusion deliberately intended by the author" – is temporarily effaced by the second, parallel murder (of the criminal by the detective), discovered in the Old Cathedral "under the spots of light" (p. 174). In *L'Emploi du temps,* similarly, the retrospective diary with its quest for lost time initially obscures the reader's perception of the forward-moving novel Revel is writing. Burton proposes that a murder mystery can be solved only by a second "murder," that is, by an act that is similar to, yet different from, the first murder and that the first murder "prefigures" (p. 215). Translated into a theory of fiction, his observation implies that mysteries, absent "points of intersection," generate solutions that relate to the original problem but nevertheless constitute new and different entities in themselves. In other words, a nonexistent center can be equated with a permanent "fissure" or a perpetual open end.[55]

Jean Pouillon has written that *L'Emploi du temps* is a novel about the problems of writing a novel.[56] This statement is certainly true in the sense in which Pouillon intended it, namely, that Butor wishes to show the novelist in the process of attempting to create a fiction adequate to reality and failing in that attempt. But Pouillon's statement is true in other ways as well. Although one might be tempted to read the novel as a drama of Revel's perception and his imagination – and indeed such dramatization would seem to be the best means a novelist has for presenting theory in the guise of fiction – *L'Emploi du temps* is not a psychological novel. Butor considers consciousness only as it relates to, and functions within, language, and he proposes a movement of language in consciousness – a movement that, after an initial push, after an original, arbitrary choice of descriptive words, is self-perpetuating and autonomous, progressing from a simple naming to a creating of myth. One is tempted to say that Butor replaces "involuntary memory" by "involuntary language." The noncharacter Revel is simply a mouthpiece whose "personality" has no effect on what happens to language. He is just a force to set the play of words in motion, a curtain raiser for the drama in which language is the main actor. Perceived changes in the external world can at best make indentations in the basically autonomous self-production of language and send the discourse off in new creative directions. That is, Butor does not deny that something like perception takes place, although it would be more nearly correct to describe the interplay of perceived exterior reality and language's procreations in Piaget's terms of assimilation (the assimilation of new information to a preexisting schema) and accommodation (the accommodation of an old schema to new information) than to use the word "perception," which has idealistic overtones.

The process of language formation that *L'Emploi du temps* demonstrates by example corresponds closely to that which Butor describes analytically in his critical essays. Since Butor formulates his theses most

compactly in the late "La Critique et l'invention" (1968), it is convenient to draw statements from this article, although the same ideas
occur in earlier essays in a more diffused form, even in the very early
"Petite Croisière préliminaire à une reconnaissance de l'archipel Joyce"
(1948), in which Butor proposes that the principal character in *Ulysses* is
language.[57] Butor begins with the premise that at the beginning of
human creation, that is, at the origins of language, the primary confrontation between human beings and external reality led to a malaise
and resulted in a naming of things (description): "The invention of
language itself was the natural result of a difficult situation: the malaise
of the first men." Besides the basis provided by "things," there is a
basis constituted by pretexts, which are formative in every stage of the
process of creating the text: "Most writers, whether they know it or
not, take the famous books of the past and put makeup on their
wrinkles." Any text will be received creatively by other readers, and its
mythology will thus be "continued." "The poet or novelist who realizes he is a critic at the same time considers not only the work of others
but also his own work unfinished; he knows he is not the only author,
and that his work appears in the context of older works and will be
continued by his readers."[58]

Clearly, the diary form is a particularly appropriate vehicle for the
allegory of language in *L'Emploi du temps*. By choosing to embed his
narrator's attempt to recover the past in the forward-marching, incre-
mental structure of the diary, Butor can maintain the two different
levels of discourse I have called the narrative of the signifier and the
narrative of the signified. Much like Frisch in *Stiller,* he uses the diary
to create a double narrative, a narrative with two senses rolled into one.
Whereas Frisch experiments with point of view, hiding Stiller's perspective in White's, Butor experiments with temporality in order to
fuse Revel's attempt to use language as a transparent medium with the
independent chain of words he actually creates. By multiplying chronologies, Butor achieves much the same effect as Frisch does by multiplying viewpoints. While Frisch aims to show that no single point of
view is valid, Butor, by letting Revel's thread of words shuttle back
and forth and come to rest repeatedly on the same past period of time,
suggests that a multiplicity of texts, no one more representationally
"correct" than any other, can be generated "about" a given subject.
Revel recalls Flaubert's Bouvard and Pécuchet in their blundering quest
for knowledge: The "truth" simply cannot be found in books.

As we have seen, the diary form as Revel conceives it, as an instrument of retrospection, is consistently undermined by the diary form as
it actually functions, as a vehicle for the unfolding of language. Butor
turns the novel into a battlefield, and because language ultimately wins,

L'Emploi du temps comes to occupy a strange, parodistic position vis-à-vis the tradition of the diary and the diary novel. The diary traditionally performed the function of creating order. In *L'Emploi du temps* the diary form is used instead to debunk the idea of order, for the order Revel attempts to impose on his days in Bleston fails. Of course, as we have seen, Revel misuses his chosen form, the journal, by trying to recapture the past in its pages. At the same time, the diary's successiveness makes it possible for a meta-order of language to take over and to succeed. The traditional journal and its order carry the personal stamp of the diarist; order, character, and the diary are intimately related. In *L'Emploi du temps* the meta-order of language is not the product of Revel's individuality; order and character are discontinuous. Under normal circumstances the diary is a tool in the hands of the diarist, but in Butor's novel it is the character Revel who occupies a secondary, instrumental, even locative position. Language is a self-generating thread that Revel merely follows, and Revel's consciousness is only the place where language unwinds from day to day.

As a text whose stated purpose is to reconstruct the past, *L'Emploi du temps* participates in the myth of depth. *L'Emploi du temps,* seen now not as Butor's allegory but as Revel's attempt to recapture the past, begins in evident support of the assumption that an a priori dichotomy exists between event and consciousness, that a valueless second instance obscures and makes inaccessible an authentic layer of experience. The split is much more pessimistically pronounced than in *A la recherche du temps perdu,* for Revel never recovers the past. There is no saving second instance, no involuntary memory that can magically re-create the absolute presence of the forgotten experience. And on this level of the implicit theoretical argument that arises out of Revel's diary, Butor abides by his pessimism. Yet the myth of depth attains a new dimension in *L'Emploi du temps.* Whereas the question of the limitation of human knowledge is thus definitively answered, Butor implies that the whole question was in fact not asked, or rather that the first question was a red herring, a point of order that needed clarification before the real question could be asked. The double question in the novel is mirrored by the peculiar admixture of two styles: on the one hand, the extreme pedantry of the diary and its reconstruction of the past and, on the other, the unrestricted fantasy of Revel's metaphors. The emphasis gradually begins to center on what, in terms of the myth of depth, would be the inauthentic half, the interpretation, as if the secondariness of the redemptive moment or saving microcosm had been recognized and the value of second things had been acknowledged. What is secondary gradually becomes primary; the text itself begins to lay claim to reality. Revel's metaphors, which carry us further and further away from the plain dusts and fogs of Bleston, are not, for us, a guide to the reality of the city, which after all is a fiction we cannot know from experience. For the reader, Revel's experience is not *like* something (e.g., Theseus's story); instead, it *is* something, namely, what Revel conceives it and describes it as being. The novel undergoes a metamorphosis from unsuccessful report to successful thing.

Its title – which is, in the tradition of Butor's titles, a pun – supports this interpretation.[59] "L'Emploi du temps" means "timetable" and "the use of time." Cast in the form of a complicated retrospective diary, the novel is a timetable; it also "uses time" in the sense of using up time. Even Revel recognizes toward the end that his writing has not recovered time but has, rather, consumed time and that precisely for this reason the writing is valuable and should under no circumstances be burned: "It was the number of these pages, of these sentences, which saved them and saved me, it was the time I would have needed; it was the weight of hours spent; it was this number, this time, this weight" (p. 378). In the sense of "timetable" the title describes the book as a thing; in the sense of "the use of time" it describes the novel as a created object and an object for reception. It is as if one were to call the *Comédie humaine* "Experiment with Recurrent Characters," or *Finnegans Wake* "Difficult Book."

The idea of the text as a thing made out of words poses the question of referentiality anew. For Butor, the object-book does not imply a simple reversal of the myth of depth or art for its own sake at the expense of a referent. Instead, a new kind of relation to the layer still considered primary, the social and environmental context, legitimizes the text. Twentieth-century antirealist writers typically design their theories of literature in watchful deference to this primary layer, which is seen as extraordinarily dominated, either exhilaratingly or dismayingly, by speed and change. Marinetti called for linguistic reproduction of the manner, rather than the matter, of this new world of speed; many other writers of our century express a compulsion to the same referentiality of manner. Butor likewise writes:

> It is clear that the world we live in is being transformed with great rapidity. Traditional narrative techniques are incapable of integrating all the new relations that have thus supervened. The result is a perpetual malaise; it is impossible for our consciousness to organize all the information that assails it, because we lack adequate tools.[60]

All these experimental and to all appearances antirealistic tendencies can be seen to be a quest for a more accurate realism; Butor writes, "Formal invention in the novel, far from being opposed to realism as shortsighted critics too often assume, is the *sine qua non* of a greater realism."

Butor composed his own later mobile and aleatory texts with an eye to reproducing a sense of our constantly changing reality. Especially in his ealier essays, however – written before *L'Emploi du temps* – Butor is less concerned that the text imitate the motions of reality. Instead, he maintains that the novelist's task is to project versions of reality that our consciousness produces or is capable of producing. The novel is *"the best possible place* to study how reality appears to us, or might appear."[61] Such novels are therefore meant to be realistic at one highly articulated remove from reality. This new realism of consciousness relates to linguistic experimentation in an obvious way: Because language forms our view of the world, expression in words automatically reflects the world as we see it or creates a world we could potentially see.

20

Doris Lessing:
The Golden Notebook

Doris Lessing, like Michel Butor, is a novelist who is remarkably frank about her aims. Unlike Butor, however, who believes that a work of fiction is enhanced by the variety of interpretations it draws in its wake, and that if critics interpret his novels in ways that never occurred to him this is a testimony to the work's creative and seminal power, Lessing thinks that a successful novel is one that readers understand as the author intended they should. If readers misunderstand, then they should be told. Consequently, Lessing writes openly and concretely about what she intended in her novels. In particular, she has said and written a good deal about the diary novel *The Golden Notebook,* which appeared in 1962 and which she has called a "failure"[62] because she thought it was badly misunderstood by critics. It will be well to discuss the work against a backdrop of Lessing's stated intentions, both because her explanations are illuminating and because the novel, indeed, does not always achieve precisely what the author says she set out to accomplish. The novel was not meant to be a banner for women's liberation, Lessing says; it is not primarily about the sex war, about politics, or about madness, although these are among its themes.[63] Instead, it was written to demonstrate the inadequacy of language to express experience, and in particular to make a statement on the crisis of the novel. In an interview conducted by Florence Howe in 1966, she said:

> I was really trying to express my sense of despair about writing a conventional novel. . . . So you've written a good novel or a moderate novel, but what does it actually say about what you've actually experienced. The truth is, absolutely nothing. Because you can't. I don't know what one does about novels. I shall write volume five [of the *Children of Violence* series] with my usual enthusiasm. I know perfectly well, when I've finished it, I shall think, Christ, what a lie. Because you can't get life into it. That's all there is to it, no matter how hard you try.[64]

In a later essay, written in 1971 and printed as the introduction to the third edition of *The Golden Notebook,* she also says that she intended to show "the dissatisfaction of a writer when something is finished: 'How little I have managed to say of the truth, how little I have caught of all that complexity; how can this small neat thing be true when what I experienced was so rough and apparently formless and unshaped' " (p. xvii).

The sentiment that motivated the composition of *The Golden Notebook,* doubt in language's expressive power, is closely related to the complex of ideas we encountered in Max Frisch's *Stiller* and Michel Butor's *L'Emploi du temps.* Like Frisch and Butor, Lessing chose a complex permutation of the diary form as the structural principle for her work, and she too conceived of her novel as an experiment in stating through form. She has made the point over and over again in interviews, no doubt in self-defense, since the first reviewers overlooked its formal construction entirely. "That was an extremely carefully constructed book,"[65] she has said; "the meaning is in the shape."[66] She meant the novel to be "a book of literary criticism" that used "various literary styles, in such a way that the shape of the book would provide the criticism."[67] The critique was to be directed at the lifelessness and ineffectuality of the conventional novel: "Another idea was that if the book were shaped in the right way it would make its own comment about the conventional novel. . . . My major aim was to shape a book which would make its own comment, a wordless statement: to talk through the way it was shaped" (p. xvii).

Despite these points of tangency with Frisch's and Butor's novels, the experience of reading *The Golden Notebook* is entirely unlike that of reading *Stiller* and still less like that of reading *L'Emploi du temps.* Its complicated formal structure notwithstanding, the work's texture lacks the polish, the artistry, and the artificiality of the two earlier novels. Instead of confining itself, exerciselike, to one theme or variations on a theme, it embraces half a dozen major themes, among which two of the most striking are the problems of independent women and the ambiguities of British communism in the 1950s. The novel incorporates an enormous cast of characters, long stretches of plain storytelling, a great deal of factual information as well as discussion of politics, and many convoluted subplots. The abundance of material threatens to overwhelm the carefully contrived formal divisions. Most of the material is not supportive of Lessing's avowed metacritical intention in any strict sense, so that *The Golden Notebook* is anything but "claustrophobic" and "enclosed," as Lessing herself describes it.[68] As a work that is meant to state through form, it might be judged uneconomical. Paradoxically, however, its strength as a novel lies in its breadth.[69] Doris

Lessing is a writer who has a great deal to say, whether she presents it in the guise of fiction or tells her readers outright in essays and interviews. She is a self-educated woman who has always been deeply committed to leftist politics and humanitarian causes: She was a member of the Communist Party until 1956; her vocal opposition to apartheid caused her to be prohibited from her native Southern Rhodesia; she has spoken out for committed literature and believes that writers have an obligation to dramatize the political conflicts of their time in their fiction. Her concern for literature has always been a part of a larger concern with actualities. Until she wrote *The Golden Notebook,* she was never a novelist remarkable for her interest in form. As she states in the essay "The Small Personal Voice," written in 1957,[70] her strongest commitment as a writer of fiction is to literary realism. Though her Communist Party affiliation did not have the effect of making her a supporter of the contemporaneous dogma of socialist realism, which she dismisses as inane, her ideas and even more particularly the style of her novels correspond to Marxist literary theories, in particular to the views of Georg Lukács.[71] Especially in the first volumes of her *Children of Violence* series, which describe the youth of the autobiographical character Martha Quest in prewar and wartime Africa, Lessing achieves the criteria of realism as Lukács formulates them: She creates a seemingly "total picture of objective reality"[72] populated by typical characters who represent the social classes from which they come, and filled with situations that illustrate the general through the particular.

Considering her political background, it is not surprising that Doris Lessing explains the crisis of language and of the novel, the stated theme of *The Golden Notebook,* in terms of the political situation and the resulting texture of life in the twentieth century. She believes that the decline of the novel since its peak in the nineteenth century can be traced to a rapidly changing environment and the anxiety of living in the shadow of the bomb. Writers no longer find it possible to create out of a shared climate of ethical judgment and a compassionate humanism that, according to Lessing, are the defining qualities of nineteenth-century realism. Twentieth-century writers, profoundly unsettled by the consciousness that their world is "so dangerous, violent, explosive, and precarious that it is in question whether soon there will be people left alive to write books and to read them," can no longer produce great works of art that are, like the great nineteenth-century novels, "a statement of faith in man himself." Instead they fall prey to "emotional anarchy" and "the luxury of despair." According to Lessing it is no longer possible to use the words and expressions that make nineteenth-century literature attractive, because they have become too simple and no longer correspond to the complexity of experience. She writes:

It would be hard, now, for a writer to use Balzacian phrases like "sublime virtue" or "monster of wickedness" without self-consciousness. Words, it seems, can no longer be used simply and naturally. All the great words like love, hate; life, death; loyalty, treachery; contain their opposite meanings and half a dozen shades of dubious implication. Words have become so inadequate to express the richness of our experience that the simplest sentence overheard on a bus reverberates like words shouted against a cliff.[73]

These views on the contemporary novelist's frustration at the inefficacy of his medium to express experience without reducing and falsifying it are not new to the reader of *The Golden Notebook*. Lessing's diarist, Anna Wulf, a novelist herself, elucidates the same ideas in even greater depth. At the beginning of the novel Anna, who has a writing block, tries in particular to spell out why it is no longer possible to write fiction. According to Anna, a good novel is one that has a "quality of philosophy," that is "powered with an intellectual or moral passion strong enough to create order, to create a new way of looking at life" (p. 59). The last writer to have written such novels, Anna thinks, was Thomas Mann. She explains the contemporary crisis of the novel as a consequence of a more general fragmentization of life, a derangement so profound that writers of fiction in our time are impotent either to comprehend or to transcend it. Novels are written as a reaction against helplessness, out of a desire to achieve a wholeness that ultimately proves unreachable. Anna thinks that two types of novels, neither of them satisfactory, result from these efforts to attain wholeness. The first type moves away from fiction in the direction of reportage. Unable to comprehend reality in a superior philosophical order, novels of this type offer readers detailed factual information, as a newspaper article does, about small segments of reality and thus help satisfy the hunger for comprehensive information. The other type of novel tends in the direction of a particular kind of illusionism. Such stories are written out of what Anna condemns as an unhealthy emotion, a nostalgia for times and places more exciting than our own, and a desire to re-create the mood of abandonment that such periods of upheaval brought with them.

Anna disapprovingly assesses her own best-selling first novel *Frontiers of War,* the story of an interracial love affair in British Africa during World War II, as a nostalgic novel. Her disgust with fictionalizing, and hence with novels, causes her to turn to journals. She writes: "It struck me that my doing this – turning everything into fiction – must be an evasion. . . . Why do I never write down, simply, what happens? Why don't I keep a diary?" (p. 197). The "pretext" as well as the reason for the diary novel *The Golden Notebook* is thus a concern with expressing the truth of experience. For Anna, this issue is closely connected to the question of the relative truth value of fictive and factual narration. Her views on writing change significantly in the course of her journal keeping. Whereas she was at first "blocked" for novels, by the end, she feels there is an irreconcilable split not just between fiction and a real experience but between any kind of expression in language, from an oral remark to a written sentence to longer pieces of writing, and any experience it tries to describe. She speaks of the "thinning of language against the density of our experience" (p. 259). Words, for her, suddenly start to detach themselves from any sort of meaning. Even the always unfinished, unrevised journals seem to her unwritable, unless she writes them extremely fast, with never a backward glance. The more she reflects on what she is writing or has written, or on any writing at all, the more acute her sense of the breakdown of language becomes:

> Words mean nothing. They have become, *when I think,* not the form into which existence is shaped, but a series of meaningless sounds, like nursery talk, and away to one side of experience. Or like the sound track of a film that has slipped its connection with the film. *When I am thinking* I have only to write a phrase like 'I walked down the street,' or take a phrase from a newspaper 'economic measures which lead to the full use of . . .' and immediately the words dissolve, and my mind starts spawning images which have nothing to do with the words, so that every word I see or hear seems like a small raft bobbing about on an enormous sea of images. So I can't write any longer. Or only when I write fast, without looking back at what I have written. For if I look back, then the words swim and have no sense and I am conscious only of me, Anna, as a pulse in a great darkness, and the words that I, Anna, write down are nothing, or like the secretions of a caterpillar that are forced out in ribbons to harden in the air. [p. 407]

By the end Anna finds journal keeping tolerable only inasmuch as she can push her journal style away from a meditative taking of account and toward the limit of the automatic and unstoppable flow of consciousness itself, or, in other words, inasmuch as writing a diary can be made to approach nonwriting.

The Golden Notebook is the record of Anna's experiments with different kinds of writing as well as of the progressive stages of her despair over the impotence of language. As we shall see, Lessing devises a variation on the traditional diary form in order to expose the truth it would not suffice to state explicitly: language's inability to express what is real. In its general conception her technique resembles Frisch's and Butor's. As we recall, Frisch presents several points of view to show the inadequacy of any single point of view, and Butor multiplies temporal relations to demonstrate the nonreferentiality of the evolving text. Lessing's purpose is to discredit the authority of any given narrative style, and she does so by juxtaposing segments of different notebooks her diarist keeps about different subjects and in different styles. Finally, a positive message emerges out of the work as well, as it did in *Stiller* and *L'Emploi du temps*. Stiller clears falsifications out of his way and comes close to the truth of his self by keeping a diary; Revel succeeds in writing a novel; and Anna Wulf finally attains Lessing's ideal of "wholeness." Lessing's solution is somewhat problematical, however: She substitutes a mystical intuition of oneness for a "total picture of objective reality," a puzzling transposition considering her political background, though one not unprecedented among Marxist critics.

By exploring the terrain between fact and fictionality in writing by example, Doris Lessing's use of the journal is if anything more complicated and differentiated than either Frisch's or Butor's. First, because *The Golden Notebook* is meant to debunk the conventional novel, it contains such a novel for the debunking. This novella functions as a frame for the journals. Lessing says that she "wanted to write a short formal novel which would enclose the rest and put in the experience it came out of, showing how ridiculous the formal novel is when it can't say a damned thing."[74] This short novel is called "Free Women"; it describes, from an omniscient narrator's point of view, Anna Wulf's life starting with the summer of 1957 and ending probably not much more than a year later. The rest of *The Golden Notebook* consists of Anna's journals, which she writes from about 1950 to about 1957 and which consequently contain "the experience" the short novel came out of. Anna finds that different aspects of her life call forth different styles of writing, so she keeps not one but four notebooks, which she herself describes as "a black notebook, which is to do with Anna Wulf the writer; a red notebook, concerned with politics; a yellow notebook, in which I make stories out of my experience; and a blue notebook which tries to be a diary" (p. 406).

Finally, Lessing has a fictive editor arrange the notebooks after the fact in an artificial order. The editor divides *The Golden Notebook* into five sections, the first four of which begin with an installment from the novella "Free Women" and contain selections from Anna's experiments in the order Black-Red-Yellow-Blue.[75] The purpose is to juxtapose examples of Anna's stylistic experiments written during the same time; the notebooks in section 1 were all written during the period 1950–4; in section 2, 1954–5; in section 3, 1955–6; and in section 4, 1955–7. The contents of the notebooks both complement and contradict one another. The contradictions confuse the reader and discourage him from keeping the information provided by the notebooks separately in mind; especially in the third and fourth sections the separate stories tend to melt together into one enormous, complicated plot. At the end of the fourth section there is an additional part entitled "The Golden Notebook." The fifth section contains only the conclusion of "Free Women."

Lessing's device of having her diarist write not one but several journals is not without precedent; the idea of multiple or multi-track diaries has come up from time to time in the history of the real diary. Amiel repeatedly contemplated introducing order into his journals by arranging them systematically according to different topics, while Hermann Hesse decided that only a plurality of diaries could do justice to the multidimensionality of his soul.[76] Lessing has Anna Wulf write in four notebooks for entirely different reasons, however. Most immediately, Anna's "split" diary reflects her increasingly acute psychic crisis, which could be described as a case of "split personality" and which, by the fourth section of the novel, degenerates into a pathological condition resembling schizophrenia. Anna's mental disorder is to be understood, in turn, as an extreme form of the alienation the fragmentization of individual experience in contemporary society must inevitably provoke. According to the Marxist Lessing, neurosis is not a personal problem or an abnormality. It is rather the logical consequence of an individual perception struggling to assimilate a reality as splintered and multifarious as our own.[77] An individual requires a sense of equilibrium, yet he is confronted, in our time, with incomprehensible and uncoordinatable diversity, which he perceives, and can only perceive, partially. He desires a totality that eludes him. Moreover, the onus of social perception channels his partial perception into prefabricated and only tenuously related subdivisions of false understanding, just as it obliges him to play and accept himself in a variety of different and incompatible roles.

Thus, Anna's four diaries are the concrete formal result of a concatenation of greater and lesser splits. The division is meant to be understood as pejorative, just as its causes are pernicious. Lessing writes in her introduction: "The essence of the book, the organization of it, everything in it, says implicitly and explicitly, that we must not divide things off, must not compartmentalize" (p. xiv). It is not hard to see how the dilemma of expression in language fits into a theory of society, perception, and mental health that posits irreconcilable division.[78] For Doris Lessing and Anna Wulf language is not a means of evoking dimensions of an experience that might otherwise have passed unobserved but, rather, an additional shrinking of the totality, an ineffective, distorted rendering of a perception that itself is only partial. Anna writes:

> Literature is analysis after the event. . . . To show a woman loving a
> man one should show her cooking a meal for him or opening a bottle of

> wine for the meal, while she waits for his ring at the door. Or waking in
> the morning before he does to see his face change from the calm of sleep
> into a smile of welcome. Yes. To be repeated a thousand times. But that
> isn't literature. Probably better as a film. Yes, the physical quality of
> life, that's living, not the analysis afterwards. [pp. 196–97]

The professional writer Anna is naïvely wistful about a medium that
involves visual images instead of words. It seems to her that a film
would bypass the analytical moment that makes linguistic representation a rendering of reality at a second remove. The camera eye would
not only avoid translating a visual experience into a different medium;
it would outwit the eye of the director and circumvent his partial perception by reproducing, without analysis, the entirety of what is there.

The negative theme of division in *The Golden Notebook* has its opposite, the theme of unity. Like the concept of fragmentization, the theme
of unity pervades the novel on all of its levels; it is applicable as a
solution in all the cases in which fragmentization constitutes the problem. Unity means transsubjective unity, or the breakdown of the individual personality; temporal unity, or the experience of presence; and
artistic unity, including "formlessness" as a criterion for verbal expression. It should be noted that the words "formlessness" and "breakdown" belong to the vocabulary both of unity and of fragmentization
and thus may potentially be given either a positive or a negative value.
At the beginning, Lessing uses the terms primarily in their pejorative
sense: Anna Wulf keeps four diaries out of a "fear of chaos," of "formlessness" (p. xi) and she is approaching a nervous "breakdown." Both
facts are symptoms of the effects of fragmentization and chaos. Later,
Lessing assigns a positive value to the terms, so that "formlessness"
becomes the solution to false order and therefore the opposite of chaos,
and Anna's "breakdown" is reevaluated as a desirable mode of passage
to transsubjective vision. Lessing writes in the introduction:

> In the inner Golden Notebook, things have come together, the divi-
> sions have broken down, there is formlessness with the end of frag-
> mentization – the triumph of the second theme, which is that of unity.
> Anna and Saul Green the American "break down." They are crazy,
> lunatic, mad – what you will. They "break down" into each other,
> into other people, break through the false patterns they have made up
> of their pasts, the patterns and formulas they have made to shore up
> themselves and each other, dissolve. [p. xi]

In the inner Golden Notebook, the last diary Anna writes, Anna records a series of illuminations, including an extraordinary dream trans-
mitted in the medium of film. The film rolls out the story of her years
in Africa, the elusive and challenging segment of her life that she tried

without success to describe twice, once in her novel *Frontiers of War* and once in her Black Notebook. The movie succeeds in breaking down the subjective viewpoint that has shaped her memories and shows her the reality of her past transsubjectively. The inner Golden Notebook thus symbolizes unity and is meant as a formal manifestation of her break-through out of mental illness.

The transsubjectivity Anna attains is expressed particularly in terms of her peculiar relationship to her lover, Saul. Lessing writes: "In the inner Golden Notebook, which is written by both of them, you can no longer distinguish between what is Saul and what is Anna" (p. xii). The two characters are in fact less indistinguishable than Lessing would have it, but an intermeshing of their personalities is evident. Saul is the film projectionist in Anna's dream. The film shows her not only the trans-subjective reality of her own experiences but experience that is foreign to her and familiar to Saul, like heroism and courage. From this foreign experience an image emerges that Anna will later use in her suggestion for the first sentence of Saul's new novel: "A man stood on a dry hillside in the moonlight, stood eternally, his rifle ready on his arm" (p. 543). Saul, meanwhile, also writes in the Golden Notebook, and he helps Anna overcome her writer's block by giving her the first sentence of her new novel.

In contrast to the Golden Notebook, Anna's four notebooks represent false form. In each notebook Anna experiments with a different kind of content or style, with a different modality of expression, each of which she hopes will prove the right means of reproducing the reality of her experience.

The Red Notebook, which is about Anna's relationship to the Communist Party and about politics, is most obviously a product of her desire for wholeness. Anna becomes a Communist because she is attracted to a view of the world that is total and to the idea of unity of purpose and action among men and women. Membership in the Communist Party proves unsatisfactory, however, for in contrast to the party Anna idealistically imagines and is drawn toward, the actual party merely upholds a falsified totality by ignoring facts incompatible with its political line and suppressing the claims of subjective individuality. The record of contemporary political events that Anna keeps in the Red Notebook also proves to be no solace. The Red Notebook trails off in a collection of newspaper clippings that mainly describe violent acts.

The Black and Yellow Notebooks represent the theoretical poles of truth-in-fact versus truth-in-fiction between which Anna oscillates in her doomed search for an adequate mode of verbal representation. In the Black Notebook, Anna takes the African experience she had fictionalized in *Frontiers of War* and tries to find the truth of the experience below the fiction. But she finds that in looking back on her youth in wartime Africa she always produces the same falsifying nostalgia for which she chastises her novel. In the Yellow Notebook she "alienates" her present experiences by presenting them fictively, and, of course, fails to capture the truth of her experience for that very reason.

The Blue Notebook is Anna's most straightforward attempt to equate truth with fact. Here she simply keeps a record of daily events. This sometimes means that she pastes newspaper clippings in her note book, but more often she writes up what happened to her from day to day, on the assumption that "the real things that happened in [the] day were the ordinary things." She finally decides, when she looks back on what she wrote, that she was wrong; factuality is not the right rubric under which to shelve experience either. She writes:

> The Blue Notebook, which I expected to be the most truthful of the notebooks, is worse than any of them. I expected a terse record of the facts to present some sort of pattern when I read it over, but this sort of record is as false as the account of what happened on 15th September, 1954, which I read now embarrassed because of its assumption that if I wrote 'at nine-thirty I went to the lavatory to shit and at two to pee and at four I sweated,' this would be more real than if I simply wrote what I thought. [p. 400]

At the end of *The Golden Notebook,* Lessing performs a sleight of hand in order to place her authorial stamp of approval on Anna's increasing despair at the various gradations of fact-in-fiction and fiction-in-fact her notebooks represent. In the final, or golden, notebook, Anna says that she starts writing a novel whose first sentence is, "The two women were alone in the London flat" (p. 547). This is the first sentence of Lessing's novel *The Golden Notebook,* or Part I of "Free Women." The novel therefore does not end but rather circles back to its starting point. It also becomes clear that not Doris Lessing but Anna Wulf is the author of "Free Women." The last-minute attribution of the novella to Anna has important consequences for the theme of narrative fictionality versus factuality. *The Golden Notebook* is constructed so that on first reading, the reader assumes that the "Free Women" narrative is the standard of reliability against which the subsequent journals can be measured. Because an installment of "Free Women" introduces each section of the novel, the conventional logic of the frame narrative, according to which the frame is more "real" than what it encloses, becomes operative. Moreover, the omniscient narrator of "Free Women" seems much more credible as a source of "fact" than Anna with her perpetual revisions and her four separate journals. Finally, the information in the "Free Women" sections really does stand uncontradicted for a long time, because it concerns a later period than the journals and is the sole source of information about that period until the notebooks catch up in the fourth section. Eventually, Lessing drops hints that the factuality of "Free Women" is contestable, hints that invariably occur in the form of a contradiction between some fact in "Free Women" and a corresponding fact in Anna's "factual" Blue Notebook. Thus in the Blue Notebook I, Tommy, Anna's friend's disturbed son, is described as being seventeen in 1950 (p. 197), whereas in "Free Women" he is twenty in 1957; in the Blue Notebook IV, Anna refers to Tommy's wife (p. 468), although the "Free Women" story never indicated that Tommy was married; and although according to the "Free Women" narrative Tommy is blind, Anna never describes him as such in the notebooks. The first hint is easily overlooked, and the others tend to mystify the reader rather than enlighten him about the expressly fictive status of "Free Women." It is not until after we find out that Anna is the author of "Free Women" that Lessing inserts a glaring discrepancy: Anna's lover, Saul, is referred to as "Milt" in the last section of the novella. Thus, by the end, the reader discovers that on the scale of Anna's fictions, "Free Women" is the most fictive of all. It is not a diary of daily events or a retelling of the past or even a fictionalization that closely follows Anna's day-to-day experiences, but an outright autobiographical novel. By making Anna the author of the novella, Lessing reverses the relationship of the frame narrative to the journals and thus deprives the reader of what has been his point of orientation for distinguishing the "facts" of Anna's story from the fictions.

If the "Free Women" narrative is invalidated as a source of reliable information about Anna's hypothetical "real" life, what can be put in its place? The Yellow Notebook is, of course, fictional; the Red Notebook may be "true," but it mainly concerns politics and deals with Anna's life too peripherally to stand alone as a source of fact; the Black Notebook purports to be the purely factual account of Anna's African past, but its reliability is impaired when Anna in the Blue Notebook recasts her wartime lover, Willi Rodde of the Black Notebook, as her husband and refers to him as "Max Wulf" (p. 400). Here, as in the "Free Women" narrative, Lessing interpolates a minor factual discrepancy in order to signal that the text is fictive. The Blue Notebook, which is allegedly painstakingly factual and is also the fixed point of reference from which both "Free Women" and the Black Notebook deviate, is the likeliest candidate for superseding the frame narrative. Yet Doris Lessing draws it and its successor the Golden Notebook into the realm of fictionality too. At the end of the third section of the Yellow Notebook, Anna's fictional alter ego, Ella, who is herself a novelist, begins thinking in terms peculiar to the novel's primary plot.

She conceives of a story that will achieve what is her author Anna's main obsession, the breaking of form. Anna writes of Ella:

> Looking for the outlines of a story . . . , she finds herself thinking: I've got to accept the patterns of self-knowledge which mean unhappiness or at least a dryness. But I can twist it into a victory. A man and a woman – yes. Both at the end of their tether. Both cracking up because of a deliberate attempt to transcend their own limits. And out of chaos, a new kind of strength.
> Ella looks inwards, as into a pool, to find this story imaged; but it remains a series of dry sentences in her mind. She waits, she waits patiently, for the images to form, to take on life. [pp. 339–40]

We recognize what Ella imagines as the story of Anna and Saul, which is described as "fact" in the last section of the Blue Notebook and the Golden Notebook. Ella's idea for a story has the effect of discrediting the last source of authority in *The Golden Notebook,* the Blue and Golden Notebooks, for pure factuality becomes an image in the mind of a fictional character.[79]

Doris Lessing thus has Anna end her diary in such a way that the structure of *The Golden Notebook* as a whole provides final verification for her contention that the truth of experience is irreproducible in language. Lessing's idea of splitting the diary into four allows her, as we have seen, to make her point in several different ways. First, the fourfold diary mirrors Anna's split personality; second, the protagonist's problem stands for a universal condition of partial perception that is caused by social fragmentization and aggravated by the restrictive categories language imposes on our understanding. Third, the division into four also gives Lessing room to show the failure of language by example, by having Anna Wulf explore four different variations on a scale from fictional to factual writing and to fail in four different, exemplary ways. The contrasting Golden Notebook establishes the theme of unity. In it Anna experiences pure presence and attains transsubjectivity, which means a breakthrough out of mental illness. Presence is mediated through a cinematic form that is supposed to represent the dissolution of all artistic form. The Golden Notebook also, supposedly, effaces point of view (symbolized by the dual point of view) and therefore, in theory, achieves and symbolizes the ideal of transsubjectivity.

Lessing's novel appeared eight years after *Stiller.* We noted already that the ideas expressed in *Stiller* were by no means new. Lessing does not take the step Butor took in *L'Emploi du temps,* that of reexamining the myth of depth; she never doubts that it is the purpose of language to be referential. The question arises of why Lessing chose to make much the same statement as Frisch by using much the same form. And since Lessing did write such a novel, why were her formal intentions overlooked by critics? Doris Lessing herself conjectures that "one reason for this is that the book is more in the European than in the English tradition of the novel" (p. xvii). She is probably right. The breakdown of language is not a conventional theme in twentieth-century English literature, and experimentation with structure as an alternative means of expression has not been a central concern of English fiction. But it is also true that the technical complexity of Doris Lessing's novel brings serious problems with it that the novels of Frisch and Butor do not. The most obvious problem is the discrepancy between Lessing's theory and her execution, between her aim to express a message through form and the fullness of content in the novel that tends to engulf the formal message. Moreover, the illumination that represents the breakthrough out of schizophrenia solves the problem of split experience and partial seeing, but it does not, logically, solve the problem of Anna's writer's block. Instead, the illumination makes the problem of words acute, for the experience is, as Anna says, inexpressible. Yet Anna's new beginning as a writer, her composition of "Free Women", implies that she overcomes her sterility.[80] The only way to resolve the discrepancy – a solution that is not very satisfactory – is to assume that Anna writes the novella ironically, juxtaposes it ironically to the notebooks, publishes the whole to make a point about the valuelessness of language, and immediately gives up writing to become a social worker – as the end of "Free Women" indicates.

One could also argue, as I did in discussing *Stiller,* that Anna publishes the notebooks plus the novella because this additive construct comes closer to the truth than a normal novel would.[81] According to this interpretation, the multiple and contradictory notebooks of the novel are a diminishment in the sense that they invalidate each other and thus demask the *idea* that representation is possible; but at the same time they are a summation that, by its very heterogeneity, approaches something like representation. Like the idea of formlessness, which points in two different directions in the novel and has a negative and a positive value, the idea of simultaneous variations might be seen to suggest infinity and thus totality rather than zero. The combination of the versions into a single novel could likewise be interpreted as an attempt to achieve artistic fusion rather than as a negative model of fragmentization and false form. Thus, Doris Lessing herself, who has repeatedly affirmed that her novel has a negative message, also says of *The Golden Notebook,* "Well at least I think it's more truthful because it's more complex."[82]

Notes

PREFACE

1 Peter Brang, "Über die Tagebuchfiktion in der russischen Literatur," in *Typologia Litterarum, Festschrift für Max Wehrli* (Zürich: Atlantis, 1968), pp. 443–6; Valerie Raoul, *The French Fictional Journal. Fictional Narcissism/Narcissistic Fiction* (Toronto: University of Toronto Press, 1980). Raoul presents a thorough and very interesting structural analysis of the diary novel, based on a corpus of French texts. Raoul has also written "Documents of Non-Identity: The Diary Novel in Québec," *Yale French Studies*, No. 65 (1983), pp. 187–99. Other works on the diary novel include Lynn Barstis, "The Modern Diary Novel: Heir of the Journal Intime," Diss. University of Illinois 1974. Barstis focuses on a characterization of the modern diary novel as a genre and shows the similarities between novels written in the late nineteenth and early twentieth centuries and the *journaux intimes*. Gerald Prince likewise characterizes the diary novel as a genre in his article "The Diary Novel: Notes for the Definition of a Subgenre," *Neophilologus*, 54 (1975), 477–81. Juliet Willman Kincaid, "The Novel as Journal: A Generic Study," Diss. Ohio State University 1977, writes on various typical functions of the journal in fiction (the diary as a device; the spiritual, confessional, psychological, and philosophical diary novel; diary novels about novelists). H. Porter Abbott, "Letters to the Self: The Cloistered Writer in Nonretrospective Fiction," *PMLA*, 95 (1980), 23–41, writes on processes of self-discovery (or their lack) in diary and epistolary fiction with a single narrator.

Writers on narrative theory who take the diary novel into account include Kurt Forstreuter, *Die deutsche Icherzählung* (Berlin: Emil Ebering, 1924), who mentions the diary novel as one of four types of first-person narrative; Robert Petsch, *Wesen und Formen der Erzählkunst* (Halle/Saale: Max Niemeyer, 1942), who considers the form very briefly as a variation on the epistolary novel; Käte Hamburger, *Die Logik der Dichtung* (Stuttgart: Klett, 1968, 2nd ed.), who likewise mentions the diary form as a variation on the epistolary novel; Bertil Romberg, *Studies in the Narrative Technique of the First-Person Novel* (Stockholm: Almquist & Wiksell, 1962), who gives an interesting characterization of its formal structure and remarks its particular appropriateness for psychological studies of the self; Gérard Genette in "Discours du récit," in *Figures III* (Paris: Seuil, 1972), who mentions it in connection with the "intercalated" time structure it shares with the epistolary novel; and Dorrit Cohn, *Transparent Minds* (Princeton, N.J.: Princeton University Press, 1978), who discusses it as an important ancestor of the interior monologue as found in Dujardin's *Les Lauriers sont coupés* or the "Penelope" section of *Ulysses,* or in her terminology, the "autonomous interior monologue."

In addition to the works just discussed, some critics of the diary or the "literary journal" mention its fictive counterpart. In particular William LeBaron Bingham, "The Journal as Literary Form," Diss. University of New Mexico 1969, discusses not only journals written for publication but also journal novels, journals as parts of novels, and the journal as the "subconscious form" of novels. Other works on the diary that touch on the diary novel are Albert Gräser, "Das literarische Tagebuch," Diss. Saarbrücken 1955, pp. 31–4; Fritz Neubert, "Zur Problematik der französischen 'Journaux Intimes' (Tagebücher)," in *Französische Literaturprobleme* (Berlin: Duncker & Humblot, 1962), pp. 441–4; and Peter Boerner, *Tagebuch* (Stuttgart: Metzler, 1969), pp. 28–9. K. Eckhard Kuhn-Osius, "Making Loose Ends Meet: Private Journals in the Public Realm," *German Quarterly,* 59 (1981), pp. 166–76, discusses fictionalization as a technique in literary diaries (p. 173).

PART I. PROBLEMS OF DEFINITION, METHOD, AND INTERPRETATION

1 André Gide, *The Counterfeiters,* trans. Dorothy Bussy (New York: Random House, 1973), p. 287.

2 For a critical study of German Romantic genre theory, see Peter Szondi, "Von der normativen zur spekulativen Gattungspoetik," in *Poetik und Geschichtsphilosophie,* ed. Wolfgang Fietkam (Frankfurt: Suhrkamp, 1974).

3 *The Fantastic,* trans. Richard Howard (Ithaca, N.Y.: Cornell University Press, 1975), p. 21.

4 "Literary Genres," in *Current Trends in Linguistics,* XII, ed. Thomas A. Sebeok (The Hague: Mouton, 1974), 957.

5 E.g., Paul Hernadi, *Beyond Genre* (Ithaca, N.Y.: Cornell University Press, 1972), p. 4, and Todorov, *The Fantastic,* p. 5.

6 "Der Zusammenhang zwischen den Verfahren der Sujetfügung und den allgemeinen Stilverfahren," in *Texte der russischen Formalisten,* ed. Jurij Striedter (München: Fink, 1969), I, 51.

7 Jurij Tynjanov, "Das literarische Faktum" (1924), in Striedter, speaks of the "Vorherrschaft oder . . . Vorhandensein eines bestimmten Genres" in a certain period (p. 397). Boris Tomachevski, "Thématique" (1925), in *Théorie de la littérature,* ed. and trans. Tzvetan Todorov (Paris: Seuil, 1965), speaks of genres as "des classes particulières des oeuvres" (p. 302).

8 See Tynjanov, in Striedter, pp. 395–9; also Tynjanov, "On Literary Evolution" (1927), in *Readings in Russian Poetics,* ed. Ladislav Matejka and Krystyna Pomorska (Cambridge, Mass.: MIT Press, 1971).

9 Tomachevski, "Thématique," p. 306.

10 *Literature as System* (Princeton, N.J.: Princeton University Press, 1971), pp. 72, 73.

11 Preface to Tzvetan Todorov, *The Poetics of Prose,* trans. Richard Howard (Ithaca, N.Y.: Cornell University Press, 1977), p. 11.

12 See, e.g., Jonathan Culler, *Structuralist Poetics* (Ithaca, N.Y.: Cornell University Press, 1975), p. 136, and Todorov, "Literary Genres," p. 958.

13 An expanded form of this argument can be found in Robert Scholes, *Structuralism in Literature* (New Haven, Conn: Yale University Press, 1974), pp. 130–1.

14 *S/Z,* trans. Richard Miller (New York: Hill & Wang, 1974), p. 3.

15 *Die Struktur des künstlerischen Textes* (Frankfurt: Suhrkamp, 1973), pp. 99–115.

16 Jacques Derrida, "La Loi du genre/The Law of Genre," in *Glyph,* 7 (1980), formulates what he calls the "law of genre" as follows: "A text cannot belong to no genre, it cannot be without or less a genre. Every text participates in one or several genres, there is no genreless text; there is always a genre and genres, yet such participation never amounts to belonging" (p. 212).

17 Saussure writes, "La langue est nécessaire pour que la parole soit intelligible et produise tous ses effects; mais celle-ci est nécessaire pour que la langue s'établisse; historiquement, le fait de parole précède toujours. . . . Enfin, c'est la parole qui fait évoluer la langue: ce sont les impressions reçues en entendant les autres qui modifient nos habitudes linguistiques." Ferdinand de Saussure, *Cours de linguistique générale,* ed. Tullio de Mauro (Paris: Payot, 1973), p. 37.

18 Ludwig Wittgenstein, *Philosophical Investigations,* trans. G.E.M. Anscombe (New York: Macmillan, 1958), § 18.

19 Modest versions of such a method have been used by critics who have chosen as their corpus all the novels written in a certain language within a span of three years, or the like, e.g., Eva Becker, *Der deutsche Roman um 1780* (Stuttgart: Metzler, 1964).

20 *Norm and Form* (London: Phaidon, 1966), p. 88.

21 René Wellek and Austin Warren, *Theory of Literature* (New York: Harcourt, Brace, 1942), p. 241.

22 I borrow the term "normal discourse" from Richard Rorty, *Philosophy and the Mirror of Nature* (Princeton, N.J.: Princeton University Press, 1979), p. 11.

23 Saussure, *Cours de linguistique générale,* p. 31.

24 Tomachevski, "Thématique," p. 303. My translation.

25 Michał Głowiński, "Der Dialog im Roman," *Poetica,* 6 (1974), 1–16, uses almost identical terminology; he speaks of "formaler Mimetismus" (p. 5). He gives as examples the Russian *skaz* and the Polish *gawęda* as imitations of oral forms, and the diary, epistolary, and memoir novels as imitations of written forms.

26 The diary has not, like the diary novel, suffered from critical neglect. Many scholarly studies on the diary and the so-called literary journal written for publication are available. There is, however, no good comprehensive history of the diary. The studies that touch on historical questions either give only a general outline of the development of the form, or present the results of investi-

gations conducted within limited national and historical boundaries. The longest and most ambitious work to date, Gustav René Hocke's *Das europäische
Tagebuch* (Wiesbaden: Limes, 1963), is comparative inasmuch as it deals with
diaries written by Western Europeans of all nationalities, but it concerns itself
primarily with establishing a typology of diaries rather than with the history of
the genre. Good bibliographical research on the diary, which would have been
especially useful for this study, is also lacking, with three notable exceptions.
These are the bibliographies by William Matthews, *American Diaries – An Anno-
tated Bibliography of American Diaries Written Prior to the Year 1861* (Berkeley and
Los Angeles: University of California Press, 1945), and *British Diaries – An An-
notated Bibliography of British Diaries Written Between 1442 and 1942* (Gloucester,
Mass.: Peter Smith, 1967), and the bibliography of nineteenth-century *journaux
intimes* presented by Alain Girard in the text of the excellent work *Le Journal
intime* (Paris: Presses universitaires de France, 1963). The latest and most complete summary of the history of the diary is contained in Peter Boerner's *Tagebuch* (Stuttgart: Metzler, 1969). Boerner provides a bibliography of all the critical literature on the diary and a summary of the main issues. For a quick
orientation, this work is recommended. Of the works that have appeared since
Boerner's bibliography, Béatrice Didier's *Le Journal intime* (Paris: Presses universitaires de France, 1976), an interpretive study of the diary as a cultural,
psychological, and literary phenomenon, stands out for bringing new insights
rather than merely reorganizing old material. Didier's remarks on journal style
are especially illuminating.

27 Cf. Hocke.

28 Gerald Prince, "The Diary Novel. Notes for the Definition of a Subgenre," *Neophilologus,* 59 (1975), 477–81, proposes a thematic rather than a
formal orientation: "What makes a diary novel unlike any other kind of narrative is . . . a theme – or, more precisely, a complex of themes and motifs – . . .
the theme of the diary, the theme of writing a diary and its concomitant themes
and motifs. Why does the narrator begin keeping a diary? . . . What does
writing mean to the narrator, or come to mean to him? . . . Where and when
exactly is the diary written?" (pp. 479, 480). Prince proposes a perfectly legitimate set, and one that offers an interesting theme for study in the diary novel. It
is not identical with the set defined by the formal characteristics I propose at the
start of Chapter 3, although it overlaps with it: The complex of themes Prince
distinguishes are not always treated in works written in diary *form* and therefore
considered diary novels by me. One reason why I do not adopt this definition is
that it is essentially synchronic, limited to the period when diaries such as we
understand them today were written. It is based on a certain conception of the
diary, on the assumption that we know what a diary *is*. If one were to write the
history of the set, one would place one's emphasis on the mimetic tie of the
diary novel to the real diary.

Prince finds that the diary novel's formal characteristics do not suffice to set it
apart from all other fiction. In fact, however, he shows that no *one* of the
diary's formal characteristics, taken *separately,* distinguishes the diary novel
from other genres. The *conjunction* of these characteristics does seem typologi-

cally adequate; the theme of the diary, in contrast, implies self-reference, which is a possible quality of all texts.

29 See, for example, Jean Marc Blanchard, "Of Cannibalism and Autobiography," *Modern Language Notes,* 93 (1978), 654, 666.

30 *The Logic of Literature,* trans. Marilynn J. Rose (Bloomington: Indiana University Press, 1973), pp. 313, 312.

31 Johannes Anderegg, *Fiktion und Kommunikation* (Göttingen: Vandenhoeck & Ruprecht, 1973), argues very similarly. Anderegg divides fictional narration into two categories, the "Ich-Du-Text" and the "Er-Text," which are similar to but not completely identical with Käte Hamburger's "Ich-Erzählung" and "Er-Erzählung," and notes that some "Ich-Du-Texte," unlike any "Er-Text," could mistakenly be supposed to be nonfiction (p. 43).

32 Valerie Raoul makes much the same point in *The French Fictional Journal: Fictional Narcissism/Narcissistic Fiction* (Toronto: University of Toronto Press, 1980), p. 5. Raoul's discussion of the relation of the fictional journal to the real journal is quite extensive, and generally I agree with it. Raoul likewise takes issue with Käte Hamburger's conclusions; she asserts that there are obvious differences between the real and the fictional journal (pp. 5, 6, 23). She discusses these differences in terms of *discours* (the real journal) and *récit* (the fictional journal) (pp. 10–11), in an argument similar to mine later in this text. Raoul also works with triangles in her structural analysis of diary fiction and gives a triangle similar to mine above in order to illustrate the relation of the journal to the novel (p. 72). Her ensuing discussion of the relation of intradiegetic and extradiegetic narrative levels in a formally mimetic genre is extremely interesting (pp. 72–6).

33 Gershon Shaked, "The Grace of Reason and the Disgrace of Misery: Zweig and Roth – A Correspondence," *Hebrew University Studies in Literature,* 10 (1982), 247–70.

34 I borrow the term "naturalization" from Jonathan Culler, *Structuralist Poetics.* Culler uses "naturalization" to mean rendering "the text intelligible by relating it to various models of coherence" (p. 159). Thus the writer can present his text as *vraisemblable* or natural at a variety of different levels (Culler enumerates five), and the reader "naturalizes" the narrative in order to make sense of it (pp. 140–60). According to Culler, identifying a narrator (e.g., as crazy) is a common method of naturalization (p. 200).

35 *Love's Pilgrimage: A Story Founded on Facts* (Philadelphia: John Bioren, 1799), p. 172. On the part- and multiple-diary novel, see also Juliet Willman Kincaid, "*The Novel as Journal: A Generic Study,*" Diss. Ohio State University, 1977, pp. 88 ff.

36 *Redgauntlet* (London: Routledge, n.d.), p. 141.

37 *Transparent Minds* (Princeton, N.J.: Princeton University Press, 1978), pp. 138–9.

38 "Letters to the Self: The Cloistered Writer in Nonretrospective Fiction," *PMLA,* 95 (1980), 23–41. I do not agree with all of Abbott's interpretations, which put too great an emphasis on what the diarist says or does in the end; thus Werther, it seems to me, is an endorsed narrator, as are many other narrators who commit suicide (Upton Sinclair's Arthur Stirling would be another example).

39 *Berlin Alexanderplatz* (Olton: Walter-Verlag, 1961), p. 327.

40 See, e.g., John Freccero, "Zeno's Last Cigarette," *Modern Language Notes*, 77 (1962), 3.

41 Paul Valéry, in fragments of 1934 and 1935, notes that the knowable self is a linguistic self (*Cahiers* I [Paris: Gallimard, 1973], 446). Contemporary critics, e.g., Paul de Man, "Autobiography as De-Facement," *Modern Language Notes*, 94 (1979), 920, and Eugenio Donato, "The Ruins of Memory: Archeological Fragments and Textual Artifacts," *Modern Language Notes*, 93 (1978), 575–6, echo this idea, claiming that the act of signification turns the self into language. Louis A. Renza, "The Veto of the Imagination: A Theory of Autobiography," *New Literary History*, 9 (1977), 6–7, maintains that writing isolates what is signifiable from its "prelinguistic background."

42 *Roland Barthes*, trans. Richard Howard (New York: Hill & Wang, 1977), p. 56. Blanchard, "Of Cannibalism and Autobiography," argues similarly: "The self does not exist; it writes; it is *l'écriture*" (p. 673).

43 "Imaginary and Symbolic in Lacan: Marxism, Psychoanalytic Criticism, and the Problem of the Subject," in *Yale French Studies*, No. 55/56 (1977), pp. 362–3.

44 "Autobiography in the Third Person," *New Literary History*, 9 (1977), 32. Renza, p. 9, likewise writes: "The autobiographer must come to terms with a unique pronominal crux: how can he keep using the first-person pronoun . . . without its becoming . . . a de facto third-person pronoun?" See also Louis Marin, "The Autobiographical Interruption: About Stendhal's *Life of Henry Brulard*," *Modern Language Notes*, 93 (1978), 602.

45 Lejeune, p. 29.

46 Cf. Käte Hamburger, *The Logic of Literature*, p. 140. Johannes Anderegg, *Fiktion und Kommunikation*, similarly designates this style as having no narrator, as being accepted by the reader, and as clearly fictive. Cf. also Michał Głowiński, "On the First-Person Novel," *New Literary History*, 9 (1977), 103, and Stanisław Eile, "The Novel as an Expression of the Writer's Vision of the World," *New Literary History*, 9 (1977), 120. S. Y. Kuroda in "Where Epistemology, Style, and Grammar Meet," *Festschrift for Morris Halle*, ed. P. Kiparsky and S. Anderson (New York: Holt, Rinehart & Winston, 1973), distinguishes between reportive style (a first-person narrator, or an effaced or neutral narrator who is not omniscient in a non–first-person story), and nonreportive style, which does not conform to the basic paradigm of linguistic performance in terms of speaker and hearer. It is more correct, he asserts, to say that there is no subject of consciousness whose judgment the statement is taken as representing, rather than to speak of an "omniscient narrator."

47 Reliable first-person discourse in fiction can be generated in a number of ways. For example, the first person can take his authority from the third person by borrowing forms of discourse appropriate only to the third person (Sartre uses this technique in *La Nausée*). Eile, pp. 118, 122, notes that in such narratives as *Robinson Crusoe* and *Moby Dick* the first person acquires reliability by virtue of his "ideal understanding, excellent memory, and extraordinary omnipresence."

48 *How to Do Things with Words* (Cambridge, Mass.: Harvard University Press, 1975).

49 Jean-Jacques Rousseau, *The Confessions,* trans. J. M. Cohen (London: Penguin, 1953), pp. 17, 169.

50 Anton Marty, *Untersuchungen zur Grundlegung der allgemeinen Grammatik und Sprachphilosophie* (Halle: Niemeyer, 1908), pp. 363–4.

51 Roman Jakobson, "Closing Statement: Linguistics and Poetics," in *Style in Language,* ed. Thomas A. Sebeok (Cambridge, Mass.: MIT Press, 1960), p. 354.

52 They need not, of course, occur in this form – for example, such expressions as "Woe!" or "Alas!" would also be expressives.

53 Marty, pp. 353–5.

54 Jakobson, p. 380. C. K. Ogden and I. A. Richards, *The Meaning of Meaning* (New York: Harcourt, Brace, & World, 1956, first pub. 1923) arrived at the same distinction, apparently independently. They speak of a division between the "symbolic" (referential) and the "emotive" use of words, and see in "emotive language," or "the use of words to express or excite feelings or attitudes" (p. 149), a way of explaining "meaning" in poetry. They assert that poetry is "the supreme form of emotive language" (p. 159). See also I. A. Richards, *Principles of Literary Criticism* (London: Kegan, Paul, Trench, Trubner, 1924), pp. 267–8, 273.

55 See Ludwig Wittgenstein, *The Blue and Brown Books* (New York: Harper & Row, 1965), pp. 66–9.

56 Wittgenstein, *Philosophical Investigations,* § 246, 288.

57 Ibid, § 412, 417.

58 Garth Hallett, *A Companion to Wittgenstein's "Philosophical Investigations"* (Ithaca, N.Y.: Cornell University Press, 1977), p. 28.

59 Wittgenstein, *Philosophical Investigations,* § 256, 284, 404, 288. In the *Zettel,* ed. G.E.M. Anscombe and G. H. von Wright, trans. G.E.M. Anscombe (Berkeley: University of California Press, 1967), §472, he writes: "Psychological verbs characterized by the fact that the third person of the present is to be verified by observation, the first person not. Sentences in the third person of the present: information. In the first person present: expression [Äußerung]. ((Not quite right.))"

60 Wittgenstein, *Philosophical Investigations,* p. 178.

61 Ibid., § 244.

62 *Critical Dissertation on the Poems of Ossian* (1763), in *The Poems of Ossian* (New York, n.d.), p. 175. Quoted by Meyer Abrams, *The Mirror and the Lamp* (New York: Oxford University Press, 1953), p. 83.

63 Wittgenstein, *Philosophical Investigations,* pp. 187e–9e.

64 Abrams, *The Mirror and the Lamp,* pp. 72–8.

65 Johann Wolfgang von Goethe, *Die Leiden des jungen Werthers,* in *Werke,* ed. Erich Trunz (Nördlingen: Beck, 1973), VI, 36–7. Translation from *The Sorrows of Young Werther,* trans. Elizabeth Mayer and Louise Bogan (New York: Random House, 1971), pp. 43–4.

66 Goethe, *Werther*, p. 10, my translation; Rainer Maria Rilke, *Die Aufzeich-nungen des Malte Laurids Brigge*, in *Sämtliche Werke*, XI (Frankfurt: Insel, 1955), 755, 756; translation from *The Notebooks of Malte Laurids Brigge*, trans. M. D. Herter Norton (New York: Norton, 1964), pp. 51, 52.

67 Though he makes no reference to predecessors, Wittgenstein seems to stand in the tradition of eighteenth-century theories on the origin of languages (and also of such studies as Charles Darwin's *The Expression of the Emotions* [1872], which treats the "language" of the body). Thus, the abbé de Condillac in the *Essai sur l'origine des connoissances humaines* (1746) writes that human language was motivated by passion; the "natural signs" of perception were cries of passion and gestures, whereas naming and spoken language came later. Jean-Jacques Rousseau in *On the Origin of Languages* (1749, ca. 1755) goes a step further; according to Rousseau, the passions stimulated the first *words* (rather than the first gestures, which were dictated by need). The first language was expressive, passionate, and melodious; it spoke to the listener's heart rather than to his reason, persuaded without convincing.

PART II. THE DIARY NOVEL IN THE EIGHTEENTH AND EARLY NINETEENTH CENTURIES

1 See Peter Boerner, *Tagebuch* (Stuttgart: Metzler, 1969), p. 42, and Gustav René Hocke, *Das europäische Tagebuch* (Wiesbaden: Limes, 1963).

2 Wolfgang Schmeisser in "Studien über das vorromantische und romantische Tagebuch," Diss. Berlin 1952, shows a line of development from the Pietist to the German Romantic diaries, asserting that the Pietist diary is the "Urtypus" of the modern diary (Ch. I). For the French *journaux intimes* the influence of Rousseau's *Confessions* is usually cited rather than a formal source; see Fritz Neubert, "Zur Problematik der französischen 'Journaux Intimes' (Tagebü-cher)," in *Französische Literaturprobleme* (Berlin: Duncker & Humblot, 1962), p. 412 et passim, and Alain Girard, *Le Journal intime* (Paris: Presses universitaires de France, 1963), p. 44 ff.

3 E.g., Godfrey Frank Singer, *The Epistolary Novel: Its Origin, Development, Decline, and Residuary Influence* (New York: Russell & Russell, 1963; first pub. 1933); Robert Adams Day, *Told in Letters: Epistolary Fiction Before Richardson* (Ann Arbor: University of Michigan Press, 1966), Ch. II; Vivienne Mylne, *The Eighteenth-Century French Novel: Techniques of Illusion* (New York: Barnes & Noble Books, 1965), p. 144.

4 The novel was attacked for lacking verisimilitude, and also for falsely presenting itself as real. See Mylne, pp. 13–15, 75, and Eva Becker, *Der deutsche Roman um 1780* (Stuttgart: Metzler, 1964), p. 12.

5 *Diacritics* 10 (1980), 15–26.

6 See Henry Knight Miller, "Augustan Prose Fiction and the Romance Tradition," *Studies in the Eighteenth Century* III, ed. R. F. Brissenden and J. C. Eade (Toronto: University of Toronto Press, 1976), 247. Day writes in *Told in Letters*, "After the 'Augustan' reader had salved his moral or aesthetic conscience . . . with the preliminary premise that he was reading a true history, he (or she) settled down contentedly to tales of the wildest improbability" (p. 110).

7 See Meyer Abrams's survey of the history of aesthetic theory before the Romantics in *The Mirror and the Lamp* (New York: Oxford University Press, 1953), p. 11.

8 "Wirklichkeitsbegriff and Möglichkeit des Romans," in *Nachahmung und Illusion,* ed. Hans Robert Jauß (München: Eidos Verlag, 1964), p. 9.

9 One of the most persuasive explanations for literary change proposes that art is continually called on to justify its privileged status as art. As society changes, fiction that derives its legitimation from outdated assumptions about its purpose within the framework of what is believed to be reality is no longer accepted, and more up-to-date fiction takes its place. Blumenberg argues thus, as does Erich Köhler, "Zur Selbstauffassung des höfischen Dichters," in *Wege der Literatursoziologie,* ed. Norbert Fügen (Neuwied: Luchterhand, 1968).

10 Mylne, *Eighteenth-Century French Novel,* makes a similar point, p. 147.

11 Fabienne Gégou, *Lettre-traité de Pierre-Daniel Huet sur l'origine des romans* (Paris: Editions A.-G. Nizet, 1971), p. 47.

12 See the essays of Morhof and Rotth in *Romantheorie. Dokumentation ihrer Geschichte in Deutschland 1620–1880,* ed. Eberhard Lämmert et al. (Berlin: Kiepenheuer & Witsch, 1971).

13 Marie-Thérèse Hipp, *Mythes et Réalités. Enquête sur le roman et les mémoires (1660–1700)* (Paris: Klincksieck, 1976), pp. 42–3.

14 Abrams, *The Mirror and the Lamp,* pp. 263–4.

15 "Die Wandlung des Nachahmungsbegriffes in der französischen Ästhetik im 18. Jahrhundert," in *Nachahmung und Illusion,* ed. Hans Robert Jauß (München: Eidos, 1964).

16 Werner Krauss, "Zur französischen Romantheorie des 18. Jahrhunderts," and Hans Robert Jauß, "Nachahmungsprinzip und Wirklichkeitsbegriff in der Theorie des Romans von Diderot bis Stendahl," both in *Nachahmung und Illusion.* See also Jacques Rustin, "Mensonge et vérité dans le roman français du XVIIIe siècle," *Revue d'Histoire littéraire de la France* 69 (1969), 13–38.

17 *Imitation and Illusion in the French Memoir-Novel, 1700–1750* (New Haven, Conn.: Yale University Press, 1969), pp. 25–6.

18 Mylne's remarks on Prévost's novels of the 1730s indicate that he already used the device playfully then (pp. 73–5). See also Frédéric Deloffre, "Le Problème de l'illusion romanesque entre 1700 et 1715," in *La Littérature narrative d'imagination* (Paris: Presses universitaires de France, 1961), pp. 115–33, on Marivaux and others. J. M. S. Tompkins says in *The Popular Novel in England, 1770–1800* (London: Methuen, 1969; first pub. 1932) in reference to editors' introductions to novels written from 1770 to 1800 that "the trick was stale" (p. 4). Valerie Raoul, *The French Fictional Journal: Fictional Narcissism/Narcissistic Fiction* (Toronto: University of Toronto Press, 1980), discusses the ironic use of the editorial preface in the diary novel (pp. 15–18).

19 E. T. A. Hoffman, *Sämtliche poetischen Werke* (Wiesbaden: Emil Vollmer Verlag, n.d.), I, 52.

20 Søren Kierkegaard, *Either/Or,* trans. David F. Swenson and Lillian Swenson (Princeton, N.J.: Princeton University Press, 1949), p. 9.

21 *A Cruising Voyage Round the World* (London: Bell & Lintot, 1712), p. xxi.

22 *The Rise of Puritanism* (New York: Columbia University Press, 1938), p. 96.

23 *An Account of some Remarkable Passages in the Life of a Private Gentleman; with Reflections thereon* (London: J. Downing, 1711), p. 245.

24 Protestant works published under the title of "Journal" before *Robinson Crusoe* (e.g., the "journals" of George Fox, Stephen Crisp, and William Penn, all 1694) are in fact autobiographies, just as sea journals before Cooke's and Rogers's are retrospective travel accounts.

25 André Gide, *L'Ecole des femmes* (Paris: Gallimard, 1944), p. 53.

26 Jean-Paul Sartre, *La Nausée* (Paris: Gallimard, 1938), p. 9.

27 Addison, Steele, and others, *The Spectator*, ed. G. Gregory Smith (London: J. M. Dent, 1958), II, 460.

28 Samuel Johnson, *Works* (Oxford: Talboys & Wheeler, 1825), IV, 346.

29 It is known that Defoe had a copy of Alexandre Exquemelin's *The Bucaniers of America* (1685), which contained two sea journals, in his library. Arthur Wellesley Secord, *Studies in the Narrative Method of Defoe* (New York: Russell and Russell, 1963; first pub. 1924), also notes that Robert Knox's published story of his life in Ceylon was almost certainly one of Defoe's sources, and conjectures that the writer might have met Knox personally and gained access to his manuscript, which included "a sort of diary or journal" (p. 41).

30 *Defoe and Spiritual Autobiography* (Princeton, N.J.: Princeton University Press, 1965), pp. ix, 6–7.

31 Several critics have commented on this aspect of the work. See, e.g., J. Donald Crowley's editor's introduction to Daniel Defoe, *The Life and Strange Surprizing Adventures of Robinson Crusoe, of York, Mariner* (New York: Oxford University Press, 1972), p. xv, and Robert Weimann, "Defoe-Robinson Crusoe," in *Der englische Roman*, ed. Franz K. Stanzel (Düsseldorf: August Begel Verlag, 1969), I, 118 ff.

32 Three critics who advance the interpretation that *Robinson Crusoe* was primarily influenced by the model of spiritual autobiography are G. A. Starr, *Defoe and Spiritual Autobiography;* Martin J. Greif, "The Conversion of Robinson Crusoe," *Studies in English Literature, 1500–1900,* II (1966), 551–74; and J. Paul Hunter in *The Reluctant Pilgrim: Defoe's Emblematic Method and Quest for Form in "Robinson Crusoe"* (Baltimore, Md.: Johns Hopkins University Press, 1966) and "The Un-Sources of Robinson Crusoe," in *Twentieth Century Interpretations of Robinson Crusoe*, ed. Frank H. Ellis (Englewood Cliffs, N.J.: Prentice-Hall, 1969).

33 Arthur Wellesley Secord, *Studies in the Narrative Method of Defoe*, views *Robinson Crusoe* primarily as an adventure story rather than as an autobiography and presents the results of his extensive research on Defoe's probable sources in contemporary travel literature.

34 Defoe, *The Life and Strange Surprizing Adventures of Robinson Crusoe, of York, Mariner*, pp. 70, 69. Further references to this edition will be given in parentheses in the text.

35 See Starr, *Defoe and Spiritual Autobiography*, Ch. 2.

36 J. Paul Hunter in *The Reluctant Pilgrim*, who also notes the temporal inconsistencies in Crusoe's journal, similarly links Crusoe's retrospective style to the allegorical dimension of the work (pp. 144–6).

37 See Hermann Ullrich, *Robinson und Robinsonaden, Litterarhistorische Forschungen,* ed. Josef Schick and M. Frh. v. Waldberg, Heft 7 (Weimar: Emil Felber, 1898), for a bibliography.

38 [Peter Longueville], *The Hermit: Or, The Unparalled* [!] *Sufferings and Surprising Adventures of Mr. Philip Quarll* (Westminster: T. Warner & B. Creake, 1727), p. 59.

39 *Hannah Hewit, or, the Female Crusoe* (London: Dibdin, 1792), p. 83.

40 The story of the Dutch sailor evidently did have its source in fact: Commodore Roggeveen, who stopped at Ascension Island in 1723 after a voyage around the world, is said to have recorded in his journal the story of a man who was marooned there several years earlier (Robert Kerr, *General History and Collection of Voyages and Travels,* IX [Edinburgh: W. Blackwood, 1814], 67, 193). No published source for the fictive narrative is known, however. Isaac James in *Providence Displayed: or, The Remarkable Adventures of Alexander Selkirk* (Bristol: Riggs & Cottle, 1800) conjectures that the fiction can be traced to "a Passage in Roggewein, concerning a Dutch Book-Keeper" (p. iv), but the attribution cannot be accepted because the story of the sailor is not included in any of Roggeveen's travel descriptions published before 1728, the date of the *Authentick Relation.*

41 James, *Providence Displayed,* p. iv.

42 Samuel Richardson, *Pamela, or, Virtue Rewarded* (London: C. Rivington & J. Osborn, 1741), I, 123.

43 *Reise in die mittäglichen Provinzen von Frankreich, Sämmtliche Werke* (Leipzig: Göschen, 1844), I, 124, 209.

44 *Journal to Stella,* ed. Harold Williams (New York: Clarendon Press, 1948), I, 153.

45 Laurence Sterne and Elizabeth Draper, *The Journal to Eliza and Various Letters,* ed. Wilbur L. Cross (New York: J. F. Taylor, 1904), p. 51.

46 *Hermione, or The Orphan Sisters* (London: William Lane, 1791), I, 167.

47 *Memoirs of Mary* (London: J. Bell, 1793), I, 93.

48 *Swift, Journal to Stella,* p. 153.

49 *Memoirs of Miss Sidney Bidulph* (London: Dodsley, 1769), I, 10.

50 The historian of the English epistolary novel Frank Gees Black, *The Epistolary Novel in the Late Eighteenth Century* (Eugene: University of Oregon Press, 1940), considers the eighteenth-century diary novel to be a kind of epistolary novel (p. 57). Jean Rousset, who discusses the letter-journal novel briefly in *Forme et Signification* (Paris: Corti, 1962), comes to the same conclusion I do, that the letter journal is a transitional type between the epistolary novel and the *journal intime* (p. 72).

51 Black, pp. 2–3, 19–22, and 174 (chart). Godfrey Frank Singer in *The Epistolary Novel* also concludes that the strongest influence on the epistolary novel in the same peak period was Richardson's, although his figures do not coincide with those of Black (Ch. VI).

52 E.g., Black, pp. 57–60; Ilse Weymar, "Der deutsche Briefroman," Diss.

Hamburg 1942, pp. 107–9; Rousset, p. 70 et passim; Natascha Würzbach, "Die Struktur des Briefromans und seine Entstehung in England," Diss. München 1964, pp. 85 ff.

53 See Vivienne Mylne, *The Eighteenth-Century French Novel,* and Janet Gurkin Altmann, "Epistolary: Approaches to a Form," Diss. Yale University 1973, for extensive discussions of the epistolary form.

54 Godfrey Frank Singer, *The Epistolary Novel,* and Robert Adams Day, *Told in Letters,* pp. 194 ff. Both argue that in England the epistolary novel probably evolved from the drama. Epistolary novels were first written by playwrights-turned-novelists when it became unfeasible for them to write for the stage, and they cast their novels in the form closest to dialogue, exchanges of letters.

55 Gabriel Joseph de Lavergne, comte de Guilleragues [?], *Lettres portugaises, Valentins et autres oeuvres de Guilleragues,* ed. J. Rougeot (Paris: Garnier, 1962), p. 58.

56 Frances Sheridan, I, 15.

57 *Hermione,* III, 64.

58 Sheridan, I, 299. Italics mine.

59 Richardson, I, 199–200.

60 Becker, Der deutsche Roman um 1780, p. 189.

61 *Anton Reiser,* III (Berlin: Friedrich Maurer, 1786), 92–3.

62 *Charles et Marie* in *Oeuvres* (Paris: Garnier, 1865), p. 210.

63 *Le Peintre de Saltzbourg,* in *Oeuvres* (Geneva: Slatkine Reprints, 1968), II, 9.

64 Peter Brang writes in "Über die Tagebuchfiktion in der russischen Literatur," in *Typologia Litterarum, Festschrift für Max Wehrli,* ed. Stefan Sonderegger, Alois M. Haas, Harald Burger (Zürich: Atlantis, 1969), that *Werther* influenced the origins of the diary novel in Russia (p. 443).

65 "Aus den Papieren eines Selbstmörders," in *Erzählungen* (Frankfurt: Johann David Sauerländer, 1837), p. 306.

66 Cf. Jean Delay, *La Jeunesse d'André Gide* (Paris: Gallimard, 1956), pp. 379, 442.

67 *Michael: Ein deutsches Schicksal in Tagebuchblättern* (München: Frz. Eher Nachf., 1934), p. 133.

68 *Le Second Werther* (Paris: Ferenczi, 1932), p. 9.

69 *Goethe-Vigilien* (Stuttgart: Klett, 1953), pp. 21–3.

70 *Dya Na Sore* (Karlsruhe: Stahlberg, 1958), pp. 273–4, 269.

71 For a detailed discussion of this question, see Norbert Miller, *Der empfindsame Erzähler* (München: Hanser, 1968), pp. 198–214.

72 Victor Lange, "Die Sprache als Erzählform in Goethes *Werther,*" in *Formenwandel: Festschrift zum 65. Geburtstag von Paul Böckmann,* ed. Walter Müller-Seidel and Wolfgang Preisendanz (Hamburg: Hoffman & Campe, 1964), p. 270.

73 See Erich Trunz's commentary, *Goethes Werke* (Hamburger Ausgabe), (München: Beck, 1973), VI, 555–7.

74 See Friedrich Sengle, *Biedermeierzeit,* II (Stuttgart: Metzler, 1972), 199–214.

75 *Le Journal intime* (Paris: Presses universitaires de France, 1963), p. ix.

76 "Studien über das vorromantische und romantische Tagebuch," Diss. Berlin 1952.

77   "Die guten Weiber," in *Sämmtliche Werke*, XVI (Stuttgart: Cotta, 1858), 522.

78   "Ein Tagebuch," in *Schriften*, XV (Berlin: G. Reimer, 1829), 323.

79   Johann Martin Miller, *Siegwart. Eine Klostergeschichte* (Faksimiledruck nach der Ausgabe von 1776; Stuttgart: J. B. Metzlersche Verlagsbuchhandlung, 1971), II, 518–19, 524.

80   Karl Philipp Moritz, III, 51.

81   *Charles et Marie, Oeuvres*, p. 173. Italics mine.

82   *Madeline, A Tale* (London: Longman, Hurst, Rees, Orme, and Brown, 1822), pp. 1, 2. Her emphasis.

83   Ibid, p. 17.

84   Friedrich Bouterwek, *Ramiros Tagebuch* (Leipzig: Gottfried Martini, 1804), pp. 8–9.

85   Ibid, p. 85.

86   August Kuhn, *Blätter aus Edmunds Tagebuch*, in *Mimosen: Erzählungen für gebildete Frauen* (Berlin: Heinrich Philipp Petri, 1822), pp. 4–5.

87   Johann Wolfgang von Goethe, *Die Leiden des jungen Werthers* (1774 edition) (Berlin: Akademie Verlag, 1954), p. 7.

88   Johann Gottfried von Pahl, *Herwart, der Eifersüchtige* (Basel: Flick, 1797), p. 3.

89   Goethe, *Werther*, p. 10.

90   Rostand, p. 9.

91   Goethe, *Werther*, p. 113.

92   Pahl, p. 186.

93   Lorenz von Westenrieder, *Leben des guten Jünglings Engelhof*, II (München: Strobl, 1782), 200.

94   Bouterwek, pp. 162–3.

95   Goethe, *Werther*, p. 45.

96   Norbert Miller writes in *Der empfindsame Erzähler*, "Aus stehenden Sprachwendungen und Bildern, aus abgegriffenen und unwägbaren Begriffen der Innerlichkeit (*Ruhe, Schwermut, Heiligkeit, usw.*) formiert sich ein verwirrendes Geflecht von Signalen, von 'Losungsworten,' wie es im 'Werther' heißt, die nicht ein Gefühl beschreiben, sondern es evozieren" (p. 192).

97   See Sengle's remarks on the "empfindsamen Ton," *Biedermeierzeit* II, 926–9.

98   Karl Philipp Moritz, III, 397–8.

99   "Werther-Studie," in *Gestaltprobleme der Dichtung*, ed. Richard Alewyn, Hans-Egon Hass, Clemens Heselhaus (Bonn: Bouvier, 1957), pp. 102–3. Hans Heinrich Borcherdt, *Der Roman der Goethezeit* (Urach: Port, 1949), is of the same opinion (pp. 25–6).

100   *Deutscher Geist im 18. Jahrhundert* (Göttingen: Vandenhoeck & Ruprecht, 1956), p. 181.

101   *Georg Lukács, Goethe und seine Zeit* (Bern: Francke, 1947), esp. p. 29.

102   Goethe, *Werther*, p. 2.

103   Black, pp. 93–7.

104   Mikhail Lermontov, *A Hero of Our Time*, trans. Reginald Merton (London: Philip Allan & Co., 1928), p. 65.

105   *Either/Or*, trans. David F. Swenson and Lillian M. Swenson (Princeton, N.J.: Princeton University Press, 1949), p. 432.

106 Ivan Turgenev, "The Diary of a Superfluous Man," in *The Novels*, trans. Constance Garnett, XIII (New York, Macmillan, 1920), 3.

107 On Turgenev and Goethe, see, e.g., Eva Kagan-Kans, *Hamlet and Don Quixote: Turgenev's Ambivalent Vision* (The Hague: Mouton, 1977), pp. 13–14. For a more extensive discussion and an interpretation that is somewhat different from mine, see Vytas Dukas and Richard H. Lawson, "*Werther* and *Diary of a Superfluous Man*," *Comparative Literature*, 21 (1969), 146–54.

108 "Ein Tagebuch," in *Schriften*, XV (Berlin: G. Reimer, 1829), 299, 320.

109 Miller, *Der empfindsame Erzähler*, p. 30; see also Peter Michelsen, *Laurence Sterne und der deutsche Roman des 18. Jahrhunderts* (Göttingen: Vandenhoeck & Ruprecht, 1962).

110 *Diary of an Ennuyée* (Philadelphia: E. Littel, 1826), p. 2.

111 *The Moonstone* (New York: AMS Press, 1970), pp. 318, 319, 320.

112 *Dracula* (New York: Dell, 1965), p. 416.

PART III. THE DIARY NOVEL IN THE LATE NINETEENTH AND EARLY TWENTIETH CENTURIES

1 Michel Raimond, *La Crise du roman: Des lendemains du naturalisme aux années vingt* (Paris: Corti, 1967).

2 "Zur Entwicklungsgeschichte des Tagebuchs," *Cosmopolis*, 10 (1898), 856–73.

3 *Le Journal intime* (Paris: Presses Universitaires de France, 1963). Girard shows (pp. 57 ff.) that there were two generations of intimists in France. The first wrote from ca. 1800 to ca. 1820 without models. The major intimists of this first generation were Joseph Joubert (who wrote the first leaves of his intimate diary in 1774), Maine de Biran, Benjamin Constant, and Stendhal; others include Restif de la Bretonne, Madame de Staël, Madame de Lamartine, Chênedollé, Lucile Desmoulins, and André-Marie Ampère. The second generation of intimists wrote from ca. 1830 to ca. 1860. These writers knew either of the diaries of their predecessors or of others (Byron's journal was translated and published in France in 1830) and were consequently aware that they were following a tradition. The major writers of the second period were Alfred de Vigny, Eugène Delacroix, Jules Michelet, Maurice de Guérin, and Henri-Frédéric Amiel (who kept his journal to the year of his death, 1881). Minor intimists were Jean-Jacques Ampère, Fontaney, George Sand, Barbey d'Aurevilly, Eugénie de Guérin, and Edmond Schérer. The Goncourts also began to keep their famous nonintimate journal during this period.

4 Richard Meyer, writing in 1898, notes the "unheilvolle Wirkung der vielen Veröffentlichungen" and concludes that as a consequence it is no longer possible for a public figure to keep a genuinely sincere private diary: "Die Drucklegung, die Kritiken, die Beeinflussung der früheren Meisterwerke haben in den neuren Schreibern die Unbefangenheit zerstört." "Zur Entwicklungsgeschichte des Tagebuchs," p. 297.

5 See Elizabeth Czoniczer, *Quelques antécédents de "A la recherche du temps perdu"* (Genève: Droz, 1957), especially Ch. II.

6 Girard, pp. 3–4, 495 ff.

7 Some intimate journals or parts of intimate journals were published in France before the 1880s, primarily in the period from ca. 1845 to ca. 1855; they include those of Maine de Biran, Maurice Guérin, Eugénie de Guérin, Vigny, Chênedollé, and Barbey d'Aurevilly (Girard, pp. 59–66, 68–9). In Germany, Hebbel's intimate journal was published in 1885–7, and Platen's had been published in 1860. None of these works had any immediate effect on the production of diary fiction, however.

8 *Essais de psychologie contemporaine* (Paris: Plon, 1899), p. 462.

9 See Jean Delay, *La Jeunesse d'André Gide* (Paris: Gallimard, 1956), pp. 328, 379.

10 See Michael G. Lerner, "The Unpublished Manuscripts of Edouard Rod's 'La Course à la Mort' and his Departure from Zola's Naturalism," *Studi Francesi*, 43 (1971), 71.

11 Rod, *La Course à la mort,* 5th ed. (Paris: Perrin, 1891), p. 1.

12 Rod, Preface to *Les Trois coeurs* (Paris: Perrin, 1890), pp. 14–15.

13 Rod, *La Course à la mort,* p. 70.

14 For information on the diary novel in Scandinavia, see Lynn Barstis, "The Modern Diary Novel: Heir of the Journal Intime," Diss. University of Illinois 1974. She devotes a chapter each to *Trætte mænd* and to Hjalmar Söderberg's *Doktor Glas.*

15 Rod, *La Course à la mort,* p. 68.

16 Arne Garborg, *Müde Seelen,* trans. Marie Herzfeld (Berlin: S. Fischer, 1893), p. 5.

17 *Le Fantôme* (Paris: Plon, 1901), pp. 219, 109.

18 *Doctor Glas,* trans. Paul Britten Austin (Boston: Little Brown, 1963), p. 19.

19 *Monsieur de Phocas* (Paris: Paul Ollendorff, 1901), pp. 287–8.

20 "Tagebuch 1900," in *Gesammelte Werke* (Frankfurt: Suhrkamp, 1970), XII, 332.

21 Rod, *La Course à la mort,* p. 6.

22 See Karl D. Uitti, *The Concept of Self in the Symbolist Novel* (S'-Gravenhage: Mouton, 1961), pp. 22 ff.

23 Czoniczer, pp. 63–90, and Raimond, *La Crise du roman,* pp. 416 ff.

24 *The Art of the Novel* (New York: Scribner, 1935), p. 321.

25 Edouard Rod, *Le Sens de la vie,* 10th ed. (Paris: Perrin, 1894), pp. 54–5.

26 According to Czoniczer, a long work on déjà-vu appeared in 1898, Eugène Bernard-Leroy's *L'Illusion de fausse reconnaissance* (p. 146).

27 Söderberg, *Doctor Glas,* p. 91.

28 "Eine Suggestion," in *Orchideen* (München: Albert Langen, 1905), p. 61.

29 Bourget, pp. 225–8.

30 For French influences on Schnitzler, see Elisabeth Eisserer, "Arthur Schnitzler als Seelenforscher in den Novellen," Diss. Wien 1950; for Schnitzler's narrative techniques, see Peter Spycher-Braendli, *Gestaltungsprobleme in der Novellistik Arthur Schnitzlers,* Diss. Zürich 1971.

31 In the other diary stories, "Der Sohn" (1892) and "Fritzi" (written in 1893 and published posthumously as the second part of "Komödiantinnen"), the diarists chiefly report the stories of third persons.

32 Robert Humphrey, *Stream of Consciousness in the Modern Novel* (Berkeley: University of California Press, 1954), p. 3.

33 Arthur Schnitzler, *Die erzählenden Schriften* (Frankfurt: Fischer, 1961), I, 44, 220, 344.

34 E.g., by Richard Ellmann, *James Joyce* (New York: Oxford University Press, 1972), p. 368.

35 "Über die Tagebuchfiktion in der russischen Literatur," in *Typologia Litterarum, Festschrift für Max Wehrli* (Zürich: Atlantis, 1969), p. 462.

36 He refers to *La Course à la mort* in his journal (*Journal 1889–1939* [Bruges: Editions de la Nouvelle revue française, 1939], p. 306).

37 *The Journals of André Gide,* trans. Justin O'Brien, I (London: Secker & Warburg, 1947), 19.

38 W. Wolfgang Holdheim, *Theory and Practice of the Novel. A Study on André Gide* (Genève: Droz, 1968), studies the tensions that continue to inform Gide's work and sees them as a tension between vitalism and a variety of other values.

39 It appears in Lilian's remarks on the necessity of chopping off the hands of drowning people who try to clamber into an overloaded lifeboat; in Edouard's discussion of real versus imaginary feelings; in Armand's musings about existence and nonexistence; and, above all, in Edouard's many reflections on the novelist's craft.

40 André Gide, *The Counterfeiters,* trans. Dorothy Bussy (New York: Random House, 1973), p. 189.

41 *Journal of "The Counterfeiters"* in Gide, *The Counterfeiters,* p. 425.

42 Gide, *The Counterfeiters,* pp. 187–8.

43 In particular, Irvin Stock, "A View of *Les Faux-Monnayeurs*," *Yale French Studies,* No. 7 (1951), pp. 72–80; also Holdheim, p. 258. David A. Steel's analysis in "Lettres et Argent: L'économie des *Faux-Monnayeurs*," *La Revue des Lettres Modernes,* No. 439–44 (1975), pp. 61–79, is also interesting in this regard.

44 The biographical circumstances were first researched by Charles Parnell, "André Gide and his *Symphonie pastorale*," in *Yale French Studies,* No. 7 (1951), pp. 60–71. More extensive accounts are given by Francis Pruner, "*La Symphonie pastorale*" *de Gide: de la tragédie reçue à la tragédie écrite,* Archives des Lettres Modernes, No. 54 (Paris: Lettres Modernes, 1964); G. W. Ireland, *André Gide. A Study of his Creative Writings* (Oxford: Clarendon Press, 1970), pp. 283–308; and especially Claude Martin, *La Symphonie pastorale* (Paris: Lettres Modernes, 1970), in his introduction to this critical edition.

45 Martin, p. xciii. See also Ireland, esp. p. 299.

46 Ireland, p. 300. See also Martin, p. xciv.

47 Ireland, p. 302.

48 Ireland, p. 307. Pruner goes so far as to conjecture that Gide changed his plan in midstream: Although he set out to write a book critical of the pastor, by the time he started the second notebook his relationship with Marc had so transformed his views that finishing the novella in the same spirit was an impossibility. According to Pruner, Gide himself noted in his journal that he was having great difficulty interesting himself again in his pastor's state of mind, and he evidently rushed the composition. Thus the tenor changes in the second notebook; Jacques becomes increasingly odious, and the blame for Gertrude's death is finally pinned on him rather than on the pastor (p. 24).

49 Critics who find the pastor self-deluding include W. G. Moore, "André Gide's *Symphonie pastorale*," *French Studies*, 4 (1959), 16–26; Parnell; Ralph Freedman, "Imagination and Form in André Gide: 'La Porte étroite' and 'La Symphonie pastorale,' " *Accent*, 17 (1957), 217–28; Lawrence E. Harvey, "The Utopia of Blindness in Gide's *Symphonie pastorale*," *Modern Philology*, 54 (1958), 188–97; Günter Schweig, "Über A. Gide's 'Symphonie pastorale,' " in *Die Neueren Sprachen, Neue Folge*, 9 (1960), 38–43; and Martin.

50 "Feuillets" (of 1924–5?), in *Oeuvres complètes*, XIII (n.p.: Nouvelle revue française, 1937), 440.

51 Mischa Harry Fayer, *Gide, Freedom and Dostoevsky* (Burlington, Vt.: The Lane Press, 1946), p. 2. My translation.

52 Harvey, p. 192.

53 *La Symphonie pastorale* (Paris: Gallimard, 1925), pp. 99–100; translation from *Two Symphonies*, trans. Dorothy Bussy (New York: Knopf, 1970), p. 231. Further references to these editions will be given in parentheses in the text.

54 Herbert Greenberg, "Time Discrepancies and Gide's Impatience: A Note on the Composition of *La Symphonie pastorale*," *Romance Notes*, 4 (1963), 102–6, has drawn attention to two remarks of the pastor's on March 8 and March 20 respectively, which seem to mean that the pastor knew he was in love with Gertrude *before* starting the second notebook. The pastor says of his dissatisfaction at Jacques's love for Gertrude, "c'est ce qui ne devait s'éclairer pour moi qu'un peu plus tard," and of Amélie's innuendos about his passion, "les phrases d'Amélie, qui me paraissaient alors mystérieuses, s'éclairèrent pour moi peu ensuite." Greenberg interprets these "time discrepancies" as evidence that Gide changed his mind about how to enlighten the pastor in the course of writing. Martin interprets them as evidence of the pastor's lying to himself (pp. civ–cv), and Arthur E. Babcock, "*La Symphonie pastorale* as Self-Conscious Fiction," *French Forum*, 3 (1978), 65–71, as evidence that we are meant to understand the pastor as a novelist rather than a diarist. All of these interpretations are possible. However, it is not absolutely necessary to interpret the two phrases as references to the pastor's ultimate understanding of his own passion. The references are not unambiguous, and especially considering the pastor's befuddled state, his "understanding" might well have been a misunderstanding. Of course, if the pastor is not referring to the revelation that he finally admits to at the beginning of the second notebook, we do not know exactly what he is referring to. Conceivably the first passage might refer to his threatening sense that his son is growing up, and the second to a later recognition that his son's love was more serious than he at first supposed. Valerie Raoul's interpretation, that the discrepancy is simply a discrepancy, is also plausible (*The French Fictional Journal. Fictional Narcissism/Narcissistic Fiction* [Toronto: University of Toronto Press, 1980], pp. 54–5).

55 Babcock, pp. 65–71, basing his interpretation largely on time discrepancies and other lapses in verisimilitude, finds a radically different interpretation for the "second voice" in the novel: We are to understand the pastor as a novelist who is consciously fashioning his own novel. This interpretation would have the effect of attributing what I call Gide's level of narration to the pastor.

56 E.g., by Moore, Parnell, Harvey, Martin, and Ireland.

57 *Divers* (Paris: Gallimard, 1931), p. 162. Parnell, pp. 67–9, shows that Gide copied almost word for word his meditations on Romans 15:14–15 in *La Symphonie pastorale* but attributed part of them to the pastor and part to Jacques. Specifically, the pastor cites "Je sais et je suis persuadé par le Seigneur Jésus que rien n'est impur en soi, et qu'une chose n'est impure que pour celui qui la croit impure"; and "Mais si, pour un aliment, ton frère est attristé, tu ne marches plus selon l'amour!" The pastor, in his interpretation, stresses the idea of *amour*, and adds, "C'est au défaut de l'amour que nous attaque le Malin." Gide, in contrast, follows his discussion of these verses in *Numquid et tu . . . ?* with the following remarks: "Et Paul continue, et ceci entre en moi comme un glaive: 'Ne cause pas, par ton aliment, la perte de celui pour lequel le Christ est mort.' " In *La Symphonie pastorale*, it is Jacques who cites this verse. Parnell correctly concludes, "We see that the two contradicting moral tendencies coexisting earlier in Gide are incarnated in the novel by the father and the son, each of whom corresponds to one of the author's points of view" (p. 69).

58 *Journal 1889–1939*, pp. 589–90.

59 Gide constructs the sentence so that it reveals an ironic second meaning, however. "Sin is that which darkens the soul – which prevents its joy" is a correct self-commentary. Sin has made the pastor spiritually blind. If he recognized his sin *as sin,* this recognition would indeed oppose his happiness. Gertrude will adopt this second meaning later herself. The passage with which she seems to justify her suicide is "Pour moi, étant autrefois sans loi, je vivais; mais quand le commandement vint, le péché reprit vie, et moi je mourus" (p. 146). In interpreting the passage, Gide establishes a connection between knowing the law and sinning (*Journal 1889–1939,* p. 589). Jacques, who reads the passage to Gertrude and surely cannot wish for her suicide, probably has a similar interpretation in mind. Jacques could be applying the quotation to his own situation; it could then be taken to mean that on account of his father's commandment, which suggested that his relationship to Gertrude was sinful, he is dying, or metaphorically leaving the world by taking orders. When Gertrude opens her eyes, however, she thinks she sees and understands sin and must therefore die.

60 For example, by Peter Ruppert, "The Aesthetic Solution in *Nausea* and *Malte Laurids Brigge,*" *Comparative Literature,* 29 (1977), 17–34; Inca Rumold, *Die Verwandlung des Ekels; Zur Funktion der Kunst in Rilkes "Malte Laurids Brigge" und Sartres "La Nausée"* (Bonn: Bouvier, 1979); and Laurence Gill Lyon in a particularly interesting essay, "Related Images in *Malte Laurids Brigge* and *La Nausée,*" *Comparative Literature,* 30 (1978), 53–71.

61 *Mythologies,* trans. Annette Lavers (New York: Hill & Wang, 1976), p. 133.

62 Letter to Gräfin Manon zu Solms-Laubach, April 11, 1910.

63 August Stahl, *Rilke-Kommentar* (München: Winkler, 1979), pp. 152–3.

64   Letter to Lili Schalk, May 14, 1911.

65   Letter to Lou Andreas-Salomé, December 28, 1911.

66   Letter to Fürstin Marie von Thurn und Taxis-Hohenlohe, September 6, 1915.

67   Maurice Betz, "Über die *Aufzeichnungen des Malte Laurids Brigge,*" in *Materialien zu Rainer Maria Rilke, Die Aufzeichnungen des Malte Laurids Brigge,* ed. Hartmut Engelhardt (Frankfurt: Suhrkamp, 1974), p. 162.

68   See Betz, p. 161 et passim, and Borge Gedso Madsen, "Influences from J. P. Jacobsen and Sigbjörn Obstfelder on Rainer Maria Rilke's 'Die Aufzeichnungen des Malte Laurids Brigge,' " *Scandinavian Studies,* 26 (1954), 112–14. Werner Kohlschmidt, "Rilke und Obstfelder," in *Die Wissenschaft von deutscher Sprache und Dichtung,* ed. Siegfried Gutenbrunner et al. (Stuttgart: Klett, 1963), pp. 458–77, shows that the conclusions of these commentators about Rilke's relations with Obstfelder are imprecise if not actually wrong. He concludes that the person of Obstfelder should not be overestimated as a model for Malte but that the parallels in style and motif between *Malte* and Obstfelder's writings generally are striking. For example, *Malte* and *En præsts dagbog* both lack typically diarylike references to dates and places; both are "ein Mosaik von assoziativen Impressionen" (p. 474); each new impression begins as if anew.

69   See Stahl, p. 154, on the chronological structure. J.-F. Angelloz, *Rilke* (Paris: Mercure de France, 1952), already noted that Malte could be compared to "une composition musicale orchestrée autour de quelques grands thèmes fondamentaux, qui sont la ville, la mort, l'enfance, l'amour" (p. 216). Ulrich Fülleborn, "Form und Sinn der *Aufzeichnungen des Malte Laurids Brigge,*" in *Materialien* (first pub. 1961), finds that *Malte* is structured according to a law of complementarity and a law of association. This conclusion is accepted by Theodore Ziolkowski, *Dimensions of the Modern Novel* (Princeton, N.J.: Princeton University Press, 1969), p. 26. Walter Seifert, *Das epische Werk Rainer Maria Rilkes* (Bonn: Bouvier, 1969), also speaks of "Gegenbilder" (p. 205). Anthony R. Stephens, *Rilkes Malte Laurids Brigge: Strukturanalyse des erzählerischen Bewußtseins* (Bern: Lang, 1974), finds that Malte is constructed according to a pattern of three cycles of recurrent themes (e.g., p. 147).

70   *The Notebooks of Malte Laurids Brigge,* trans. M. D. Herter Norton (New York: Norton, 1964), p. 15. Page numbers for further references to this edition will be given in the text. Where I use my own translations, volume and page numbers for Rainer Maria Rilke, *Sämtliche Werke* (Insel Werkausgabe) (Frankfurt: Insel, 1976) will be given in text.

71   Today, five of the tapestries are understood to be allegories of the five senses. Sight is the tapestry that Rilke describes last; Hearing is his third; Taste, his first; Smell, his second; and Touch, his fourth. The tapestry "A mon seul désir" (Rilke's fifth) is considered not to be part of the sequence. This interpretation of the tapestries was not proposed until 1921, however (see J. J. Marquet de Vasselot, *Les Tapisseries dites La Dame à la licorne* [Paris: Lapina, n.d.], p. 5. Rilke thus could not have known of it when he wrote *Malte.* The tapestries are now hung in an order that conforms to the new interpretation, but when the Cluny museum first acquired them in 1882, they were hung in precisely the same order in which Rilke describes them in *Malte* (see *Musée des Thermes et de l'Hôtel de Cluny, Catalogue* by E. du Sommerard [Paris: Hôtel de Cluny, 1883], pp. 678–80). It therefore seems likely that Rilke adopted an existing order, rather than inventing his own.

72 Letter to Fürstin Marie von Thurn und Taxis-Hohenlohe, August 30, 1910.

73 Rilke, *Sämtliche Werke* (Insel Werkausgabe) (Frankfurt: Insel, 1976), IX, 180.

74 Cf. Ernst Fedor Hoffmann, "Zum dichterischen Verfahren in Rilkes 'Aufzeichnungen des Malte Laurids Brigge' " in *Materialien* (first pub. 1968), p. 240; Judith Ryan, " 'Hypothetisches Erzählen': Zur Funktion von Phantasie und Einbildung in Rilke 'Malte Laurids Brigge' " in *Materialien* (first pub. 1971), pp. 247–8, and Brigitte L. Bradley, *Zu Rilkes Malte Laurids Brigge* (Bern: Francke, 1980), p. 41.

75 Fülleborn calls the episode Malte's "Gottesbeweis" (p. 195); Seifert, p. 287, and Stephens, pp. 197–8, argue similarly.

76 Thus, Hoffmann, p. 239, suggests that we read *Die Aufzeichnungen* as "poetry in statu nascendi"; Ziolkowski, p. 14 et passim, finds that with *Die Aufzeichnungen,* Malte overcomes his fear of time by creating an atemporal work of art and counteracts his sense of the chaos around him by creating an aesthetic order; Ryan, "Hypothetisches Erzählen," pp. 278–9, disagrees with these critics but argues along the same lines, finding that Malte's writing remains too subjective to be considered a success in its own terms. Stephens argues that Malte is not primarily about the problems of the artist; he writes, "die Künstlerproblematik darf als Metapher der im Rahmen der Romanfiktion herrschenden, existentiellen Problematik betrachtet werden" (p. 25). He shows, persuasively, the self-validating aspect of an argument that takes the artistic achievement of Rilke's novel as evidence for Malte's own success (p. 228).

77 My discussion of Rilke's metaphors in the *Neue Gedichte* and of the significance of the mirror that follows largely agrees in its conclusions with Judith Ryan's more extensive discussion in *Umschlag und Verwandlung* (München: Winkler, 1972), Ch. I.

78 My interpretation is very similar to that of Stephens; what I call "mirrors" he calls "Vorwände." He traces the "Vorwand" concept (and the word) in Rilke's work back to the late 1890s and shows how it is consistent with Rilke's theory of artistic creation in the same period. One difference is that Stephens uses the "Vorwand" concept to explain Rilke's puzzling and frequent attribution of negative and positive connotations to the same phenomenon, asserting that a "Prinzip der entgegengesetzten Darstellung" is a primary element in the concept. The implication is that one can potentially interpret the "Zentrum" of any given phenomenon in the *Aufzeichnungen* as having the opposite value of the "Vorwand." I find this implication risky. Moreover, I believe that such ambiguities in *Malte* are traceable not to the mirror (or "Vorwand") technique but to another source, such as differences between Malte's momentary and still limited perception of an event and another possible interpretation that Rilke wishes to suggest.

79 *Materialien*, p. 131.

80 See especially Armand Nivelle, "Sens et Structure des 'Cahiers de Malte Laurids Brigge,' " in *Revue d'Esthetique,* 12 (1959), 128. Various critics have argued persuasively that the novel presents a clear system of values, even though it is unclear whether Malte himself succeeds or fails. Hoffmann first elucidates the problem in its most general terms, and I think quite correctly: "Während die Person, wie erwähnt, zurücktritt, sich geradezu hinter dem Erleben auflöst, bleibt dieses in seiner Qualität als subjektiv Erlebtes weiter bestehen und gültig, ja, es gewinnt seinen breiten Gültigkeitsanspruch eben daraus, daß es nicht auf eine Person rückbezogen wird" (p. 225). Other critics propose different systems of values. Walter Sokel, "Zwischen Existenz und Weltinnenraum," in *Rilke heute,* ed. Ingeborg H. Solbrig and Joachim W. Storck (Frankfurt: Suhrkamp, 1975), believes that the novel's ideal is "Ent-Ichung," and that many of the work's ambiguous passages can be explained because "Ent-Ichung" is both desirable and terrifying. Seifert finds that the novel's ideal is totality and that it demonstrates this ideal through a dialectic structure. Stephens finds that "die 'Einheit' des Werkes liegt in der genau strukturierten Uneinheitlichkeit der 'Person des Schreibenden' und der positive Sinn des Werkes in der gegensätzlichen Symbolik von Maltes Erleben selbst" (p. 261).

81 *Madeleine au miroir* (Paris: Calmann-Lévy, 1912), p. 6. Cf. Guy Chantepleure's *Malencontre* (Paris: Calmann-Lévy, 1910), where the diarist's father tells her that keeping a journal is advisable because "on prend de ses actes une notion plus juste, on classe ses idées, on éprouve ses sentiments, on délibère avec soi-même, on voit plus clair en soi et autour de soi, on évite ainsi quelques sottises" (p. 12). In Léontine Zanta's *La Science et l'amour* (Paris: Plon, 1921), the narrator's teacher tells her, "Pour vivre intérieurement, profondément, . . . il n'y qu'un moyen, c'est d'écrire votre journal. Chaque soir, à la fin de votre labeur, à l'heure où, vous sentant bien seule, vous vous recueillerez, tout comme l'enfant fait sa prière, vous écrivez sur le feuillet blanc la parole intérieure, vous ferez votre examen de conscience" (p. 5).

82 Richard J. Evans, *The Feminist Movement in Germany 1894–1933* (London: Sage Publications, 1976), Ch. II. Evans sees 1894, the year of the founding of the Bund Deutscher Frauenvereine, as a turning point in German feminism; the original German women's organization, the Allgemeiner Deutscher Frauenverein, had, since its founding in 1865, occupied itself with little except for welfare work and the issue of improved education for women.

83 See Gabriele Strecker, *Frauenträume, Frauentränen* (Weilheim/Oberbayern: Otto Wilhelm Barth Verlag, 1969), pp. 48–9.

84 *The Journal of a Young Artist,* trans. Mary J. Serrano (New York: Cassell, 1889), p. 406.

85 See Gretl Jansen, "Frauenpsychologie und Frauenpädagogik bei Marcel Prévost," Diss. Würzburg 1927, and Jules Bertaut, *Marcel Prévost* (Paris: E. Sansot, 1904).

86 *A Sorrow Beyond Dreams,* in *Three by Peter Handke* (New York: Avon, 1977), p. 264.

87 *Tagebuchblätter einer Emancipierten* (Leipzig: Hermann Seeman Nachfolger, 1902), p. 3.

88 Women were first admitted to the faculty of medicine at the University of Heidelberg in 1891; in 1901 they were admitted to all disciplines at Freiberg and Heidelberg; but in 1905 there were still only eighty full-time women students in Germany. See Evans, p. 19, and Richard Hamann and Jost Hermand, *Naturalismus* (Frankfurt: Fischer, 1977), p. 101.

89 Asenijeff, p. 25.

90 Margarete Böhme, *Tagebuch einer Verlorenen* (Berlin: F. Fontane, 1906), p. 228.

91 *Das flüchtige Spiel* (Einsiedeln/Köln: Benziger, 1940), p. 184.

92 Maïté Albistur and Daniel Armogathe, *Histoire du féminisme français* (Paris: Editions des Femmes, 1977), pp. 380, 383.

93 Tinayre, p. 137.

94 Albistur and Armogathe, p. 381.

95 "Trends in Literary Theory: The Female Aesthetic and German Women's Writing," *German Quarterly*, 54 (1981), 70.

PART IV. THE CONTEMPORARY DIARY NOVEL

1 The heroines of Margarete Böhme's *Tagebuch einer Verlorenen* (Berlin: Fontane, 1905) and Carl Bulcke's *Das Tagebuch der Susanne Övelgönne* (Dresden: Carl Reissner, 1906), for instance, both receive diaries as confirmation presents from their aunts.

2 Works that study the phenomenon of the literary diary intended for publication include Albert Gräser, *Das literarische Tagebuch* (Saarbrücken: West-Ost Verlag, 1955); Wilhelm Grenzmann, "Das Tagebuch als literarische Form," *Wirkendes Wort*, 9 (1959), 84–93; and Klaus Günther Just, "Das Tagebuch als literarische Form" in *Übergänge* (Bern: Francke, 1966), pp. 25–41. The collection *Das Tagebuch und der moderne Autor,* ed. Uwe Schulz (München: Hanser, 1965), presents essays by contemporary German authors on journals and journal keeping.

3 "Zur Entwicklungsgeschichte des Tagebuchs," *Cosmopolis*, 10 (1898), 293.

4 *Tagebuch* (Stuttgart: Metzler, 1969), p. 53.

5 O. Schreiter, "Das fingierte Tagebuch im Aufsatzunterricht," *Zeitschrift für Deutschkunde*, 35 (1921), 340–2; Kurt Forstreuter, *Die deutsche Icherzählung* (Berlin: Emil Ebering, 1924), pp. 54–5.

6 *Diary in Exile*, trans. Elena Zarudnaya (Cambridge, Mass.: Harvard University Press, 1924), pp. 3, 4.

7 John Fletcher, "Sartre's *Nausea*: A Modern Classic Revisited," *The Critical Quarterly*, 18 (1976), 12.

8 Friedrich Nietzsche, "Über Wahrheit und Lüge im außermoralischen Sinne," *Gesammelte Werke*, VI (München: Musarion, 1922), 81.

9 Hugo von Hofmannsthal, "Ein Brief," in *Erzählungen, Erfundene Gespräche und Briefe, Reisen,* in *Gesammelte Werke in zehn Einzelbänden*, pp. 465–6.

10 Letter to Countess Manon zu Solms-Laubach, April 11, 1910, in *Letters of Rainer Maria Rilke 1892–1910,* trans. Jane Barnard Greene and M. D. Herter Norton (New York: Norton, 1969), p. 363.

11 "Der Erzähler," in *Illuminationen* (Frankfurt: Suhrkamp, 1969), pp. 409–13.

12 *Leave-taking* [*and*] *Vanishing Point,* trans. Christopher Levenson (London: Calder and Boyars, 1966), p. 248. Cf. Peter Boerner, "The Significance of the Diary in Modern Literature," *Yearbook of Comparative and General Literature,* No. 21 (1972), pp. 41–5. Taking ten of the best-known twentieth-century writers' diaries as examples, Boerner lists tendencies "toward the concrete, the documentary and fragmentary, toward rejection of a synoptic view, toward experimentation and the disintegration of poetic structure" as typical (pp. 44–5).

13 *Sincerity and Authenticity* (Cambridge, Mass.: Harvard University Press, 1971), p. 55.

14 *Molloy,* trans. Patrick Bowles in collaboration with the author (New York: Grove Press, 1955), p. 83.

15 *Malone Dies,* trans. Samuel Beckett (New York: Grove Press, 1977), p. 88.

16 *Der Schatten des Körpers des Kutschers* (Frankfurt: Suhrkamp, 1971), p. 48.

17 For a discussion of this use of the diary form – where the diary is used for its connotations of verisimilitude in order to make a statement about the theory of the novel – as well as further examples, see Juliet Willman Kincaid, "The Novel as Journal: A Generic Study," Diss. Ohio State University 1977, pp. 200 ff.

18 Frisch himself calls the whole novel a diary. See his interview with Horst Bienek, in Horst Bienek, *Werkstattgespräche mit Schriftstellern* (München: Hanser, 1962), p. 24, and "An Interview with Max Frisch," conducted by Rolf Kieser (1971), *Contemporary Literature,* 13 (1972), 6.

19 Bienek, p. 24.

20 In particular Rolf Kieser, "Man as His Own Novel: Max Frisch and the Literary Diary," *Germanic Review,* 47 (1972), 109–17, and *Max Frisch: Das literarische Tagebuch* (Frauenfeld: Huber, 1975); and Horst Steinmetz, *Max Frisch: Tagebuch, Drama, Roman* (Göttingen: Vandenhoeck & Ruprecht, 1973), present extensive analyses. Erich Franzen also discusses Frisch's use of the diary form in his article "Über Max Frisch," in *Über Max Frisch,* ed. Thomas Beckermann (Frankfurt: Suhrkamp, 1971).

21 Max Frisch, *Tagebuch 1946–1949* (Frankfurt: Suhrkamp, 1973), pp. 42, 294, 118, 122, 43.

22 " 'Stiller,' Roman von Max Frisch. Fragment einer Kritik," in *Über Max Frisch,* ed. Beckermann, pp. 7, 11.

23 For a detailed analysis of the novel's formal organization, see Karlheinz Braun, "Die epische Technik in Max Frischs Roman 'Stiller' als Beitrag zur Formfrage des modernen Romans," Diss. Frankfurt 1959.

24 Max Frisch, *Stiller* (Frankfurt: Fischer, 1965), p. 39. Further references to this edition of *Stiller* will be given in parentheses in the text.

25 In the later interview with Bienek, Frisch no longer speaks of the true self. Instead he states that "Jedes Ich, auch das Ich, das wir leben und sterben, ist eine Erfindung" (Bienek, p. 25).

26 For a more extensive discussion of this theme, see Monika Wintsch-Spiess's *Zum Problem der Identität im Werk Max Frischs* (Zürich: Juris-Verlag, 1965). Eduard Stäuble, *Max Frisch: Gesamtdarstellung seines Werkes* (St. Gallen: Erker-Verlag, 1967), also deals with these themes briefly (pp. 46 ff.).

27 *Tagebuch 1946–1949,* pp. 22–3.

28 See *Tagebuch 1946–1949,* p. 37.

29 Ibid., p. 33.

30 Ulrich Weisstein interprets Stiller's profession similarly in *Max Frisch* (Boston: Twayne, 1967), pp. 51–2.

31 *Oeuvres de Jean Rotrou* (Genève: Slatkine Reprints, 1967), V, 25.

32 *Tagebuch 1946–1949,* p. 200.

33 Cf. Steinmetz, p. 58. Manfred Jurgensen, *Max Frisch: Die Romane* (Bern & München: Francke, 1972), also finds that "es fällt schwer, Rolf zuzustimmen" (p. 68).

34 " 'Stiller,' " in *Über Max Frisch,* p. 10.

35 The significance of Stiller's retreat into the country after he is released from prison and his subsequent mode of life is the most controversial aspect of the novel. Critics are in disagreement as to whether the end of *Stiller* is to be understood in a positive sense, in accordance with the public prosecutor's evaluation, or in the negative sense of a reacceptance of his old role. Interpretations that see Stiller's withdrawal from society and his existence as a potter as a positive fulfillment of his true inclinations include those of Monika Wintsch-Spiess, pp. 96 ff., and Ulrich Weisstein, pp. 52–5. The majority of Frisch's critics judge Stiller's self-acceptance to be mere resignation and his solitary existence in Glion, which I interpret as the completion of the step to autonomy, to be defeat: see Karlheinz Braun, p. 18 ff.; Hans Mayer, "Anmerkungen zu 'Stiller,' " in Beckermann, ed., *Über Max Frisch,* p. 38; Charles W. Hoffmann, "The Search for Self, Inner Freedom, and Relatedness in the Novels of Max Frisch," in Robert R. Heitner, ed., *The Contemporary Novel in German* (Austin, 1967), pp. 98, 103–6; Stäuble, p. 166; Jurgensen, pp. 68, 83, 90; and Steinmetz, pp. 48–9.

36 "Les 'moments' de Marcel Proust," *Répertoire* [vol. I] (Paris: Editions de minuit, 1960).

37 See Jean Pouillon, "Les Règles du je," *Les Temps Modernes,* 12 (1957), 1591–8; Leo Spitzer, "Quelques Aspects de la technique des romans de Michel Butor," *Archivum Linguisticum,* 13 (1961), 171–95; Jean Rousset, "Trois Romans de la mémoire (Butor, Simon, Pinget)," *Cahiers Internationaux de Symbolisme,* 9–10 (1965–6), 75–84.

38 Michel Butor, *L'Emploi du temps* (Paris: Editions de Minuit, 1957), p. 117. Further references to this edition will be given in parentheses in the text. An English translation of this book has been published as *Passing Time,* trans. Jean Stewart (New York: Simon & Schuster, 1969).

39 "Les Figures," in *L'Exemple,* published in one volume with *L'Emploi du temps* (Paris: Editions de Minuit, 1957).

40 "Recherches sur la technique du roman," *Répertoire II* (Paris: Editions de Minuit, 1964), pp. 91–2.

41 "Petite Croisière préliminaire à une reconnaissance de l'archipel Joyce," *Répertoire* [I], p. 195. Butor also mentions the intimate journal in Kierkegaard's *Repetition,* p. 105.

42 Butor, "Recherches sur la technique du roman," *Répertoire II,* p. 92. Butor gives a detailed explication of Kierkegaard's work in *Répertoire* [I], p. 100.

43 Robbe-Grillet, "Nature, Humanism, Tragedy" (1958), in *For a New Novel,* trans. Richard Howard (New York: Grove Press, 1965), pp. 49–75.

44 For an excellent discussion of the mirrors in Butor's own works, see Lucien Dällenbach, *Le Livre et ses miroirs dans l'oeuvre romanesque de Michel Butor,* Archives de Lettres Modernes, 135 (Paris: Minard, 1972).

45 Dällenbach finds that the myths *introduce* the metaphors into the text (p. 17). It seems to me, however, that the production of the metaphors *precedes* the myths both logically and in the sequence of the text and that the myths represent the culmination of the metaphoric expansion.

46 "La Critique et l'invention," *Répertoire III* (Paris: Editions de Minuit, 1968), p. 8.

47 *Butor* (Paris: Gallimard, 1968), p. 113.

48 It is not to be assumed that Butor is punning unconsciously. In his essay "Le Roman et la poésie," in writing about ancient texts, he adds for clarification: "*textus:* tissu, enlacement, contexture" (*Répertoire II,* p. 18). *L'Emploi du temps* abounds with references to itself; I have singled out those that appear to me most important for mention in this essay. Trevor Field shows in his excellent article "Les Anagrammes révélatrices de *L'Emploi du temps,*" *Australian Journal of French Studies,* 12 (1975), 314–25, how the novel is full of anagrams for *livre,* "wrote," "words," *texte,* and the like.

49 Butor is of course aware of the double meaning of "reflection." He writes in "La Critique et l'invention," *Répertoire III,* p. 17, that the activity of the writer "va se réfléchir [instead of *refléter*] comme dans un miroir." He also puns on *réflexion* in "Intervention à Royaumont," *Répertoire* [I], p. 271.

50 "Recherches sur la technique du roman," *Répertoire II,* p. 97.

51 Jean Pouillon, "Les Règles du je," and Peter Brooks, "In the Laboratory of the Novel," *Daedalus,* 92 (1963), 265–80, find that Revel fails. This opinion is shared by Michael Spencer, *Michel Butor* (Boston: Twayne, 1974), and Arnold Weinstein, "Order and Excess in Butor's *L'Emploi du temps,*" *Modern Fiction Studies,* 16 (1970), 41–55, but with qualifications: Spencer thinks that Revel at least achieves the insight that the past is complicated (p. 55), and Weinstein finds that at the end Revel finally does succeed in seeing Bleston as it really is, which is Revel's own opinion (p. 52). Leo Spitzer accounts for the puzzling end of *L'Emploi du temps* by diagnosing Revel as schizophrenic (p. 195). As will be seen, I do not agree wholly with any of these interpretations of the novel's ambiguous end.

52 Butor, "La Critique et l'invention," *Répertoire III,* pp. 8, 12.

53 The view that the New Cathedral symbolizes either Butor's or Revel's *L'Emploi du temps* is shared by several critics. Spencer calls it a "paradigm" for the novel (p. 58) and Dällenbach, "une image préfigurative" for Revel's work (p. 21), while Georges Raillard, in *Butor,* calls the book "le Temple-Livre" (p. 119). Weinstein interprets the church differently, as a symbol for the "real Bleston" that Revel finally sees (p. 52).

54 Butor, "Les Oeuvres d'art imaginaires chez Proust," *Répertoire II,* p. 291.

55 In an interview published in 1974, Butor explicitly relates the "gaps" he perceives in reality to those in *L'Emploi du temps:* "Reality is not a continuous thing; it is full of holes. . . . We fill the gaps of reality with fiction. . . . When Revel does his writing, it is also full of gaps; and the book is finished with a hole; the last day of February is a leap year" (Kathleen O'Neill, "On Passing Time," *Mosaic*, 8 [Fall 1974], 35–36).

56 Pouillon, "Les Règles du je," pp. 1591–2.

57 Butor, "Petite Croisière préliminaire à une reconnaissance de l'archipel Joyce," *Répertoire* [I], pp. 201–2.

58 Butor, "La Critique et l'invention," *Répertoire III*, pp. 12, 9, 17.

59 Butor says in an interview: "Je fais très attention au titre; le titre est un mot qui est en plus gros que tous les autres mots du livre, c'est comme si ce mot était répété 100 fois ou 1000 fois. Donc, je choisis les titres soigneusement" (Georges Charbonnier, *Entretiens avec Michel Butor* [Paris: Gallimard, 1967], p. 11). He says that *L'Emploi du temps* is a pun and demonstrates how the pun in *Passage de Milan* works (p. 136).

60 Butor, "Le Roman comme recherche," *Répertoire* [I], p. 9.

61 Ibid., pp. 9, 8. Italics mine.

62 Florence Howe, "A Conversation with Doris Lessing (1966)," *Contemporary Literature*, 14 (1973), 429.

63 Introduction to *The Golden Notebook* (New York: Simon & Schuster, 1962), third printing. Further references to this edition will be given in parentheses in the text.

64 Howe, pp. 428–9.

65 Ibid., p. 424.

66 *Queen*, August 21, 1962, p. 32. Quoted from Paul Schlueter, *The Novels of Doris Lessing* (Carbondale, Ill.: Southern Illinois University Press, 1973), p. 82.

67 Written for the book jacket of the original British edition of *The Golden Notebook;* quoted by Schlueter, p. 83.

68 Ibid.

69 Cf. the judgments of Frederick R. Karl, "Doris Lessing in the Sixties: The New Anatomy of Melancholy," *Contemporary Literature*, 13 (1972), 15, and Lynn Sukenick, "Feeling and Reason in Doris Lessing's Fiction," *Contemporary Literature*, 14 (1973), 528.

70 Available in Doris Lessing, *A Small Personal Voice*, ed. Paul Schlueter (New York: Knopf, 1974), pp. 3–21.

71 Anne M. Mulkeen in "Twentieth-Century Realism: The 'Grid' Structure of *The Golden Notebook*," *Studies in the Novel* (NTSU), 4 (1972), 262–3, also finds that Lessing's theories are similar to those of Lukács.

72 Georg Lukács, *The Historical Novel*, trans. Hannah and Stanley Mitchell (Boston: Beacon Press, 1963), p. 90.

73 Lessing, "The Small Personal Voice," pp. 7, 6, 11, 5.

74 *Queen*, August 21, 1962, p. 32. Quoted from Schlueter, *Novels*, p. 82.

75 The best analysis of the structure of *The Golden Notebook* is Joseph Hynes's "The Construction of *The Golden Notebook*," *Iowa Review*, 4, No. 3 (1973), 100–13. Roberta Rubenstein, "Doris Lessing's *The Golden Notebook:* The Meaning of its Shape," *American Imago*, 32 (1975), 40–58, has an interesting interpretation for the order of the notebooks: "The five sections present . . .

five angles of vision, with the focus altering from distance to close-up analogous to the effect created by focusing a camera at infinity and then gradually rotating the lens adjustment until only what is very close is 'in focus' " (p. 45).

76 See Gustav René Hocke, *Das europäische Tagebuch* (Wiesbaden: Limes, 1963), p. 939.

77 Nancy Shields Hardin, who discusses Doris Lessing's involvement with Sufism and the philosophy of her later novels in "Doris Lessing and the Sufi Way," *Contemporary Literature* 14 (1973), 565–81, shows that Lessing's belief in a compartmentalizing and separating mental reflex becomes increasingly pronounced and explicit in her recent works such as *The Four-Gated City*. For an analysis of fragmentization and false form as it applies specifically to women's lives, see Barbara Bellow Watson, "Leaving the Safety of Myth: Doris Lessing's *The Golden Notebook* (1962)," in *Old Lines, New Forces*, ed. Robert K. Morris (Rutherford: Fairleigh Dickinson University Press, 1976), pp. 12–37, esp. pp. 26–8.

78 Sydney Janet Kaplan in "The Limits of Consciousness in the Novels of Doris Lessing," *Contemporary Literature*, 14 (1973), 541, analyzes the psychological implications of the failure of words for the writer Anna and concludes that it is a chief cause of her schizophrenia.

79 Other critics interpret differently. For Rubenstein, *The Golden Notebook*'s message is that "the synthesis of fact and fiction . . . will yield the truth" (p. 45). In her view, the film in the Golden Notebook, which merges fact and fiction (p. 54), mirrors the success of *The Golden Notebook* as a whole. Rubenstein's interpretation is based on taking the Blue Notebook as fact. She thus continues to see *The Golden Notebook*'s structure as a distance to close-up focus, not as a self-swallowing loop, as I do. Valerie Carnes, " 'Chaos, That's the Point'. Art as Metaphor in Doris Lessing's *The Golden Notebook*," *World Literature Written in English,* 15 (1976), 17–28, also thinks Lessing supports the idea of a fusion of fiction and reality. According to her, the first sentence of "Free Women" symbolizes Anna's success in "creating" her own life, in a context where "the boundaries between illusion and reality fade" and where " 'novel' and 'ordinary life' shade imperceptibly into one another" (p. 28).

80 Critics' attempts to interpret *The Golden Notebook* from the perspective of its "resolution," Anna's overcoming her writing block, necessarily run aground on the logical incompatibility of the problem of words and the solution. John L. Carey, "Art and Reality in *The Golden Notebook*," *Contemporary Literature,* 14 (1973), 455, for example, is obliged, in order to account for Anna's breakthrough out of sterility, to interpret the "Free Women" novella as a piece of model writing instead of the wooden short novel Doris Lessing herself describes it as being.

81 Hynes, who sees the main theme of the novel as the impossibility of reproducing Anna rather than the impossibility of reproducing any kind of experience in words, argues that Anna's promise to "put all of herself into one book" is technically fulfilled not by the Golden Notebook but rather by *The Golden Notebook* (pp. 103–5). Marjorie S. Lightfoot, "Breakthrough in *The Golden Notebook*," *Studies in the Novel* (NTSU), 7 (1975), 277–84, also finds a solution in the complexity of the form (pp. 281–3). Dennis Porter, "Realism and Failure in *The Golden Notebook*," *Modern Language Quarterly*, 35 (1974), rightly perceiving that Lessing uses "the techniques of . . . literary realism" (p. 56) in *The Golden Notebook* despite her explicit quarrel with the realistic novel, concludes that Lessing finally decides to support realism. She falls back on "varieties of realism as the only appropriate style" although "she has no illusions as to their truth-bearing power" (p. 65). This interpretation has its advantages; it makes sense of the novel and illuminates one of Lessing's – evidently overlapping – objectives. Yet this reading, like Carey's, depends on seeing Anna's breakthrough and the composition of "Free Women" as the solution to the problems of the novel, a reading that is at variance with Doris Lessing's own interpretation of "Free Women."

82 Howe, p. 429.

Bibliography of
Diary Fiction

The bibliography lists novels and stories that are entirely or primarily in diary form. Some borderline cases that might be of interest to students of the genre have also been included.

The lists of diary fiction in English, French, and German are extensive, although they do not claim completeness. They are based on searches in large collections. The bibliographies of diary fiction in other languages, as well as the separately listed American bibliography, simply list works that happen to have come to my attention; they are intended to give interested readers an impression of what exists.

Within each language group, works are listed chronologically, according to the date of first publication. If the date of first publication is not known, the first available publication date is given. In cases where the date of composition significantly antecedes the date of first publication, the work is listed under the date of composition.

ENGLISH
1710–19
"Journal of a Sober Citizen," in *The Spectator*. March 4, 1712.
"Clarinda's Journal," in *The Spectator*. March 11, 1712.
An Hue and Cry after Dr. S- - -t. London, 1714.
Dr. S——t's Real Diary. London, 1715.

1720–9
"A Journal of Four Days," in *Letters Sent to the Tatler and Spectator*. London, 1725.
Authentick Relation Of The Many Hardships and Sufferings Of A Dutch Sailor. London, 1728.

1730–9
The Just Vengeance of Heaven Exemplify'd. London, 1730.

274

1750–9

"Journal of a Senior Fellow, or Genuine Idler," in *The Idler*. Dec. 2, 1758.
["Journal of three days' employment"], in *The Idler*. July 28, 1759.

1760–9

Sheridan, Frances. *Memoirs of Miss Sidney Bidulph, Extracted from her own Journal, and now first published*. London, 1761–7.

1790–9

Hermione, or the Orphan Sisters. London, 1791.

1800–9

Mrs. Parsons. *Murray House*. London, 1804.

1810–19

Byron, Medora. *The Bachelor's Journal*. London, 1815.
Byron, Medora. *The Spinster's Journal*. London, 1816.

1820–9

Opie, Amelia. *Madeline. A Tale*. London, 1822.
Boswell, Thomas Alexander. *The Journal of an Exile*. London, 1825.
[Jameson, Anna B.] *Diary of an Ennuyée*. Philadelphia, 1826.

1830–9

Bell, Henry Glassford. "Journal of Two Days, with an interval of Forty
    Years," in *The Rainbow, or Tales and Sketches*. London, 1830.
Bury, Charlotte. *Journal of the Heart*. London, 1830.
Warren, Samuel. *Passages from the Diary of a late Physician*, in *Blackwood's Maga-
    zine*. 1830–7.
Sherwood, Mary Martha. *Roxobel*. London, 1831.
Gore, Catherine Grace Frances. *The Diary of a Désennuyée*. London, 1836.
Marryat, Frederick. *Diary of a Blasé*. Philadelphia, 1836.
Thackeray, William Makepeace. "Passages from the Diary of the Late Dolly
    Duster; with Elucidations, Notes, etc; by Various Eds," in *Fraser's
    Magazine*. Oct., Nov. 1838.
Thackeray, William Makepeace. "Skimmings from 'The Diary of George
    IV,' " in *The Yellowplush Correspondence*. Philadelphia, 1838.

1840–9

Baxter, George R. Wythen. "The Diary of a Detenu for Debt," in *Humor and
    Pathos*. London, 1842.
Baxter, George R. Wythen. "Passages from the Diary of a Late Clergyman," in
    Humor and Pathos. London, 1842.
Manuscripts from The Diary of a Physician. London, 1844.
Rathbone, Hannah Mary. *So much of the Diary of Lady Willoughby as relates to her*

Domestic History, and to the eventful Period of the Reign of Charles the First. London, 1844–7.

Thackeray, William Makepeace. *Jeames's Diary,* in *Punch.* 1845–6.

Brontë, Emily. *Wuthering Heights.* London, 1847.

Lever, Charles James. *Diary and Notes of Horace Templeton, Esq., Late Secretary of Legation at – – –.* London, 1848.

1850–9

[Manning, Anne]. *The Maiden and Married Life of Mary Powell, Afterwards Mistress Milton.* London, 1850.

Manning, Anne. *The Household of Sir Thomas More.* London, 1851.

Craik, Dinah Maria. *Bread upon the Waters; a Governess's Life.* London, 1852.

Ephemeris or Leaves from the Journal of Marion Drayton. London, 1853.

[Skene, Harriet]. *The Diary of Martha Bethune Baliol, from 1753 to 1754.* London, 1853.

[Manning, Anne]. *Deborah's Diary.* London, 1856.

1860–9

Charles, Elizabeth. *Chronicles of the Schönberg-Cotta Family.* London, 1863.

Charles, Elizabeth. *Diary of Mrs. Kitty Trevylyan.* London, 1864.

Charles, Elizabeth. *The Diary of Brother Bartholomew, a Monk of the Abbey of Marienthal, in the Odenwald, in the Twelfth Century.* New York, 1865.

Charles, Elizabeth. *The Draytons and the Davenants.* London, 1866.

Sewell, Elizabeth Missing. *Journal of a Home Life.* London, 1867.

1870–9

Oliphant, Laurence. *Piccadilly. A Fragment of Contemporary Biography.* Edinburgh, 1870.

Smith, Jane Mary Fowler. *Journal of the Lady Beatrix Graham, Sister of the Marquis of Montrose.* London, 1870.

Marshall, Emma. *Mrs. Mainwaring's Journal.* London, 1874.

1880–9

Gip's Journal: A Dog's Diary of a Tour in Europe. Oxford, 1880.

Pater, Walter. "A Prince of Court Painters," in *Imaginary Portraits.* London, 1887.

Hudson, Frank. *A Very Mad World.* London, 1889.

1890–9

Lee, Vernon. "Amour Dure: Passages from The Diary of Spiridion Trepka," in *Hauntings. Fantastic Stories.* London, 1890.

Jerome, Jerome K. "The Diary of a Pilgrimage," in *Diary of a Pilgrimage.* Bristol, 1891.

Marshall, Emma. *Winifrede's Journal.* New York, 1891.

Grossmith, George and Weedon. *The Diary of a Nobody.* Bristol, 1892.

Zangwill, Israel. "Diary of a Meshumad," in *Ghetto Tragedies.* London, 1893.

Dowson, Ernest. "The Diary of a Successful Man," in *Dilemmas*. London, 1895.

Frith, Walter. *In Search of Quiet, A Country Journal, May-July*. London, 1895.

Maitland, Ella Fuller. *Pages from The Day-book of Bethia Hardacre*. London, 1895.

Sharp, William. "Fragments of the Lost Journals of Piero di Cosimo," in *Ecce Puella and other Prose Imaginings*. London, 1895.

Stoker, Bram. *Dracula*. Westminster, 1897.

Russell, Mary Annette. *Elizabeth and Her German Garden*. London, 1898.

1900–9

Fowler, Ellen Thorneycroft. "Scattered Leaves," in *Cupid's Garden*. New York, 1900.

Phillpotts, Eden. "The Diary of a Perfect Gentleman," in *Fancy Free*. London, 1901.

Cornwall, Nellie. *The Little Don of Oxford*. London, 1902.

Collins, T. *Such is Life; being certain extracts from the diary of Tom Collins*. Sydney, 1903.

Gissing, George. *The Private Papers of Henry Ryecroft*. Westminster, 1903.

1910–19

Baring, Maurice. *Lost Diaries*. London, 1913.

1920–9

Maconechy, J. *The Secret Journal of Charles Dunbar*. London, ca. 1923.

Steel, Flora Annie. "A Precession of Equinoxes," in *Tales of the Tides, and Other Stories*. London, 1923.

King-Hall, Magdalen. *The Diary of a Young Lady of Fashion in the Year 1764–1765*. London, 1925.

Marshall, Archibald. *Miss Welby at Steen*. London, 1929.

1930–9

De La Pasture, Edmée. *Diary of a provincial lady*. London, 1930.

Barrie, Sir James Matthew. *Farewell Miss Julie Logan*. London, 1931.

Stevenson, Dorothy Emily. *Mrs. Tim of the Regiment; Leaves from the Diary of an Officer's Wife*. London, 1932.

De La Pasture, Edmée. *The Provincial Lady in London*. New York, 1933.

De La Pasture, Edmée. *The Provincial Lady in America*. New York, 1934.

Creswell, Harry Bulkeley. *Diary from a Dustbin*. London, 1935.

Durrell, Lawrence. *The Black Book, an Agon*. Paris, 1938.

1940–9

De La Pasture, Edmée. *The Provincial Lady in Wartime*. New York, 1940.

MacManus, Francis. *Flow on Lovely River*. Dublin, 1941.

Stevenson, Dorothy Emily. *Mrs. Tim Carries On*. London, 1941.

Thompson, Sylvia. *The Gulls Fly Inland*. Boston, 1941.

Travers, Pamela. *I Go by Sea, I Go by Land*. New York, 1941.

Creswell, Harry Bulkeley. *Grig*. London, 1942.
Bottome, Phillis. *Survival*. Boston, 1943.
Creswell, Harry Bulkeley. *Grig in Retirement*. London, 1943.
Maclean, Catherine Macdonald. *Farewell to Tharrus*. New York, 1944.
Jameson, Storm. *The Journal of Mary Hervey Russell*. London, 1945.
Davies, William Robertson. *The Diary of Samuel Marchbanks*. Toronto, 1947.
Stevenson, Dorothy Emily. *Mrs. Tim Gets a Job*. London, 1947.
Drake, Margaret Evelyn. *Chrysantha*. Philadelphia, 1948.
Farjeon, Joseph Jefferson. *Death of a World*. London, 1948.
Smith, Dorothy Gladys. *I Capture the Castle*. Boston, 1948.
Wheatley, Dennis. *The Haunting of Toby Jugg*. London, 1948.

1950–9
Kennedy, Margaret. *Troy Chimneys*. New York, 1952.
Sargeson, Frank. *I for one . . .* , in *Landfall,* a New Zealand quarterly, June 5, 1952.
Stevenson, Dorothy Emily. *Mrs. Tim Flies Home; Leaves from the Diary of a Grass-widow*. London, 1952.
Hartley, Leslie Poles. *The Go-between*. London, 1953.
Hawthorn, E. M. D. *Quietly She Lies*. New York, 1953.
Aldiss, Brian Wilson. *The Brightfount Diaries*. London, 1955.
Grun, Bernard. *The Golden Quill, a Novel Based on the Life of Mozart*. London, 1956.
Williams, David F. *Agent from the West*. London, 1956.
Baldwin, Monica. *The Called and the Chosen*. London, 1957.
Huxley, Elspeth. *The Red Rock Wilderness*. London, 1957.
O'Connor, Mary. *Fool's Question*. London, 1957.
Tweedsmuir, Susan. *Cousin Harriet*. London, 1957.
Berger, John Peter. *A Painter of Our Time*. London, 1958.
Blumenfeld, Josephine. *Pin a Rose on Me*. London, 1958.
Byrne, Marie. *Softly, Softly*. London, 1958.
Chitty, Susan. *Diary of a Fashion Model*. London, 1958.
O'Connor, Mary Garland. *Thy Wedded Husband*. Boston, 1958.
Bell, Neil. *At the Sign of the Unicorn*. London, 1959.
Blakeston, Oswell. *Hop Thief*. London, 1959.
Janeway, Elizabeth. *The Third Choice*. Garden City, New York, 1959.
Phillpotts, Eden. *There Was an Old Man*. London, 1959.
Wadsworth, Phyllis. *Young Miss Isotope*. London, 1959.

1960–9
Trocchi, Alexander. *Cain's Book*. New York, 1960.
Brenan, Gerald. *A Holiday by the Sea*. London, 1961.
Dashwood, R. M. *Provincial Daughter*. London, 1961.
Lowry, Malcolm. *Through the Panama,* in *Hear Us O Lord from Heaven Thy Dwelling Place*. Philadelphia, 1961.
Sackville-West, Victoria. *No Signposts in the Sea*. London, 1961.

Lessing, Doris. *The Golden Notebook*. London, 1962.
Fowles, John. *The Collector*. London, 1963.
Goudge, Elizabeth. *The Scent of Water*. London, 1963.
Lambert, Gavin. *Inside Daisy Clover*. New York, 1963.
Phelps, Gilbert. *The Winter People*. London, 1963.
Wilson, Colin. *The Sex Diary of Gerard Sorme*. New York, 1963.
Andrew, Prudence. *A Sparkle from the Coal*. London, 1964.
Mott, Michael. *Helmet and Wasps*. London, 1964.
Bois, Helma de. *The Incorruptible*. New York, 1965.
Bermant, Chaim. *Diary of an Old Man*. London, 1966.
Banks, Lynne Reid. *Children at the Gate*. London, 1968.
Household, Geoffrey. *Dance of the Dwarfs*. London, 1968.
Maugham, Robin. *The Second Window*. London, 1968.
Quin, Ann. *Passages*. London, 1969.
Wollheim, Richard. *A Family Romance*. London, 1969.

1970–9
Maugham, Robin. *The Last Encounter*. London, 1972.
Hoban, Russell. *Turtle Diary*. London, 1975.

AMERICAN
1830–9
Poe, Edgar Allan. "Ms. Found in a Bottle," in *Saturday Visiter*. Oct. 19, 1833.

1840–9
Poe, Edgar Allan. "The Journal of Julius Rodman," in *Gentleman's Magazine*.
    Philadelphia, 1840.
Sargent, Lucius Manlius *Diary of the Rev. Solomon Spittle*. Boston, 1847?
Whittier, John Greenleaf. *Leaves from Margaret Smith's Journal in the Province of
    Massachusetts Bay. 1678–9*. Boston, 1849.

1860–9
Woods, Caroline H. *The Diary of a Milliner*. New York, 1867.

1870–9
James, Henry. "The Diary of a Man of Fifty," in *Harper's New Monthly Maga-
    zine* and *Macmillan's Magazine*. July 1879.

1880–9
Gray, Walter T. *The Bad Boy at Home*. New York, 1885.

1890–9
The Journal of "The Clover." A Summer Day-book. August, 1892. New York,
    1893.
Twain, Mark. "Extracts from Adam's Diary," in *The Niagara Book . . . By W.
    D. Howells, Mark Twain, . . . and Others*. Buffalo, 1893.

1900–9

Flandrau, Charles Macomb. *The Diary of a Freshman.* New York, 1901.

Wiggin, Kate Douglas Smith. *The Diary of a Goose Girl.* Boston, 1902.

Sinclair, Upton. *The Journal of Arthur Stirling ("The Valley of The Shadow").* Pasadena, ca. 1903.

Twain, Mark. "Eve's Diary," in *Harper's Magazine.* 1905.

Babcock, Winnifred. *The Diary of Delia.* New York, 1907.

1910–19

Bosher, Kate. *Mary Cary.* New York, 1910.

Lindley, Elizabeth. *The Diary of a Book-Agent.* New York, 1911.

Furman, Lucy. *Mothering on Perilous.* New York, 1913.

Stringer, Arthur John Arbuthnott. *The Prairie Wife.* Indianapolis, 1915.

1920–9

Stringer, Arthur John Arbuthnott. *The Prairie Mother.* Indianapolis, 1920.

Rinehart, Mary Roberts. *The Red Lamp.* New York, 1925.

Cher, Marie. *Up at the Villa.* New York, 1929.

1930–9

Waller, Mary Ella. *The Windmill on the Dune.* Boston, 1931.

Stringer, Arthur John Arbuthnott. *The Mud Lark.* Indianapolis, 1932.

Bernstein, Hillel. *L'Affaire Jones.* New York, 1934.

Blake, Dorothy. *The Diary of a Suburban Housewife.* New York, 1936.

Davis, Clyde Brion. *The Great American Novel.* New York, 1938.

Parrish, Anne. *Mr. Despondency's Daughter.* New York, 1938.

Douglas, Lloyd Cassel. *Doctor Hudson's Secret Journal.* Boston, 1939.

1940–9

Thielens, Gerrie. *Awake! My Heart.* New York, 1940.

Patchen, Kenneth. *The Journal of Albion Moonlight.* New York, 1941.

Boyle, Kay. *Primer for Combat.* New York, 1942.

Field, Hope. *Stormy Present.* New York, 1942.

Morris, Edita. *My Darling from the Lions.* New York, 1943.

Robinson, Dorothy Atkinson. *It's All in the Family.* New York, 1943.

Bellow, Saul. *Dangling Man.* New York, 1944.

Boynton-Hamilton, Mathi. *On Winter's Traces.* New York, 1945.

Hillyer, Laurie. *Time Remembered.* New York, 1945.

Weekley, William. *The Ledger of Lying Dog.* Garden City, New York, 1947.

Davis, Clyde B. *Playtime Is Over.* Philadelphia, 1949.

Wernher, Hilda. *My Indian Son-in-law.* Garden City, New York, 1949.

1950–9

Hersey, John. *The Wall.* New York, 1950.

Davidson, Louis. *Captain Marooner.* New York, 1952.

Leslie, Jean. *The Intimate Journal of Warren Winslow.* Garden City, New York, 1952.

Stolz, Mary. *In a Mirror*. New York, 1953.

Haydn, Richard. *The Journal of Edwin Carp*. New York, 1954.

Herbert, Frederick Hugh. *I'd Rather Be Kissed*. New York, 1954.

Shirer, William Lawrence. *Stranger, Come Home*. Boston, 1954.

Zara, Louis. *Blessed Is the Land*. New York, 1954.

Finletter, Gretchen. *The Dinner Party*. New York, 1955.

Vidal, Gore. "Pages from an Abandoned Journal," in *A Thirsty Evil*. New York, 1956.

Heymann, Lucie. *By Appointment Only*. New York, 1957.

Roschwald, Mordechai. *Level 7*. New York, 1959.

Wellman, Paul Iselin. *The Fiery Flower*. New York, 1959.

1960–9

Cohen, Peter. *Diary of a Simple Man*. New York, 1962.

O'Grady, Rohan. *Pippin's Journal*. New York, 1962.

Wilchek, Stella. *Ararat*. New York, 1962.

Arroway, Francis M. *Diary of a Candid Lady*. Garden City, New York, 1964.

Hutchins, Maude. *Honey on the Moon*. New York, 1964.

Downey, Harris. *The Key to My Prison*. New York, 1965.

Hawes, Evelyn. *The Happy Land*. New York, 1965.

Linney, Romulus. *Slowly, by Thy Hand Unfurled*. New York, 1965.

Merrill, James. *The (Diblos) Notebook*. New York, 1965.

Nathan, Robert. *The Mallot Diaries*. New York, 1965.

Connell, Evan S. *The Diary of a Rapist*. New York, 1966.

Keyes, Daniel. *Flowers for Algernon*. New York, 1966.

Vonnegut, Kurt. *Mother Night*. New York, 1966.

Arnold, Michael. *The Archduke*. Garden City, New York, 1967.

Kaufman, Sue. *Diary of a Mad Housewife*. New York, 1967.

Mather, Melissa. *One Summer in Between*. New York, 1967.

Matthews, Jack. *Hanger Stout, Awake!* New York, 1967.

Vining, Elizabeth Gray. *I, Roberta*. Philadelphia, 1967.

Elman, Richard. *Lilo's Diary*. New York, 1968.

Prokosch, Frederic. *The Missolonghi Manuscript*. New York, 1968.

Vidal, Gore. *Myra Breckinridge*. Boston, 1968.

Elman, Richard. *The Reckoning; The Daily Ledgers of Newman Yagodah, Advokat and Factor*. New York, 1969.

Graves, Wallace. *Trixie*. New York, 1969.

1970–9

Flynn, Robert. *The Sounds of Rescue, the Signs of Hope*. New York, 1970.

Horwitz, Julius. *The Diary of A. N.* New York, 1970.

Matthews, Jack. *Beyond the Bridge*. New York, 1970.

Walker, T. Mike. *Voices from the Bottom of the World; a Policeman's Journal*. New York, 1970.

Adams, Hazard. *The Truth About Dragons: An Anti-romance*. New York, 1971.

Herlihy, James Leo. *The Season of the Witch*. New York, 1971.

Webb, Lucas. *Eli's Road*. New York, 1971.
Bryant, Dorothy. *Ella Price's Journal*. New York, 1972.
Carlisle, Henry. *Voyage to the First of December*. New York, 1972.
Lieber, Joel. *Two-Way Traffic*. New York, 1972.
McCormack, Eliza. *Would You Believe Love?* New York, 1972.
Schiff, Ken. *Passing Go*. New York, 1972.
Sarton, May. *As We Are Now*. New York, 1973.
Boynton, Peter. *Stone Island*. New York, 1973.
Rhodes, Richard. *The Ungodly*. New York, 1973.
Clark, Eleanor. "A Summer in Puerto Rico," in *Dr. Heart*. New York, 1974.
Pratt, John Clark. *The Laotian Fragments*. New York, 1974.
Swados, Harvey. *Celebration*. New York, 1974.
Vidal, Gore. *Myron*. New York, 1974.
Updike, John. *A Month of Sundays*. New York. 1975.
Updike, John. "From the Journal of a Leper," in *The New Yorker*. July 19, 1976.

FRENCH
1800–9
Souza-Botelho, Adélaïde. *Charles et Marie*. Paris, 1802.
Nodier, Charles. *Le Peintre de Saltzbourg, journal des émotions d'un coeur souffrant*. Paris, 1803.
Souza-Botelho, Adélaïde. *Eugène de Rothelin*. Paris, 1808.

1820–9
Hugo, Victor. *Le Dernier jour d'un condamné*. Paris, 1829.

1830–9
Flaubert, Gustave. "Mémoires d'un fou" [1839], in *Oeuvres complètes*. Paris, 1973.

1840–9
Sand, George. *Isidora*. Paris, 1846.
Porchat, Jacques. *Trois mois sous la neige, journal d'un jeune habitant du Jura*. Paris, 1848.

1850–9
Du Camp, Maxime. *Le Livre posthume, mémoires d'un suicidé*. Paris, 1853.
Frémy, Arnould. *Journal d'une jeune fille*. Paris, 1853.
Second, Albéric. "Le Journal d'une jeune femme," in *Contes sans prétention*. Paris, 1854.
Sand, George. *La Daniella*. Paris, 1857.
Feuillet, Octave. *Le Roman d'un jeune homme pauvre*. Paris, 1858.

1860–9
Champfleury. *Les Demoiselles Tourangeau. Journal d'un étudiant*. Paris, 1864.
Zola, Emile. *La Confession de Claude*. Paris, 1865.

Taine, Hippolyte. *Notes sur Paris. Vie et opinions de M. Frédéric Thomas Graindorge*. Paris, 1867.

1870–9

Daudet, Alphonse. *Robert Helmont, journal d'un solitaire*. Paris, 1874.

Rambert, Eugène. "La Marmotte au collier," in *Les Alpes suisses*, 4. Bâle, 1875.

Belot, Adolphe. *Folies de jeunesse*. Paris, 1876.

Maupassant, Guy de. "Sur l'eau," in *La Maison Tellier*. Paris, 1881. First pub. as "En Canot" in 1876.

Feuillet, Octave. *Le Journal d'une femme*. Paris, 1878.

Theuriet, André. *Sous-bois, impressions d'un forestier*. Paris, 1878.

1880–9

France, Anatole. *Le Crime de Sylvestre Bonnard*. Paris, 1881.

Uzanne, Octave. "Les Hasards des petits papiers," in *Les Surprises du coeur*. Paris, 1881.

Des Perrières, Carle. *Rien ne va plus*. Paris, 1882.

Loti, Pierre. "Pasquala Ivanovitch," in *Fleurs d'ennui*. Paris, 1883.

Loti, Pierre. "Suleïma," in *Fleurs d'ennui*. Paris, 1883.

Loti, Pierre. "Voyage de quatre officiers de l'escadre internationale au Monténégro," in *Fleurs d'ennui*. Paris, 1883.

Maupassant, Guy de. "Aux eaux," in *Le Gaulois*. July 24, 1883.

Droz, Gustave. *Tristesses et sourires*. Paris, 1884.

Theuriet, André. *Le Journal de Tristan, impressions et souvenirs*. Paris, 1884.

Maupassant, Guy de. "Mes vingt-cinq jours," in *Le Gil Blas*. Aug. 25, 1885.

Maupassant, Guy de. "Nos Anglais," in *Le Gil Blas*. Feb. 17, 1885.

Maupassant, Guy de. "Un Fou," in *Le Gaulois*. Sept. 10, 1885.

Rod, Edouard. *La Course à la mort*. Paris, 1885.

Maupassant, Guy de. "Le Horla," in *Le Gil Blas*. Oct. 26, 1886.

Cherbuliez, Victor. *La Bête*. Paris, 1887.

Fabre, Ferdinand. *Mlle Abeille (fragments de mon journal)*. Paris, 1887.

Maupassant, Guy de. "Livre de bord," in *Le Gaulois*. Aug. 17, 1887.

Bazin, René. *Une Tache d'encre*. Paris, 1888.

Loti, Pierre. *Madame Chrysanthème*. Paris, 1888.

[Schulz, Jeanne.] *La Neuvaine de Colette par ★ ★ ★,* " in *La Revue des Deux Mondes*. 1888.

Rod, Edouard. *Le Sens de la vie*. Paris, 1889.

1890–9

Adam, Paul. *Robes rouges*. Paris, 1891.

André Gide. *Les Cahiers d'André Walter*. Paris, 1891.

Rod, Edouard. "Pension de famille. Carnet d'hiver d'un vieux garçon," in *Nouvelles romandes*. Paris, 1891.

Loti, Pierre. *Fantôme d'Orient*. Paris, 1892.

Adam, Paul. "L'Inéluctable," in *Critique des moeurs*. Paris, 1893.

Le Roux, Hugues. *Gladys*. Paris, 1894.

Ardel, Henri. "Au cours!," in *Rêve blanc*. Paris, 1895.

Gide, André. *Paludes*. Paris, 1895.

O'Monroy, Richard. "Mes Jours de l'an," in *Histoires tendres*. Paris, 1895.

O'Monroy, Richard. "Les Trois accolades," in *Histoires tendres*. Paris, 1895.

Prévost, Marcel. *Le Jardin secret*. Paris, 1897.

Gyp. *Journal d'un grinchu*. Paris, 1898.

Prévost, Marcel. "Le Mariage de Julienne," in *Trois nouvelles*. Paris, 1898.

1900–9

Mirbeau, Octave. *Le Journal d'une femme de chambre*. Paris, 1900.

Bourget, Paul. *Le Fantôme*. Paris, 1901.

Lorrain, Jean. *Monsieur de Phocas. Astarté*. Paris, 1901.

Prévost, Marcel. *L'Heureux ménage*. Paris, 1901.

Bazin, René. "Une Excursion de chasse en Hollande," in *Récits de la plaine et de la montagne*. Paris, 1903.

Bazin, René. "Journal de route au bord du Rhône," in *Récits de la plaine et de la montagne*. Paris, 1903.

Bordeaux, Henry. *Le Lac noir,* in *Journal des Débats*. 1903.

Favre de Coulevain, Hélène. *Sur la branche*. Paris, 1903.

Bordeaux, Henry. *La Jeune fille aux oiseaux*. Paris, 1905.

Loti, Pierre. *La Troisième jeunesse de Madame Prune*. Paris, 1905.

La Vrille. *Le Journal d'une masseuse*. Paris, 1906.

Farrère, Claude. *L'Homme qui assassina*. Paris, 1907.

Prévost, Marcel. "Mon petit voisin," in *Femmes*. Paris, 1907.

Prévost, Marcel. "Un Voluptueux," in *Femmes*. Paris, 1907.

Bazin, René. *Mémoires d'une vieille fille*. Paris, 1908.

Boylesve, René. *Mon Amour*. Paris, 1908.

1910–19

Bordeaux, Henry. *La Robe de laine*. Paris, 1910.

Chantepleure, Guy. *Malencontre*. Paris, 1910.

Tinayre, Marcelle. *Madeleine au miroir, journal d'une femme*. Paris, 1912.

Larbaud, Valéry. *A. O. Barnabooth*. Paris, 1913.

Bazin, René. "Journal d'une soeur française de Jérusalem," in *Récits du temps de la guerre*. Paris, 1915.

Barbusse, Henri. *Le Feu. Journal d'une escouade*. Paris, 1916.

D'Honville, Gérard. *Jeune Fille*. Paris, 1916.

Le Roux, Hugues. *Au champ d'honneur*. Paris, 1916.

Moselly, E. *Le Journal de Gottfried Mauser*. Paris, 1916.

Fribourg, André. *Croire. Histoire d'un soldat*. Paris, 1917.

Parn, Francisque. *En suivant la flamme*. Paris, 1918.

Rolland, Romain. *Colas Breugnon*. Paris, 1918.

Burnat-Provins, Marguerite. *Vous*. Paris, 1919.

Gide, André. *La Symphonie pastorale*. Paris, 1919.

Jaloux, Edmond. *Les Amours perdues*. Paris, 1919.

1920–9

Arnoux, Alexandre. *Indice 33.* Paris, 1920.

Prévost, Marcel. *Mon cher Tommy.* Paris, 1920.

Rostand, Maurice. *Le Cercueil de cristal.* Paris, 1920.

Gilbert de Voisins, Auguste. *Le Démon secret.* Paris, 1921.

Zanta, Léontine. *La Science et l'amour, journal d'une étudiante.* Paris, 1921.

Haraucourt, Edmond. *Vertige d'Afrique.* Paris, 1922.

Lens, A.-R. de. *Derrière les vieux murs en ruines.* Paris, 1922.

Valdagne, Pierre. *Constance, ma tendre amie.* Paris, 1922.

Jaloux, Edmond. *L'Amour de Cécile Fougères. Roman inédit.* Paris, 1923.

Le Breton, André. *Le Tourment du passé, journal intime d'un inconnu.* Paris, 1923.

Pérochon, Ernest. *Les Ombres.* Paris, 1923.

Charbonneau, Louis. *Mambu et son amour.* Paris, 1924.

Gide, André. *Les Faux-Monnayeurs.* Paris, 1925.

Mistler, Jean. *Châteaux en Bavière.* Paris, 1925.

Dekobra, Maurice. *Flammes de velours.* Paris, 1927.

Duhamel, Georges. *Journal de Salavin.* Paris, 1927.

Kessel, Joseph. *La Rage au ventre.* Paris, 1927.

Rostand, Maurice. *Le Second Werther.* Paris, 1927.

Malraux, André. *Les Conquérants.* Paris, 1928.

Gide, André. *L'Ecole des femmes.* Paris, 1929.

1930–9

Chardonne, Jacques. *Eva ou le Journal interrompu.* Paris, 1930.

Henry-Bordeaux, Paule. *Antaram de Trébizonde.* Paris, 1930.

Bove, Emmanuel. *Journal écrit en hiver.* Paris, 1931.

Escholier, Raymond. *L'Herbe d'amour.* Paris, 1931.

Jouhandeau, Marcel. *Le Journal du coiffeur.* Paris, 1931.

Deffoux, Léon. *Pipe-en-bois, témoin de la Commune.* Paris, 1932.

Mauriac, François. *Le Noeud de vipères.* Paris, 1932.

Robert, Louis de. *Journal d'un mari.* Paris, 1932.

Fauconnier, Geneviève. *Claude.* Paris, 1933.

Drieu la Rochelle, Pierre. "Journal d'un homme trompé" in *Journal d'un homme trompé.* Paris, 1934.

Danemarie, Jeanne. *La Possédée de Vauverdane.* Paris, 1935.

Bernanos, Georges. *Journal d'un curé de campagne.* Paris, 1936.

Blond, Georges. *Journal d'un imprudent.* Paris, 1936.

Sartre, Jean-Paul. *La Nausée.* Paris, 1938.

Romains, Jules. *La Douceur de la vie.* Paris, 1939.

1940–9

Pourrat, Henri. *Vent de mars.* Paris, 1941.

Berr, Henri. *L'Hymne à la vie.* Paris, 1942.

Dubois la Chartre, André. *Du Héros, de la Femme et de Dieu. Journal de Bellérophon.* Paris, 1942.

Queffélec, Henri. *Journal d'un salaud.* Paris, 1944.

Daninos, Pierre. *Méridiens*. Paris, 1945.
Gautier, Jean-Jacques. *L'Oreille*. Paris, 1945.
Gracq, Julien. *Un Beau ténébreux*. Paris, 1945.
Malraux, Clara. *Portrait de Grisélidis*. Paris, 1945.
Bataille, Georges. *La Haine de la poésie*. Paris, 1947. Later as *L'Impossible* [1962],
    in *Oeuvres Complètes* 3. Paris, 1971.
Daninos, Pierre. *Le Carnet du Bon Dieu*. Paris, 1947.
Bataille, Georges. "La Scissiparité," in *Les Cahiers de la Pléiade*. 1949.

1950–9
Pezeril, Daniel. *Rue Notre-Dame*. Neuchâtel, 1950.
Beckett, Samuel. *Malone meurt*. Paris, 1951.
Beckett, Samuel. *Molloy*. Paris, 1951.
Duhamel, Georges. *Cri des profondeurs*. Paris, 1951.
Poulet, Robert. *L'Enfer-ciel. Journal d'un condamné à mort*. Paris, 1952.
Daninos, Pierre. *Les carnets du Major Thompson*. Paris, 1954.
Lallemand, Ferdinand. *Journal de bord de Maarkos Sestios*. Paris, 1955.
Butor, Michel. *L'Emploi du temps*. Paris, 1956.
Dubois la Chartre, André. *Journal intime d'Hercule*. Paris, 1957.
Lesort, Paul André. *Le Fer rouge*. Paris, 1957.
Masson, Loys. *La Douve*. Paris, 1957.
Gennari, Geneviève. *Journal d'une bourgeoise*. Paris, 1959.
Pinsonneault, Jean Paul. *Les Abîmes de l'aube* [1959]. Montréal, 1962.

1960–9
Bessette, Gérard. *Le Libraire*. Paris, 1960.
Daninos, Pierre. *Un Certain monsieur Blot*. Paris, 1960.
Fabre-Luce, Alfred. *La Voyageuse de nuit*. Paris, 1961.
Montaurier, Jean. *Comme à travers le feu*. Paris, 1962.
Queneau, Raymond. *Les Oeuvres complètes de Sally Mara*. Paris, 1962.
Drieu la Rochelle, Pierre. "Journal d'un délicat," in *Histoires déplaisantes*. Paris,
    1963.
Pouillon, Fernand. *Les Pierres sauvages*. Paris, 1964.
Soubiran, André. *Journal d'une femme en blanc*. Paris, 1964.
Audiberti, Jacques. *Dimanche m'attend*. Paris, 1965.
Beauvoir, Simone de. "La Femme rompue," in *La Femme rompue*. Paris, 1967.
Del Castillo, Michel. *Gerardo Laïn*. Paris, 1967.
Dutourd, Jean. *Pluche ou l'Amour de l'art*. Paris, 1967.
Fournier, Roger. *Journal d'un jeune marié*. Montréal, 1967.
Godbout, Jacques. *Salut Galarneau!* Paris, 1967.
Cayrol, Jean. *Je l'entends encore*. Paris, 1968.

1970–9
Sagan, Françoise. *Des Bleus à l'âme*. Paris, 1972.
Gautier, Jean-Jacques. *Cher Untel*. Paris, 1974.
Tournier, Michel. "Amandine ou les deux jardins," in *Le Coq de bruyère*. Paris,
    1978.

GERMAN

1770–9
Planck, Gottlieb Jakob. *Tagebuch eines neuen Ehmanns*. Leipzig, 1779.

1790–9
Brakenbusch. *Tagebuch eines Menschenbeobachters*. Hannover, 1791.
Thümmel, Moritz August von. *Reise in die mittäglichen Provinzen von Frankreich*. Leipzig, 1791–1805.
Pahl, Johann Gottfried von. *Herwart, der Eifersüchtige – Auszüge aus seinem Tagebuch*. Basel, 1797.
Tieck, Ludwig. "Ein Tagebuch," in *Straußfedern. Eine Sammlung kleiner Romane und Erzählungen, 7*. Berlin, 1798.

1800–9
Richter, Johann Paul Friedrich. "Des Luftschiffers Giannozzo Seebuch," in *Komischer Anhang zum Titan*. Berlin, 1801.
Arnim, Achim von. "Aloys und Rose. Französische Miscellen aus Wallis. Aus dem Tagebuche eines hypochondrischen Reisenden," in *Französische Miscellen, 3*. Tübingen, 1803.
Bouterwek, Friedrich. *Ramiros Tagebuch*. Leipzig, 1804.
Kotzebue, August von. "Fragmente aus dem Tagebuch des letzten Königs von Polen, Stanislaus Augustus," in *Kleine Romane, Erzählungen, Anecdoten und Miscellen*. Leipzig, 1805.
Weitzel, Johannes Ignatz. *Lindau oder der unsichtbare Bund*. Frankfurt, 1805.

1810–19
Hoffmann, Ernst Theodor Wilhelm (Amadeus). "Kreisleriana," in *Fantasiestücke in Callot's Manier. Blätter aus dem Tagebuche eines reisenden Enthusiasten*. Bamberg, 1814–15.
Tarnow, Fanny. "Das Tagebuch Augustens," in *Frauentaschenbuch für 1815*.
Heun, Carl. "Auszug aus dem Tagebuche Kilians, des Seminaristen zu Schnabelschanzhausen," in *Vergißmeinnicht. Ein Taschenbuch für 1818*. 1818.
Zschokke, Heinrich. "Das Neujahrsgeschenk. (Aus den Tagebüchern des armen Pfarr-Vikars von Wiltshire)," in *Erheiterungen. Eine Monatsschrift für gebildete Leser*. 1819.

1820–9
Birkenstock, Wilhelm Christian. *Hugo's Tageblätter an Max*. Hamburg, 1821.
Meine Reise und Ich. Jena, 1821.
Tarnow, Fanny. "Jugendansichten," in *Lilien, 2*. Leipzig, 1821.
Kuhn, August. "Blätter aus Edmunds Tagebuche," in *Mimosen: Erzählungen für gebildete Frauen*. Berlin, 1822.
Arnim, Achim von. "Die Verkleidungen des französischen Hofmeisters und seines deutschen Zöglings," in *Frauentaschenbuch für das Jahr 1824*. Nürnberg, 1824.

[Hudtwalcker]. *Bruchstücke aus Karl Berthold's Tagebuch*. Berlin, 1826.

Märcker, Friedrich Adolf. *Julius. Eine Lebensgeschichte aus der Zeit*. Berlin, 1829.

Spindler, Carl. "Denkwürdigkeiten eines Wahnsinnigen," in *Kettenglieder, Gesammelte Erzählungen*, 3. Stuttgart, 1829.

1830–9

Selten, J. *Luise, oder Was ein Mädchen durch Sittsamkeit, Selbstprüfung und Fleiß werden kann*. Braunschweig, 1830.

Spindler, Carl. "Skizzen aus dem Badejournal eines Sechzigers," in *Moosrosen*, 1. Stuttgart, 1830.

Tarnow, Fanny. "Blätter aus Theresens Tagebuch," in *Auswahl aus Fanny Tarnow's Schriften*, 6. Leipzig, 1830.

Tarnow, Fanny. "Paulinens Jugendjahre," in *Auswahl aus Fanny Tarnow's Schriften*, 9. Leipzig, 1830.

Lewald, August. "Aus dem Tagebuche eines Guillotinirten," in *Novellen*. Hamburg, 1831.

Braun von Braunthal, Johann Karl. *Fragmente aus dem Tagebuche eines jungen Ehmann's*. Wien, 1833.

Kühne, Gustav. *Eine Quarantäne im Irrenhause*. Leipzig, 1835.

Gaudy, Franz von. *Aus dem Tagebuch eines wandernden Schneidergesellen*. Leipzig, 1836.

Biedenfeld, Ferdinand Leopold Karl von. "Aus den Papieren eines Selbstmörders," in *Erzählungen*. Frankfurt, 1837.

Vogl, Johann R. "Der Gedankenräuber. Aus dem Tagebuche eines Freundes," in *Novellen*. Wien, 1837.

Brentano, Clemens. "Tagebuch der Ahnfrau," in *Gockel, Hinkel und Gackeleia*. Frankfurt, 1838.

1840–9

Stifter, Adalbert. "Feldblumen" [1840] in *Studien*, 1. Pesth, 1844.

Weisser, Adolph. *Hinterlassene Papiere eines geistlichen Selbstmörders*. Pforzheim, 1841.

Schubar, L. *Memoiren eines Verurtheilten*. Berlin, 1842.

Schirges, Georg. "Tagebuchblätter eines unglücklichen Apothekers," in *Zwei Gräber*. Leipzig, 1843.

Stolle, Ferdinand. "Valerie. Frühlingsnovelle," in *Kleinere Erzählungen*, 1. Leipzig, 1844.

Herloßsohn, Carl. "Schwester Anna und ihr Tagebuch," in *Phantasiegemälde. Taschenbuch romantischer Erzählungen für 1846*. Leipzig, 1846.

Nordmann. "Eine Grabschrift," in *Ein Novellenbuch*, 1. Wien, 1846.

Nieritz, Gustav. *Jacob Sturm, oder: Tagebuch eines Dorfschulmeisters*. Berlin, 1847.

Stelzhamer, Franz. "Morgensturm und Abendroth," in *Heimgarten*, 1. Leipzig, 1847.

Lentner, Joseph Friedrich. "Veränderungen. Roman in Bruchstücken. Nach den Papieren einer Tänzerin," in *Novellenbuch*, 3. Magdeburg, 1848.

1850–9

Lisettens Tagebuch. Leipzig, 1852.

Nathusius, Marie. *Tagebuch eines armen Fräuleins.* Berlin, 1853.

Spindler, Carl. *Der Teufel im Bade. Aufzeichnungen eines Kurgastes in Homburg.* Stuttgart, 1853.

Raabe, Wilhelm. *Die Chronik der Sperlingsgasse.* Berlin, 1857.

1860–9

Religion und Liebe. Roman aus dem Tagebuche eines Anonymen. Hamburg, 1860.

Raabe, Wilhelm. *Nach dem großen Kriege.* Berlin, 1861.

Heyse, Paul. "Unheilbar. (Ein Mädchentagebuch)," in *Meraner Novellen.* Berlin, 1864.

Holtei, Karl. *Noch ein Jahr in Schlesien.* Breslau, 1864.

1870–9

Seidel, Heinrich. *Der Rosenkönig.* Breslau, 1871.

Hopfen, Hans. *Juschu. Tagebuch eines Schauspielers.* Stuttgart, 1875.

Hoefer, Edmund. "*In doloribus.* Tagebuchblätter eines Verschollenen," in *Fünf neue Geschichten.* Stuttgart, 1877.

Wellmer, Arnold. "Fröhliche Weihnachten. Drei Blätter aus dem Tagebuche eines Einsamen. Eine Weihnachtsgeschichte," in *Fröhliche Feste!* Berlin, 1878.

1880–9

Jensen, Wilhelm. *Das Tagebuch aus Grönland.* Berlin, 1885.

Hartleben, Otto Erich. "Um den Glauben. Ein Tagebuch," in *Zwei verschiedene Geschichten.* Leipzig, 1887. Also published as "Die Serenyi."

Conradi, Hermann. "Sein erstes Buch," in *Das literarische Anhalt,* ed. Jean Bernard Muschi and Hermann Wäschke. Dessau, 1888.

Lienhard, Friedrich. *Die weiße Frau.* Dresden, 1889.

Liliencron, Detlev von. "Der Mäcen," in *Der Mäcen.* Leipzig, 1889.

Liliencron, Detlev von. "Die Mergelgrube," in *Der Mäcen.* Leipzig, 1889.

Schnitzler, Arthur. "Der Andere," in *An der schönen blauen Donau.* Wien, 1889.

Walter, Gerhard. "Allein," in *Fernab von der Straße. Vier Novellen.* Jena, 1889.

1890–9

Panizza, Oskar. *Aus dem Tagebuch eines Hundes.* Leipzig, 1892.

Conrad, Michael Georg. *Die Beichte des Narren,* vol. 3 of *Was die Isar rauscht.* Leipzig, 1893.

Scheerbart, Paul. *Das Paradies, die Heimat der Kunst.* Berlin, 1893.

Schnitzler, Arthur. "Blumen," in *Neue Revue.* Wien, August, 1894.

Mann, Thomas. "Der Tod," in *Simplicissimus,* Nos. 21–23, 1896.

Huch, Rudolf. *Aus dem Tagebuche eines Höhlenmolches.* Leipzig, 1897.

Reuter, Gabriele. "Im Sonnenland," in *Der Lebenskünstler.* Berlin, 1897.

Schnitzler, Arthur. "Die Frau des Weisen," in *Die Zeit.* Wien, January, 1897.

Bierbaum, Otto Julius. "Emil der Verstiegene; aus dem Tagebuch eines blümeranten Dichters," in *Kaktus und andere Künstlergeschichten*. Berlin, 1898.

Hauptmann, Gerhart. "Rovio" [ca. 1899–1903], in *Sämtliche Werke*, 11, ed. Hans-Egon Hass. Frankfurt, 1974.

1900–9

Reuter, Gabriele. *Ellen von der Weiden. Ein Tagebuch*. Berlin, 1900.

[Hesse, Hermann]. "Tagebuch 1900," in *Hinterlassene Schriften und Gedichte von Hermann Lauscher*, ed. Hermann Hesse. Basel, 1901.

Asenijeff, Elsa. *Tagebuchblätter einer Emancipierten*. Leipzig, 1902.

Esswein, Hermann. "Das Annerl" [1899], in *Das Atelier. Studien in Prosa*. München, 1902.

Walser, Robert. "Ein Maler," in *Fritz Kocher's Aufsätze*, in *Der Bund*, Nos. 12–14, 1902.

Musil, Robert. "Tagebuch Hippolyte" [ca. 1903], in *Gesammelte Werke*, 7, ed. Adolf Frisé. Hamburg, 1978.

Sternheim, Carl. "Drei Tage aus einem Tagebuch" [1903] in *Gesamtwerk*, 9, ed. Wilhelm Emrich. Neuwied, 1970.

Meyrink, Gustav. "Eine Suggestion," in *Orchideen*. München, 1904.

Suttner, A. Gundaccar von. *Die Nixe*. Dresden, 1904.

Blei, Franz. "Der Beau" [1905], in *Erdachte Geschehnisse – Vermischte Schriften*, 1. München, 1911.

Böhme, Margarete. *Tagebuch einer Verlorenen. Von einer Toten*. Berlin, 1905.

Flaischlen, Cäsar. *Jost Seyfried*. Berlin, 1905.

Bulcke, Carl. *Das Tagebuch der Susanne Övelgönne*. Dresden, 1906.

Das Tagebuch eines Glücklich-Verheirateten, unterschlagen und mitgeteilt von Karlchen. München, 1906.

Wedekind, Frank. "Bei den Hallen," in *Feuerwerk*. München, 1906.

Wedekind, Frank. "Ich langweile mich," in *Feuerwerk*. München, 1906.

Huch, Rudolf. *Max Gebhard. Eine Studie*. Berlin, 1907.

Ernst, Otto. *Überwunden. Aus den Aufzeichnungen eines Schulmeisters*. New York, 1908.

Ewers, Hanns Heinz. "Aus dem Tagebuche eines Orangenbaumes," in *Das Grauen. Seltsame Geschichten*. München, 1908.

Ewers, Hanns Heinz. "Die Mamaloi," in *Das Grauen. Seltsame Geschichten*. München, 1908.

Brod, Max. "Ausflüge ins Dunkelrote," in *Die Erziehung zur Hetäre; Ausflüge ins Dunkelrote*. Stuttgart, 1909.

Müller, Hans. "Der segnende Schatten," in *Geheimnisland. Novellen*. Berlin, 1909.

Walser, Robert. *Jakob von Gunten*. Berlin, 1909.

1910–19

Meyer, Alfred Richard. *Triole. Das Tagebuch der Margot B.* Wien, 1910.

Nathusius, Annemarie von. *Der stolze Lumpenkram*. Berlin, 1910.

Rilke, Rainer Maria. *Die Aufzeichnungen des Malte Laurids Brigge*. Leipzig, 1910.

Heym, Georg. "Das Tagebuch Shakletons" [1911], in *Dichtungen und Schriften,* 2, ed. Karl Ludwig Schneider. n.p., 1962.

Mühlau, Helene von. *Nach dem dritten Kind. Aus dem Tagebuch einer Offiziersfrau.* Berlin, 1911.

Forbes-Mosse, Irene. *Der kleine Tod.* Berlin, 1912.

Müller-Guttenbrunn, Adam. *Es war einmal ein Bischof.* Leipzig, 1912.

Scheerbart, Paul. "Professor Kienbeins Abenteuer. Eine Laboratoriums-Novellette," in *Astrale Novelletten.* Karlsruhe, 1912.

Carossa, Hans. *Doktor Bürgers Ende. Letzte Blätter eines Tagebuchs.* Leipzig, 1913.

Ehrenstein, Carl. *Klagen eines Knaben.* Leipzig, 1913.

Goering, Reinhard. *Jung Schuk.* Frankfurt, 1913.

Reventlow, Franziska, Gräfin zu. *Herrn Dame's Aufzeichnungen.* München, 1913.

Voß, Richard. *Kundry. Die Geschichte einer Leidenschaft.* Stuttgart, 1913.

Walser, Robert. "Tagebuch eines Schülers," in *Geschichten.* Leipzig, 1914.

Adler, Paul. *Nämlich.* Dresden-Hellerau, 1915.

Keller, Paul. *Ferien vom Ich.* Breslau, 1915.

Ulitz, Arnold. "Der geträumte Thron. Aus den Aufzeichnungen eines Kronprätendenten," in *Die Narrenkarosse.* München, 1916.

Strobl, Karl Hans. "Das Grabmal auf dem Père Lachaise," in *Lemuria. Seltsame Geschichten.* München, 1917.

Brod, Max. *Das große Wagnis.* Leipzig, 1918.

Grimm, Hans. *Der Ölsucher von Duala. Ein Tagebuch.* Berlin, 1918.

Keller, Paul. *Hubertus. Ein Waldroman.* Breslau, 1918.

Latzko, Andreas. "Der Kamerad – ein Tagebuch," in *Menschen im Krieg.* Zürich, 1918.

Schaefer, Heinrich. *Gefangenschaft.* Berlin, 1918.

Goll, Claire. "Myriel," in *Der gläserne Garten. Zwei Novellen.* [Von Claire Studer]. München, 1919.

Seeger, Johann Georg. *Kilian Kötzler.* Leipzig, 1919.

Siemsen, Hans. *Auch ich, auch du. Aufzeichnungen eines Irren.* Leipzig, 1919.

1920–9

Birkenbihl, Michael. "Mondleid," in *Dämonische Novellen.* München, 1920.

Halbach, Fritz. *Jud Günther, der böse Geist der Etappe. Ein Roman nach Tagebuchblättern aus dem Weltkrieg.* München, 1920.

Hennings, Emmy. *Das Brandmal. Ein Tagebuch.* Berlin, 1920.

Janstein, Elisabeth. *Die Kurve. Aufzeichnungen.* Wien, 1920.

Klabund. *Marietta. Ein Liebesroman aus Schwabing.* Hannover, 1920.

Kokoschka, Bohuslav. *Adelina oder der Abschied vom neunzehnten Lebensjahr.* München, 1920.

Lichnowsky, Mechtild. *Geburt.* Berlin, 1921.

Vesper, Will. *Die Wanderungen des Herrn Ulrich von Hutten. Ein Tagebuch-Roman.* Gütersloh, 1921.

Hauptmann, Gerhart. *Phantom. Aufzeichnungen eines ehemaligen Sträflings.* Berlin, 1923.

Reimann, Hans. "Das Kronprinzenbuch," in *Von Karl May bis Max Pallenberg in 60 Minuten*. München, 1923.

Johst, Hans. *Consuela. Aus dem Tagebuch einer Spitzbergenfahrt*. München, 1925.

Claudius, Hermann. *Meister Bertram van Mynden, Maler zu Hamburg. Ein hansisch Tagebuch um 1400 quasi gesetzet*. Hamburg, 1927.

Meyrink, Gustav. *Der Engel vom weltlichen Fenster*. Leipzig, 1927.

Goebbels, Joseph. *Michael. Ein deutsches Schicksal in Tagebuchblättern*. München, 1929.

1930–9

Hauptmann, Gerhart. *Buch der Leidenshaft*. Berlin, 1930.

Johst, Hanns. *Die Torheit einer Liebe*. München, 1930.

Schneider-Weckerling, Meta. *Cornelia Goethe. Roman in Tagebuchblättern*. Jena, 1930.

Thomas, Adrienne. *Die Katrin wird Soldat*. Berlin, 1930.

Bonne, Georg. *Im Kampf gegen das Chaos*. München, 1931.

Keun, Irmgard. *Das kunstseidene Mädchen*. Berlin, 1932.

Schultze-Pfaelzer, Gerhard. *Der unbekannte Bürger. Historie von heute*. Berlin, 1932.

Ey, Adolf. *Marianne. Eine Studentenliebe am Genfer See*. Hannover, 1933.

Bonsels, Waldemar. *Der Reiter in der Wüste. Eine Amerikafahrt*. Stuttgart, 1935.

Siegmund, Walter. *Der Fähnrich*. Berlin, 1935.

Waterboer, Heinz. *Das Tagebuch des Dr. Sarraut*. Berlin, 1935.

Carossa, Hans. *Geheimnisse des reifen Lebens. Aus den Aufzeichnungen Angermanns*. Leipzig, 1936.

Keun, Irmgard. *Das Mädchen mit dem die Kinder nicht verkehren durften*. Amsterdam, 1936.

Keun, Irmgard. *Nach Mitternacht*. Amsterdam, 1937.

Hauptmann, Gerhart. "Siri. Selbstbekenntnisse eines jungen Humanisten" [1938–39], in *Die großen Erzählungen*. Berlin, 1967.

Kästner, Erich. *Georg und die Zwischenfälle*. Basel, 1938; title of 2nd ed., *Der kleine Grenzverkehr*.

Lützkendorf, Felix. *Märzwind. Die Aufzeichnungen des Leutnants Manfred Kampen und ein Nachbericht*. Berlin, 1938.

Landgrebe, Erich. *Die neuen Götter. Aus den Papieren des Architekten Hemrich*. Berlin, 1939.

Simpson, Margot von. "Nur ein Hund (Aus den Aufzeichnungen des Regierungsrats S.)," in *Liebesquintett*. Dresden, 1939.

Witzany, Rudolf. *Der Freiheit Mutter war die Not*. Karlsbad, 1939.

1940–9

Brenner, Hans Georg. *Nachtwachen. Die Aufzeichnungen eines jungen Mannes*. Berlin, 1940.

Müller-Einigen, Hans. *Das Glück, da zu sein. Ein Tagebuch*. Bern, 1940.

Seidel, Ina. *Unser Freund Peregrin. Aufzeichnungen des Jürgen Brook*. Stuttgart, 1940.

Blümner, Heinz Hubertus. *Mexikanisches Erlebnis*. Berlin, 1941.

Lothar, Ernst. *Die Zeugin*. First published as *A Woman Is Witness: A Paris Diary*. New York, 1941.

Martens, Kurt. *Verzicht und Vollendung*. Berlin, 1941.

Wolf, Siegfried. *Flammen und Lichter. Aus den Aufzeichnungen des Soldaten Kerstan*. Stuttgart, 1941.

Klipstein, Editha. *Der Zuschauer*. Hamburg, 1942.

Watzlik, Hans. *Das Glück von Dürrnstauden*. Leipzig, 1942.

Andres, Stefan. "Sommerliche Elegie," in *Wirtshaus zur weiten Welt. Erzählungen*. Jena, 1943.

Bagier, Guido. *Das tönende Licht*. Berlin, 1943.

Brock, Paul. *Das Opfer der Unbekannten. Aufzeichnungen des Amadeus Metauge*. Berlin, 1943.

Höwing, Hanns. *Tage mit Dorette*. Wiesbaden, 1946.

Schwarz, Georg. "Das verborgene Licht," in *In der Kelter Gottes. Zwei Erzählungen*. München, 1946.

Eitel, Paul. *Heinrich Selbander*. Hamburg, 1948.

Lichtenberg, Wilhelm. *Die Himmelsleiter. Das Leben einer Schauspielerin*. Zürich, 1948.

Podewils, Sophie Dorothee. *Wanderschaft*. Berlin, 1948.

Longoni, Andreas. *Weg ohne Ende*. Bern, 1949.

Schmidt, Arno. "Enthymesis oder W. I. E. H.," in *Leviathan*. Hamburg, 1949.

Schmidt, Arno. "Gadir oder Erkenne dich selbst," in *Leviathan*. Hamburg, 1949.

Schmidt, Arno. "Leviathan oder Die beste der Welten," in *Leviathan*. Hamburg, 1949.

1950–9

Goll, Claire. *Tagebuch eines Pferdes*. Thal/St. Gallen, 1950.

Schmidt, Arno. *Schwarze Spiegel*, in *Brand's Haide; zwei Erzählungen*. Hamburg, 1951.

Selinko, Annemarie. *Désirée*. Köln, 1951.

Hildesheimer, Wolfgang. "Aus meinem Tagebuch," in *Lieblose Legenden*. Stuttgart, 1952.

Stromberg, Kyra. *Das Nadelöhr*. Hamburg, 1952.

Windthorst, Margarete. *Das lebendige Herz. Aufzeichnungen vor Tau und Tag von Hyacinth Henricus Holm*. Hamm, 1952.

Büchner, Johannes. *Nacht. Aus den Notizen eines Priesters*. Basel, 1953.

Kühner, Otto Heinrich. *Nikolskoje*. München, 1953.

Barthel, Ludwig Friedrich. *Runkula. Tagebuch eines Karnickels*. München, 1954.

Frisch, Max. *Stiller*. Frankfurt, 1954.

Fussenegger, Gertrud. *In Deine Hand gegeben*. Düsseldorf/Köln, 1954.

Kneip, Jakob. *Johanna. Eine Tochter unserer Zeit*. Köln, 1954.

Lerber, Helene von. *Im Glashaus*. St. Gallen, 1954.

Mühlberger, Josef. *Die schwarze Perle. Tagebuch einer Kriegskameradschaft*. Esslingen, 1954.

Ihlenfeld, Kurt. "Schwieriger Einzug," in *Eseleien auf Elba*. Witten, 1955.

Wille, Hanns Julius. *Feuer im Wind. Leben und Vergehen des Dichters Johann Christian Günther.* Berlin, 1955.
Bürki, Roland. *Das große Finden.* St. Gallen, 1956.
Holthusen, Hans Egon. *Das Schiff. Aufzeichnungen eines Passagiers.* München, 1956.
Richter-Ruhland, Walter. *Die Jahre hinab. Aufzeichnungen eines Sonderlings.* Köln, 1956.
Brecht, Bertolt. *Die Geschäfte des Herrn Julius Caesar.* Berlin-Schöneberg, 1957.
Roth, Edgar. . . . *Auf daß wir Frieden hätten.* Zürich, 1957.
Bernard, Denis F. *Mensch ohne Gegenwart.* Wien, 1958.
Böll, Heinrich. "Hauptstädtisches Journal," in *Doktor Murkes gesammeltes Schweigen.* Köln, 1958.
Koch, Werner. *Pilatus. Erinnerungen.* Düsseldorf, 1959.

1960–9
Kaschnitz, Marie Luise. "Am Circeo," in *Lange Schatten. Erzählungen.* Hamburg, 1960.
Kroneberg, Eckart. *Der Grenzgänger.* Olten, 1960.
Weiss, Peter. *Der Schatten des Körpers des Kutschers.* Frankfurt, 1960.
Henz, Rudolf. *Die Nachzügler.* Graz, 1961.
Hilty, Hans Rudolf. *Parsifal.* München, 1962.
Bernhard, Thomas. *Frost.* Frankfurt, 1963.
Marwitz, Roland. *Die Wandlung.* Köln, 1963.
Kaschnitz, Marie Luise. "Der Schriftsteller," in *Neue Rundschau, 76.* 1965.
Andres, Stefan. *Der Taubenturm.* München, 1966.
Kein, Ernst. *Die Verhinderung.* Salzburg, 1966.
Kopp, Josef Vital. *Der Forstmeister. Dokumente einer Krise.* Luzern, 1967.

1970–9
Grass, Günther. *Aus dem Tagebuch einer Schnecke.* Neuwied, 1972.
Stiller, Klaus. *Tagebuch eines Weihbischofs.* Berlin, 1972.
König, Barbara. *Schöner Tag, dieser 13.* München, 1973.
Struck, Karin. *Klassenliebe.* Frankfurt, 1973.

ITALIAN
Papini, Giovanni. *Gog.* Firenze, 1931.
Seminara, Fortunato. *Il vento nell'oliveto* [*Wind in an Olive Grove*]. Torino, 1951.
De Céspedes, Alba. *Quaderno proibito* [*The Secret*]. Milano, 1952.
Papini, Giovanni. *Il libro nero.* Firenze, 1952.
Tobino, Mario. *Le libere donne di Magliano* [*The Mad Woman of Magliano*]. Firenze, 1953.
Ottieri, Ottiero. *Donnarumma all'assalto* [*Men at the Gate*]. Milano, 1959.
Moravia, Alberto. *L'attenzióne* [*The Lie*]. Milano, 1965.

SPANISH
Parra, Teresa de la. *Diario de una señorita que se fastidia.* Caracas, 1922.

Delibes, Miguel. *Diario de un cazador*. Barcelona, 1955.

Delibes, Miguel. *Diario de un emigrante*. Barcelona, 1957.

Benedetti, Mario. *La Tregua* [*The Truce*]. Montevideo, 1960.

Desnoes, Edmundo. *Memorias del subdesarrollo*. [*Inconsolable Memories*]. Havana, 1965.

PORTUGUESE AND BRAZILIAN

Machado de Assis, Joachim Maria. *Memorial de Ayres* [*Counselor Ayres's Memorial*]. Rio de Janeiro, 1908.

ROMANIAN

Horia, Vintilă. *Dieu est né en exil*. Paris, 1960.

SCANDINAVIAN

DANISH

Blicher, Steen Steensen. "Brudstykker af en Landsbydegns Dagbog" ["The Journal of a Parish Clerk"], in *Læsefrugter*, 23, ed. A. F. Elmquist. Aarhus, 1824.

Blicher, Steen Steensen. "Præsten i Vejlbye" ["The Parson at Vejlbye"]. 1829.

Kierkegaard, Søren. "Forførerens Dagbog" ["Diary of a Seducer"], in *Enten-Eller*, [*Either/Or*], Kjøbenhavn, 1843.

Kierkegaard, Søren. "Skyldig-Ikke Skyldig" [" 'Guilty?'/'Not Guilty?' "], in *Stadier paa Livets Vej* [*Stages on Life's Way*]. Kjøbenhavn, 1845.

Nansen, Peter. *Julies Dagbog* [*The Diary of Julie*]. Kjøbenhavn, 1893.

Nansen, Peter. *Guds Fred* [Ger: *Gottesfriede*]. København, 1895.

Nansen, Peter. "Af en Forelskers Dagbog" [Ger: "Aus dem Tagebuch eines Verliebten"], in *Samlede Skrifter*, vol 3. København, 1909.

Michaëlis, Karin. *Den farlige Alder* [*The Dangerous Age*]. København, 1910.

Hansen, Martin A. *Løgneren* [*The Liar*]. København, 1950.

NORWEGIAN

Garborg, Arne. *Trætte mænd* [Ger: *Müde Seelen*]. Kristiania, 1891.

Obstfelder, Sigbjørn. *En præsts dagbog* [Ger: *Tagebuch eines Pfarrers*]. København, 1900.

SWEDISH

Bremer, Fredrika. *En dagbok* [*A Diary*]. Stockholm, 1843.

Levertin, Oscar. "Ur ett hjärtas dagbok" [Ger: "Aus dem Tagebuch eines Herzens"], in *Rococo-noveller*. Stockholm, 1899.

Söderberg, Hjalmar. *Doktor Glas* [*Doctor Glas*]. Stockholm, 1905.

Krusenstjerna, Agnes von. *Ninas dagbok* [*The Diary of Nina*]. Stockholm, 1917.

ORIENTAL

JAPANESE

Dazai, Osamu. *No Longer Human* [trans. of *Ningen shikkaku*]. 1948. New York, 1958.

Tanizaki, Jun'ichirō. *The Key* [trans. of *Kagi*]. 1956. New York, 1960.
Tanizaki, Jun'ichirō. *Diary of a Mad Old Man*. 1962. New York, 1965.
Kawabata, Yasumari. "Tagebuch eines Sechzehnjährigen," in *Tagebuch eines Sechzehnjährigen* [trans. of *Jūrokusai no nikki*]. München, 1969.

AFRICAN
CAMEROON
Beti, Mongo. *Le pauvre Christ de Bomba*. Paris, 1956.

EAST EUROPEAN
RUSSIAN
Radiščev, Aleksandr. "Dnevnik odnoj nedeli" [Diary of a Week], in *Sobranie ostavšixsja sočinenij pokojnogo A. N. Radiščeva*, 4. 1811.
Gogol', Nikolaj. "Zapiski sumasšedšego" ["The Diary of a Madman"], in *Arabeski*. Sankt-Peterburg, 1835.
Lermontov, Mixail. *Geroj našego vremeni* [*A Hero of Our Time*]. Sankt-Peterburg, 1840.
Turgenev, Ivan. "Dnevnik lišnego čeloveka" ["The Diary of a Superfluous Man"], in *Otečestvennye zapiski*. 1850.
Dostoevskij, Fëdor. *Zapiski iz podpol'ja* [*Notes from Underground*]. Sankt-Peterburg, 1864.
Garšin, Vsevolod. "Xudožniki" [Ger: "Die Künstler"], in *Otečestvennye zapiski*. 1879.
Gorbunov, Ivan. "Dnevnik Dvoreckogo" ["The Diary of Dvoretsky"], in *Novoe vremja*. Dec. 12, 1882.
Čexov, Anton. "Iz dnevnika pomoščnika buxgaltera" [From the Diary of a Bookkeeper's Assistant], in *Oskolki*. June 1883.
Čexov, Anton. "Iz dnevnika odnoj devicy" [From the Diary of a Young Lady], in *Oskolki*. Oct. 1883.
Tolstoj, Lev. "Posmertnye zapiski starca Fëdora Kuzmiča" ["Fëdor Kuzmič"] [1890–1905], in *Posmertnye xudožestvennye proizvedenija L. N. Tolstogo*. Berlin, 1912.
Veresaev, V. *Bez dorogi* [Ger: *Ohne Weg*]. Moskva, 1895.
Ropšin, V. *Kon' blednyj* [*The Pale Horse*]. Sankt-Peterburg, 1909.
Andreev, Leonid. *Confessions of a Little Man*. New York, 1917.
Zamjatin, Evgenij. *My* [*We*] [1920]. New York, 1952. First pub. as *Nous Autres*. Paris, 1924.
Andreev, Leonid. *Dnevnik Satany* [*Satan's Diary*]. Gelsingfors [Helsinki], 1921.
Ognëv, Nikolai. *Dnevnik Kosti Rjabceva* [*Diary of a Communist Schoolboy*] [1923–4]. Moskva, 1927.
Ropšin, V. *Kon' voronoj* [*The Black Horse*]. Paris, 1923.
Tolstoj, Aleksej. "Rukopis', najdennaja pod krovat'ju," in *Nedra*. Moskva, 1923.
Rachmanowa, Alexandra. *Studenten, Liebe, Tscheka und Tod. Tagebuch einer russischen Studenten*. Salzburg, 1931.
Rachmanowa, Alexandra. *Ehen im roten Sturm*. Salzburg, 1932.

Amosov, Nikolaj. *Zapiski iz buduščego* [*Notes from the Future*], in *Nauka i žizn'*. Moskva, 1965.

POLISH

Sienkiewicz, Henryk. *Bez Dogmatu* [*Without Dogma*]. Warszawa, 1891.

FINNISH

Waltari, Mika. *Johannes Angelos* [*Dark Angel*]. Porvoo, 1952.

HUNGARIAN

Just, Béla. *La Potence et la croix, récit*. Paris, 1954.

Index of Names and Titles

Index of Subjects

authentic-document convention, 57–63,
111, 112, 179, 189, 191
see also fiction of writing
author
in diaries vs. diary fiction, 33–5, 47–8
endorses narrator (consonance), x, 37–
8, 41, 47, 50; *see also* reliable narration
undermines narrator (dissonance), x,
37–8, 41, 47, 50, 138–9, 145; *see also*
unreliable narration
voice of, in first-person narration, 34–6,
39
autobiography, 31–4, 56, 57, 188
problems in interpreting, 39–41, 46
Puritan, 66, 68–70, 72–3, 190

consonance, *see* author, endorses narrator
constatives, 42, 45–7, 49, 50
constative statements of interiority, 42–3,
46, 136

diary (*see also* fiction of writing, connotations of; *journal intime;* letter journal;
literary journal; Protestant diaries; sea
journal; travel journal), 25, 34–5, 48,
185–7
and connotations of closeness to reality,
144, 145, 193–4, 242
and connotations of order, 66, 67, 125,
141, 151, 192, 214, 230, *see also* Protestant diaries, Puritan diaries
and connotations of sincerity, 124, 131,
141, 145, 190, 200, 206, *see also* sincerity
criticism on, 248n26
history of, 24–5, 55–6, 64, 100, 115,
173, 185
and history of word "diary" and synonyms, 27–30, 75, 80
importance of, for diary novel, x, 24–6,
55–6
diary novel
contrasted with diary, 26, 31–5, 187–8
contrasted with epistolary novel, 5, 77–8
contrasted with memoir novel, 4–5

criticism on, ix, 246n1
definition of, reconsidered and method
of study, 24–7, 249n28
origins of, 25, 55–6, 64–74
problems of definition of, 6–8
typologically defined, 3–4
dissonance, *see* author, undermines narrator

emotives, *see* expressives
epistolary novel
characterized and contrasted with diary
novel, 4, 5, 7, 77–8, 82
decline of, 100–1
and diary novels about women, 88,
101, 173
and expressive mode, 49
influence of, on early diary novel, 22–3,
25, 56, 72, 76–7
influence of, on Wertherian diary novel,
88, 91–2
as mimetic form, 24, 56–9, 61, 62
origins of, 56
and unreliable narration, 138
Werther as, 86, 90
expressive form, xi, 34, 189–96
in Butor's *L'Emploi du temps,* 217–18,
229–30
in Frisch's *Stiller,* 198, 201–2, 207–8, 210
in Gide's *Les Faux-Monnayeurs,* 143–4
in Lessing's *Golden Notebook,* 234, 237–
8, 241–5
expressive mode, 46, 49, 50
and consonance, 47
and metaphor, 46, 50, 98
in Wertherian diary novel, 96–9, 156
expressives, 39, 43–50, 136

fiction of writing, x, 5, 201, 216
as characteristic of diary novel, 4, 7,
194
connotations of, 90–1, 108, 124–5, 211
in history of diary novel (*see also* authentic-document convention), 133–
7, 181, 191–3

fictive narrator, 4, 5, 33, 35
fictive reader, 4, 5, 33, 48, 77, 151
    lack of, in diary novel, 5, 7, 25, 26, 33,
        51
    in letter-journal novel, 78–9
    trouble getting rid of, in diary novel, 92
fictive sea-adventure journal, 73–4
fin-de-siècle diary novel, 89–90, 105, 115–
    17, 119–25
first-person discourse, 39, 41, 46–7, 50–2,
    192
    question of authority in, x, 39–43, 46,
        see also reliable narration; unreliable
        narration
    see also first-person narration
first-person narration
    advantages and disadvantages of, 36–7,
        49, 81–2, 126–7, 188
    as characteristic of diary novel, 4, 8,
        22–3, 25, 26, 194
    differences between fictional and nonfic-
        tional, 32–5, 47–8
    and expressives, 39, 44, 46–9
    interpretation of, x, 35, 39–41, 46–7,
        50–1
    manipulation of, in Frisch's Stiller, 206–
        7, 210–11
    and reliable narration, 156–7, 166, 169,
        171
    types of, 4–8, 136
    and unreliable narration, 39–41, 138,
        145
    see also first-person discourse
first-person pronoun, 40, 225
first-person statements, 41–4, 47, 50
Frauenroman, 174

genre, ix–x, 3, 9–23
    as code, norm, or convention, x, 12–23
    descriptive concept of, 9–12, 15, 16, 20
    and finding bibliography, 18–19, 21–2,
        24
    Formalist concept of, 12
    and generic names, 22–3
    as group of texts, 15–19, 21–2
    and imitation or encoding, 11, 21–2, 25
    methods of studying, 21–2
    problems of definition of, x, 6, 9–11,
        18, 21
    problems of studying, 14–17, 19–20
    relation of individual texts to, 12–18
    structuralist concept of, x, 10, 12
    typological or theoretical concept of, x,
        9–12
Gothic novel, 100

historical novel, 100

imitation, see mimesis
interior monologue, 84, 96, 97, 201
    closeness of late-nineteenth-century di-
        ary novel to, 7, 133–7
    contrasted with diary form, 5–6
    displaces diary in psychological fiction,
        135–6, 189
intimate journal, see journal intime

journal, see diary
journal intime, 29, 38, 66, 67, 86, 115–18,
    173, 174, 185, 186, see also diary, and
    connotations of sincerity; sincerity
    Amiel's, 115, 117–18
    Gide's, 140–2
    history of, 55–6, 91, 101, 259n3
    as model for diary novel, 56, 92–3,
        116–22, 189
    publication history of, 115–17, 260n7
    and Stiller, 207, 211

letter, 34, 46, 84–5
    history of, 56, 57, 91, 100
letter journal, 75–6
letter-journal novel, 75–86, 109, 190
    contrasted with Wertherian diary novel,
        90, 93–6
    contrasted with women's diary fiction
        around 1900, 173, 175
    and Richardson, 75–7, 79, 84
literary journal, 185, 186, 197
    criticism on, 267n2

memoir, see autobiography
memoir novel
    characterized and contrasted with diary
        novel, 4–5
    as mimetic form, 24, 56–9, 62
    and unreliable narration, 138
metaphor
    in Butor, 218–25, 230–1
    and expressive style, 46, 50, 98
    and reliable narration, 157, 171–2
    in Rilke, 157–64, 166–72
metaphors of body, 50
metaphors of vision, 42–3, 159–64
mimesis, 57
    as criterion for art, 59–62
    of diary by diary novel, 6, 24–6, 34,
        51–2, 55–6, 191–2, 195
    formal, 24, 190–2, 195
    in genre formation, 11–12, 25
    of nonfictional forms by eighteenth-
        century novel, 56–62, 191
mystery novel, 111–12

narrative triangle, 4, 5, 17, 48, 52, 96
    second, 33–5, 38, 39, 48